Environmental
Politics
and Policy

require

Neutral lab
—testing
Constantly change
employees so
cant be built

Environmental Politics and Policy

Eighth Edition

Walter A. Rosenbaum
University of Florida

CQ PRESS

A Division of SAGE

Washington, D.C.

CQ Press
2300 N Street, NW, Suite 800
Washington, DC 20037

Phone: 202-729-1900; toll-free, 1-866-4CQ-PRESS (1-866-427-7737)

Web: www.cqpress.com

Cover design: Paula Goldstein, Blue Bungalow Design
Typesetting: C&M Digitals (P) Ltd.

⊗ The paper used in this publication exceeds the requirements of the
American National Standard for Information Sciences—Permanence of
Paper for Printed Library Materials, ANSI Z39.48-1992.

Printed and bound in the United States of America

14   13   12   11   10   1   2   3   4   5

Library of Congress Cataloging-in-Publication Data

Rosenbaum, Walter A.
    Environmental politics and policy / Walter A. Rosenbaum. — 8th ed.
        p. cm.
    Includes bibliographical references and index.
    ISBN 978-1-60426-607-8 (pbk. : alk. paper) 1. Environmental
policy—United States. I. Title.

    GE180.R66 2011
    363.7′05610973—dc22

                                                    2010022970

For Ashley, Leanna, and Karley

Contents

Figures, Tables, Boxes, and Maps

Boxes

Maps

Preface

We have passed the threshold of the twenty-first century, and any author with a social conscience who writes a book about environmentalism should do so with deliberation. It is a time to measure distances: How far have we come? How far must we go? It is a time to talk about time and change: What have we lost? What have we gained? This book is addressed to an audience who will live well into the new century, a generation with its ambition and imagination resolutely fixed on tomorrow, so it is also a time to talk about what might be: What will this generation accomplish? What ideas and visions will challenge its imagination and come to fruition? In short, an author should write accurately and responsibly not only about what has happened but also about its meaning in social and historical time. Therefore, this is a book about the more enduring institutions and processes of American environmental policymaking as well as their ongoing transformation and implications.

Readers familiar with *Environmental Politics and Policy* will recognize a continuity with previous editions in conceptual framework and substantive policy concerns. They will also notice some significant editorial improvements. The foundational chapters that explain and illustrate the essential components of the policymaking process (Chapters 2 and 3) still cover these key areas, but they have been carefully reorganized for greater clarity and continuity. Chapter 2 now focuses entirely on the policymaking process, whereas Chapter 3 covers the institutions and politics of policymaking. Throughout the book, case studies and other examples have been updated comprehensively, where appropriate, to ensure timeliness and relevance. Each chapter has been edited rigorously to eliminate material from previous editions that is no longer essential. The result is a more concise narrative that does not sacrifice such fundamentals as the conceptual design, the careful explanation of substantive policy, and the abundant illustrations that have appealed to the readers of previous editions. As always, a major subtext is the continuing challenge, inherent to environmental policymaking, of reconciling sound science with practical politics.

This edition also records significant events and illuminates the strategic transformations that have taken place in domestic environmental politics and policy at the advent of the Barack Obama administration. These include:

- A new discussion in Chapters 1 and 8 of the energy policy agenda of the Obama administration, with particular attention to the administration's renewable energy proposals and their environmental significance.
- A greatly expanded exploration in Chapter 10 of global climate change as a domestic policy issue and the implications of its global setting. That discussion includes an assessment of the relevance for the United States of the highly contentious 2009 Conference of Parties to the United Nations Framework Convention on Climate Change in Copenhagen, the impact of its aftermath on domestic energy policy, and the crucial role of the Intergovernmental Panel on Climate Change (IPCC) in the domestic climate policy debate.
- The shifting texture and discontinuities of public opinion about the environment and its impact on environmental policymaking. Chapter 2, for example, examines a number of potentially significant aspects of public opinion trends since the 2008 presidential election. These include the increasing polarization of opinion between Republican and Democratic partisans over important domestic energy issues such as climate change, the credibility of science and scientists in environmental policymaking, the importance of environmental regulation compared to economic growth in national policymaking, and the continuing failure of environmentalism to become a salient factor in presidential voting. Chapter 8 discusses the shift of public opinion toward a more benign view of commercial nuclear power and the implications of this shift; Chapter 10 explores the significant impact of the 2009 climategate issue on public opinion.
- The continuing change in environmental trends and indicators. The shelf life of environmental data is short. Data need continual updating and pruning to remain relevant. Tables and figures from earlier editions that are no longer useful have been removed. The remaining tables and figures presenting the most essential data—current trends in national air pollution emissions, water quality, and toxic waste discharges, for example—have been updated as much as possible. The discussion of environmental justice in Chapter 4 has been expanded to emphasize the growing domestic infrastructure of the movement.

- The emergence of new issues and the evolving status of old issues. The introductory and concluding chapters bracket the entire narrative with attention to the impact of the Obama presidency and its environmental agenda on understanding both our domestic environmental politics and our international environmental diplomacy. Elsewhere, in Chapter 4, domestic risk assessment methods are now contrasted with the precautionary principle, an alternative approach widely used in the European Union and receiving increasing attention in the United States. This chapter also updates the continuing controversy over the human cancer risk associated with exposure to the chemical dioxin and to chemical plasticizers in materials used in making children's toys. The discussion of water pollution regulation in Chapter 6 includes a description of the technically complex, economically expensive problem now confronting the states in determining the "Total Maximum Daily Loading" for contaminants in runoff water from agriculture and other sources of non-point pollution. Chapter 8 introduces the issue of mountain top removal, a growing and increasingly controversial method of coal surface mining, and the newly emerging challenge posed by coal ash disposal from power-generating plants. Chapter 10 for the first time discusses the most widely advocated domestic emissions control strategy to control climate warming emissions, Carbon Capture and Sequester (CCS).

I have tried to keep faith with colleagues, students, reviewers, and others who have found the narrative design informative, accessible, and durable. That includes an implicit commitment to material that is interesting as well as balanced and teachable—in the end, a book that is both a good read and a fair read.

Acknowledgments

As usual, the talents of many other people were enlisted in the writing of this new edition, and I am deeply indebted to them for the continuing acceptance of this book. Like most teachers, I recognized long ago that my students are often my best instructors and critics. To them, I express my continuing gratitude. A number of reviewers made constructive suggestions during the revision and writing of this edition. I thank Marjorie Hershey, Indiana University; Lilias Jones Jarding, South Dakota State University; Karoline Mortensen, University of Maryland; and Shannon Orr, Bowling Green State University for their thorough reviews. To CQ Press, I owe a special appreciation: this edition marks my thirtieth year of very rewarding collaboration with its talented staff. To my current CQ Press editors Charisse Kiino and Gwenda Larsen, and to copyeditor Julie Nemer, I offer a well-deserved thanks for the many hours of planning, reviewing, and patience invested in the work. Faults of omission and commission—alas!—are my own.

—*Walter A. Rosenbaum*

*Environmental
Politics
and Policy*

Chapter 1

After Earth Day

The difficulty of converting scientific findings into political action is a function of the uncertainty of the science and the pain generated by the action.
          —William D. Ruckelshaus, former administrator of
          the U.S. Environmental Protection Agency

Wind persistently scours the High Plains. In Wyoming, wind is virtually a constant presence that often seems intrusive, unwelcome, even malevolent. This wind can blow hard and unceasing for days or weeks, eroding rich farm topsoil; plunging the state into a prolonged, bitter subzero freeze; and unpredictably disrupting commerce and industry. Prosperity rarely seems to ride the wind. Throughout most of Wyoming's history, it was carbon—the buried energy of coal, petroleum, and oil shale—that seemed the certain path toward Wyoming's future economic vitality.

Then came the Barack Obama presidency and with it a prediction that promised to transmute Wyoming wind into benign, even welcome energy. But wind energy and the towering wind turbines it might sow across the Wyoming horizon also pitch the state into the midst of colliding forces that typify many of the challenges confronting twenty-first-century environmental policy and reveal the enduring qualities of the nation's environmental policymaking.

Prelude: "The Best Wind in America"

Before a national audience, newly elected President Barack Obama celebrated Earth Day 2009 from a wind tower assembly plant in Newton, Iowa, where he declared his intention to put the United States on "the clean energy superhighway" leading to a safer environment and greater energy efficiency. He envisioned "a new era of energy exploration for

1

America" and predicted that by 2030 wind power could create 20 percent of all energy produced in the United States. "After decades of dragging our feet," promised Obama, his new national energy agenda "will finally spark the creation of a clean energy industry that will create hundreds of thousands of jobs over the next few years, manufacturing wind turbines and solar cells."[1] To redeem that promise, the American Recovery and Reinvestment Act of 2009—the Obama' administration's $781 billion economic stimulus package—dedicated $61 billion to promote wind energy and other clean energy alternatives. "Green energy" had now become a priority in the continually evolving politics and policy of American environmentalism

No state seems better situated to take advantage of this clean energy money than Wyoming. The state is home of the nation's strongest and most persistent wind, the "best wind in North America," claims the American Wind Energy Association, a developers' trade group.[2] But the energy superhighway comes at a cost. The highway is proving less a swift and certain road to a new green energy era than a challenging, arduous, and sometimes problematic pathway through America's policymaking labyrinth.

A New Wind Rush. As if to confirm Obama's prophecy, operating and planned wind farms are rapidly appearing across Wyoming. The state is experiencing a twenty-first-century equivalent of Wyoming's historic gold and coal rushes—what enthusiastic wind power proponents call a wind rush. To its proponents, wind power is nearly ideal for Wyoming: it releases no polluting air and climate changing emissions, creates renewable and efficient energy, stimulates economic development, and reduces American dependence on imported oil. In short, it is an environmentally benign, inherently attractive twenty-first-century technology.

Electric utilities are ready to exploit Wyoming's wind power potential. In April 2009, Duke Power, among the nation's largest electric utilities, announced plans to build its fourth Wyoming wind farm. When completed, Duke's Wyoming wind power portfolio will include more than 250 wind towers generating 5,000 megawatts of electricity, mostly for southern California, with enough capacity to power 50,000–60,000 homes.[3] PacifiCorp, another ambitious High Plains utility, is already producing 551 megawatts of power from its 85 wind towers, while Rocky Mountain Power plans to build a 74-tower farm near Medicine Bow. Horizon Wind Energy wants to build a 196-turbine wind farm in Carbon County costing $600 million. And there are others.

All Wyoming's other planned and operating wind farms, however, will be overshadowed by the Power Company of Wyoming's proposed Chokecherry and Sierra Madre Wind Energy Project in Carbon County, near

Laramie. The project will become the largest wind farm in the United States, sprawling over 150 square miles; costing $4–6 billion; and consisting of 1,100 wind towers, each 240 feet tall, and collectively generating as much electric energy as Hoover Dam.[4] If the essential TransWest power line is also constructed to transport this energy to southern California and Arizona, more than 600,000 homes can be served.

"Get Used to Those Turbines." Proponents of Wyoming wind power predict that sowing more wind farms across the state will transform Wyoming into a national wind power leader. The state currently ranks twelfth in state wind power production, but the American Wind Power Association estimates the state could rise to seventh place, producing about 8,500 megawatts of electricity, enough to serve 1.5 million households. Jonathon Naughton, director of the Wind Energy Research Center at the University of Wyoming, predicts that the number of Wyoming wind turbines could multiply as many as twelve times by 2030. "You should get used to those turbines on the horizon if this happens," Naughton said.[5]

Wind power could become an economic cornucopia for Wyoming. Thousands of new jobs might be created in transporting wind turbines, manufacturing wind towers, building and servicing wind power facilities, and constructing power lines. Landowners accepting wind turbines on their property could receive more than $10,000 yearly for each tower. And wind power, unlike coal and petroleum, produces no polluting air emissions or climate-warming chemicals imposing regulatory costs on other industries.

No Certain Wind Rush. The wind rush is no certain thing, however. The public is divided and tentative about the wind farms. Many Wyoming residents don't want to see those wind turbines or their transmission lines arrayed against the horizon, at least not across their view of the horizon. "If you want to have a contentious public meeting, talk about transmission," remarked Wyoming governor William Freudenthal. "It brings out the 'not-in-my backyard' people," he adds, "whom I have known to be so pro-development you could practically scrape it off them. Generally, in this state we support economic development … and when all of a sudden it ends up in our backyard, our view changes a lot."[6] Numerous citizen groups, like the Northern Laramie Range Alliance, have organized rapidly across Wyoming to limit the visual and biological impact of the wind farms. The environmental community itself cannot agree about the environmental risks of wind farms.[7]

There are economic, political, and technological uncertainties. Electric utilities contemplating new Wyoming wind farms are vulnerable to the energy market. They are unlikely to develop aggressively unless wind power can compete commercially in the future with oil and natural gas. The utilities will depend on federal and state governments to create an economically congenial regulatory scheme and to issue the required permits for wind turbines and transmission lines. The utilities must also depend on the credit markets to provide the billions of dollars in capital essential for constructing wind farms. Moreover, the state's governor, legislature, and local governments must become and remain dependable allies. Ultimately, federal regulators must also approve both wind towers and their transmission lines. Wind turbine technologies, yet to be tested over long time spans, must also prove durable, efficient, and economically profitable over their whole life cycle. And the industrial and technical infrastructure essential to manufacture and sustain wind turbines must remain resilient.

It is the environmental impact of wind towers, however, that suffuses all discussion of Wyoming's wind farms with the greatest uncertainty. And the most potent environmental disrupter of ambitious wind energy plans is the otherwise inconspicuous sage grouse.

"That Bird." Half the nation's remaining sage grouse population inhabits Wyoming.[8] The sage grouse, a chicken-size ground dweller, is poised precariously on the threshold of becoming a federally listed endangered species. Unfortunately for wind power promoters, the sage grouse is living in all the wrong places. The land required to accommodate the wind towers, roads, and transmission lines of Wyoming's proposed new wind farms could disastrously fragment the grouse's essential habitat. For example, half of Carbon County, the proposed site of the most ambitious wind farms, is also the bird's essential core area and any significant reduction of these core areas would almost certainly accelerate the grouse's decline into a federally endangered species. The U.S. Fish and Wildlife Service is currently studying the status of the grouse population, and environmentalists oppose any development that nudges the grouse toward possible extinction.

If the grouse becomes endangered, no further energy development of any kind—and that includes coal, oil, and natural gas—could be accommodated on any core area. Wyoming policymakers understandably want to steer all energy development away from the core areas. But 80 percent of Wyoming's potential coal production, 83 percent of its natural gas, and 60 percent of petroleum reserves also lie in or near core areas. And Governor Freudenthal is determined to keep energy production out of the core areas: "What I have is an obsession with making sure that the economy of this state continues to function, and it won't if that bird gets listed."[9] Whether it is possible to reconcile satisfactorily the sage hen's survival, wind power's vigorous development, Wyoming's economic vitality, and the High Plain's ecological resiliency (and at what cost) will be ultimately depend on the interplay of conservation science, the energy market, state and federal policy decisions, the public mood, and technological innovation.

In one perspective, what happens to "that bird" and the wind turbines, whose dual destinies have become inextricably joined, is a uniquely regional matter. In a larger perspective, however, the High Plains have become a stage on which are displayed issues, actors, and institutions that characteristically converge in national environmental policymaking marking its continuing transformation, and setting the agenda for the chapters to follow.

The Environmental Legacy

By the time Barack Obama pledged his administration to a "new energy superhighway," America's environmental movement had already transformed the nation's environment and its politics in many enduring ways. The evidence of important gains in environmental quality is substantial. One influential report card on international environmental performance, for example, commended the United States for its continuing improvement in environmental management between 1996 and 2004, especially in regulating air, water, and pesticide pollutants during a period when the U.S. economy was vigorously growing. In addition, the report noted that, although the United States was disengaging from international negotiations to regulate climate warming during the George W. Bush administration, the United States still continued its support of numerous other international programs.[10]

Perhaps most impressive has been the improvement of the nation's air quality. Ambient concentrations of sulfur oxides, carbon monoxide, nitrogen oxides, and particulates—all associated with serious human health disorders—have been reduced significantly; and many more acutely dangerous ambient air toxics, especially formaldehyde and lead, have been reduced drastically or virtually eliminated. Dangerous chemical and biological pollutants of major U.S. waterways, such as the Mississippi, Potomac, and Ohio rivers, have been reduced sharply. Aggressive regulatory programs have reduced significantly the number of abandoned hazardous waste sites across the United States and, for the first time, compelled the manufacturers and distributors of hazardous or toxic chemicals to comply with national standards for their transport and disposal. National testing programs now require more rigorous screening and testing of newly manufactured chemicals to protect human health and the environment. Numerous plant and animal species that were threatened with extinction, including the American bald eagle and the American panther, have been protected and, in some instances, restored to vitality. Equally important, the United States is committed to numerous regional and international treaties, such as the Montreal Protocol to reduce the global ozone hole, testifying to a growing recognition that the quality of the nation's domestic environment and global environmental quality have become interdependent. Most important politically, these transformations are grounded in a durable national consensus that environmental protection must now be a first-order public concern—a remarkable emergence of a national ecological consciousness that was nonexistent a few decades ago.

Substantial though these transformations are, the American environment remains significantly degraded in critical respects. More than 60 percent of the U.S. population—over 186 million Americans—live in 390 counties where unhealthful levels of either ozone or particulate pollution still prevail.[11] More than half the total area of the nation's biologically essential estuaries and almost half the nation's river miles are considered unacceptably polluted. The primary cause of this water degradation is still largely unregulated. Although testing may now be required to assess the public health risk from newly manufactured chemicals, surprisingly little information is available about the extent to which Americans are exposed to thousands of existing chemicals or about the possible health risks involved. Federal government estimates suggest that information on public exposure is available for less than 6 percent of more than 1,400 naturally occurring and manufactured chemicals considered to pose a human health threat.[12] The U.S. Environmental Protection Agency (EPA) has been able to assess the public health risks for an even smaller proportion of the about seven hundred new chemicals introduced annually into commerce and industry. "EPA's review of new chemicals provides only limited assurance that health and environmental risks are identified," according to a report by the U.S. Governmental Accountability Office (GAO; formerly the Government Accounting Office), "because the agency has limited information with which to review them."[13] In fact, one of the most compelling national environmental problems is the pervasive lack of reliable scientific information about current environmental quality and human exposure to environmental contaminants—data that are absolutely essential for sound environmental policymaking. When environmental scientists convened in 1998 to create the first comprehensive detailed assessment of the nation's environmental conditions, they discovered that they lacked sufficient information for almost half of the indicators considered essential to adequately characterize national environmental quality.[14]

It is increasingly apparent that the scope and scale of this ecological degradation were often gravely underestimated and that the social and economic costs of pollution regulation were frequently miscalculated badly when the nation's major environmental policies were enacted. For instance, when Congress wrote legislation in 1976 requiring the EPA to ban or regulate any chemicals posing an unreasonable risk to human health, it did not anticipate that more than 62,000 chemical substances might have to be evaluated to determine their toxicity. Nor did Congress predict when it wrote the Comprehensive Environmental Response, Compensation, and Liability Act of 1980 (CERCLA, popularly known as Superfund) to clean up the nation's worst abandoned chemical waste sites that more than 40,000 sites would be discovered by 2007; that 500 new sites would be identified annually; and that the initial funding would be virtually exhausted by the mid-1990s, thus requiring annual additional appropriations of $1.2 billion through at least 2010.[15] Similar examples of this sort are found in every domain of environmental concern. We know now that the seemingly inexorable expansion in the scale and costs of environmental restoration is often the consequence of better environmental monitoring and research revealing, often to considerable surprise, the true reach and complexity of environmental problems. These issues, and more, are inevitable yet essential to policymaking in a democratic society. Thus, environmental protection is a work in progress.

The Evolution of American Environmentalism

"When President [Richard] Nixon and his staff walked into the White House on January 20, 1969," writes Nixon adviser John C. Whitaker, "we were totally unprepared for the tidal wave of public opinion in favor of cleaning the nation's environment that was about to engulf us." What followed was no less a surprise. "Yet only 17 months after the election, on April 22, 1970, the country celebrated Earth Day, with a national outpouring of concern for cleaning up the environment. Politicians of both parties jumped on the issue. So many politicians were on the stump on Earth Day that Congress was forced to close down. The oratory, one of the wire services observed, was "as thick as smog at rush hour."[16]

That first Earth Day in April 1970 was the Big Bang of U.S. environmental politics, launching the country on a sweeping social learning curve of ecological management never before experienced or attempted in any other nation. No challenge has been more fundamental to American environmentalism since Earth Day 1970 than the constructive adaptation of the original vision of environmental conservation and renewal, once written into law and embedded into the political and economic structure of American life, to domestic and global changes.

The Environmental Decade: From Richard Nixon to Ronald Reagan

The 1970s, the decade spanning the presidencies of Richard Nixon, Gerald Ford, and Jimmy Carter, remains the most remarkably creative legislative period in the history of American environmentalism.[17] During this decade, almost all of the major environmental laws, federal environmental regulatory institutions, and environmental interest groups that now define the contours of the nation's environmental politics and policy appeared. Although Nixon himself was no environmentalist, he and congressional Republicans recognized the enormous political capital to be gained by riding the crest of the upwelling public concern for environmental protection. In Congress, a vigorous broad coalition of Democrats and Republicans in both chambers collaborated in creating the legislative majorities essential to firmly establish the legal and political foundations of the U.S. environmental era.[18]

By the time Richard Nixon's presidency abruptly ended in 1974, Congress had written the National Environmental Policy Act of 1969 (NEPA), which required all federal agencies to prepare environmental impact statements for any significant actions affecting the environment, declared a national policy "to encourage productive and enjoyable harmony between man and his environment," and created the Council on Environmental Quality (CEQ) within the White House to advise the president on environmental matters. During this period, the Clean Air Amendments of 1970 for the first time mandated national air pollution standards and regulatory laws to enforce them. Two years later, the Federal Water Pollution Control Act Amendments of 1972 (Clean Water Act) set national water quality goals, established a national pollution discharge permit system, and created federal grants to the states to improve municipal waste treatment plants. To administer these new laws, Nixon created by executive order the EPA, the largest federal regulatory agency and the first of its kind in any national government.

This cascade of environmental legislation continued with the Coastal Zone Management Act (1972), creating federal grants to the states to establish coastal zone management plans under federal guidelines. The Endangered Species Act (1973) broadened federal authority to protect all endangered and threatened species; the Safe Drinking Water Act (1974) authorized the federal government for the first time to set standards protecting the quality of the nation's drinking water. During Jimmy Carter's tumultuous presidential term (1977–1981), the catalog of federal environmental legislation was further enlarged with the addition of the Toxic Substances Control Act of 1976 (TSCA), requiring premarket testing of chemical substances and authorizing the EPA to regulate or ban the manufacture, sale, and use of chemicals posing "an unreasonable risk of injury to health or to the environment," and the Resource Conservation and Recovery Act of 1976 (RCRA), requiring the EPA to set national standards for hazardous waste treatment, storage, and disposal.

By the time Jimmy Carter entered the White House in 1977, public support for environmental protection had become so broadly and deeply founded that it was, in effect, now part of the national consensus—that array of issues publicly accepted as an essential and priority concern of government. Concurrently, the number of, membership in, and political effectiveness of environmental organizations continued to grow to the point that environmentalism was recognized among the nation's major political constituencies.

Unlike Richard Nixon and Gerald Ford, who preceded him in the White House, Jimmy Carter portrayed himself firmly as environmentalist and actively courted the environmentalist vote in his 1976 campaign. Environmentalists, however, anticipated an outpouring of successful new White House environmental initiatives and legislative accomplishments that never quite materialized.[19] Carter's term began well enough with his successful promotion of the Surface Mining Control and Reclamation Act (1977), establishing for the first time federal standards for strip mining and requiring mine operators to environmentally restore mined lands. Carter was also instrumental in the congressional passage of amendments to the Clean Air Act and Clean Water Act in 1977. Powerfully aided by national revelation of the extensive buried toxic waste dump discovered under the suburban settlement at New York's Love Canal, Carter was able to collaborate with Congress in the creation of CERCLA (or Superfund). It was also a bleak decade for proponents of nuclear-generated electricity. Their ambitious vision of an expansive commercial nuclear power industry was shattered by the precipitous drop in public approval and political support in the aftermath of the 1979 near-catastrophic reactor meltdown at Pennsylvania's Three Mile Island power plant.

Carter's administration was beset from the outset by the energy crisis, created earlier when the Organization of Petroleum Exporting Countries (OPEC) in 1973 imposed an embargo on American imports of Middle Eastern petroleum.[20] The economic shock of the embargo and the political turbulence in its aftermath compelled the federal government for the first time since World War II to regulate domestic petroleum prices and supply, to set energy-efficiency standards for transportation and consumer products, and to create a national energy plan. In an effort to rationalize U.S. energy policy, Carter proposed and Congress enacted legislation establishing the new Department of Energy, bringing together many scattered and uncoordinated federal energy programs and administrative agencies. The energy crisis also immersed the Carter administration in the inherently contentious and unpopular business of regulating national energy consumption, thus entangling Carter in protracted rancorous policy controversies that largely displaced other environmental initiatives and set the stage for the bitterly adversarial environmental politics of the 1980s.

The Politics of Deadlock: From Ronald Reagan to Bill Clinton

The Reagan and George Bush presidential years (1981–1993) rise like a great divide between environmental eras. The environmental movement had prospered through the 1970s in a benign political climate assured by a succession of White House occupants who were tolerant of, if not always sympathetic to, environmentalism and by a vigorous bipartisan congressional coalition committed to the floodtide of environmental legislation it had created in the 1970s. All that changed with the advent of the Reagan administration (1981–1989). Reagan and his advisers, abetted by a new cadre of sympathetic congressional Republicans and the collapse of bipartisan congressional environmentalism, believed they had been elected to bring regulatory relief to the U.S. economy, and environmental regulations were an early priority on their hit list of laws needing regulatory reform. The environmental movement regarded the Reagan administration as the most environmentally hostile in a half century and Reagan's regulatory reform as the cutting edge of an implacable assault on the institutional foundations of federal environmental laws enacted during the 1970s.[21]

The environmental movement, thrown on the defensive, expended most of its energy and resources defending the legislative and administrative achievements of the Environmental Decade from President Reagan's regulatory relief. The Reagan years severely tested the foundations of the environmental movement. Although the foundations held, little was done to advance the implementation of existing policies or to address new and urgent environmental issues. The result was a political standoff and congressional deadlock over new environmental initiatives. To environmentalists, the Reagan years were, above all, a period of dangerous drift and indecision, almost a decade of lost opportunities and intensifying environmental ills. The Reagan years, however, did have one bright aspect for environmentalists—the administration's aggressive regulatory reform and the highly visible political battles it spawned proved a magnificent recruitment weapon for environmental interest groups, which experienced an unprecedented surge of new memberships.

Accompanied by polarizing partisan infighting and protracted legislative delays, Congress was able to pass important amendments to the Clean Water Act, the Safe Drinking Water Act, Superfund, and the RCRA. What seemed perhaps the most significant legislative achievement of the turbulent Reagan years was the Nuclear Waste Policy Act of 1982, which established a national plan for the highly contentious permanent disposal of high-grade nuclear waste and authorized the Energy Department to implement a strategy for constructing and operating geological repositories for the mounting volume of domestic commercial nuclear power wastes. The act soon proved so politically vexing—no state wanted the waste—that Congress abandoned the strategy in 1987 and awarded the waste site to a very unhappy Nevada. The future of commercial nuclear power seemed to plunge from bleak to barren when the deadly 1984 reactor meltdowns at the Soviet Union's Chernobyl nuclear power facility released a catastrophic cloud of high levels of atmospheric radioactivity over the Soviet Union and its adjacent European neighbors. The lethal radioactivity brought death and severe chronic illness to thousands of Russians and Europeans exposed to the radioactive fallout.

President George Bush (1989–1993) awakened in the environmental movement expectations of major reform and seemed to bring to the White House a more sympathetic and active environmentalism after the Reagan years. Bush's performance never kept his promise to be the environmental president, but his administration ended the pernicious impasse of the Reagan years with important, if episodic, new policy initiatives and administrative reforms. The EPA's morale and resources, severely depleted during the Reagan years, were improved. The Bush administration sponsored and adeptly promoted the Clean Air Act Amendments of 1990, a long-overdue reform of the Clean Air Act of 1970. Among the more important elements of the amendments were new requirements and deadlines for urban air pollution regulation, stricter emissions standards for motor vehicles, cleaner automobile fuel standards, mandated reductions of sulfur oxide and nitrogen oxide emissions from power plants to reduce acid deposition, and creation of a market system for the emission allowances. The Pollution Prevention Act of 1990 created an Office of Pollution Prevention in the EPA to promote pollution waste reduction and minimization. The Energy Policy Act of 1992 for the first time created a comprehensive federal energy plan to reduce U.S. dependence on imported oil, encouraged energy efficiency and conservation, and promoted renewable energy. The Department of Energy finally ended decades of federal deception and negligence by acknowledging publicly the federal government's responsibility for the appalling environmental contamination of military nuclear weapons facilities.

But the backside of Bush environmentalism was equally conspicuous: a reluctance to address global environmental issues such as climate warming or the preservation of biodiversity, a progressively hardening resistance to any new domestic environmental regulations, and a low priority for environmentalism on the policy agenda. By the end of Bush's single term, it was apparent that his administration had restored only partially the resources essential for governmental management of the environment and had enacted only a few urgently needed policy initiatives.

Great Expectations: The Clinton Years

Sometime deep in the twilight of the 1980s the political winds shifted again, bringing back to the White House in the 1990s a president friendly to the environmental movement and aggressively committed to environmental regulation, even if that meant tough rethinking about its goals and accomplishments. The environmental movement expected much of Bill Clinton, especially since then vice president Al Gore was an outspoken environmentalist and Clinton had cultivated the environmentalist vote. In the end, the Clinton administration was distinguished more by its ambitions than by its accomplishments.[22] Clinton generally reinvigorated environmental regulation and installed aggressive environmentalist administrators in strategic executive agencies such as the Department of the Interior and the EPA. He revived U.S. engagement in international environmental policymaking, eventually committing the United States to the Kyoto Protocol to control global climate warming (which the U.S. Senate, for its part, refused to ratify).

But Clinton confronted throughout most of his administration a hostile Republican congressional majority that thwarted most of his legislative initiatives. Moreover, during his second term (1997–2001) Clinton was increasingly preoccupied with the bitterly divisive congressional battle over his impeachment, and the White House environmental agenda was all but ignored. During his first term, however, Congress passed the important Food Quality Protection Act of 1996. The act created a new approach to regulating pesticides used in food, fiber, and other crops by requiring the EPA to determine the health risk in foods by considering all the ways in which people were exposed to harmful chemicals and created a reasonable risk health standard for raw and processed food that replaced the earlier standard barring processed food containing even a trace of chemicals thought to cause cancer. Despite its failed expectations, the Clinton administration's turbulent two terms nonetheless resonated with a vision of environmental governance akin to the ambitious environmentalism of the 1970s, even as the mood of discontent with the existing regulatory regime hardened.

Confrontation Renewed: The Second Bush Presidency

Then came Republican George W. Bush (2001–2009). To the wary environmental movement, Bush's succession to the White House seemed to announce a profoundly unsettling new regime emerging from the shadows of the bitterly remembered Reagan administration and enthusiastically embracing its environmental attitudes. The environmental movement and most passionate environmentalists vigorously opposed Bush's election, even though Bush strongly rejected any implication that he would renew Reagan's assault on environmental regulation. Instead, Bush represented himself as a moderate environmentalist, a prudent reformer rather than an antienvironmental zealot.

Nonetheless, Bush's relationship with the environmental movement was confrontational from the outset. His appointment of individuals closely associated with energy production and natural resource consumption to strategic leadership positions in the executive branch, especially in the Department of the Interior and the Department of Energy, and the close association of Vice President Dick Cheney with the oil and gas industry provoked deep misgivings among environmentalists. Subsequent events, including the president's energy plan; his persistent efforts to open federal lands, particularly the Arctic National Wildlife Refuge, to energy exploration; and his repudiation of an earlier commitment to an international agreement combating global climate warming seemed to confirm the dark suspicions about his environmental sensibilities already pervasive among environmental organizations.[23] The Energy Policy Act of 2005 and the subsequent Energy Independence and Security Act of 2009 exemplified the Bush administration's ambitious effort to create a long-term energy strategy for the United States. The 2005 legislation was intended to increase the supply of energy resources; improve energy efficiency; and accelerate energy research, development, and exploration with a heavy reliance on fossil fuels and nuclear power. The Energy Independence and Security Act set the mandated national automobile fuel-economy standard at 35 miles per gallon by 2020 and sought to increase the availability of alternative fuels, especially biofuels. Although the environmental community generally welcomed the initiatives aimed at increasing energy efficiency and developing renewable energy resources, environmentalists continued to criticize the heavy emphasis on accelerated fossil fuel exploration, new commercial nuclear power, and coal-fired utilities in the Energy Independence and Security Act.

During the Bush administration, the EPA did strengthen national air pollution controls on particulates and mercury emissions, but to environmentalists these and other administration initiatives were too laggard and limited. Environmentalists also complained that the Bush administration routinely suppressed or rewrote scientific data to satisfy its ideological prejudices on environmental issues. As U.S. involvement and public frustration with the war in Iraq escalated, environmental affairs seemed increasingly marginalized in the Bush White House—Republican strategists, in any case, had largely conceded the environmentalist vote to the Democrats. Christie Todd Whitman, Bush's first EPA administrator, had complained at the end of her term that the Bush administration seemed condemned to "an eternal fistfight" with environmental groups.[24] Her remark became prophetic. "George W. Bush will go down in history as America's worst environmental president," snapped a leading environmentalist spokesperson, as if to confirm Whitman's prediction.[25]

Expectations Reawakened: The Obama Presidency

The election of Barack Obama and the return of Democratic majorities to both congressional chambers in 2009 seemed to signify a renewed White House commitment to ambitious environmental initiatives and relief from the adversarial, polarizing environmental legislative politics of the Bush administration. Obama actively and successfully cultivated the environmentalist vote, pledging his administration to new policy initiatives concerning global climate change, energy conservation, and domestic pollution regulation.

Obama's early appointment of Lisa P. Jackson, director of the New Jersey Department of Environmental Protection and an experienced EPA official, as EPA administrator seemed to environmentalists a sure portent that the Obama White House meant to give environmental issues a high priority. This was followed by the administration's American Recovery and Reinvestment Act of 2009, the massive economic recovery program that included more than $100 billion in spending, tax incentives, and loan guarantees to promote energy efficiency, renewable energy development, fuel efficient cars, and control of climate-warming emissions, among other programs appealing to environmentalists. But Obama also quickly encountered the inevitable conflicting claims of other compelling issues and constituencies—national health reform, the Iraq and Afghanistan wars, federal budget deficits, a depressed economy, and more—deflecting White House resources from the environmental agenda and inciting environmentalist criticism of what seemed a glacial pace of environmental agenda initiatives.

Ongoing Challenges: Present and Future

On that first Earth Day in 1970, more than half the Americans living today had not been born, and the new movement's youthful leaders are now well into middle age. A whole new generation has since matured, and with that generation, U.S. environmental politics has been, and continues to be, transformed. Several years into the twenty-first century, Americans now have almost four decades of collective experience of unprecedented experimentation in environmental management. The ultimate test of the ambitious U.S. regime of environmental regulation will be not how well it was conceived but how well it endures. That endurance depends largely on how well American science, political culture, and environmental leadership can learn from past experience and creatively apply the lessons learned to several profound problems now recognized as inherent in all environmental policymaking—issues that run as deep and defining themes throughout every chapter in this book.

Implementation Issues

The character and pace of policy implementation change continually in response to shifting public moods; to ebbs and flows in crucial resources such as money and personnel invested in carrying out environmental policies; to changes in political party control of Congress, the White House, and state governments; and to other changes discussed in later chapters. In short, policy implementation is unfolding and variable, powerfully driven by economic, political, and cultural forces. Practically every important environmental ill has been targeted by a major federal law, but delays and difficulties in program implementation routinely impede enforcement. The majority of important environmental laws have been implemented at a plodding pace, and portions of all the laws exhibit regulatory rigor mortis. Although practically all factions agree on the need for a remedy, a laggardly pace is the norm.

One reason for this plodding pace is the growing complexity of the regulatory process. The average size of major environmental statutes has inflated from about fifty pages in the 1970s to more than five hundred pages currently. The original Clean Air Act (1970) was 68 pages, the Clean Air Act Amendments of 1990 weighed in at 788 pages, and the regulations required for their implementation will exceed 10,000 pages. Like an augury of the future, the American Clean Energy and Security Act (2009), the first climate change regulatory legislation to be proposed by the House of Representatives, bloated to more than 1,400 pages. To create the elephantine regulations necessary to implement these complex laws and to apply the procedures in the appropriate instances can consume an enormous amount of time, as subsequent chapters in this book reveal. The regulation of toxic substances provides an illustration. The average time needed for the complete testing of sixteen common chemicals required by TSCA (1976)—a small fraction of the total that must be evaluated under the law—from their initial selection through the final EPA review of the test data has been eight years.[26]

Another important source of regulatory delay is the increasing mismatch between the responsibilities assigned to environmental agencies and the budgetary resources required to accomplish them. Although the EPA's workload has increased enormously since its creation in 1970, its budget has failed to keep pace. At the beginning of George W. Bush's administration, for instance, the EPA's annual appropriations were 25 percent below the 1980 level and shrank an additional 12 percent by 2009, when measured in constant dollars (that is, after adjustment for inflation).[27] Decades of underfunding has left the EPA overwhelmed by the scientific and administrative complexity of its regulatory tasks. For example, by 1990, the EPA was able to reassess and register only 31 of more than 20,000 older pesticides whose reevaluations had been ordered by Congress as long ago as 1972 and again in 1988. Despite a congressionally mandated deadline of 1997 to complete the job, the GAO reported that "the program may not be completed until 2006"—and it wasn't completed then.

Enforcement of most environmental legislation also depends on voluntary compliance by regulated interests, public and private, but the responsible federal and state agencies often lack the resources to monitor compliance with the law. Few states, for example, routinely inspect public and private drinking water systems, even though such inspections are required by the Safe Drinking Water Act (1974). One-half of the nation's 59,000 large water systems and one-fifth of the 139,000 small ones are not monitored to ensure that water is not contaminated by sewage or pesticide runoff.[28] Quite often, the information essential to effective regulation is missing or fragmentary, and the available information is often surprisingly haphazard. Many states, for instance, lack the technical resources to develop numerical standards for many groundwater contaminants and, instead, depend on evidence of environmental damage or public health risks before acting to control these substances.

Economic growth and population expansion often diminish the effectiveness of pollution controls over time. The automobile emission controls and reduced lead levels in gasoline required by the Clean Air Act together have lowered the average new car's hydrocarbon and carbon monoxide emissions significantly. But the number of automobiles in the United States has increased nearly 71 percent, from 80.4 million in 1970 to 137 million in 2006, with an additional 60 million new trucks since 1970. This vehicle population explosion counteracts the emission reductions achieved for individual vehicles and leads eventually to widespread urban violations of federal air quality standards.

Other potent impediments to program implementation include the litigation virtually predestined for any major regulation, difficult coordination between state and federal governments, bureaucratic infighting, and much else. Collectively these implementation problems constitute one of the most urgent, and daunting, political and administrative tasks of the twenty-first century.

Rising Costs

By most estimates, the national cost of environmental regulation does not seem excessive or likely to inhibit healthy economic growth. Currently, the United States spends about $120 billion annually for environmental control, or about 2 percent of the gross national product.[29] Overall, the annual proportion of national expenditures invested in pollution control appears to have decreased since 1990.[30] Although aggregate expenditures increased only moderately after 2000, these expenditures conceal troublesome details. The cost of individual regulatory programs is soaring, often inflicting heavy unanticipated costs on specific economic sectors, depleting regulatory resources, and compelling a search for scarce new funding sources. For example:

- *Superfund* was created to clean up the nation's numerous abandoned hazardous waste sites. After originally authorizing $1.6 billion for the project, Congress was compelled in the mid-1980s to increase spending to $15.2 billion, and estimates now suggest the program will require annual congressional supplements of at least $1.5 billion after 2010.[31]
- *Diesel fuel regulations for school buses* are soon to be proposed by the federal government and already required in some states. Meeting the standard can cost from $7,500 to $100,000 per bus. California, the first state to require stricter standards, will spend $715 million to implement them.[32]
- *Federal storm water runoff regulations* will require the District of Columbia to spend $1.9 billion to completely renovate its antiquated sewer system.[33]
- *Groundwater samples for water pollution control* can exceed $200,000 for digging a required well, while soil samples may cost from $500 to $5,000, depending on the number of contaminants present.

The roster of inflationary programs has become a virtual catalog of the nation's major environmental laws.

Unanticipated environmental problems, unexpected scientific complexities, and inexperience with new regulations are the common causes of massive cost overruns. Proponents of regulatory programs, particularly the congressional committees and staff writing the laws, are often ignorant (sometimes intentionally) about hidden costs. When Congress ordered the EPA to issue regulations requiring communities to filter and chlorinate their drinking water—a safeguard against giardiasis, a waterborne intestinal disease—it did not specify that the cost might approach $5 billion plus $500–700 million in annual operating expenses.[34] In another instance, the unanticipated difficulties in controlling the formation of low-level ozone and the emission of nitrogen oxides by trucks and automobiles are two major reasons why achieving the goals of the Clean Air Act is estimated to have cost at least $80 billion more than the $60 billion already spent by federal, state, and local governments before the act was amended in 1990.[35] The litany of other inflationary provocations includes administrative delay, litigation, bureaucratic bungling, waste, missing information, and political obstruction. Whatever the reasons, excessive costs divert public and private capital from more productive investment, promote economic inefficiency, impair competitiveness in some industries, and increase consumer costs. And bloated budgets become a cudgel in the hands of opponents eager to beat back demands for essential improvements in environmental management.

Environmentalists traditionally have approached discussions about the cost of environmental regulation with considerable wariness. They suspect, often correctly, that the estimates of regulatory costs produced by business or other regulated interests are inflated deliberately. (However, they are not equally dubious about the considerably lower estimates they usually produce.) They also believe that benefit-cost comparisons applied to environmental policies are usually biased because it is much easier to monetize the costs of regulation than the benefits. Even more controversial is the problem of ecological valuation—assigning a value to wetlands, for example, when deciding whether to convert them to commercial development or to protect an endangered species whose habitat is threatened. Moreover, many environmentalists consider it ethically irresponsible to allow economic costs to weigh heavily in making environmental regulations.

But spiraling costs are changing traditional environmental attitudes. Leaving aside predictable and usually unresolvable arguments over the "real" costs of environmental regulations, the fact of sharply rising costs has compelled many major environmental leaders to seek creative strategies for reducing the expense and to collaborate in this effort with the businesses and industries being regulated. This search for creative new approaches has affected the current policy debate in several ways. First, proposals to shift the primary objective of many current pollution laws, such as the Clean Air Act, from eliminating pollution to reducing exposure to the pollutants have become a major reform issue. This debate is explored in Chapter 4. Suffice it to note here that the proponents of reform believe that reducing the risk of exposure, rather than attempting to eliminate pollutants, is a far less expensive and more technologically feasible objective. Second, rising regulatory costs have focused more attention on eliminating pollutants (referred to as pollution prevention) in production processes as an alternative to "end of the pipe" pollution treatment. Finally, many environmental leaders and organizations have become more receptive to economic incentives and other market strategies as substitutes for traditional administrative procedures in securing compliance with environmental regulations on the assumption that market approaches may be more economically efficient and environmentally effective. Recently, national and international trading in "emission rights" has become an increasingly popular proposal by those favoring market-oriented strategies for pollution control.

Still, any debate about the importance of economic considerations in environmental regulation excites an ideological passion among many environmental leaders and groups that profoundly believe environmental values must never be compromised by marketplace logic. The environmental movement probably will remain divided over the wisdom of economic reform. Reform will come anyway, slowly and divisively.

Evolving Science and Technology

When the political leadership of American environmentalism set out its initial policy agenda following Earth Day 1970, the ozone hole, global climate warming, genetically altered foods, endocrine disrupters, leaking underground toxic storage tanks, ionizing radiation, indoor air pollution, and a multitude of other environmental issues—as well as many thousands of chemicals now common in U.S. commerce and industry—were unimagined or unknown. All these matters, and many more currently on the environmental movement's priority list, are largely the product of scientific research in the past several decades. In later chapters, we observe how science contributes constructively to environmental management through, for example, the discovery of environmentally benign substitutes for more harmful chemicals such as chlorofluorocarbons (CFCs). But the relentless evolution of scientific research can also frustrate, confuse, and discredit existing environmental policy by producing all sorts of new and unexpected discoveries. For example, twenty-five years after the EPA set the original air pollution standard for airborne particulates, a serious public health problem, the agency had to revise the standard, making it significantly more stringent. The result was enormous new public and private costs, attended by a nasty political backlash, largely because later research convincingly demonstrated that the earlier standard had been based on insufficient data—although it was the best available at the time.

Ironically, the environmental movement's success often contributes inadvertently to this disruptive research. Environmental advocacy has greatly enlarged the resources and productivity of U.S. environmental science, thereby accelerating the pace of new discoveries that often reveal deficiencies in the scientific basis of existing environmental policy.

This rising tide of ecological science poses several continuing challenges to environmental scientists and policymakers. First, it can produce new data indicating that prior policy decisions may have been based on inadequate information and must be revised—perhaps with great political or legal difficulty and at considerable expense. Policymakers can easily and unjustly appear to have been ignorant, or impetuous, for having made decisions (although often based on the best currently available information and frequently under strong public pressure) that later and better research shows were incorrect. For example, to meet the public health standards of the Clean Air Act, the EPA in 2006 slightly lowered the short-term threshold for public exposure to particulates (soot) as a result of scientific research conducted since the original standard had been set several decades previously. Although the new standard, described by the EPA as "the most health-protective in U.S. history," is assumed to create from $9–70 billion in long-term health and visibility benefits, it is also estimated to cost electric utilities alone about $400 million yearly to implement.[36]

Scientific research can also produce ambiguous, fragmentary, or contradictory data concerning the existence or extent of an environmental problem—especially at an early stage in the research—at a time when policymakers feel compelled nonetheless to do something about the issue. Sometimes a solution—or the appearance of one—seems so urgent that policymakers believe that they cannot wait for additional research or perhaps that additional research may never satisfactorily resolve the issue. Sometimes the scientific evidence about the impact of an environmental regulation may also be inconclusive. The continuing scientific ambiguity about the ecological impact of humanmade chemicals mimicking human hormones (often called endocrine disrupters) and the persisting controversy about the ecological impact of species loss illustrate this sort of science problem.

Science is also slowly, sometimes painfully, teaching the public and its policymakers that ecological reality is often more complex than had been assumed. And it can surprise. Consider an outbreak of cryptosporidiosis, a potentially severe human intestinal infection caused by a waterborne parasite, that occurred in Milwaukee, Wisconsin, in 1997, infecting 403,000 people and killing more than 50 of them. At the time, Milwaukee's public water supply complied with all federal drinking water standards intended to protect the public from such well-known health hazards, and public officials were initially perplexed by the disease outbreak. Subsequent research implied that Milwaukee's epidemic of cryptosporidiosis was related to the turbidity (the concentration of sediment) of the city's drinking water, although turbidity in large public water systems had not previously been associated with microbial contamination. "Milwaukee was a wake-up call," observed one of the EPA's drinking water experts in explaining why the agency would carefully reevaluate its drinking water standards for turbidity from that point on.[37] Milwaukee's problem reveals characteristics common to the ecological surprises that often challenge policymakers. It involved a complex web of causality spanning great geographical distances, embracing different environmental media, and posing many alternative modes of explanation. Cause and effect could not easily be documented and sometimes spanned years or decades. The puzzle also implied related problems not yet discovered, reminding those involved that ecology itself remains a science rich with uncertainty.

Finally, scientific research can complicate environmental policymaking and, in the process, drive up the cost and time involved in remedying environmental ills by disclosing, instead of timely solutions or quick answers to an ecological problem, the unanticipated need for new information. Pentagon planners call these discoveries the "unk-unks"—the unknown unknowns, the kinds of information we don't know are needed until a problem is investigated. Consider, for instance, the experience of scientists trying to explain the sudden dramatic increase in fish kills between 1991 and 1993 in North Carolina's vast estuaries. An unprecedented millions of fish were floating to the water surface with large bleeding sores, often accompanied by a strange smell that burned the eyes and throat—not the smell of decaying fish. At first, investigators assumed the familiar explanation—lack of dissolved oxygen in the water, a seasonal deficiency in the estuarine environment that sometimes becomes severe enough to kill fish. But additional study disclosed no severe oxygen deficiency. Instead, extensive fish biopsies gradually revealed something wholly unexpected—the presence of enormous quantities of a tiny one-celled creature, a dinoflagellate of the species *Pfiesteria piscicida,* an apparently harmless organism seldom studied and never associated with extensive fish kills. So biologists began to observe *Pfiesteria* habits intensively. They discovered that when estuarine nutrient levels of nitrogen and phosphorous increased significantly, *Pfiesteria* can transform into a murderous little organism with a personality akin to the star of the science fiction movie *Alien*, multiplying in staggering numbers and aggressively attacking and consuming huge fish populations. The *Pfiesteria*, in turn, were stimulated to multiply by the high nutrient levels in the water, apparently caused by agricultural and animal feedlot run-off. Thus, an unk-unk—in this case, the complete life cycle of *Pfiesteria*—was unexpectedly uncovered in the course of investigating a fish kill and became a critical component in understanding and eliminating the problem itself.[38]

Sustainable Development and Ecosystem Management

Presently underway between the Florida Keys and Orlando, Florida, is what is predicted to be the largest, most expensive, and most scientifically complex environmental restoration project ever attempted anywhere. The South Florida Ecosystem Restoration Project, popularly called the Everglades Restoration, intends to restore and protect for future generations the ecologically endangered Everglades, a globally unique, irreplaceable subtropical ecosystem gravely damaged by urban development and agricultural cultivation. The project embraces 25,000 square miles of Florida's interior, coastal lands, and water. It will cost more than $10.9 billion and require at least thirty years to complete—if the plan is successful.[39] The Everglades Restoration is one of a half dozen massive federal ecosystem management projects underway across the United States. These projects are markers along the way of a profound transformation in environmental policy associated with the growing importance of sustainable development as a foundation for environmental management.

The Challenge of Sustainability

The 1987 publication of *Our Common Future* (often called the Brundtland Report) by the World Commission on Environment and Development (WCED) rapidly advanced an already growing concern with sustainable development into a transcendent goal for the international environmental movement. The WCED's definition of *sustainable development* as "meeting the needs of the present without compromising the ability of future generations to meet their own needs"[40] has become virtually synonymous with the concept itself. Over time, as Jonathan M. Harris, an international environmental scholar, has observed, this definition has been interpreted to include three components:

- *Economic:* "An economically sustainable system must be able to produce goods and services on a continuing basis, to maintain manageable levels of government and external debt, and to avoid extreme sectoral imbalances which damage agricultural and industrial production."

- *Social:* "A socially sustainable system must achieve distributional equity, adequate provision for social services including health and education, gender equality, and political accountability and participation."
- *Environmental:* "An environmentally sustainable system must maintain a stable resource base, avoiding over-exploitation of renewable resource systems ... and depleting non-renewable resources.... This includes maintenance of biodiversity, atmospheric stability, and other ecosystem functions."[41]

A multitude of governmental entities, private institutions, and advocacy organizations worldwide (most created since 1990) testify to the expanding impact of sustainable development as a strategic goal for environmental policy and politics. In 1992, the United Nations Commission on Sustainable Development was created, and the next year President Clinton signed an executive order creating the President's Council on Sustainable Development, directed by then vice president Gore. [42] In 1996, the EPA created its Sustainable Communities Network. The global salience of sustainability as an environmental concern was reaffirmed in 2002 by the UN World Summit on Sustainable Development in Johannesburg, South Africa. By 2007, an international directory listed 51,500 organizations claiming some concern for sustainable development. A U.S. national directory cited more than 2,700 private or public entities involved with environmental sustainability.[43]

The concept of sustainable development is loaded with ambiguities that can reduce it to a cliché and weighted with goals that can seem competitive, even contradictory. Protection of nonrenewable resources, for instance, may appear inconsistent with sustained economic production. Adequate provision of health and education services may appear to require reduction of public spending to protect biodiversity. Some of the most divisive political controversies within the environmental movement arise over these issues.

Implementing Sustainability: Ecosystem Management

Despite the difficulties, policies intended to promote sustainability are being created and implemented through public policy at all U.S. governmental levels. One significant illustration is the growing importance of ecosystem management in federal resource planning. The rapid development of environmental science and increasing experience with environmental policymaking has compelled a realization that a greater emphasis must be given to the inherent ecological value of natural resources and that successful ecological restoration often requires planning on a vast spatial and temporal scale never previously attempted.

A fundamental principle of ecosystem management is that wise resource use must involve "the integration of ecological, economic, and social principles to manage biological and physical systems in a manner safeguarding the long term sustainability, natural diversity, and productivity of the landscape." This means that the primary goal of natural resource planning should be "to develop and implement management that conserves, restores and maintains the ecological integrity, productivity, and biological diversity of public lands."[44] In short, a natural resource should not be managed primarily to satisfy human economic interests nor valued mostly in dollar terms. From this perspective, forests, rivers, wetlands, and other natural resources such as the Everglades should be administered in a manner protecting *all* their natural benefits, including as habitats for fish and wildlife; as clean drinking water for communities; and for wood, fiber, forage, and ecological functions, as well as for human recreational and economic uses.

A second premise of ecosystem management is that large endangered natural systems such as river valleys, forestlands, and wetlands—often the most ecologically valuable natural resources—should be restored or protected as whole interrelated ecosystems, even if they are geographically enormous, rather than divided geographically and managed by different agencies and governments with different missions and often conflicting policies.

Sustainable development through ecosystem management is also politically contentious and inherently risky in the United States. It seems to defy two hundred years of past federal, state, and local natural resource planning, with its deeply embedded assumption that government should manage natural resources primarily for their economic value and human utility. Powerful private interests, such as energy producers, timber companies, livestock managers, land developers, recreation industries, and their allies, compete relentlessly for access to natural resources administered by public agencies. Indeed, almost every economic interest associated with natural resource consumption strives persistently to preempt competing claims on such resources. Furthermore, numerous governmental bureaucracies responsible for public resource management, agencies whose historical mission has been to facilitate private access to resources in the public domain, cannot easily adapt their deeply rooted organizational cultures to the newer ideas of ecosystem management and sustainable development. Moreover, many states are at best ambivalent about the new planning principles because the traditional economic exploitation of their natural resources, however ecologically disruptive it might be, also brought new jobs, increased tax revenues, and accelerated local economic development.

Plan for the Book

This chapter has introduced, broadly and briefly, the major themes that later chapters explore in more depth and detail. It has also provided a review of many significant events since Earth Day 1970 that define the political setting for environmental policymaking today, thus creating a present sense of place in the rapidly evolving politics of American environmentalism. The chapters that follow progress from a broad overview of the major governmental institutions, private interests, and political forces shaping all environmental policy today to an increasingly sharp focus on the distinctive issues, actors, and interests involved with specific environmental problems.

Chapter 2 (Making Policy: The Process) describes the phases of the policy cycle that shapes all major environmental policies. Included is an exploration of the influence of the U.S. Constitution and U.S. political culture on this process. Also discussed are the nature of environmental pressure groups and other stakeholders in the policy process and the important role of public opinion and the scientific community in policymaking.

Chapter 3 (Making Policy: Institutions and Politics) describes the specific U.S. governmental institutions, private interests, and political forces engaged in environmental policymaking. The narrative includes a discussion of the presidency, the important bureaucracies, Congress, and the courts. Also discussed is the importance of political events such as changing congressional majorities, economic growth or recession, and shifting public moods.

Almost all environmental policymaking entails some common issues. Chapter 4 (Common Policy Challenges: Risk Assessment and Environmental Justice) explores two of the most scientifically contentious and politically controversial of these issues: risk analysis and environmental justice. Risk analysis is concerned with determining whether specific chemicals, industrial processes, consumer products, and environmental contaminants, among many other things, pose a significant threat to public health or the environment and, if they do, how they should be regulated. Environmental justice investigates whether various social groups, particularly minorities of color and economically disadvantaged individuals, are disproportionately exposed to environmental risks or denied reasonable opportunity to protect themselves from such risks.

Among the longest running and least resolvable conflicts in environmental policymaking is over the economic cost and fairness of environmental regulations. Chapter 5 (More Choice: The Battle over Regulatory Economics) looks at two major aspects of this issue: the use of benefit-cost analysis to evaluate environmental regulations and proposals to replace current methods of environmental regulation with policies that rely on market forces to achieve results. Discussed are the major arguments and interests aligned on different sides of these issues, together with evidence about the impact of proposed economic reforms when they have been instituted.

Chapter 6 (Command and Control in Action: Air and Water Pollution Regulation) describes the nation's major air and water pollution control laws and evaluates their impact. The chapter explains how these laws illustrate the command-and-control style of regulation now common in the United States. Also described are the substantive elements of the Clean Air Act (1970) and the Federal Water Pollution Control Act Amendments (1972). The accomplishments and deficiencies resulting from these major air and water pollution laws are reviewed, together with characteristic policymaking challenges created by the scientific and economic requirements of air and water pollution control.

Chapter 7 (A Regulatory Thicket: Toxic and Hazardous Substances) focuses on the major regulatory legislation to control environmental dangers posed by chemical, biological, and radioactive agents. The major laws examined include the TSCA (1976), the RCRA (1974), and Superfund legislation. The chapter briefly describes the major elements of these important laws and examines their impact in the context of determining whether these laws have accomplished their purpose to control the manufacture and distribution of ecologically harmful chemicals and to safely regulate toxic waste from the cradle to the grave.

Chapter 8 (Energy: Nuclear Dreams, Black Gold, and Vanishing Crude) describes the nation's primary energy resources and increasing reliance on fossil fuels, together with the ecological, economic, and political risks entailed. The chapter focuses special attention on diminishing petroleum supplies, the attractions and environmental dangers associated with increased coal production, and the environmental problems linked to nuclear power. Also explored are future energy policy options and the ecological implications, especially in the contentious trade-off between coal and nuclear power as future energy sources and the challenges created by greater reliance on energy conservation and energy efficiency as alternatives to major reliance on traditional energy sources.

Chapter 9 (635 Million Acres of Politics: The Battle for Public Lands) focuses on the historic political battle over the use of more than 700 million acres of public land, mostly controlled by the federal government. The narrative examines the major economic and environmental interests engaged in a century-long battle over access to timber, natural gas, petroleum, grazing land, hydroelectric power, and other important resources on federal land. Described are the major federal agencies caught in the middle of these conflicts, such as the Department of the Interior and the U.S. Forest Service. The chapter also discusses the major legislation these agencies are expected to implement in managing these resources and the resulting problems, including the obstacles to achieving ecosystem management on federal lands.

Chapter 10 (Climate Change, Domestic Politics, and the Challenge of Global Policymaking) explains why the United States can no longer satisfactorily regulate or protect its own environment without a growing engagement in regional and international environmental policymaking; it then reviews the nation's erratic involvement in global environmental policymaking. Discussed are the ozone hole, acid precipitation, global climate warming, and sustainable development; these illustrate the compelling need for this international involvement and illuminate some of the major political opportunities and difficulties posed for the United States by international environmental diplomacy. Finally, the chapter identifies the implications of U.S. environmental diplomacy for achieving sustainable national and international development.

Conclusion

In calendar time, the presidential election of Barack Obama preceded the fifth decade of the environmental era proclaimed in the 1970s. In political time, it commenced an uncertain season for environmentalists now deep into that era, a season of conflicting implications and richly contradictory experiences. From the perspective of policymaking, a sense of frustration and impasse nurtured by the bitterly divisive conflict between organized environmentalism and the White House has permeated the era, yet evidence is abundant that environmental leaders have enormously enlarged the temporal and geographical scope of their policy vision to embrace sustainable development, ecosystem management, and global ecological restoration. Improvements in environmental quality have become increasingly apparent, and sometimes impressive, yet regulatory achievements often fall gravely below expectations. Environmentalism has matured to the point where its organizational advocates can reflect critically on past experience and accept the need for rethinking and reforming their policy agenda, especially the need to moderate the escalating cost of environmental protection and to find more effective ways to implement pollution regulation. At the same time, the rapid progress of environmental science reveals with increasing acuteness the need to improve significantly the quality of the science base on which environmental policy is grounded. Environmentalism is now firmly rooted in U.S. political culture, yet its electoral force often seems surprisingly feeble.

In many ways, it is the best of times and the worst of times for environmentalism. In no other period has environmentalism seemed more politically potent, armed with powerful organized advocacy, legislative authority, public approval, and scientific credibility and seasoned with political experience. Nevertheless, as this chapter amply demonstrates, at no time have the scientific and political challenges confronting the environmental movement seemed more formidable.

Suggested Readings

Andrews, Richard N. L. *Managing the Environment, Managing Ourselves: A History of American Environmental Policy.* 2nd ed. New Haven, Conn.: Yale University Press, 2006.

Graham, Mary. *The Morning after Earth Day: Practical Environmental Politics.* Washington, D.C.: Brookings Institution Press, 1999.

Lomborg, Bjorn. *The Skeptical Environmentalist: Measuring the Real State of the World.* New York: Cambridge University Press, 2001.

Mazmanian, Daniel A., and Michael E. Kraft. *Toward Sustainable Communities: Transition and Transformations in Environmental Policy.* 2nd ed. Cambridge, Mass.: MIT Press, 2009.

Merchant, Carolyn. *American Environmental History: An Introduction.* New York: Columbia University Press, 2007.

Ophuls, William, and A. Stephen Boyan Jr. *Ecology and the Politics of Scarcity Revisited: The Unraveling of the American Dream.* New York: W. H. Freeman, 1992.

Shabecoff, Philip. *A Fierce Green Fire: The American Environmental Movement.* Washington, D.C.: Island Press, 2003.

Simon, Julian L. *Hoodwinking the Nation.* Washington, D.C.: Cato Institute, 2000.

Notes

1. Market Watch, "Text of President Barack Obama's Speech on Energy," April 22, 2009, available at: www.marketwatch.com/story/text-president-obamas-speech-energy (accessed December 3, 2009).
2. Quoted in Felicity Barringer, "Demand for Wind Power Is Spurring Ranchers in Wyoming to Join Forces," *New York Times*, November 28, 2008, A32.
3. Duke Energy, "Power Up with Wind," March 2009, available at: www.duke-energy.com/pdfs/Wind-Power-Projects-Fact-Sheet.pdf (accessed December 5, 2009).
4. *Colorado Energy News*, "Mega Wyoming Wind Project Would Contain 1,000 Turbines," September 9, 2008, available at: http://coloradoenergynews.com/2008/09/mega-wyoming-wind-project-would-contain-1000-turbines/.
5. Michelle Dynes, "Looking 20 Years into Wind Future," *Wyoming Tribune-Eagle*, August 15, 2009, A1.
6. Quoted in States News Service, "Governor's Commentary on Wyoming's Wind Energy Challenge," August 19, 2009, available at: www.allbusiness.com/government/government-bodies-offices-regional/12690402-1.html (accessed December 4, 2009).
7. Matt Joyce, "Are Wind Farms Spoiling the View? Rancher's Neighbors Have Formed an Alliance to Fight Industrial-Scale Development in Their Neighborhood," *Lewiston Morning Tribune* (Idaho), August 24, 2009, 1.
8. Reuters News Service, "Sage Grouse Supporters Take on Wind Farms," August 3, 2009, available at: http://money.cnn.com/2009/08/03/news/economy/windpower_vs_wildlife.reut/index.htm (accessed November 2009).

9. Quoted in Lydia DePhillis, "NIMBY Backlash? Not So Much," *New Republic,* September 4, 2009, available at: www.tnr.com/blog/the-vine/nimby-backlash-not-so-much (accessed December 5, 2009).

10. Norman J. Vig, "Making the Grade? OECD Environmental Performance Reviews: United States," *Environment* 48, no. 7 (2006): 40–43.

11. American Lung Association, "Executive Summary," *State of the Air 2009* (Washington, D.C.: American Lung Association, 2009).

12. U.S. General Accounting Office (GAO), "Chemical Risk Assessment: Selected Federal Agencies, Procedures, Assumptions and Policies," Document no. GAO 01-810, Washington, D.C., August 2001, 16.

13. General Accounting Office, *Chemical Regulation: Options Exist to Improve EPA's Ability to Assess Health Risks and Manage Its Chemical Review Program,* Report no. GAO-05-2005, Washington, D.C., June 13, 2005, 1.

14. Robert O'Malley, Kent Davender-Bares, and William C. Clark, " 'Better' Data: Not as Simple as It Might Seem," *Environment Magazine* (March 2003): 9–18.

15. Katherine Probst and David Konisky, *Superfund's Future: What Will It Cost?* Executive Summary (Washington, D.C.: Resources for the Future, 2001).

16. John C. Whitaker, "Earth Day Recollections: What It Was Like When the Movement Took Off," *EPA Journal,* July–August 1988, available at: www.epa.gov/history/topics/earthday/10.htm (accessed December 7, 2009).

17. A comprehensive summary of federal environmental legislation since 1970 is found in Norman J. Vig and Michael E. Kraft, "Major Federal Laws on the Environment, 1969–2008," in *Environmental Policy: New Directions for the Twenty-First Century,* ed. Norman J. Vig and Michael E. Kraft (Washington, D.C.: CQ Press, 2010), App. 1.

18. Useful analyses of the presidency's role in environmental policymaking can be found in Dennis L. Soden, ed., *The Environmental Presidency* (Albany, N.Y.: SUNY Press, 1999); Norman J. Vig, "Presidential Powers and Environmental Policy," in *Environmental Policy: New Directions for the Twenty-First Century,* ed. Norman J. Vig and Michael E. Kraft (Washington, D.C.: CQ Press, 2010), 75–98.

19. On the Carter presidency's environmental policies and politics, see Peter G. Bourne, *Jimmy Carter: A Comprehensive Biography from Plains to Post-Presidency* (New York: Scribner, 1997); Burton I. Kaufman, *The Presidency of James Earl Carter, Jr.* (Lawrence: University Press of Kansas, 1993).

20. The Carter administration's difficulties with energy policy are examined from different perspectives in Richard H. K. Vietor, *Energy Policy in America since 1945* (Cambridge, UK: Cambridge University Press, 1984); Pietro S. Nivola, *The Politics of Energy Conservation* (Washington, D.C.: Brookings Institution, 1986).

21. More detailed analyses of Reagan's environmental policies are found in Michael E. Kraft and Norman J. Vig, "Environmental Policy in the Reagan Presidency," *Political Science Quarterly* 99 (fall 1984): 414–439; Barry D. Freedman, *Regulation in the Reagan-Bush Era: The Eruption of Presidential Influence* (Pittsburgh, Pa.: University of Pittsburgh Press, 1995); V. Kerry Smith, *Environmental Policy under Reagan's Executive Order: The Role of Cost-Benefit Analysis* (Chapel Hill: University of North Carolina Press, 1984); Robert V. Bartlett, "The Budgetary Process and Environmental Policy," in *Environmental Policies in the 1980s,* ed. Norman J. Vig and Michael E. Kraft (Washington, D.C.: CQ Press, 1984); J. Clarence Davies, "Environmental Institutions and the Reagan Administration," in *Environmental Policies in the 1980s,* ed. Norman J. Vig and Michael E. Kraft (Washington, D.C.: CQ Press, 1984).

22. On the Clinton presidency, see Campbell Colin and Bert A. Rockman, eds. *The Clinton Presidency: First Impressions* (Chatham, N.J.: Chatham House, 1995); "GOP Sets

104th Congress on New Regulatory Course," *Congressional Quarterly Weekly Report,* December 10, 1994, 1693–1719.

23. The environmentalist indictment of George W. Bush's administration is summarized in Natural Resources Defense Council, *Rewriting the Rules, Year-End Report 2002: The Bush Administration's Assault on the Environment* (Washington, D.C.: Natural Resources Defense Council, January 2003); U.S. Congress, House of Representatives, Committee on Government Reform—Minority Staff, Special Investigations Division, "Politics and Science in the Bush Administration: Prepared for Rep. Henry W. Waxman," Washington, D.C., August 2003.

24. Quoted in Katherine Q. Seelye, "Whitman Quits as E.P.A. Chief," *New York Times,* May 22, 2003, 1A.

25. Robert F. Kennedy Jr., "Crimes against Nature," November 18, 2003, available at: www.rollingstone.com/politics/story/5939345/crimes_against_nature (accessed March 12, 2007).

26. GAO, "Status of EPA's Reviews of Chemicals under the Chemical Testing Program," Report no. GAO/RCED 92-31FS, Washington, D.C., October 1991, 27.

27. J. Clarence Davies, *Nanotechnology Oversight: An Agenda for the New Administration* (Washington, D.C.: Woodrow Wilson Center, 2008), 10.

28. Michael Decourcy Hines, "Survey Finds Flaws in States' Water Inspections," *New York Times,* April 15, 1993, A14; GAO, "Widening Gap between Needs and Available Resources Threatens Vital EPA Program," Report no. GAO/RCED 92-184, Washington, D.C., July 1992.

29. U.S. Department of Commerce, Bureau of the Census, *Statistical Abstract of the United States, 1996* (Washington, D.C.: Government Printing Office, 1997).

30. For estimates on national pollution expenditures and their impact, see William A. Pizer and Raymond Kopp, "Calculating the Costs of Environmental Regulation," Discussion Paper 03-06, Resources for the Future, Washington, D.C., March 2003; U.S. Environmental Protection Agency, Office of Policy Planning and Evaluation, *The Costs of a Clean Environment* (Washington, D.C.: Environmental Protection Agency, 1990), v–viii.

31. Johnathan L. Ramseur, Mark Reisch, and James E. McCarthy, "Superfund Taxes or General Revenues: Funding Policy Issues for the Superfund Program I," Document RL 31410, Congressional Research Service, Washington, D.C., February 4, 2008, 9.

32. Janet Wilson, "Aging U.S. School Buses Still Fouling Air," *Los Angeles Times,* May 25, 2006, A14.

33. Lisa Rein, "As Pressure Increases, So Do Ways to Control Pollution," *Washington Post,* May 23, 2006, A01.

34. John Cushman, "Efficient Pollution Rule under Attack," *New York Times,* June 28, 1995.

35. "Cost of Clean Air Bill Assailed," *New York Times,* March 8, 1988.

36. Andrea Fischer, "EPA Tightens Particulate Matter Rule; Manufacturers Concerned with Costs," *Transport Topics,* October 2, 2006, 4, 35.

37. Quoted in Denise Grady, "Turbid Tap Water May Be Source of Unexplained Intestinal Ailments," *New York Times,* November 4, 1997, A10.

38. Chris Reuther, "Microscopic Murderer: Pollution May Be Motivating *Pfiesteria* to Kill Fish by the Thousands," Academy of Natural Sciences, Philadelphia, May–June 1999, available at: www.acnatsci.org/ research/kye/pfiester.html (accessed August 1999).

39. For a comprehensive description of the South Florida project, see Working Group of the South Florida Ecosystem Restoration Task Force, *Success in the Making: An Integrated Plan for South Florida Ecosystem Restoration and Sustainability* (Washington, D.C.: U.S. Government Printing Office, 1998).

40. World Commission on Environment and Development (Brundtland Commission), *Our Common Future* (New York: Oxford University Press, 1987), 43.

41. Jonathan M. Harris, " Basic Principles of Sustainable Development," Working Paper 00-04, Global Development and Environment Institute, Medford, Mass., 2000, 5–6.

42. The Clinton administration's ecosystem management initiative is discussed in GAO, "Ecosystem Management: Additional Actions Needed to Adequately Test a Promising Approach," Document no. GAO/RCED 94-111, Washington, D.C., 1994.

43. Thaddeus C. Trzyna, Elizabeth Margold, and Julia K. Osborn, *World Directory of Environmental Groups*, 7th ed. (Sacramento, Calif.: International Center for the Environment and Public Policy, 2005); Harbinger Communications, *National Environmental Directory* (Santa Cruz, Calif.: Harbinger Communications, 2005), available at: www.environmentaldirectory.net/search.htm.

44. U.S. Department of the Interior, Bureau of Land Management, "Ecosystem Management in the BLM: From Concept to Commitment," Publication no. BLM/SC/Gi-94/005 Washington, D.C., 1994, 1736.

Chapter 2

Making Policy
The Process

This President believes in pursuing the best, most objective science, and the record proves it.

Brian James, spokesperson,
George W. Bush Presidential Campaign, October 14, 2004

Prof. Sharon L. Smith, an expert on arctic marine ecology at the University of Miami ... received a call from the White House. She had been nominated to take a seat about to open up on the Arctic Research Commission, a panel of presidential appointees that helps shape research on issues in the far north, including the debate over oil exploration in the Arctic National Wildlife Refuge. The woman calling from the White House office of presidential personnel complimented her resume, Dr. Smith recalled, then asked the first and—as it turned out—only question. "Do you support the president?" ... She responded that she was not a fan of Mr. Bush's economic and foreign policies. "That was the end of the interview," she said. "I was removed from consideration instantly."

New York Times, October 14, 2004[1]

James E. Hansen is a senior scientist at the National Aeronautics and Space Administration (NASA), director of NASA's Goddard Institute for Space Studies, and one of the nation's best-known and most respected atmospheric scientists. One October day in 2004, Hansen sent an angry message from Iowa to the White House and received a predictably disagreeable response. It was the opening public round in an acrimonious battle between Hansen and the White House that prevailed throughout the George W. Bush administration over the federal government's

32

response to the issue of climate warming. The struggle exposed deep, persistent, and fundamental disagreements within the federal government over which institutions and officials should shape the government's environmental policies.

The White House and the Greenhouse

From its beginning, the George W. Bush administration's approach to climate change policy was contentious. Soon after his inauguration, Bush retracted an earlier pledge to restrict power plant discharges of carbon dioxide (CO_2), the major gas associated with climate warming. The administration also rejected participation in the Kyoto Protocol, the 1997 global treaty in which 149 other nations had pledged to a scheduled reduction in their CO_2 emissions. Bush strongly promoted voluntary industrial cutbacks in CO_2 emissions, endorsed a gradual and moderate decrease in national greenhouse gas reductions, and repeatedly emphasized the scientific uncertainties involved in predicting future climate change—actions provoking vigorous opposition from segments of the scientific community, sharp congressional debate, and division among policy experts.

A Public Challenge

That October day, Hansen directly contradicted the White House position by assuring the University of Iowa audience that the scientific community generally agreed that temperatures on Earth are rising because of the greenhouse effect—emissions of CO_2 and other materials into the atmosphere that trap heat. Moreover, he noted, scientists believed these rising temperatures could damage crops and human health, cause sea levels to rise, and trigger other problems.[2]

Hansen's presentation seemed designed to infuriate the White House. Hansen told his audience that the George W. Bush administration wants to hear only findings that "fit predetermined, inflexible positions" and that the Bush administration "consistently downplayed" information confirming global climate warming. In addition, Hansen asserted, reports that outline the potential dangers of global warming were edited by the Bush administrators to make the problem appear less serious "in direct opposition to the fundamental precepts of science." If these remarks were not sufficiently inflammatory, Hansen turned to the forthcoming November presidential election between Bush and John Kerry. "Speaking as a private citizen," he said, he believed that "John Kerry has a far better grasp than

President Bush on the important issues that we face, as far as the area for which I have expertise, climate change and its relation to energy use."[3]

The Bush administration responded by further increasing its already substantial pressure on the administration's political appointees to control the flow of scientific information from NASA by delaying or altering public documents released by the agency. Until mid-2004, however, the simmering conflict between Hansen and the Bush White House seldom erupted publicly. In fact, Hansen had earlier twice been invited to brief the Bush cabinet on climate issues, and the president himself had cited Hansen's research on occasion. By late 2004, however, the White House–Hansen relationship had frayed badly. The Iowa speech revealed the widening depth of their disagreement about climate warming.

Dire Consequences?

Rising White House irritation at Hansen's continuing outspoken views throughout 2005 on climate warming policy culminated in December. That month, Hansen warned the American Geophysical Union that, without leadership in the United States, climate change would eventually leave Earth "a different planet" and, later, released information that 2005 was probably the warmest year in at least a century. Hansen soon received telephone warnings from NASA's public affairs office that "dire consequences" might follow if his statements continued, including the possibility that public affairs officials might stand in for him at news media interviews. About the same time, a novice NASA public affairs officer, remarking that his job was to "make the president look good," rejected a request from National Public Radio to interview Hansen. Hansen insisted, however, that he had an obligation to speak out because part of NASA's official mission was "to understand and protect our home planet."[4]

Conflict between the White House and agency scientists over where science ends and politics begins was not peculiar to the Bush administration, however. Hansen and other NASA scientists had sparred with both the previous Clinton and George Bush administrations over climate warming data and policies. However, Hansen reported to several national newspapers, "nothing in 30 years equated the push made since early December to keep him from publicly discussing what he says are clear-cut dangers for further delay in curbing carbon dioxide."[5] What followed revived public controversy over two of the enduring issues in American environmental policymaking: which government institutions and leaders should shape the nation's environmental policies and what role science, and the scientific community, should assume in this process.

Competing Interests and Institutions

Hansen found important allies. Shortly after the revelation of "direct threats," NASA administrator Michael D. Griffin issued a message to NASA's 19,000 employees reassuring them it was not the job of NASA's public affairs officers "to alter, filter or adjust engineering or scientific material produced by NASA's technical staff."[6] The public affairs officer who wanted to "make the president look good" was fired. Sherwood Boehlert, the influential chair of the House Science Committee, himself a Republican, warned that the Hansen affair revealed "NASA is clearly doing something wrong" because "good science cannot exist in an atmosphere of intimidation."[7] And the prestigious American Association for the Advancement of Science hastily convened a crowded session at its 2006 annual conference to denounce political interference in governmental science.

Others saw the controversy differently. "It seems that Dr. Hansen, once again, is using his government position to promote his own views and political agenda, which is a clear violation of governmental procedure in any administration," said a spokesperson for James M. Inhofe, the Republican chair of the Senate Committee on the Environment and Public Works.[8] NASA's deputy assistant administrator for public affairs noted that public affairs officials routinely reviewed the public statements of employees in most federal agencies and such reviews were essential to ensure an orderly flow of information and to avoid surprises. And he added—in words heard often among Bush White House officials and agency leaders—"while governmental scientists were free to discuss scientific findings, policy statements should be left to policy makers and appointed spokesmen."[9] Undaunted, Hansen warned a House committee in mid-2008 that it is almost, but not quite, too late to start defusing what he called the "global warming time bomb." He offered a plan for cuts in emissions and also a warning about the risks of further inaction.[10]

The controversy churned into the twilight of the Bush administration, drawing more partisans into the fray and enlarging the conflict. Hansen's supporters were delighted when the nonpartisan Government Accountability Office (GAO), responsible to Congress for oversight of the executive branch, reported in 2007 that communications policies at NASA were inhibiting some scientists from openly discussing their research.[11] Predictably, scientific and environmental interest groups sympathetic to Hansen aggressively rose to his defense. As if to publicly embarrass the Bush administration, early in 2009 the American Meteorological Society, the leading professional association of climate scientists, awarded Hansen its highest honor for "outstanding contributions to climate modeling, understanding climate ... and for clear communication of climate science in the public arena." And the National Audubon Society followed several months later with an award established to recognize "demonstrated courage and integrity in defense of the environment."[12]

None of these actions, however, could eliminate the deep disagreement between governmental institutions, public officials, and scientists over their appropriate roles in environmental policymaking nor guarantee that the Obama administration would avoid them. These conflicts arise from the many divisions of power embedded in the U.S. Constitution and the ambiguities of authority that result from these divisions. The White House–Hansen dispute, for example, fed on historic controversies over the limits of the president's power as the nation's chief executive and major public policymaker and on conflicting understandings about the responsibility of federal administrators to the White House and to their own professions or agency mission. In addition, to many scientists inside and outside Washington, the Hansen controversy was the raw edge of the always contentious dispute over how much policymakers should defer to scientific data and opinions.

Policymaking Is a Process

The Hansen controversy exemplifies the multitude of actors and institutions; the complex fabric of decisions; and the sometime glacial, disjointed, and frequently contentious sequence of events involved in the making of national environmental policy.

Although environmental policies usually develop less tumultuously, this incident features some characteristics common to environmental policymaking. First, policymaking is a process that involves a number of related decisions originating from different institutions and actors ranging across the whole domain of the federal government and private institutions. As policy analyst Hugh Heclo observes, policy is "a course of action or inaction rather than a specific decision or action."[13] Moreover, policymaking is continuous; once made, decisions rarely are immutable. Environmental policy is therefore in some respects fluid and impermanent, always in metamorphosis. Second, policymakers—whether of the legislative, White House, or bureaucratic type—can seldom act without restraint. Their discretion is bounded and shaped by many constraints: the constitutional separation of powers, institutional rules and biases, statutory laws, shared understandings about the "rules of the game" for conflict resolution, political realities, and more. These constraints collectively are a given in the policy setting, which means government resolves almost all issues in a predictable style. Third, environmental policymaking is a volatile mixture of politics and science that readily erupts into controversy among politicians, bureaucrats, and scientists over their appropriate roles in the process as well as over the proper interpretation and use of scientific data in policy questions.

One useful way to understand public policy, and environmental policy specifically, is to view the process as a cycle of interrelated phases through which policy ordinarily evolves. Each phase involves a different mix of actors, institutions, and constraints. Although somewhat simplified, this approach illuminates particularly well the interrelated flow of decisions and the continual process of creation and modification that characterizes governmental policy development. This chapter begins by describing the significant phases of environmental policymaking and then examines important constitutional and political influences, deeply embedded in U.S. political culture, that continually animate and shape the environmental policies emerging from this policy cycle.

The Policy Cycle

Public policies usually develop with reasonable order and predictability. Governmental response to public issues—the business of converting an issue into a policy—customarily begins when an issue can be placed on the governmental agenda. The successful promotion of issues to the agenda does not ensure that public policies will result, but this step initiates the policy cycle. An environmental issue becomes an environmental policy as it passes through several policy phases.

Agenda Setting

Political scientist Charles O. Jones aptly calls agenda setting "the politics of getting problems to government."[14] It is the politics of imparting sufficient importance and urgency to an issue so that the government will feel compelled to place the matter on the official agenda of government—that is, the "set of items explicitly up for the serious and active consideration of authoritative decision-makers."[15] This means getting environmental issues on legislative calendars, before legislative committees, on a priority list for bill introduction by a senator or representative, on the schedule of a regulatory agency, or among the president's legislative proposals. In brief, getting an issue on the agenda means placing it where institutions and individuals with public authority can respond and feel a need to do so. Especially if an environmental issue is technical and somewhat esoteric, its prospects for making the agenda are bleak unless political sponsors are attracted to it. Former EPA assistant administrator and environmental activist Clarence Davies observes, "New technical information by itself does not significantly influence the political agenda. It must be assisted by some type of political propellant," such as an interest group, congressional committee, or the president.[16] Thus, the discovery of the stratospheric ozone hole, and the ability of scientists to portray it in the most literal way—scientific photography enabled the public to *see* a hole—immensely hastened the Montreal Protocol to completion.

Formulation and Legitimation

The governmental agenda also can be a graveyard for public problems. Few issues reaching the governmental agenda (environmental or otherwise) reach the phase of policy formulation or legitimation. Policy formulation involves setting goals for policy, creating specific plans and proposals for these goals, and selecting the means to implement such plans. Policy formulation in the federal government is especially associated with the presidency and Congress. The State of the Union address and the avalanche of bills introduced annually in Congress represent the most obvious examples of formulated policies. Policies, once created, must also be legitimated, invested with the authority to evoke public acceptance. Such legitimation usually is done through constitutional, statutory, or administrative procedures, such as voting, public hearings, presidential orders, or judicial decisions upholding the constitutionality of laws—rituals whose purposes are to signify that policies have now acquired the weight of public authority.

Implementation

Public policies remain statements of intention until they are translated into operational programs. Indeed, the impact of policies depends largely on how they are implemented. What government is doing about environmental problems relates primarily to how the programs have been implemented. Policy analyst Eugene Bardach compares the implementation of public policies to "an assembly process"; according to him, it is

> as if the original mandate ... that set the policy or program in motion were a blueprint for a large machine that has to turn out rehabilitated psychotics or healthier old people or better educated children.... Putting the machine together and making it run is, at one level, what we mean by the "implementation" process.[17]

Policy implementation involves especially the bureaucracy, whose presence and style shape the impact of all public policies.

Assessment and Reformulation

All the procedures involved in evaluating the social impact of governmental policies, in judging the desirability of these impacts, and in communicating these judgments to the government and the public can be called policy assessment. Often the federal courts assume an active role in the process, as do the mass media. The White House, Congress, and the bureaucracy continually monitor and assess the impacts of public policy. As a consequence, once a policy has been formulated, it may pass through many phases of reformulation. All major institutions of government may play a major role in this process of reformulation.

Termination

The "deliberate conclusion or succession of specific governmental functions, programs, policies or organizations" amounts to policy termination, according to political scientist Peter deLeon.[18] Terminating policies, environmental or otherwise, is such a formidable process that most public programs, in spite of intentions to the contrary, become virtually immortal. Policies usually change through repeated reformulation and reassessment.

Policymaking Is a Combination of Phases

Because policymaking is a process, the various phases almost always affect each other, an important reason why understanding a policy often requires considering the whole development pattern. For instance, many problems encountered by the EPA when enforcing the Federal Water Pollution Control Act (1956) arose from the congressional failure to define clearly in the law what was meant by a *navigable waterway,* to which the legislation explicitly applied. Congress deliberately built in this ambiguity to facilitate the passage of the extraordinarily complicated legislation. In turn, the EPA sought early opportunities to bring the issue before the federal courts—to compel judicial assessment of the law's intent—so that the agency might have reliable guidance for its implementation of the provision. Also, many aspects of environmental policy may occur simultaneously. While the EPA was struggling to implement portions of the Superfund legislation allocating grants to the states for cleaning up abandoned toxic waste sites, Congress was considering a reformulation of the law to increase funding authorization to support more state grants.

Constitutional Constraints

The design of governmental power intended more than two centuries ago for a nation of farmers still rests heavily on the flow of policymaking in a technological age. Like other public policies, environmental programs have been shaped, and complicated, by the enduring constitutional formula.

Checks and Balances

The Madisonian notion of setting "ambition against ambition," which inspired the constitutional structure, creates a government of countervailing and competitive institutions. The system of checks and balances disperses power and authority within the federal government among legislative, executive, and judicial institutions and thereby sows tenacious institutional rivalries that are repeatedly encountered in discussions of specific environmental laws. Yet, as former presidential adviser Richard E. Neustadt has observed, these are separated institutions sharing power; effective public policy requires that public officials collaborate by discovering strategies to transcend these institutional conflicts.[19]

The U.S. federal system disperses governmental power by fragmenting authority between the national and state governments. Despite the growth of vast federal powers, federalism remains a sturdy constitutional buttress supporting an edifice of authority—shared, independent, and countervailing—erected from the states within the federal system. "It is difficult to find any governmental activity which does not involve all three of the so-called 'levels' of the federal system."[20] No government institution monopolizes power. "There has never been a time when it was possible to put neat labels on discrete 'federal,' 'state' and 'local' functions."[21]

Regulatory Federalism

Federalism introduces complexity, jurisdictional rivalries, confusion, and delay into the management of environmental problems. Authority over environmental issues inherently is fragmented among a multitude of governmental entities. Moreover, almost all new federal regulatory programs since 1970 permit, or require, implementation by the states. Thirty-five states, for instance, currently administer water pollution permits under the Clean Water Act. State implementation of federal laws may vary greatly in scope and detail. Management of water quality in the Colorado River basin, for instance, is enormously complicated because seven states have conflicting claims on the quantity and quality of Colorado River water to which they are entitled. No overall plan exists for the comprehensive management and protection of the river, and none can exist in this structure of divided and competitive jurisdictions. The federal government often attempts to reduce administrative complications in programs administered through the states by the use of common regulations, guidelines, and other devices to impose consistency on implementation. However, the practical problems of reconciling so many geographical interests within the arena of a single regulatory program often trigger major problems in implementing the programs.

Federal and state collaboration in environmental regulation is often amiable but is just as often contentious. Many state authorities believe that numerous environmental problems that are now federally regulated would be best managed by state and local governments. Many such state authorities also resent the expense and administrative difficulty they must endure to implement the numerous environmental laws and regulations they believe the federal government has negligently piled on them. During the 1980s, for example, almost one-third of all major federal legislative mandates affecting the states related to environmental issues. During that decade, EPA regulations to implement these laws are estimated to have cost the states more than $24 billion in state capital expenses and operating costs while federal financial support for these state activities was diminishing.[22]

Organized Interests

The Constitution encourages a robust pluralism of organized interests. Constitutional guarantees of freedom of petition, expression, and assembly promote constant organization and political activism at all governmental levels among thousands of economic, occupational, ethnic, ideological, and geographical interests. To make public policy in the United States requires public officials and institutions to reconcile the conflicting interests of organized groups whose claims not only to influence but also to authority in making public policy have resulted in an unwritten constitutional principle. The constitutional architecture of the U.S. government also provides numerous points of access to public power for such groups operating in a fragmented governmental milieu. The political influence broadly distributed across this vast constellation of organized private groups clouds the formal distinction between public and private power.[23] Instead, the course of policymaking moves routinely and easily between public institutions and private organizations mobilized for political action.

These constitutional constraints have important implications for environmental policy. It is easier to defeat legislation and other governmental policies than to enact them, to frustrate incisive governmental action on issues than to create it. Furthermore, most policy decisions result from bargaining and compromise among institutions and actors all sharing some portion of diffused power. Formulating policy usually means coalition building in an effort to engineer consensus by reconciling diverse interests and aggregating sufficient strength among different interests to support effective policies. As economist James V. DeLong observes, agencies "like to achieve consensus on issues and policies. If they cannot bring everyone into the tent, they will try to get enough disparate groups together so as to make the remainder appear unreasonable. If the interested parties are too far apart for even partial consensus, then the agency will try to give everybody something."[24]

Bargaining and compromise often purchase consensus at the cost of disarray and contradiction in the resulting policies. "What happens is not chosen as a solution to a problem but rather results from compromise, conflict and confusion among officials with diverse interests and unequal influence," notes presidential adviser Graham Allison.[25]

Incrementalism

Public officials strongly favor making and changing policy incrementally. "Policy making typically is part of a political process in which the only feasible political change is that which changes social states by relatively small steps," writes social analyst Charles A. Lindblom.[26] Gus Speth, a former chair of the Council on Environmental Quality and a veteran environmental policymaker, describes incrementalism as "working within the system." He explains:

> When today's environmentalism recognizes a problem, it believes it can solve that problem by calling public attention to it, framing policy and program responses for government and industry, lobbying for those actions, and litigating for their enforcement. It believes in the efficacy of environmental advocacy and government action. It believes that good-faith compliance with the law will be the norm.... Today's environmentalism tends to be pragmatic and incrementalist—its actions are aimed at solving problems and often doing so one at a time.... In the end, environmentalism accepts compromises as part of the process. It takes what it can get.[27]

In general, such incrementalism favors relying on past experience as a guide for new policies, carefully deliberating before changing policy, and rejecting rapid or comprehensive policy innovation.

Incrementalism is politically seductive. It permits policymakers to draw on their own experiences in the face of unfamiliar problems and encourages the making of small policy adjustments "at the margins" to reduce anticipated, perhaps irreversible, and politically risky consequences. But incrementalism also can become a prison of the imagination by inhibiting policy innovation and stifling new solutions to issues. Especially when officials treat new policy issues as if they were familiar ones and deal with them in the customary ways, a futile and possibly dangerous repetition of the past can result in the face of issues requiring a fresh approach.

The National Environmental Policy Act (NEPA, 1969), the Clean Air Act (1970), and the other innovative legislation of the early 1970s came only after Congress repeatedly failed when dealing with environmental issues incrementally.[28] For more than thirty years previously, and despite growing evidence of serious environmental degradation, Congress had continued to treat pollution as a "uniquely local problem" requiring a traditional "partnership" between federal and state governments in which Washington gently prodded the states to deal more effectively with pollution. This deference to the states was a prescription for inaction. Despite three major new federal air and water pollution laws between 1950 and 1970, all appealing to this governmental partnership, few states voluntarily wrote or enforced effective pollution controls, to the mounting frustration of environmentalists and public health advocates. Finally, Congress put an end to this incrementalism with the avalanche of new, forceful federal environmental laws in the 1970s mandating national pollution standards and regulations that compelled state compliance and enforcement. To many observers, this was a sudden outburst of environmental reform. In fact, its rise to the national policy agenda had been achieved by years of increasingly skilled, patient, and persistent promotion by a multitude of groups. The Clean Air Act, for instance, had been supported for almost five years by a national environmental alliance, the Clean Air Coalition, before it achieved national attention. Nonetheless, the time consumed in attempts to attack problems incrementally, the degree of environmental damage necessary to convince Congress that new approaches were needed, and the effort invested by the environmental movement in political action all testify to the tenacity of incrementalism in the policy process.

Interest Group Politics

It is an implicit principle in U.S. politics, assumed by most public officials as well as those groups seeking access to them, that organized interests affected by public policy should have an important role in shaping those policies. Few special interests enjoy such a pervasive and unchallenged access to government as business, but almost all major organized groups enjoy some measure of influence in public institutions. Many officials, in critic Theodore Lowi's terms, conduct their offices "as if it were supposed to be the practice of dealing only with organized claims in formulating policy, and of dealing exclusively through organized claims in implementing programs."[29]

Structuring Groups into Government

Arrangements exist throughout governmental structures for giving groups access to strategic policy arenas. Lobbying is accepted as a normal, if not essential, arrangement for ensuring organized interests a major role in lawmaking. More than one thousand advisory committees exist within the federal bureaucracy to give interests affected by policies some access and voice in agency deliberations. Hundreds of large, quasi-public associations bring together legislators, administrators, White House staff, and private-group representatives to share policy concerns, thereby blurring the distinction between public and private interests. The National Rivers and Harbors Congress, for example, looks after water resource projects; the Highway Users Federation for Safety and Mobility diligently promotes the interstate highway system; and the Atomic Industrial Forum pursues the interests of commercial nuclear power corporations. Successful organized groups so effectively control the exercise of governmental power that, in historian Grant McConnell's words, significant portions of the U.S. government have witnessed "the conquest of segments of formal state power by private groups and associations."[30] In effect, group activity at all governmental levels has been practiced so widely that it has become part of the constitutional order.

Business: An Unusual Kind and Degree of Control

No interest has exploited the right to take part in the governmental process more pervasively or successfully than has business. In environmental affairs, the sure access of business to government assumes enormous importance because business is a major regulated interest whose ability to represent itself and secure careful hearing before public agencies and officials often delays or complicates such regulation. In 2008, for instance, about 70 percent of the more than 770 companies and organizations hiring 2,340 lobbyists to work on climate change and spending at least $90 million lobbying were business groups.[31] But, historically and institutionally, the influence of business on government has transcended the agencies and officials concerned with environmental affairs.

Business traditionally has enjoyed what Lindblom calls a "special relationship" with government.[32] Business weighs especially heavily in the deliberations of public officials because its leaders collectively manage much of the economy and perform such essential economic functions that the failure of these businesses would produce severe economic disorder and widespread suffering. According to Lindblom,

Government officials know this. They also know that widespread failure
of business ... will bring down the government. A democratically elected
government cannot expect to survive in the face of widespread or prolonged distress.... Consequently, government policy makers show constant
concern about business performance.[33]

So great is this concern that public officials usually give business not
all it desires but enough to ensure its profitability. Out of this grows the
privileged position of business in government, its widely accepted right to
require that government officials often "give business needs precedence
over demands from citizens through electoral, party, and interest-group
channels."[34]

Business also enjoys practical political advantages in competition with
other interests for access to and influence on government: far greater
financial resources, greater ease in raising money for political purposes,
and an already existing organization available for use in political action.
These advantages in strategic resources and salience to public officials do
not ensure the uncompromised acceptance of business's demands on government, nor do they spare business from defeat or frustration by opponents. But business often, if not usually, is able to exploit its privileged
status in U.S. politics to ensure that its views are represented early and
forcefully in any policy conflicts, its interests are pursued and protected
carefully at all policy phases, and its forces are mobilized effectively for
long periods of time. These are formidable advantages, often enough to
give a decisive edge in competitive struggles with environmental or other
interests that do not have the political endurance, skill, or resources to be
as resolute in putting pressure on government when it counts.

Environmentalism's Enlarging Access

Prior to the 1970s, environmentalists were at a considerable disadvantage in achieving effective access to government compared to the
environmentally regulated interests, particularly business. The environmental lobby could claim, with considerable justification, to be political
outsiders compared to business. However, environmental groups—along
with public interest groups, consumer organizations, and others advocating broad public programs—were quick to promote a number of new
structural and legal arrangements that enlarged their governmental
influence. Indeed, Congress and administrative agencies often created
these structural and legal arrangements deliberately for the advantage
of environmental interests. These new arrangements, defended fero-
ciously by environmental organizations against continuing assaults by
their political opposition, have diminished greatly the disparities in
political access and influence that once so conspicuously distinguished

environmentalists from their political opponents. Environmental groups, in fact, have acquired the finesse to be formidable adversaries in traditional political confrontations with well-endowed opponents. "The perception is that environmentalists are a bunch of unwashed kids tying themselves to trees," remarked a political media expert observing environmental activists promoting national climate warming regulation. "That's not the case anymore. These are very sophisticated and well-funded campaigns."[35] In a reversal of form, for instance, during the opening congressional battle over the president's climate warming program shortly after Barack Obama's election, environmentalist supporters of a proposal to limit greenhouse-gas emissions outspent their opposition in the media $8 million to $7.4 million. However, environmentalists gain no advantage when the skilled legislative advocacy of lobbyists is involved. During the early months of the Obama administration, oil and gas interests spent more than $82 million on lobbying concerned with climate warming regulation; environmental groups spent $9.8 million.[36] Still, the political season has turned. In the rough calculus of governmental influence, environmentalists may not yet claim parity with organized business, but environmentalism no longer wears comfortably the rags of the politically disadvantaged and the establishment outsider. In the vernacular of Washington, D.C., environmentalists are now "major players"—so major that a closer look at organized environmentalism and its impact on public opinion is essential to understand the fundamental driving forces of environmental policymaking.

Strategies and Tactics

Organization is the bedrock on which the politics of successful environmental policymaking is built. Estimates of environmentalism's organizational membership vary. About 5 percent of Americans report membership in an environmental organization, and between 15 and 21 percent customarily report they have been active in an environmental group.[37] In 2003, about 14 percent reported they were participants in the environmental movement.[38] Careful estimates suggest that more than 5,600 organized environmental groups are active, together with hundreds more transient, local, and regional organizations defying enumeration.[39] The thousands of organized national, state, and local groups, collectively enrolling several hundred thousand active members, arm the movement with absolutely essential political resources that only organized groups provide—dependable, active, informed, and experienced advocacy.[40] Organized groups create the kind of constant pressure on policymakers and the continual aggressive surveillance of policy administration required for effective policy influence in government.

The many groups marching under the environmental banner continue to grow in number, sophistication, and political aggressiveness. To the media and public surprised by Earth Day 1970, the environmental movement seemed to materialize from a political vacuum. In fact, between 1960 and 1970 the national groups sponsoring the event had already grown from 123,000 to almost 820,000 members.[41] As always, behind the public politics of environmentalism was the driving force of calculated organizational action and adroit media manipulation—the evidence of skilled political advocacy.

The environmental movement is also changing. The growth in membership has enlarged the political clout of environmental interests at the state and local levels at a time when state and local governments have become increasingly important actors in American environmental policy-making.[42] Even though federal environmental leadership lapsed during the George W. Bush administration, many innovative initiatives, particularly concerning climate warming, emerged from numerous state and regional governments. Between 2000 and 2008, for instance, environmental organizations successfully promoted three unprecedented regional agreements to regulate climate warming emissions: the Regional Greenhouse Gas Initiative (RGGI) among Northeastern states, the Midwest Climate Initiative, and the Western Climate Initiative.[43] Many leading environmental groups are also moderating the habitually contentious political style that once characterized their confrontations with business and industry groups in favor of a more cautious exploration of the opportunities for collaboration and compromise.[44]

The proliferation of organizations manifests an increasingly divisive pluralism within the movement as well: ideologically, organizationally, and tactically. The ideological cleavages between moderates and radicals and between the national leaders and local grassroots constituencies have widened and solidified. After two decades of sometimes spectacular growth following Earth Day 1970, membership in the mainstream national environmental organizations has slackened in recent years and, in some instances, declined moderately. Nonetheless, the organizational base of environmentalism remains potent politically.

Ideological Consensus and Cleavage

Environmentalism has never been a church of one creed. The reformist politics of the 1990s exacerbated ideological, programmatic, and tactical disagreements that have always existed among the faithful. Although pluralism, and the conflicts born of it, are inherent in environmentalism, this pluralism is still bounded by general values, attitudes, and beliefs—a way of looking at nature, humanity, and U.S. society—widely shared with many nuances by environmental leaders and activists. Although this pluralism lacks the coherence of an ideology, it sets environmentalists apart from mainstream American culture.

Essential Principles

Reduced to essentials, environmentalism springs from an attitude toward nature that assumes that humanity is part of the created order, ethically responsible for the preservation of the world's ecological integrity and ultimately vulnerable, as are all Earth's other creatures, to the good or ill that humans inflict on nature. In the environmentalist perspective, humans live in a world of limited resources and potential scarcities; like the good stewards of an inheritance, they must use their scientific genius to manage global resources. An enlightened approach to managing nature, the environmentalists argue, should stress the interdependency of all natural systems (the ecosystem concept), the importance of ecological stability and resource sustainability, and the enormously long time span in which the impact of ecological change occurs. In its approach to nature, environmentalism emphasizes the sanctity of the created order as a warning against the human assumption that we stand above and apart from the created order by virtue of our intelligence and scientific achievements. All this is summed up for many ecologists in the metaphor of "spaceship Earth," the image of a unique and vulnerable ecosystem traveling through space and time, dependent on its crew for survival.

In its cultural stance, environmentalism sharply criticizes marketplace economics generally and capitalism particularly, and it denigrates the growth ethic, unrestrained technological optimism, and the political structures supporting these cultural phenomena. Such an attitude places environmentalists on a collision course with dominant American values. Environmentalism challenges U.S. confidence in market mechanisms to allocate scarce resources for several reasons. Environmentalists assert that market economics esteem economic growth and material consumption above concern for ecological balance and integrity. Therefore, the market cannot be relied on to signal resource scarcity efficiently enough to prevent possibly catastrophic resource exhaustion. Many, like environmental philosopher William Ophuls, believe marketplace economies are ecologically reckless:

> An unregulated market economy inevitably fosters accelerated ecological degradation and resource depletion through ever higher levels of production and consumption. Indeed, given the cornucopian assumptions upon which a market system is based, it could hardly be otherwise; both philosophically and practically, a market economy is incompatible with ecology.[45]

Environmentalism is less hostile to technology itself than to blind faith in the power of technology to cure whatever ecological ills it begets and to bland confidence in technological expertise to meet humanity's material and spiritual needs. Environmentalists regard the public's confidence in American know-how as responsible for many of the nation's most difficult environmental problems, such as the management of commercial nuclear technologies. The environmental movement's initial political agenda arose from these attitudes toward the natural world and contemporary culture. From its inception, the movement has expressed an ambivalence toward the nation's dominant social structures that frequently translates into calls for major institutional as well as policy reforms. Many environmentalists believe that the nation's dominant political institutions and processes must be reformed because they are committed to the preservation of ecological, economic, and technological values that are hostile to prudent ecological management. For some, this is summed up as suspicion of the establishment and the traditional institutions and processes associated with it. Political scientist A. Susan Leeson argues, "If American political ideology and institutions have been successful in encouraging the pursuit of happiness through material acquisition, they appear incapable of imposing the limits which are required to forestall ecological disaster."[46] Many fear the power of an interlocking economic and political structure committed to controlling technology in environmentally reckless ways.

Until the 1980s, the national organizations representing the environmental movement were largely untroubled by impassioned, divisive ideological cleavages. During the 1980s, however, an emergent radicalism and ideological conflict within the movement cohered into a multitude of newly dissident organizations and opened acrimonious schisms within many of the older established groups. The environmental movement has now become an uneasy alliance of numerous, often discordant political camps spread across a widening ideological terrain.

The Ideological Mainstream

Organized environmentalism today is divided into several ideological enclaves. The movement's dominant ideological and political style has been crafted by *pragmatic reformers*, the largest, most politically active and publicly visible organizations, represented by national groups such as the Sierra Club and the National Wildlife Federation. These large organizations emphasize political action through government; traditional styles of politics such as bargaining and coalition building; and national environmental agendas focusing on pollution, resource conservation, and land use. Their priorities are "influencing public policy in incremental steps, forging pragmatic alliances issue by issue with those with whom they could agree," explains Michael McCloskey, former executive director of the Sierra Club. McCloskey emphasizes that the pragmatists do not believe "that the entire political or economic system needed to be changed and were confident that environmental protection could be achieved within the framework of existing institutions of governance."[47]

The robust ideological diversity among the pragmatists, however, makes them appear more an ecumenical movement than a denomination. One important factional conflict pits preservationist groups, such as the Sierra Club and the Wilderness Society, which emphasize the preservation of resources rather than their economic or recreational exploitation, against groups such as the Izaak Walton League and the National Wildlife Federation, which favor prudent resource development for public use and economic growth. Another significant cleavage divides the pragmatists from antiestablishment groups such as Friends of the Earth and Environmental Action, which are impatient at the moderation and slowness of political action among the leading national groups but still committed to traditional forms of political activity. The national leadership in almost all mainstream environmental organizations, in fact, contends with their own grassroots factions, which, in the words of critic Brian Tokar, believe "the voices of 'official environmentalism' [are] hopelessly out of step with the thousands of volunteers who largely define the leading edge of locally based environmental activism."[48] To these critics, the leaders of official environmentalism have become just another political elite, absorbed in promoting their careers and accommodating the corporate interests that they should be opposing. When the World Wildlife Fund, for instance, selected a former executive of Weyerhaeuser Company, an international timber industry giant, for a major management position, the organization was bitterly flayed by one grassroots environmentalist publication:

> The World Wildlife Fund functions more like a corporate enterprise than public interest group. It ... has made millions upon millions hawking its panda logo, a brand as zealously marketed as Nike's "swoosh." But, of course, it's done almost nothing to save the panda ... except peddle pictures to trophy wives and innocent third graders. Call it Panda porn.... The World Wildlife Fund also rakes in millions from corporations.... As a result, WWF's budget has swelled to over $100 million a year.... Most of it goes to pay for plush offices, robust salaries, and a tireless direct mail operation to raise even more money.[49]

These critics, who agree on little else, complain about the amount of foundation money flowing into the coffers of pragmatic environmental groups. Such generous underwriting—often by large donors such as the

Pew Memorial Trusts and the Heinz Foundation—has sometimes exceeded $400 million annually and, in the opinion of the critics, compels mainstream environmentalism to compromise its programs and tactics to suit its foundation patrons. "It's like throwing a huge steak in among a bunch of starving lions," complained a spokesman for Oregon's Native Forest Council. "The lions will jump on it even if it is laced with arsenic."[50] Undoubtedly, foundations do prod their environmentalist clientele toward political moderation, but such influence is highly variable. The hardliners, moreover, have had their own foundation angels, such as the Turner Foundation, created by broadcast entrepreneur Ted Turner, which contributed millions of dollars annually during the 1990s to aggressive antiestablishment environmental organizations. And many "odd couple" alliances exist between relatively moderate foundation sponsors and aggressive environmental activists such as the one between the Ford Foundation and Environmental Defense. Even without these other provocations, differing organizational agendas and constituencies are themselves divisive to environmentalism. Which organizational agendas will prevail in the competition among environmental organizations for political primacy? Will the movement's priorities be air or water pollution, land preservation, hazardous waste management, national land-use planning, species preservation, global environmental problems, recreational development, indoor air pollution, or something else?

Deep Ecologists

Another highly vocal faction within environmentalism comprises individuals and groups ideologically committed to *deep ecology* or *lifestyle transformation*. Deep ecologists believe humans are, at best, only a part of nature—and not necessarily the most significant part. They believe that all forms of life have an equal claim on existence; that social, political, and economic institutions should promote the ecological vitality of all created orders; and that fundamental changes in national institutions and lifestyles are essential to preserve global ecological integrity. The fundamental political problem, from the deep ecologists' perspective, is that social institutions have become instruments for the human exploitation of the created order for the primary benefit of humans, often through technologies that threaten to destroy essential aspects of the natural order. Deep ecology inherently challenges the fundamental institutional structures and social values on which governments, economies, and societies are presently constituted. Thus, between deep ecologists and what they call the shallow ecology of mainstream environmentalism there abides a profound philosophical tension, nourished by antagonistic principles and a sharply disparate political imagination.[51]

Deep ecologists, lacking the political leverage of organizational or numerical strength, are presently a vocal, aggressive, and dissenting minority within the environmental movement. Many within the movement, preferring social to political action, have adopted individual and collective lifestyles outside conventional American culture. Nonetheless, deep ecologists continue to be politically active, often to greatest effect at the state and local levels. They also constitute a persistent opportunistic minority in many national environmental organizations with considerable potential to become a creative as well as a disruptive influence in national environmental politics.

Radical Environmentalism

Militant and alienated from the movement's organizational mainstream, *radical environmentalism* emerged in the 1980s among environmentalists disillusioned with establishment styles and accomplishments. According to environmental historian Bill Devall, the radical environmentalists

> were discouraged by the compromising attitude of mainstream groups, by the bureaucratization of the groups, by the professionalization of leaders and their detachment from the emerging concerns of grassroots supporters, and by the lack of success of mainstream organizations in countering the Reagan anti-environmental agenda.[52]

Radical environmentalists favor direct-action tactics, including the street politics of civil disobedience, nonviolent demonstrations, and political obstruction. To environmental radicals, the harassment of commercial whaling vessels on the high seas by Greenpeace protest vessels, carefully orchestrated to attract media attention worldwide, was better politics than the inhibited reformist style of the mainstream organizations.

Radical environmentalists share a common sensibility that all life is mortally threatened by an ecological degeneration created by advanced modern cultures. Thus, radicals espouse a fundamental cultural transformation that rejects the dominant political and economic institutions of most advanced societies as incompatible with global ecological vitality. This preoccupation with transformational politics usually involves a belief in "bearing witness" through lifestyle changes emphasizing harmony with nature, conservation of resources, and cooperative living in reconstructed, ecologically sensitive societies.[53]

Despite a commitment to nonviolence, radicals betray ambivalence about, if not tolerance of, forms of violence—*ecotage* and *monkeywrenching* are euphemisms—condemned from within and outside the environmental movement. Shadowy groups such as the Animal Liberation

Front (ALF) and the Earth Liberation Front (ELF) are suspected of violent property destruction. (The ALF Web site has contained information on making arson devices, and the ELF claimed responsibility for burning down a Boise Cascade Corporation office in Oregon, causing $1 million in damages.)[54] The small but aggressive movement Earth First!, created by former staff members of mainstream environmental groups, epitomizes this tendency despite its many other conventional activities. For instance, Earth First! spokespeople sometimes assert that in defense of nature, and to save old-growth trees from the lumberyards, it may be permissible to spike these trees with metal rods that are likely to fragment viciously and cause injuries when shattered by commercial logging chain saws.

Other groups, such as Greenpeace and the Sea Shepherd Society, have been accused of nonviolent direct action that provokes violence, such as disabling the nets of commercial fishing vessels whose crews refuse to protect dolphins during deep-sea tuna harvesting. In light of the profound cultural alienation inherent in many radical ideologies, an ambivalence about political violence is inevitable, although radical environmentalism's political strategies still remain—sometimes barely—within the tradition of nonviolent direct action.

Organizational Structures and Strategies

The number and size of environmental organizations expanded through the mid-1990s, but membership subsequently declined, evidence of a familiar up-and-down cycle common to environmental organizations as public perceptions of environmental crises ebb and flow. Strong membership growth throughout the early 1990s was largely a response to aggressive organizational recruiting and the highly publicized confrontations between the White House and environmentalists during the Reagan-Bush period. By the end of the 1990s, the largest environmental organizations had collectively lost more than a million members. Nonetheless, the major national organizations retain the numbers and resources needed to ensure their influential presence in national policymaking. Moreover, to the national membership rolls should be added the thousands of grassroots state and local groups. For instance, one national organization concerned with solid waste identifies seven thousand collaborating state and local groups. Altogether, the number of national, state, and local environmental organizations is estimated to exceed ten thousand.

Membership. Although social support for environmentalism is broadly based in the United States, the organizational membership is mostly middle to upper class, white, well educated, and well off.[55] Such a socially select membership exposes environmentalists to the frequent criticism that the *criticism*

so-called greens are too white and too well off, that they are racists or elitists indifferent to minorities and the economically disadvantaged. To support these accusations, critics argue that environmentalism fights for clean air but not for equal employment opportunities, promotes wilderness preservation for upscale recreationists but not better schools for the disadvantaged, and condemns pollution in national parks but not inner-city decay. In short, the agenda of environmentalism is largely a wish list from the book of middle-class white lifestyles. Mainstream environmental organizations, increasingly sensitive to such criticism, have struggled to broaden their social constituencies and policy agendas. A number of national organizations have initiated joint action with labor and minority groups intended to make environmentalism relevant to the workplace and neighborhood. Most national environmental organizations, responding to initiatives from minority groups, also have supported the emerging environmental equity movement intended to end discrimination against the economically disadvantaged in environmental policymaking. The emergence of environmental racism as a mainstream environmentalist concern is discussed in Chapter 4.

The Organizational Mainstream. The environmental movement's national leadership is concentrated in a small number of highly visible, politically skilled, and influential organizations. Most of these organizations are included in the Group of Ten, an informal alliance of mainstream organizations that often collaborate on national issues. The Group of Ten comprises the National Wildlife Federation, the Sierra Club, the National Audubon Society, the Wilderness Society, Friends of the Earth, Environmental Defense, the National Parks and Conservation Association, the Izaak Walton League, the Natural Resources Defense Council, and the Environmental Policy Institute. The large mainstream groups, the movement's political pragmatists, are thoroughly professionalized and sophisticated in staff and organization. They are armed with the same high-technology tools and modern techniques of policy advocacy as any other powerful national lobby. The large membership rolls of the national organizations demonstrate an aptitude for direct-mail solicitation that is as good as can be found in Washington, D.C.

Growing professionalization of the leadership of the mainstream groups continues to provoke accusations from many environmentalists that the national organizations have lost their fire and vision. The critics charge that the national leadership is more bureaucratic than charismatic, that it has lost touch with the movement's grassroots and has become preoccupied with bargaining and compromise. "Increased professionalization," Robert Cameron Mitchell, Riley Dunlap, and Angela Mertig observe in their study of national environmental organizations, "carries with it the dangers of routinization in advocacy, careerism on the part of staff members, and passivity on the part of volunteers, all of which have been detected in the national organizations."[56]

Factional infighting may be an inevitable price of professional advocacy. Controversy within environmentalism over the political loyalty of the professionalized leadership now frequently erupts into nasty media brawls. A typical incident was the public street fight between environmental organizations over the North American Free Trade Agreement (NAFTA), supported by establishment regulars such as the National Wildlife Federation and the National Audubon Society. Groups opposing NAFTA, including the Sierra Club, Friends of the Earth, Greenpeace, Public Citizen, and the Rainforest Action Network, prepared newspaper advertisements asking, "Why are some 'green' groups so quick to sell off the North American environment? Maybe they are too cozy with corporate funders."[57] This increasing disaffection with the national leadership is one reason for the increase in state and local environmental organizations as well as for the growth of radical environmentalism. Another important reason for the growth of grassroots organizations has been Washington's continuing devolution of regulatory authority to the state and local governments, a trend initiated by the Ronald Reagan administration.

The Essential Politics of Procedure. Rep. John Dingell, D-Mich., a legislator of legendary political skill, once shared a lesson gleaned from thirty years in Congress: "I'll let you write the substance on a statute and you let me write the procedures, and I'll screw you every time."[58] Dingell's axiom illuminates a law as fundamental to policymaking as gravity is to physics—the decision-making rules, as much as the policy outcomes, enlarge or diminish group power. The environmental movement, always respectful of Dingell's axiom, has been as aggressive in promoting advantageous policy procedures as in creating substantive environmental laws.

The politics of procedure is always a fundamental consideration in environmentalist political agendas. Indeed, the movement's power flows, in good part, from success in procedural politics, from aggressively exploiting advantage through the intricate manipulation of policy process. Because so many environmental laws are implemented largely through bureaucracy and the courts, environmental organizations have been especially sensitive to the importance of protecting, or enhancing, decision-making procedures that work to their benefit in these institutions. The success of this strategy depends on securing these procedural advantages through law: statutory, administrative, or judicial. The public politics of environmentalism could not have succeeded so well, and perhaps not at all, had environmentalism's political power not been anchored in procedural law during the movement's rise to influence in the 1970s. "To a great extent, environmental group power ... was legal power," observes political scientist George Hoberg, and environmentalism survived because the new legal arrangements "granted environmental groups institutional and legal foundations that to a large extent solidified their power status within the regime."[59]

Environmental groups have benefited especially from changes in law and administrative procedure that enhance their access to information and their opportunities to participate in the implementation of environmental laws. A major environmental reform was the enactment of NEPA in 1969, requiring federal agencies to prepare environmental impact statements that have become a major source of substantive information and procedural influence in federal environmental policies. Other important reforms include provisions in almost every major environmental law to greatly expand citizen participation in administrative decision making and to make it easier for citizens to sue administrative agencies for failure to implement environmental laws. Equally important has been increased activism among federal judges in reviewing critically the regulatory decisions of environmental agencies—called the hard-look doctrine—that often works to the environmentalists' advantage.

Environmentalism and Its Critics

The mainstream groups are now acknowledged Washington insiders, part of the interest-group establishment. Although environmentalist organizations are committed to defending the public interest and public values, they also represent a constituency with its own ideological and material interests. As environmentalism becomes increasingly organized and politicized nationally, critics assert that it has also assumed the narrow, self-interested viewpoint of every other interest group while promoting policies that often serve no public ends.

Public Interest or Self-Interest?

Critics frequently allege that environmentalism is largely the voice of a social elite hostile to U.S. capitalism, distrustful of science inconsistent to its own viewpoint , and obsessed with imagined or exaggerated ecological problems. In one such indictment, the editors of the *Detroit News* complained that environmentalists were "a small band of environmental doomsayers, mostly upper middle-class whites, who are quick to forecast disaster but never see an upside to technology and economic progress."[60] To fortify such arguments, critics assert that the environmentalists' passion for controlled economic growth will deprive the economically disadvantaged domestically and internationally, that wilderness preservation usually benefits a handful of naturalists but deprives the average American of access to and enjoyment of wilderness resources, and that locking up resources costs jobs and inhibits economic progress. Moreover, continues the indictment, environmentalists often selfishly obstruct valuable public or private projects like power-generating plants, waste landfills, and even apparently environmentally friendly projects when these might threaten their lifestyle or property values—the same NIMBY-ism (Not-In-My-Backyard-ism; the uncompromising public opposition to living next to any potentially hazardous facility) that environmentalists criticize in others. Critics have delightedly seized on events that seem proof of perverse environmentalism, such as the opposition by some environmental spokespeople to a proposed 130-tower wind farm in Horseshoe Shoal, a shallow portion of Nantucket Sound south of Cape Cod and the vehement environmentalist battle against a vast solar-energy plant in the Mojave Desert, a very remote and reliably sunny location.[61] In these and many similar instances, however, plausible reasons exist for concern about the biological and ecological impacts of such projects and—as often happens—the environmentalist community itself is often divided over the issues. Nonetheless, to such critics, environmentalism speaks not for *the* public interest but for *a* public interest, and often a social strata, that excludes millions of Americans.

The white, comfortably middle-class ambiance of most environmental organizations does nothing to diminish such criticism, as a former executive director of the Natural Resources Defense Council, John H. Adams, acknowledges: "There is much to criticize—the predominantly white staffs, the cultural barriers that have damaged and impeded joint efforts with activists of color."[62] Many environmental organizations are striving diligently for greater social diversity in membership and programs. National environmental organizations, for example, are actively seeking, with some success, to build durable alliances with labor unions anchored by a shared concern about workplace safety and worker health, but the stigma of social exclusivity still clings to the movement.[63] In addition, increased professionalization and competition among environmental groups breeds a preoccupation with organizational needs. "There's tremendous competition out there for money," observes Les Line, a former editor of *Audubon Magazine*. "And we've gotten top-heavy with bureaucrats and accountants and fund-raisers who are all good professionals but I don't think you'd catch them sloshing through the marsh."[64] Critics frequently add that environmentalism's hidden agenda is antibusiness, maybe even economic revolution.[65]

Environmental leaders also resort to the rhetoric of crisis so habitually that environmentalism's mother tongue may seem to be the Apocalypse. This hyperbolic style begets the kind of misstatements on which critics often seize to demonstrate environmentalism's distorted vision. There have certainly been errors, as the discussion of the controversies over the chemicals disononyl phthalate (DINP) and dioxin demonstrate (see Chapter 4). In addition, the seriousness of many ecological issues declared to be crises may be, at most, a matter of unresolved scientific controversy. Nonetheless, environmentalists have aroused an appropriate sense of urgency about numerous ecological issues such as air and water pollution, groundwater contamination, radioactive wastes, and surface mining, to cite but a few. The crisis style, however, can eventually become trite and unappealing if it is habitual.

The mainstream environmental organizations are sometimes condemned as shrewd opportunists, promoting policies that enlarge their own political power at public expense. The environmentalist attitude toward the Superfund program is often cited as a flagrant case in point. The major environmental groups generally insist on the strictest possible standards for all Superfund site cleanups, as required in the original law. Others have suggested that some relaxation of standards would enormously shrink the huge program costs and greatly facilitate site cleanups without significantly increasing risks to public health. But, the critics assert, environmentalists insist on the stringent standards because it draws to their side the waste treatment industry and the legal profession, for whom the strictest standards ensure the greatest income.

Constructive Opposition or Destructive Obstruction?

It is a political axiom of organized environmentalism that only unremitting pressure on the government will ensure that environmental laws are implemented effectively. This informal ideology of countervailing power is animated by the conviction that government officials cannot be trusted to implement environmental regulations without the coercive force of pressure politics. Distrust of bureaucrats runs so deeply through environmentalism that, next to saving nature for humanity, environmentalists often seem most dedicated to protecting the public from its public servants. This sour assault on environmental regulators, for instance, comes not from regulation's embittered foes but from Michael McCloskey, the former executive director of the Sierra Club:

> [Regulatory programs] need endless follow-through and can go wrong in a thousand places. The relevant bureaucracies have minds of their own and very little loyalty to the ideas of those who lobbied the programs through.

Although the bureaucracies are somewhat responsive to Presidential direction, they are not very responsive to outside lobbying and are subject to no self-correcting process if they fail to be productive.[66]

The reliance by those within organized environmentalism on countervailing power is manifest in their customary resistance to the relaxation of strict pollution standards, which critics consider to be stonewalling. Countervailing power also means the continual resort to litigation, administrative process, citizen involvement, and any other procedures that equate with group pressure on government. More than half of all litigation initiated against federal agencies involving compliance with NEPA and the majority of all legal challenges to EPA regulations originate with environmental organizations, often in collaboration with labor unions, consumer groups, and private interests. Environmental organizations are extremely aggressive in challenging federal, state, and local agencies over compliance with Superfund cleanup standards and over the licensing of hazardous waste disposal sites and nuclear utilities, among many other issues. Citizen involvement activities at all governmental levels are exploited, if not dominated, by environmental groups and their allies, to considerable advantage.[67]

The skilled exploitation of these and other political processes has invested environmentalists with political power they probably would not otherwise have. Moreover, countervailing power often forces administrative agencies and their regulated interests to comply with laws they might prefer to ignore and frequently improves the quality of regulatory decision making. But countervailing power also has produced enormous delays in the implementation of regulations and increased significantly the cost of environmental regulation through litigation and administrative process. In addition, countervailing power at state and local levels can virtually immobilize the process of licensing hazardous waste facilities. Whether the use of countervailing power has become dangerously disruptive to environmental governance is a concern to many within the environmental movement as well as to its critics because such power can be subverted into the chronic obstruction of the processes it was intended to safeguard.

The continuing controversy over environmentalism, whatever its admitted merits, reveals some political realities—environmentalist organizations have institutional dogmas and self-serving agendas that may not always be compatible with the larger interests of the movement or even with their own professed goals. Although environmental organizations frequently speak in the name of an encompassing public interest and may unselfishly pursue it, they also speak for a distinctive social and ideological constituency that often does not include the whole public or even a majority of the public.

public. Environmentalism itself is increasingly divided over the goals and social constituencies to which it should be responsive. The rancorous pluralism already inspired by these conflicting convictions will continue to expand during the twenty-first century. In addition, the professionalization of national organizational leadership—inevitable if environmentalism is to survive the fiercely competitive struggle among interest groups for political resources—is also likely to breed a growing disunity between the national leadership and grassroots environmentalism.

The Public and Environmentalism

Whatever its internal dissonances, the environmental movement has been largely responsible for a remarkable growth in public environmental consciousness and acceptance of environmental protection as an essential public policy. These are public assets, essential to the movement's continuing political vitality, and environmental organizations are extremely adept at arousing public concern on environmental matters and turning it into political advantage. How durable and deep this public support may be, especially in times of severe political or economic hardship, is a different matter.

A Core Value

"The transformation of the environment from an issue of limited concern to one of universal concern is now complete," observed opinion analyst Everett Carll Ladd in mid-1996.[68] The strength of public support for environmental protection early in the twenty-first century, as measured by public opinion polls, certainly appears vigorous and widespread. It might even appear superficially that the United States was becoming a nation of environmentalists. From the early 1970s into the exit of George W. Bush's presidency, public opinion polls generally exemplified strong public support for environmental protection throughout most American social, ethnic, and regional groups.[69] In 2008, for example, an opinion poll by Duke University's Nicholas Institute posed this question to a representative sample of American voters: "Now, let's say you heard about a proposal that would create stronger national standards to help protect our land, air and water. Not knowing any of the specifics, but just generally, does that sound like something you would favor or oppose?" Almost 80 percent of respondents reported they would favor such a proposal, responses consistent with other polls that regularly exemplified strongly favorable public support for numerous environmental protection measures. Another national poll the same year reported that 41 percent of respondents thought of themselves "as an environmentalist."[70]

Critics sometimes assert that environmental interest groups speak for only a small portion of the public, but these polls seem to suggest otherwise. In general, opinion polls consistently report that substantial majorities in almost all major socioeconomic groups support the environmental movement and governmental programs to protect the environment and have supported them since Earth Day 1970.[71] Environmental activists have been especially gratified that the polls offer little support to the once widespread notion that concern for environmental quality is a "white thing."[72] As long as environmental questions are lofty abstractions, the public's answers can easily imply that environmentalism's roots run deeply as well as broadly across the nation. Certainly when the political bedrock of environmental regulation seems threatened—when fundamental laws such as the Clean Air Act or Clean Water Act seem imperiled—public support for environmentalism has been impressive. The most politically powerful demonstration of such support occurred during the bitter confrontation between the Reagan administration and environmental organizations in the early 1980s.

Environmentalists have also accomplished what amounts to a massive raising of the public's ecological consciousness through public education about environmental issues facing the United States and the world. On the first Earth Day, ecology and the environment were issues foreign to most Americans. Today, most Americans have a rudimentary understanding of many basic ecological precepts, including the importance of resource conservation and the global scale of environmental problems. The movement has educated the public and itself into embracing a progressively larger conception of the environment. Before the 1960s, most environmental groups were concerned primarily with land and wildlife management, not with air or water pollution or hazardous waste. The goals of the early environmentalists were nearsighted, focused mostly on domestic issues, and the supporting science was unsophisticated in its lack of sensitivity to the complex interrelationships among environmental problems. Today viewpoints are more global, ecologically informed, and expansive.

Environmental organizations also have encouraged greater public skepticism about the credibility and managerial skills of the scientists, technicians, and other spokespeople for science and technology involved in public affairs. Since the mid-1970s, environmental organizations have repeatedly challenged the competence of scientific experts and the quality of science supporting opponents in political and administrative battles. These unrelenting technical controversies over the management of commercial nuclear power, the regulation of pesticides, the setting of appropriate air- and water-quality standards, and much else have educated the public about the limits of scientific expertise. Many environmental groups have promoted local citizen involvement in decisions about the siting of real or potential environmental hazards. Critics charge that these groups are entirely too successful at grassroots activism. They blame environmentalists for the rapid spread of NIMBY-ism. This issue is discussed more fully in Chapter 7.

How Deep and Broad is Public Environmentalism?

Despite the public's ecological concern, environmentalism's public impact is still restricted in politically important ways. Environmentalism may now be a consensual value in U.S. politics, but it is what public opinion analyst Riley E. Dunlap calls a "passive consensus"—a situation of "widespread but not terribly intense public support for a goal [in which] government has considerable flexibility in pursuing the goal and is not carefully monitored by the public."[73] Carll Ladd is blunter: Americans, having affirmed their environmentalism, "have turned to other things."[74]

By 2010, several durable patterns had emerged suggesting that the "other things" to which Americans are turning seldom included sustained interest or reflection about environmental issues at home, at work, or at the voting booth. First, environmental issues have rarely risen to compelling importance or remained among the issues that most concern the public. Thus, when the Pew Research Center asked a sample of the American public in early 2009 which issues should receive priority in Congress and the White House that year, four in ten Americans said "protecting the environment" should be a top priority yet ranked many issues much higher on their preference lists. Protecting the environment scored fifteenth out of twenty issues on the public's overall priority, behind such leading issues as defending the United States from terrorist attacks, improving the educational system, strengthening the economy, and seven other concerns, as illustrated in Figure 2-1. And, as Table 2-1 indicates, the public importance of environmentalism has apparently diminished gradually over the last decade; by 2009, the percentage of respondents ranking the environment as a high presidential priority had diminished from 63 to 41 percent.

Even though the public consistently rates Democrats much higher than Republicans on environmental stewardship, being green seldom appears to help any presidential candidate get to the White House. Environmentalism, in fact, has had little impact so far on voting for president. In none of the past six presidential elections, for instance, did more than 11 percent of voters ever state that the environment was the most important issue in casting their ballots.[75] Asked in 2008 if they were likely to vote for a president who was "a strong environmentalist," 54 percent of the poll

Figure 2-1 The American Public's Top Issue Priorities for the Obama Administration for 2009

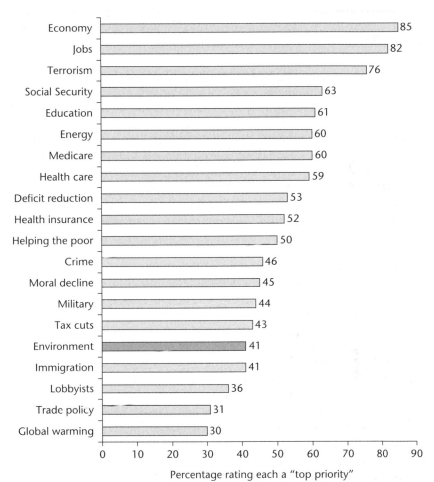

Percentage rating each a "top priority"

Source: Pew Research Center for the People and the Press, "Economy, Jobs Trump All Other Policy Priorities in 2009: Environment, Immigration, Health Care Slip Down the List," The Pew Center, Washington, D.C., January 22, 2009, 1. Reprinted by permission.

respondents reported it would matter little or not at all and another 6 percent were uncertain.[76] Despite Bill Clinton's efforts in 1996 to wrap his campaign in an environmentalist mantle with the presence of self-proclaimed environmentalist Al Gore as his running mate, fewer than 1 percent of those who voted for him cited environmentalism as the most important reason and fewer than 10 percent cited environmentalism

Table 2-1 Top Domestic Priorities for Obama and Congress

	Percentage considering each as a "top priority"									
	Jan. 2001	Jan. 2002	Jan. 2003	Jan. 2004	Jan. 2005	Jan. 2006	Jan. 2007	Jan. 2008	Jan. 2009	Change 2008–2009
Strengthening nation's economy	81	71	73	79	75	66	68	75	85	+10
Improving the job situation	60	67	62	67	68	65	57	61	82	+21
Defending U.S. against terrorism	—	83	81	78	75	80	80	74	76	+2
Securing Social Security	74	62	59	65	70	64	64	64	63	–1
Improving educational system	78	66	62	71	70	67	69	66	61	–5
Dealing with U.S. energy problems	—	42	40	46	47	58	57	59	60	+1
Securing Medicare	71	55	56	62	67	62	63	60	60	0
Reducing health-care costs	—	—	—	—	—	—	68	69	59	–10
Reducing budget deficit	—	35	40	51	56	55	53	58	53	–5
Providing health insurance to uninsured	61	43	45	54	60	59	56	54	52	–2
Dealing with problems of poor	63	44	48	50	59	55	55	51	50	–1
Reducing crime	76	53	47	53	53	62	62	54	46	–8
Dealing with moral breakdown	51	45	39	45	41	47	47	43	45	+2
Strengthening the military	48	52	48	48	52	42	46	42	44	+2
Reducing middle-class taxes	66	43	—	44	48	51	48	46	43	–3
Protecting the environment	63	44	39	49	49	57	57	56	41	–15
Dealing with illegal immigration	—	—	—	—	—	—	55	51	41	–10
Reducing influence of lobbyists	—	—	—	—	—	—	35	39	36	–3
Dealing with global trade	37	25	—	32	32	30	34	37	31	–6
Dealing with global warming	—	—	—	—	—	—	38	35	30	–5

Source: Pew Research Center for the People and the Press, "Economy, Jobs Trump All Other Policy Priorities in 2009: Environment, Immigration, Health Care Slip Down the List," The Pew Center, Washington, D.C., January 22, 2009, 3. Reprinted by permission.

among *any* reason for supporting him.[77] Conversely, environmentalists may have fiercely criticized both Ronald Reagan's and George W. Bush's records on environmental regulation, but this did not hurt either candidate at the polls.[78] Massive environmentalist criticism of George W. Bush's environmental policies following his 2000 election, moreover, did not appear to change significantly the public's evaluation of Bush as an environmental protector (indeed, in mid-2003 more than half the public polled by Gallup reported that the nation's environmental protection policies were "about the same" as when Bush was elected).[79]

It seems environmental values are linked weakly to candidate preferences for most voters at most elections and certainly in presidential contests. Among the reasons for environmentalism's electoral disconnect among voters, the Nichols Institute suggests that most voters:

- Believe significant progress has been made in environmental protection.
- Perceive the environment as "long-term issues that did not warrant the same priority as more 'immediate' concerns such as jobs and health care."
- Assume that environmental policies would have negative economic impacts such as lost jobs and higher taxes.[80]

Nonetheless, major environmental organizations remain determined to mobilize the public to support green candidates and legislation, while insisting (especially to elective officials and candidates) that environmentalism is potent at the polls. After the 2000 presidential election, the most important environmentalist political campaign organization, the League of Conservation Voters, released a public opinion poll that appeared to demonstrate, among other things, that clean air and water are "top-tier concerns among voters, that environmental issues were 'central to Americans' vote decisions in November' and at least 'important' to Presidential voting."[81] Perhaps. But, on the evidence, the message seems more like preaching to the choir.

Sudden surges of public interest or apprehension about the environment predictably rise in the aftermath of widely publicized environmental disasters or emergencies, but public concern is usually evanescent unless the issue is repeatedly dramatized and personalized. At best, it appears that deep public engagement with environmental issues is a sometime thing. "While the environment has enjoyed remarkable staying power on the national political agenda over the past thirty years," concludes political scientist Deborah Lynn Guber after studying public environmental attitudes, "public commitment to those issues can be somewhat fickle, moving in cycles that visibly advance and retreat over time."[82] This is also evident in Table 2-1, which tracks public concern for environmental protection from 2001 through 2009.

Another important trend across this decade has been increasing public concern about the possible adverse economic impact of environmental regulation. One symptom has been a gradual increase in the proportion of the public that, when asked to make a choice, agreed that economic growth should take precedence over environmental protection—evidence of the nation's growing economic malaise during these years. By 2009, Gallup reported for the first time in twenty-five years of repeated polling on the issue that a majority favored the economy over the environment, one among many indicators of how pervasively economic anxieties dominated domestic politics in the wake of the continuing recession.[83]

The severe recession, which began in late 2007, undoubtedly fueled the public's growing preoccupation with the economy and demonstrated, once again, the potency of economic issues in commanding public attention and setting national policy priorities. Environmentalism has yet to prove its political toughness by surviving the brutal test of a prolonged recession or a depression. In broader perspective, these polls exemplify what most public officials know from experience—the enormous difficulty in persuading the public to accept the sometimes substantial costs of environmental management in terms of dollars or lifestyle. (Jimmy Carter, battered by a nasty public backlash when his administration attempted to manage the 1970s energy crisis with a portfolio of new controls on public energy consumption and availability, compared that struggle to "gnawing on a rock.")[84] It may sometimes appear to environmental leaders that an environmental equivalent of the 9/11 terrorist attack on New York is required to arouse sustained public attention and acceptance for even modest personal costs that might be involved.

Finally, a deep, apparently durable partisan cleavage runs like a fault line across public alignments on most domestic environmental matters. On most major issues related to the environmental policy—how to regulate, what to regulate, and whether to regulate—Republican and Democratic partisans persistently disagree.[85] Compared to Republicans, Democrats are more receptive to environmental regulation and its management by government, more likely to attribute importance to environmental issues in domestic politics, more inclined to give environmental policy greater salience in shaping their candidate preferences, and more inclined overall to perceive environmentalists favorably. The partisan divide on environmental issues is apparent in Table 2-2, which illustrates the demographic differences in public attitudes about the importance of environmental issues in 2008 and 2009.

Perhaps another common but unstated reason that environmental policy does not engage the public more broadly and deeply is the inherent

Table 2-2 Demographic Differences in the Priority of Environmental Protection, 2008–2009

	Percentage rating environmental protection as a "top priority"		Change 2008–2009
	Jan. 2008	Jan. 2009	
Total	56	41	−15
Men	55	39	−16
Women	57	43	−14
Ages 18–34	55	43	−12
Ages 35–49	58	41	−17
Ages 50–64	56	35	−21
Ages 65+	57	45	−12
College graduate	46	35	−11
Some college	58	36	−22
High school or less	61	48	−13
Republican	39	20	−19
Independent	56	41	−15
Democrat	67	54	−13
Moderate/conservative Democrat	63	54	−9
Liberal Democrat	74	57	−17

Source: Pew Research Center for the People and the Press, "Economy, Jobs Trump All Other Policy Priorities in 2009: Environment, Immigration, Health Care Slip Down the List," The Pew Center, Washington, D.C., January 22, 2009, 5. Reprinted by permission.

scientific complexity of the issues, which may often confound or mystify the average person. No matter, science and science disputes are unavoidable in environmental policy discourse.

The Special Place of Science in Policymaking

What often distinguishes environmental policymaking from other policy domains is the extraordinary importance of science, and scientific controversy, in the policy process. The growth of environmental legislation since the 1970s is evidence of the federal government's increasing concern with science and technology after World War II. Legislation concerning atomic power, air and water pollution, workplace and consumer safety, and hazardous wastes has put before public officials and agencies the need to make determinations of public policy by depending heavily on scientific evidence and scientific judgments. Indeed, environmental issues routinely require administrative agencies, Congress, judges, the White House staff, and even the president to make these determinations.

Science as Law

The range of scientific judgments required of administrative agencies in implementing environmental programs seems to embrace the whole domain of ecological research. For instance, the Coast Guard is authorized "in order to secure effective provisions ... for protection of the marine environment ... to establish regulations for ships with respect to the design and construction of such vessels ... and with respect to equipment and appliances for ... the prevention and mitigation of damage to the marine environment."[86]

The EPA is to set effluent standards for new sources of water pollution so that each standard reflects "the greatest degree of effluent reduction ... achievable through application of the best available demonstrated control technology, process, operating methods, or other alternatives, including, where practicable, a standard permitting no discharge of pollutants."[87] The EPA is also required to establish "standards of performance" for classes and categories of new air pollution sources "which contribute significantly to air pollution or contribute to endangerment of public health or welfare."[88]

Congress, and particularly the congressional committees writing legislation, also may have to resolve a multitude of technical issues. When regulating hazardous substances, for instance, what is a reasonable period to specify for chemical manufacturers to produce reliable data on the human effects of potentially dangerous substances? Is it necessary to regulate air emissions from diesel trucks to reduce harmful air pollutants? Is it appropriate to include heavy metals in the list of water pollutants for which standards must be created by the EPA? Eventually, judges will be compelled to weigh scientific evidence and render judgment on environmental issues. For example, did the Department of the Interior have sufficient information to file a valid environmental impact statement on a proposed coal-mining lease on federal lands, as required by NEPA? Or do federal standards for nuclear reactors adequately protect public safety, as required by regulations created by the Nuclear Regulatory Commission?

Science as Politics

In policy conflicts, data become weapons and science becomes a bastion against critics. Indeed, torturing the technical data to fit some partisan position has become an art form in policy debates. Environmental issues frequently place scientists in a highly charged political atmosphere in which impartiality and objectivity, among the most highly esteemed scientific virtues, are severely tested and sometimes fail.

Scientists are consulted by public officials in good part because the scientists' presumed objectivity, as well as their technical expertise, makes them trustworthy advisers. But impartiality can be an early casualty in highly partisan and polarizing policy conflicts. Even if scientists maintain impartiality, they cannot prevent the partisans of one or another policy from distorting the technical information to gain an advantage. Scientists suspect (with justification) that their work will often be misrepresented in political debate and their credibility consequently diminished.

In any case, it is characteristic of environmental policy that scientific evidence and opinion frequently are divided for political reasons and, thus, that expert disagreements will reinforce political conflicts. Especially when political conflict tends to polarize views and force division over issues, an expert can intentionally, or unwittingly, shade opinions to fit a favored position or manipulate materials until they fit a simplistic policy position. "Experts tend to behave like other people when they engage in a controversy," Allan Mazur, a sociologist and physicist, observes. "Coalitions solidify and disagreements become polarized as conflict becomes more acrimonious."[89] Mazur further observes that experts favoring nuclear power tend to support the notion that a threshold of radiation exposure exists below which human risks are negligible; experts opposing nuclear power plants, in contrast, favor a linear conception of risk that permits no such threshold.[90] When scientific disputes erupt in the course of environmental decision making, we need not assume willful deceit on any side to suggest that political and economic bias could, and probably does, play some part in convincing experts of the truth of a position. Unfortunately, few executives or legislative agencies are innocent of data manipulation, deliberate or not, at some time.

Policy Pressures and the Scientific Method

Few public officials are scientists. Faced with the technical questions inherent in environmental policy, officials customarily turn to scientists and technicians for answers or at least for definitions of alternative solutions to clarify choices. As a matter of practical politics, solving issues by resorting to credible scientific evidence can also deflect from officials the criticism they might otherwise endure—sometimes science alone legitimizes policy. But the politician and the scientist live in fundamentally different decision-making worlds.

For instance, significant differences exist in the time frames for problem solving. "In his search for truth," biologist Roger Revelle observes, "the scientist is oriented toward the future; the politician's orientation is usually here and now. He desires quick visible pay-offs for which he often seems willing to mortgage the future. For the politician in a democratic society, infinity is the election after the next one."[91] Often, public officials are compelled to act swiftly. The Clean Air Act, for example, required the EPA administrator to set standards for sulfur oxides and nitrogen oxides within two years. The Superfund Amendments and Reauthorization Act, passed in 1986, included among its 150 deadlines a requirement that the EPA issue a plan to implement the act's radon research program, produce an annual report on radon mitigation demonstration programs, and provide a report on its national assessment of the radon problem in less than two years after the legislation was passed.[92]

If a crisis erupts—a newly discovered leaking hazardous waste dump or a potentially catastrophic oil spill, for instance—information is needed immediately. But scientific information rarely appears on demand, even in urgent situations and especially when it must be sufficiently accurate to point to a clear direction for policy.

Public officials, moreover, often must craft environmental policies amid continuing disagreement between experts and the public over the degree of risk associated with various environmental problems. For instance, whereas the public rated chemical waste disposal as the highest environmental risk, the experts ranked it considerably lower. In contrast, the experts assigned much greater risk to stratospheric ozone depletion and indoor radon than did the public. Chemical plant accidents were rated a major risk by the public but not by the experts. In effect, these differences amount to two different agendas of priority for environmental regulation. Critics of current environmental regulation, pointing to these disparate views of ecological risk, often argue that public opinion has intimidated policymakers into following the wrong environmental priorities.

Still, decisions must be made, thus confronting policymakers with an unsettling choice between a scientifically risky decision and a politically risky one.[93] Consider, for example, the decision in September 1997 by officials of the National Institute of Environmental Health Sciences (NIEHS) and the Minnesota Pollution Control Agency (MPCA) to announce publicly that samples of Minnesota surface water and groundwater had produced severe abnormalities in native frogs. Asserting they did not know which compound in the water might have caused the deformities or what human health effects might follow, the agencies offered bottled water to residents with drinking wells in the affected areas, a pronouncement quickly reported and amplified by the state and national news media. Little more than a month later, the NIEHS and the MPCA endured withering criticism from scientific colleagues who accused the agencies of making a rushed and inept decision that unduly alarmed the public without scientific justification. Researchers in the EPA's Minnesota research laboratory, as well as other research scientists, asserted that their own evidence contradicted the agencies' conclusions, that the deformities had resulted from a chemical imbalance common to Minnesota water, and that the findings were not particularly worrisome. "Now federal scientists are going to look like idiots, even ones who are ultimately proven right," complained the director of another federal research lab. Nonetheless, the NIEHS and the MPCA defended their decision. "We had no intention of going public until we were further along in interpreting the data," explained an NIEHS official, but a public announcement became unavoidable. The MPCA research scientist who made the decision to alert the public insisted that she would still make the same decision. Knowledge about the frog deformities was spreading among the public, she explained, and any attempt by her agency to distribute bottled water without a public explanation would incite a panic. "We felt as a public agency we needed to let people know exactly where research was at," she concluded.[94]

The Minnesota incident was especially discomfiting for scientific professionals because scientists prefer to measure the correctness of a policy by the standards of experimentation and empiricism. Public officials, in contrast, have to calculate a standard's correctness using several additional criteria: Will it satisfy enough public and private interests to be enforceable? Can it be enforced with existing governmental personnel and within the budget? Does the standard appear credible? (It must not be so controversial as to shake public confidence.) But scientists may measure acceptability by the single standard of accuracy; this, not acceptability, matters. Under these circumstances, it is understandable that policymakers and their scientific consultants often disagree about which data should be used, and in what manner, in policy decisions.

Conclusion

In an important sense, environmental degradation is a twenty-first-century problem resolved according to eighteenth-century rules. Fundamental government arrangements, such as institutional checks and balances, interest-group liberalism, federalism, and much else reviewed in this chapter, are explicitly created by the Constitution or are implicit in its philosophy. The explosive growth of federal environmental legislation and the distinctive role of science in environmental policymaking add distinctly new elements to the federal policy cycle and indicate that environmental management has become a permanent new policy domain within federal and state governments with its own set of institutional and political biases.

Suggested Readings

Cohen, Richard E. *Washington at Work: Back Rooms and Clean Air.* New York: Macmillan, 1992.

Gruber, Deborah Lynn. *The Grassroots of a Green Revolution.* Cambridge, Mass.: MIT Press, 2003.

Layzer, Judith. *The Environmental Case: Translating Values Into Policy.* 2nd ed. Washington, D.C.: CQ Press, 2005.

Lindblom, Charles A., and Edward J. Woodhouse. *The Policy-Making Process.* 3rd ed. Englewood Cliffs, N.J.: Prentice-Hall, 1993.

Marzotto, Toni, Vicky Moshier Burnor, and Gordon Scott Bonham. *The Evolution of Public Policy: Cars and the Environment.* Boulder, Colo.: Lynne Rienner, 2000.

Notes

1. Andrew C. Revkin, "Bush vs. the Laureates: How Science Became a Partisan Issue," *New York Times,* October 19, 2004, A1.
2. Andrew C. Revkin, "Climate Scientist Says NASA Tried to Silence Him," *New York Times,* January 29, 2006, A1
3. Quoted in Chuck Schoffner, "NASA Expert Says Bush Administration Stifles Evidence on Global Warming," Associated Press State and Local Wire, October 27, 2004, available at: www.ap.org (accessed January 5, 2007).
4. Quoted in Revkin, "Climate Scientist," A1.
5. Ibid.
6. Andrew C. Revkin, "NASA Chief Backs Agency Openness," *New York Times,* February 4, 2006, 1.
7. Quoted in Andrew C. Revkin, "Lawmaker Condemns NASA over Scientist's Accusations of Censorship," *New York Times,* January 31, 2006, A15.
8. Quoted in ibid.
9. Quoted in Revkin, "Climate Scientist," A1.
10. Andrew C. Revkin, "Years Later Climatologist Renews His Call for Action," *New York Times,* June 23, 2008, A18.
11. Andrew C. Revkin, "NASA Office Is Criticized on Climate Reports," *New York Times,* June 3, 2008, A16.
12. States News Service, "James Hansen and David Foster Share Inaugural Peter A. A. Berle Environmental Integrity Awards," April 30, 2009; PR Newswire, "NASA Climate Scientist Honored by American Meteorological Society," January 14, 2009.
13. Hugh Heclo, "Issue Networks and the Executive Establishment," in *The New American Political System,* ed. Anthony King (Washington, D.C.: American Enterprise Institute, 1979), 89.
14. Charles O. Jones, *An Introduction to Public Policy* (North Scituate, Mass.: Duxbury Press, 1978), 38.
15. Roger W. Cobb and Charles D. Elder, *Participation in American Politics* (Baltimore: Johns Hopkins University Press, 1972), 86.
16. J. Clarence Davies III, "Environmental Regulation and Technical Change," in *Keeping Pace with Science and Engineering: Studies in Environmental Regulation,* ed. Myron F. Uman (Washington, D.C.: National Academies Press, 1993), 255.
17. Eugene Bardach, *The Implementation Game* (Cambridge, Mass.: MIT Press, 1971), 36.
18. Peter deLeon, "A Theory of Termination in the Policy Process: Rules, Rhymes and Reasons," paper delivered at the annual meeting of the American Political Science Association, Washington, D.C., September 1–4, 1977, 2.

19. Richard E. Neustadt, *Presidential Power* (New York: John Wiley, 1960).
20. Morton Grodzins, "The Federal System," in *American Federalism in Perspective,* ed. Aaron Wildavsky (Boston: Little, Brown, 1967), 257.
21. Ibid. See also Charles E. Davis and James P. Lester, "Federalism and Environmental Policy," in *Environmental Politics and Policy: Theories and Evidence,* ed. James P. Lester (Durham, N.C.: Duke University Press, 1989), 57–86; James P. Lester, "A New Federalism? Environmental Policy in the States," in *Environmental Policy in the 1990s,* ed. Norman J. Vig and Michael Kraft (Washington, D.C.: CQ Press, 1990), 59–80.
22. U.S. Advisory Commission on Intergovernmental Relations, *Federal Regulation of State and Local Governments: The Mixed Record of the 1980s,* Publication A-126 (Washington, D.C.: Advisory Commission on Intergovernmental Relations, July 1993), 44–45, chaps. 4, 8.
23. This mingling of private and public power is well explored in Grant McConnell, *Private Power and American Democracy* (New York: Vintage Books, 1967). See also Helen M. Ingram and Dean E. Mann, "Interest Groups and Environmental Policy," in *Environmental Politics and Policy: Theories and Evidence,* ed. James P. Lester (Durham, N.C.: Duke University Press, 1989), 135–157.
24. James V. DeLong, "How to Convince an Agency," *Regulation* (September–October 1982): 31.
25. Graham Allison, *The Essence of Decision* (Boston: Little, Brown, 1971), 163.
26. Charles A. Lindblom, "The Science of Muddling Through," *Public Administration Review* (spring 1959): 86.
27. James Gustave Speth, "Environmental Failure: A Case for the New Green Politics," *Environment 360: Opinion,* October 20, 2008, available at: http://e360.yale.edu/content/feature.msp?id=2075.
28. The reasons for this departure are examined carefully in J. Clarence Davies III and Charles F. Lettow, "The Impact of Federal Institutional Arrangements," in *Federal Environmental Law,* ed. Erica L. Dolgin and Thomas G. P. Guilbert (St. Paul, Minn.: West, 1974), 26–191.
29. Theodore Lowi, "The Public Philosophy: Interest Group Liberalism," *American Political Science Review* 61 (March 1967): 18.
30. McConnell, *Private Power and American Democracy,* 162.
31. Center for Public Integrity, "Investigations: The Climate Change Lobby Heating Up," Center for Public Integrity, available at: www.publicintegrity.org/projects/entry/1182/ (accessed August 28, 2009).
32. Charles E. Lindblom and Edward J. Woodhouse, *The Policy-Making Process,* 3rd ed. (Englewood Cliffs, N.J.: Prentice-Hall, 1993), 90.
33. Charles A. Lindblom, *The Policy Making Process,* 2nd ed. (Englewood Cliffs, N.J.: Prentice-Hall, 1980), 73.
34. Ibid.
35. Fredreka Schouten, "Big Greens and Friends Spend $2.9 million in Aug 09 Pushing Self-Dealing Climate Bills," *USA Today,* September 2, 2009, available at: http://www.usatoday.com/news/washington/2009-09-02-climateads_N.htm.
36. Fredreka Schouten, "Backers of Climate Bill Spend More on Ads," *USA Today,* September 3, 2009, available at: www.usatoday.com/news/washington/2009-09-02-climateads_N.htm (accessed December 23, 2009).
37. Riley E. Dunlap, "The State of Environmentalism in the U.S.—Diagnosis: Neither Dead nor Rejuvenated," April 26, 2007, available at: www.ecoamerica.typepad.com/blog/2007/04/the_state_of_en.html.
38. Steve Crabtree, "Surprising Stats on 'Active' Environmentalists," *Gallup Poll Tuesday Report,* April 8, 2003, available at: www.gallup.com (accessed February 12, 2004).

39. Robert Brulle, Liesel Hall Turner, Jason Carmichael, and J. Craig Jenkins, "Measuring Social Movement Organization Populations: A Comprehensive Census of U.S. Environmental Movement Organizations," *Mobilization: An International Quarterly Review* 12 (July 2007): 195–210.

40. Dunlap, "State of Environmentalism."

41. Robert Cameron Mitchell, Angela G. Mertig, and Riley E. Dunlap, "Twenty Years of Environmental Mobilization: Trends among National Environmental Organizations," in *American Environmentalism: The U.S. Environmental Movement, 1970–1990,* ed. Riley E. Dunlap and Angela G. Mertig (Philadelphia: Taylor and Francis, 1991), 24.

42. Katrina Darlene Taylor, "The Broadening Strategy of Environmental Organizations on the Issue of Global Warming," paper presented at the annual conference of the Western Political Science Association, San Diego, Calif., 2008.

43. Committee on Energy and Commerce, "Climate Change Legislation Design White Paper: Appropriate Roles for Different Levels of Government," February 2008, available at: http://energycommerce.house.gov/Climate_Change/white%20paper%20st-lcl%20roles%20final%202-22.pdf.

44. Tom Price, "The New Environmentalism: Can New Business Policies Save the Environment?" *CQ Researcher* 16, no. 42 (2006): 985–1008.

45. William Ophuls, *Ecology and the Politics of Uncertainty* (San Francisco: Freeman, 1977), 171.

46. A. Susan Leeson, "Philosophic Implications of the Ecological Crisis: The Authoritarian Challenge to Liberalism," *Polity* 11 (spring 1979): 305.

47. Michael McCloskey, "Twenty Years of Change in the Environmental Movement: An Insider's View," in *American Environmentalism: The U.S. Environmental Movement, 1970–1990,* ed. Riley E. Dunlap and Angela G. Mertig (Philadelphia: Taylor and Francis, 1991), 78–89, quotation on 78.

48. Brian Tokar, "Questioning Official Environmentalism," *Z Magazine,* April 1997, 38.

49. Jeffrey St. Clair, "Panda Porn: The Marriage of WWF and Weyerhaeuser," *Counterpunch Magazine,* December 5, 2002, available at: http://www.counterpunch.org/stclair1205.html (accessed April 2, 2010).

50. Quoted in Scott Allen, *Boston Globe,* October 20, 1997, 8.

51. Bill Devall, "Deep Ecology and Radical Environmentalism," in *American Environmentalism: The U.S. Environmental Movement, 1970–1990,* ed. Riley E. Dunlap and Angela G. Mertig (Philadelphia: Taylor and Francis, 1991), 51–61; G. Sessions, "The Deep Ecology Movement," *Environment Review* 11 (June 1987): 105–125; Rick Scarce, *Eco-Warriors: Understanding the Radical Environmental Movement* (Chicago: Noble Press, 1992).

52. Devall, "Deep Ecology and Radical Environmentalism," 55.

53. David Foreman, *Ecodefense* (Tucson, Ariz.: Abbzug Press, 1988); G. Grossman, *And on the Eighth Day We Bulldozed It* (San Francisco: Rainbow Action Network, 1988); S. Obst Love and D. Obst Love, eds., *Ecotage* (New York: Bantam Books, 1972); D. Day, *The Environmental Wars: Reports from the Front Lines* (New York: St. Martin's, 1989).

54. John H. Cushman Jr. and Evelyn Nieves, "In Colorado Resort Fires, Culprits Defy Easy Labels," *New York Times,* October 24, 1998.

55. Robert Cameron Mitchell, "From Conservation to Environmental Movement: The Development of the Modern Environmental Lobbies," in *Government and Environmental Politics,* ed. Michael J. Lacey (Washington, D.C.: Wilson Center Press, 1989), 81–114; Michael deCourcy Hinds, "The Politics of Pollution," *American Demographics* 22 (2000): 26.

56. Robert Cameron Mitchell, Angela Mertig, and Riley E. Dunlap, "Public Opinion and the Green Lobby," in *American Environmentalism: The U.S. Environmental Movement, 1970-1990*, ed. Riley E. Dunlap and Angela G. Mertig (Philadelphia: Taylor and Francis, 1992), 21.

57. *New York Times*, September 16, 1993, A6.

58. George Hoberg, *Pluralism by Design: Environmental Policy and the American Regulatory State* (New York: Praeger, 1992), ix.

59. Ibid., 198–199.

60. Warren T. Brookes, "Here Comes Flat Earth Day," *Detroit News*, March 8, 1990, 13.

61. Amanda Little, "RFK Jr. and Other Prominent Enviros Face Off over Cape Cod Wind Farm," *Grist*, January 12, 2006, available at: www.grist.org/article/capecod; Jeffry Ball, "Power Shift: Renewable Energy, Meet the New Nimbys—Solar and Wind-Power Proposals Draw Opposition from Residents Fearing Visual Blight; a Dilemma for Some Environmentalists," *Wall Street Journal* (eastern ed.), September 4, 2009, A13.

62. John H. Adams, "The Mainstream Environmental Movement," *EPA Journal* 18, no. 1 (1992), 25–26.

63. Bryan Mayor, *Blue-Green Coalitions: Fighting for Safe Workplaces and Healthy Communities* (Ithaca, N.Y.: Cornell University Press, 2009).

64. Quoted in *New York Times*, June 9, 1993, 7.

65. Marc K. Landy and Mary Hague, "The Coalition for Waste: Private Interests and Superfund," in *Environmental Politics: Public Costs, Private Rewards*, ed. Michael S. Greve and Fred L. Smith (New York: Praeger, 1992), 75.

66. McCloskey, "Twenty Years of Change," 86.

67. Michael J. McCann, "Public Interest Liberalism and the Modern Regulatory State," *Polity* 21 (winter 1988): 373–400.

68. Everett Carll Ladd and Karlyn Bowman, "Public Opinion on the Environment," *Resources* 124 (summer 1996): 5.

69. See, for example, Riley E. Dunlap, "An Enduring Concern," *Public Perspective*, September–October 2002, 10–15.

70. Nicholas Institute for Environmental Policy Solutions, *A Presentation of Key Findings from a National Survey of 800 Likely Voters Conducted August 25–28, 2005* (Durham N.C.: Nicholas Institute, 2005), 2.

71. Steven R. Brechin and Daniel A. Freeman, "Public Support for Both the Environment and Anti-Environmental President: Possible Explanations for the George W. Bush Anomaly," *Forum* 2, no. 1 (2004), Berkeley Electronic Press, available at: http://www.bepress.com/forum.

72. Paul Mohai, "Dispelling Old Myths: African American Concern for the Environment," *Environment* 45 (June 2003): 11–26.

73. Riley E. Dunlap, "Public Opinion and Environmental Policy," in *Environmental Politics and Policy: Theories and Evidence*, ed. James P. Lester (Durham, N.C.: Duke University Press, 1989), 131.

74. Ladd and Bowman, "Public Opinion on the Environment," 5.

75. Ibid.

76. ABC News/Planet Green/Stanford University poll.

77. Ibid., 7.

78. Brechin and Freeman, "Public Support."

79. Riley E. Dunlap, "No Environmental Backlash against Bush Administration," April 19, 2007, available at: http://www.gallup.com/poll/27256/state-environmentalism-us.aspx.

80. Jim DiPeso, "The 2006 Midterm Elections: An Environmental Perspective," *Environmental Quality Management* (spring 2006), available at: www.interscience.wiley.com (accessed January 20, 2007).

81. League of Conservation Voters Education Fund, "Post-Election Polling Shows That American Voters Strongly Support Proactive Environmental Policies," www.lcveducation. org/Programs/Programs.cfm?ID=91&c=24.

82. Deborah Lynn Guber, *The Grassroots of a Green Revolution* (Cambridge, Mass.: MIT Press, 2003), 177.

83. The majority prevailed by a 51–42 margin. Frank Newport, "Americans: Economy Takes Precedence over the Environment," March 19, 2009, available at: http://www. gallup.com/poll/116962/ (accessed December 18, 2009).

84. Quoted in Neil King Jr., "A Past President's Advice to Obama: Act with Haste—Jimmy Carter Says New Administration Needs to Harness the Benefits of a Crisis Mentality to Tame Energy Policy," *Wall Street Journal* (eastern ed.), December 11, 2008, A16.

85. See, for example, Riley E. Dunlap, "Climate Change Views: Republican-Democratic Gaps Expand," May 29, 2008, available at: http://www.gallup.com/poll/107569/ClimateChange-Views-RepublicanDemocratic-Gaps-Expand.aspx.

86. Ports and Waterways Act of 1972, Pub. L. No. 92-340.

87. Federal Water Pollution Control Act Amendments of 1972, Pub. L. No. 92-500.

88. Clean Air Act, Pub. L. No. 84-159 (1955), Pub. L. No. 91-604 (1970), Pub. L. No. 101-549 (1990).

89. Allan Mazur, *The Dynamics of Technical Controversy* (Washington, D.C.: Communications Press, 1981), 29.

90. Ibid., 27.

91. Roger Revelle, "The Scientist and the Politician," in *Science, Technology, and National Policy,* ed. Thomas J. Kuehn and Alan L. Porter (Ithaca, N.Y.: Cornell University Press, 1981), 134.

92. U.S. General Accounting Office, "Superfund: Missed Statutory Deadlines Slow Progress in Environmental Programs," Report no. GAO/RCED 89-27, Washington, D.C., November 1988, chap. 2.

93. The epitome of this decision-making problem is explored in Riley Dunlap, *DDT: Scientists, Citizens, and Public Policy* (Princeton, N.J.: Princeton University Press, 1981), esp. chap. 8.

94. Quoted in "Colleagues Say Frog Deformity Researchers Leaped Too Soon," *Washington Post,* November 3, 1997, A3.

Chapter 3

Making Policy
Institutions and Politics

The right to traverse the winter wonders of the world's oldest national park in a snowmobile has become one of the nation's most complicated environmental issues.... While court challenges continue, the question is likely to be decided by whoever wins the presidential election in November—which means the fate of snowmobiling in Yellowstone is as uncertain as the nation's political future. "We can say for sure that we will welcome winter visitors to Yellowstone next December," said Cheryl Matthews, a spokesperson for the park. "What vehicles they will come in is something we don't know. It would be a great injustice to speculate on what may happen."

"We're totally confused, and we're the people who are supposed to know all about this," said Bill Dart of the Blue Ribbon Coalition, a pro-snowmobile group.... "The thing changes all the time. It's on. It's off. We're in the park. We're out." ...
—Washington Post, March 15, 2004

... by now the case has begun to resemble a procedural maze.
—Judge Neil Gorsuch, December 3, 2009[1]

It was May 2003. Christine Todd Whitman, administrator of the EPA, and Gale Norton, secretary of the interior, were meeting for lunch. Neither suspected they were about to plunge unwittingly and unwillingly into an acrimonious environmental controversy that would eventually entangle their agencies, span three presidencies, endure for eighteen years, and end—perhaps—with the presidency of Barack Obama The lunch was a convenient way for two of President George W. Bush's most important environmental administrators to facilitate cooperation between their departments by sharing common concerns and exchanging important information. The year so far had gone badly for Whitman. There were continued public disagreements with the Bush White House and pervasive rumors in Washington, D.C., that Whitman had fallen from White House favor and might quit her job or be fired. However, the lunch with Norton—a monthly arrangement—should have been unremarkable. The lunch was civil enough, but even as they ate, the EPA was publicly announcing its support for a ban on snowmobiles in Yellowstone National Park, which Norton, the Department of the Interior (DOI), and the Bush White House had all vigorously opposed since the president's inauguration.

Norton was irritated, and a "blunt conversation" followed. She telephoned the EPA administrator that same afternoon to complain: Why had Whitman failed to tell her about the announcement while they were at lunch? Whitman was surprised because *she* had not been notified either. In fact, the EPA "announcement" was just a letter written by a relatively low-level regional EPA administrator to the National Park Service (NPS) merely recommending the replacement of snowmobiles. Someone with a distaste for snowmobiles in the Denver EPA office had released the letter to the media, thus creating public confusion about the Bush administration's controversial snowmobile policy, adding to Whitman's discomfort and annoying Norton. "All the people who should have been notified on the snowmobile issue weren't," explained an EPA media spokesperson unhelpfully. Shortly thereafter, Whitman held a conference call with agency employees across the nation to remind them that politically sensitive information like the Denver letter should be cleared with her office.[2]

The EPA letter was merely one episode along a convoluted path left by the snowmobile policy as it labored through the federal government's policymaking labyrinth. The trail began when President Bill Clinton late in his second term recommended that the DOI ban the snowmobiles from Yellowstone and Grand Teton national parks and the department's NPS sought to comply. When the snowmobile industry and its many allied interests vigorously protested the ban, President Bush, who opposed the Clinton decision, announced on his first day in office that he would encourage the NPS to continue allowing the vehicles in Yellowstone and Grand Teton. The EPA's embarrassing letter appeared while the NPS was preparing to follow Bush's initiative. Opponents of the snowmobiles responded to Bush's announcement by taking their case to the federal courts and, in December 2003, the Washington, D.C., district court ordered the DOI to reinstate the Clinton ban on snowmobiles. The Republican majority in the House of Representatives then unsuccessfully attempted to counter the district court by passing a bill, ultimately unsuccessful, that would have permitted continued snowmobiles in the parks.[3]

The snowmobile issue now motored back into the federal judiciary and through the federal bureaucracy. In August 2004, the NPS proposed to permit snowmobiles in the parks for at least three years while it studied the conflicting scientific and economic data about snowmobiles. Two months later, the NPS publicly released its plan to allow limited guided daily treks for 750 snowmobiles in Yellowstone—about twice the average entering the previous year. Environmentalists and other opponents of the snowmobiles now moved to another venue, persuading the Washington, D.C., federal district court in September 2004 to order the DOI to *restore* the Clinton administration's snowmobile ban. The snowmobile industry and its allies countered by initiating other litigation in the Wyoming federal district court, resulting in an October 2004 court injunction in effect *forbidding* the DOI to enforce the Clinton ban on snowmobiles in Yellowstone and Grand Teton national parks.[4]

The Bush administration seemed to have won. It was "A common sense solution for snowmobile use that protects resources while also allowing appropriate access for employment by the public," exalted Secretary of the Interior Norton. To underscore her point, Norton appeared at Yellowstone Park in February 2005 "with a jaunty orange pennant waving from the back of her black snowmobile," reported the *New York Times*, "[and] tootled through a snowscape of hills, steaming rivers and indifferent bison this week giving an unusual personal endorsement to the machines that some consider a blight and others a blessing."[5] Even though many western political leaders in both parties, and a substantial portion of the western public, were less enthusiastic about snowmobiles—one opinion poll reported that 80 percent of the western public favored more limits on snowmobiles in the two parks— snowmobiles seemed to have overrun the opposition.[6]

But that was not the end of the story. When Norton resigned from the DOI in mid-2006, she was succeeded by former Idaho governor Kirk Kempthorne, whose nomination was vigorously opposed by environmentalists who considered him an arch-opponent and a sure partisan for more snowmobiles in the parks. Contrary to predictions, however, the DOI's proposed new park regulations in November 2006 rejected the increased use of snowmobiles in the parks, limited snowmobile access to 518 vehicles daily (less than the NPS quota originally proposed in 2003), and suspended additional snowmobile regulations for three years while a fourth environmental impact statement on the issue was created. This decision satisfied neither the proponents nor opponents of snowmobiles (snowmobiling had become "the most managed experience known to man" growled a snowmobile industry spokesman[7]), and both sides now shifted the controversy back to the federal courts, so often the last resort in environmental policy contention.

From September 2008 until December 2009, the snowmobile issue shuttled between various federal court jurisdictions as each side went venue shopping for an advantage. In September 2008, the Washington, D.C., district court rejected the NPS limit of 518 vehicles daily in

Yellowstone and Grand Teton national parks and the NPS responded with a new temporary regulation limiting the snowmobiles to 318 daily. Almost immediately thereafter, another federal district court, in Denver, Colorado, considered the issue from a different legal perspective, rejected the new limit of 318 daily vehicles, and ordered the NPS to reinstate its quota of 720 snowmobiles daily. There the matter stood until mid-July 2009 when Ken Salazar, the new Obama administration's secretary of the interior, announced that the 318-vehicle limit at Yellowstone and Grand Teton would prevail temporarily while the NPS spent the next two years working out a final snowmobile plan for both parks. Wyoming's congressional delegation, whose state's recreation industry depended substantially on park patronage, promptly blasted the new arrangement as "an insult to our state and gateway communities." A spokesman for the snowmobile industry complained that snowmobilers were "incredibly frustrated."[8] Snowmobile opponents like the National Parks Conservation Association complained that the whole process had taken too long and had been inconclusive. The NPS went to work on another environmental impact statement.

Although the discordant progress of its snowmobile policy undoubtedly annoyed the Bush White House, similar instances of publicly confused policymaking, often ending with problematic solutions, can be found in the history of any presidency and will surely appear before the end of the Obama presidency. Policymaking in the federal government is inherently time consuming, frequently highly contentious, and often mined with surprises and uncertainties. This situation arises in large part because different institutions, often with conflicting missions, are involved in the policymaking process. It could hardly be otherwise in a government of checks and balances, where institutions exercise competing and shared powers concurrently. In addition, history resonates through the policymaking process. Today's policy discussions are infused with institutional memories of past events and nuanced with expectations for the future. This chapter examines the most important of the institutions involved in this process to exemplify how competing constitutional authority, shared powers, and historical experience shape the character of policymaking in Washington.

The Presidency

"Mothers all want their sons to grow up to be president," President John Kennedy once remarked, "but they don't want them to become politicians in the process."[9] The president wields vast constitutional authority and powerful leverage over public opinion, enlarged by a century of growing public tolerance for presidential assertions of additional inherent powers. But to be a successful policymaker the president must still be a proficient politician. The essential politics of presidential leadership in environmental affairs, as with other policy issues, requires, among other things, the will as well as the ability to bargain and compromise with Congress, to know how to shape public opinion and when to be governed by it, and to know when to respect judicial independence and when to challenge it—in short, a capacity to move a government of divided powers and competitive institutions in the direction that presidential policies require.

Occupants of the White House since Earth Day 1970 have varied greatly in their concern about environmental protection and their ability to translate environmental commitments into practical policy. So-called green presidents have often been the least successful environmental policymakers. It is a lesson repeated endlessly in Washington that even presidents committed to the politics of policymaking discover they cannot always command the ends even when they summon the means for policy leadership (see Chapter 1).

Presidential Resources

Environmentalists, long irate at what they perceived to be the Bush administration's dismal environmental record, had awaited prompt signals that the new Obama administration would bring the anticipated friendlier environmentalist agenda to Washington, and they weren't disappointed. Within days of taking office, Obama had, among other welcome initiatives, exercised his constitutional authority as chief executive to revoke Bush administration policies promoting resource exploration near Utah public lands, to suspend other Bush measures facilitating increased timber production from the national forests, and to order regulators to write stringent new rules for auto emissions and fuel economy. This followed a high-profile "green inauguration" featuring a carbon-neutral ball (another was celebrated on a green carpet made from recycled rug), hybrid Lexuses for transportation, organic menus, recycled paper invitations, and valet bicycle parking. All of this demonstrated early the president's intention to summon both the inherent constitutional powers of his office and his unrivalled ability to command media attention to advance his environmental agenda. Here were potent presidential resources, a few among many, that could effectively shape the course of White House environmental policymaking—if presidential skill, historical opportunity, congressional and judicial collaboration, the economy, the public, and luck also permitted.

Constitutional Powers

As the nation's chief executive, the president can bring to environmental policymaking a vast array of constitutional powers. A short list of these resources includes:

- The authority to propose and to veto legislation.
- The ability to propose policy priorities and initiatives to Congress and the nation simultaneously in the constitutional State of the Union message.
- The power to draft and to present to Congress the annual federal budget.
- The authority to appoint a cabinet of executive department heads and to designate other executive leadership of most major federal environmental bureaucracies, such as the DOI and the EPA.
- The power to appoint federal judges when judicial vacancies occur.
- The prerogative to issue executive orders, which require no congressional approval, to all federal executive agencies.
- An ability to appoint policy advisers to the president's personal staff and to White House advisory committees required by Congress.
- The authority to negotiate and to propose international agreements and treaties for congressional approval. [10]

This inventory excludes a great deal, such as the talent of creative presidents to transmute traditional authority into new modes of influence (such as President Clinton's technique for frustrating congressional Republican opposition to new federally protected forests by creating them through executive orders immune to congressional veto). Moreover, presidential power also resides in the president's decision not to use his or her resources of policy leadership—inaction is also a form of policymaking.

In practice, presidential ability to capitalize on the presidency's political resources for environmental purposes has varied greatly. One explanation for this variability is the many ways in which circumstances can alter the political climate surrounding the White House—events such as economic recessions, changing congressional majorities, and other changes in the political "seasons." Moreover, some presidents, such as Jimmy Carter, have been less skilled than others at Washington politics.

Surprise, Crisis, and the Presidency

Sometimes presidential policymaking is blessed or plagued by the unexpected and the unpredictable—as, for instance, when the first Earth Day arrived to the complete surprise of President Richard Nixon and his staff. Often, presidents discover that their policy agenda and priorities become captive not only to unexpected events but to crises that force the pace and substance of White House politics, however much the president may wish otherwise. Crises of various kinds have compelled many crucial White House environmental initiatives such as the Superfund legislation in 1980 regulating abandoned hazardous waste sites and the creation of the Toxics Release Inventory (TRI) in 1984 to track toxic industrial air and water emissions.

The disastrous 2010 oil spill in the Gulf of Mexico is a textbook illustration of how events can shape White House policy. The Deepwater Horizon oil rig exploded and was incinerated in the Gulf of Mexico on April 20, 2010. It unleashed a catastrophic oil spill quickly accelerating into an environmental crisis, spilling 210,000 gallons of crude oil daily into the gulf. Within a month, the spill had created a vast underwater oil plume 10 miles long and 1 mile wide, a surface slick visible to astronauts in the International Space Station, hundreds of miles above Earth. For British Petroleum, the rig's owner, it rapidly became a financial and political crisis exacerbated by the global media's relentless dramatization of the event and its potentially catastrophic environmental consequences.

The Deepwater Horizon disaster was an acute embarrassment and a potential political disaster for the Obama administration. Exactly a month before the rig explosion, Obama had announced that he would propose that Congress increase significantly the scale of oil and natural gas exploration in a large portion of the eastern Gulf of Mexico. A month later, the Deepwater Horizon disaster compelled Obama to announce that his administration would stop further offshore energy exploration indefinitely—an abrupt policy reversal enthusiastically advertised by his critics as evidence of his bad judgment and poor political leadership. Obama's decision to propose new offshore exploration had been a reluctant concession made to Senate Republicans, many of whom had campaigned decades for increased exploration; it was the price he had to pay for Republican support of the administration's important climate-warming legislation. But the Deep Horizon disaster now compelled Obama, and Congress as well, to focus not on getting more oil from the gulf but on preventing further offshore drilling crises.

The Executive Office of the President

The president may be an individual but the *presidency* is also an institution surrounding the Oval Office with an array of administrative resources, collectively called the Executive Office of the President (EOP), which includes the president's personal staff and has become essential for the president to fulfill his constitutional responsibilities. Most of the EOP's 1,800 employees are permanent civil service appointees, such as the critically important personnel in the Office of Management and Budget (OMB), who provide expert administrative advice, oversee the implementation of presidential policies, and provide continuity from one presidency to the next.[1] In addition, within the EOP is an entity called the White House, containing other, personally appointed presidential staff and advisers, such as speechwriters and congressional liaison specialists, whom the president selects and who serve at his or her pleasure. Much of the daily work involved with the president's environmental policymaking is done by the individuals and offices within the EOP and by his or her personal staff. Equally important, presidents routinely turn to their personal staff and the professionals in the EOP for advice and assistance. Thus, what appears to be a presidential decision often turns out, on close inspection, to be a collaborative White House staff creation. Indeed, it is often an OMB official, not the president, who interprets and represents White House policies to Congress and the federal bureaucracy.

Within the EOP, several offices are especially strategic in environmental policymaking. Perhaps the most important (although virtually unknown to the public) is the OMB, which assists the president in preparing his annual budget, oversees the implementation of that budget within all the executive agencies including the environmentally related bureaucracies, assists the president in drafting his legislative proposals, reviews congressional legislation to determine its compatibility with the president's environmental agenda, and oversees the work of the environmental regulatory agencies such as the EPA and the Nuclear Regulatory Commission (NRC). The OMB, and particularly its director, who is appointed by the president, can become an especially powerful presence in environmental policymaking when invested by the president with considerable responsibility and discretion in implementing the president's legislative policies and budget priorities. Ronald Reagan's OMB director, David Stockman, probably set the standard for iron-fisted enforcement of the president's environmental policies within the executive branch, but his successors, regardless of who occupies the White House, customarily have acquired reputations for forceful leadership essential to their job.

Because OMB is so frequently the agent for implementing presidential policy within the executive branch, OMB readily becomes a focus for conflict over White House environmental policymaking. During the George W. Bush years, for example, a persistent controversy over alleged White House interference in EPA scientific research converged on the OMB. A governmental watchdog organization complained:

Increasingly, the OMB has waded into the waters of federal science. OMB's presence adds little if any value to the scientific process. At a minimum, OMB's insistence that it be included during scientific development delays agency efforts. At worst, it casts a political shadow over science and science-based policy and threatens public protections.[12]

Not surprisingly, environmentalists have pressed President Obama to assure that OMB during his administration is convincingly free of similar accusations. In fact, most of OMB's essential work is uncontroversial, but its placement at the intersection of so many environmental issues within the executive branch assures its continuing visibility in the inevitable controversies bound to arise.

Other environmentally important entities within the EOP are the Council on Environmental Quality (CEQ) and the Office of Science and Technology Policy (OSTP). The mission of the OSTP, created in 1976, is to:

- Advise the president and others within the EOP on the impacts of science and technology on domestic and international affairs.
- Lead an interagency effort to develop and implement sound science and technology policies and budgets.
- Work with the private sector to ensure federal investments in science and technology contribute to economic prosperity, environmental quality, and national security.
- Build strong partnerships among federal, state, and local governments; other countries; and the scientific community.
- Evaluate the scale, quality, and effectiveness of the federal effort in science and technology.

Like OMB, much of the OSTP's continuing responsibilities are uncontroversial and often commendable in the view of environmentalists—for example, promoting federal support for green energy technologies. Inevitably, however, the OSTP's daily involvement in science, technology, energy, and environmental policy within the White House often implicates it in controversial issues together with the OMB and the CEQ.

Council on Environmental Quality

The National Environmental Policy Act of 1969 (NEPA) includes a provision for establishing a commission to advise the president on environmental matters. To be headed by three members appointed by the president, the CEQ was to be part of the president's staff. Among the major responsibilities prescribed for the council in Section 203 of NEPA were (1) to gather for the president's consideration "timely and authoritative information concerning the conditions and trends in the quality of the environment both current and prospective," (2) "to develop and recommend to the President national policies to foster and promote the improvement of environmental quality," and (3) "to review and appraise the various programs and activities of the Federal Government" to determine the extent to which they comply with, among other things, the requirement for writing environmental impact statements.[13] The CEQ was created, like other major presidential advisory commissions, primarily to provide policy advice and evaluation from within the White House directly to the president.

The CEQ is a small agency with no regulatory responsibilities or major environmental programs beyond modest research activities, but early on it assumed symbolic importance and political value to environmental interests. Its presence within the White House implied a high national priority given to environmental programs, and the council's opportunities to influence the president directly meant that it might act, in the words of environmental leader Russell Peterson, as "the environmental conscience of the executive branch."[14] The council has a statutory mandate to administer the process of writing and reviewing environmental impact statements within the federal government and to advise other executive agencies on environmental issues. As with all other presidential advisory bodies, the CEQ exercises no more influence in White House decisions than the president cares to give it; it may carry on its NEPA-mandated activities, but the president is always free to ignore any of its recommendations or other initiatives.

By 2000, the CEQ's early political clout had vanished. The CEQ's rapid decline in status since the Carter administration illustrates how much its effectiveness depends on presidential favor. The council enjoyed considerable influence under President Carter, but its influence plummeted rapidly during the Reagan administration. President George Bush's pledges of environmental concern did not, to the disappointment of environmentalists, portend better days for the CEQ, nor did the arrival of the Clinton administration after the 1992 election. President Clinton's proposal to replace the CEQ with a White House environmental policy adviser appointed by the president shocked the environmental community and seemed virtually an obituary for the council, which adopted an almost minimalist agenda during Clinton's term. The CEQ experienced no reversal of fortune under the George W. Bush administration. Although the environmental community should have been its natural constituency, the CEQ often became the target of environmentalist criticism for its apparent passiveness, if not complicity, during the Bush administration's frequent attempts to influence science policy within the executive branch. "There is evidence," concluded a report written near the end of the Bush presidency by a panel including several past chairs and numerous members of the CEQ, "that the Council has been used to undermine the statutory environmental protection responsibilities of other federal agencies. There is also a perception that the Council has been used to gainsay the scientific conclusions of federal agencies on climate change and other issues." At the same time, the panel emphasized the CEQ's potential to become again a highly influential and visible presence—"the President's voice on the environment"—during the Obama administration.[15]

Congress: Too Much Check, Too Little Balance

The president may propose, but it is often Congress that ultimately disposes. In a Madisonian government of separated institutions sharing powers, presidents and environmental administrators have good reasons to look warily toward Congress. The Constitution invests Congress with enormous authority over the daily conduct of the president and the executive branch. Under ordinary circumstances, few aspects of presidential and bureaucratic behavior are untouched directly or indirectly by congressional authority and politics.

Despite a panoply of party organizations, legislative leaders, and coordinating committees, Congress is still largely an institution of fragmented powers and divided geographical loyalties. Legislative power is dispersed in both chambers among a multitude of committees and subcommittees; local or regional concerns often tenaciously claim legislative loyalties. The electoral cycle intrudes imperiously on policy deliberations. The public interest and legislative objectivity compete with equally insistent legislative concerns to deliver something from Washington to the "folks back home." In environmental affairs, Congress is an assembly of scientific amateurs who must enact programs of great technical complexity to ameliorate scientifically complicated environmental ills that most legislators only dimly understand.

The Statutory Setting. The most fundamental congressional responsibility is to craft environmental law. Current federal environmental legislation is a patchwork of several hundred congressional enactments written since the 1950s. Legal scholar Christopher Schroeder's verdict about federal toxic substance laws—that they have "resulted not in a well-designed cabin, but in a pile of logs"[16]—applies as well to the whole of federal environmental legislation. Many controversies prominent since the 1970s result from the inconsistencies, contradictions, confusions, and inadequacies of this statutory welter. At the same time, each law memorializes the success of a major environmental coalition in waging a battle for environmental protection that may have lasted decades. Each law acquires a politically vocal and potent constituency from congressional factions, private interests, bureaucratic agencies, and program beneficiaries. A huge volume of judicial opinions girding each law with court-derived interpretations and justifications further institutionalizes the legislation. These laws are the legal edifice on which environmental policy has been erected.

The major legislative enactments currently on the federal statute books relating to just one category of environmental pollutant, toxic substances, include fifteen major laws. Cataloging just one among the many categories of environmental law is sufficient to emphasize two realities about environmental policy controversies: (1) the existing law becomes a conservative force in policy debate because it is difficult to change, and (2) the incompatibilities and omissions in current environmental legislation are a continuing cause of difficulties in policy implementation and enforcement.

Committee Decentralization. Congress has been described as a "kind of confederation of little legislatures."[17] In both chambers, the committees and subcommittees—those little legislatures wielding the most consistently effective power in the legislative system—are dispersed and competitive in environmental matters. William Ruckelshaus, the first EPA administrator, complained in the early 1970s that he had to deal with sixteen different congressional subcommittees.[18] The situation has gotten more complicated since then. In the 110th Congress (2009–2011), the box score for committees with EPA jurisdiction came to seven full committees including thirteen subcommittees in the Senate and eight full committees with eighteen subcommittees in the House of Representatives. Any major environmental legislation, depending on its content, is predestined to arrive on several, perhaps many, different committee and subcommittee tables during a customarily labored progress through congressional deliberation. Thus, the Senate's massive Boxer-Kerry climate change legislation introduced in 2009 to the 110th Congress could have been pondered by some combination of five full committees (Environment and Public Works, Energy and Natural Resources, Finance, Agriculture, and Foreign Relations) and their subcommittees. Congressional jurisdictions over ocean issues is also very generously dispersed; the 109th Congress included fifty committees and subcommittees in both chambers with jurisdiction over related research and policy.

With authority over environmental policy fragmented among a multitude of committees in each chamber, competition and jurisdictional rivalry commonly occur as each committee attempts to assert some influence over environmental programs. The result is that, as a rule, environmental legislation evolves only through protracted bargaining and compromising among the many committees. This time-consuming process often results in legislation that is vague or inconsistent. Divided jurisdictions, however, provide different interest groups with some point of committee access during environmental policy formulation; as a consequence, these groups resist efforts to reduce the number of committees with overlapping jurisdictions and concentrate authority in a few major committees.

Localism. When the national taxpayer organization Citizens against Government Waste (CAGW) noted in its annual *Pig Book* that Mississippi ranked sixth among the fifty states in the amount of political pork (a common term for wasteful federal spending) its congressional delegation had delivered to the state, Sen. Trent Lott, R-Miss., seemed almost pleased with his state's ranking. "The definition of wasteful 'pork' is in the eye of the beholder," he responded. "In my eye, if its south of Memphis, it sure isn't pork.... If we must use our political acumen to get part of our money back, then so be it. In this regard, CAGW's report indicates Mississippi is doing very well."[19] Many of his Senate colleagues would have added, "Amen." Senators are unapologetically loyal to the practice of voting for each other's local public works projects, the most common political pork.

Localism is driven by a powerful tradition in congressional voting. In U.S. political culture, legislators are treated by constituents—and regard themselves—as ambassadors to Washington, D.C., from their own geographical areas. They are expected to acquire skills in the practice of pork-barrel politics, capturing federal goods and services for their constituencies. They are also expected to be vigilant in promoting and protecting local interests in the national policy arena. Congressional tenure is more likely to depend on a legislator's ability to serve these local interests than on other legislative achievements. Although not the only influence on congressional voting, such politics is deeply rooted and probably the single most compelling force in shaping voting decisions.

This localism affects environmental policy in different ways. By encouraging legislators to view environmental proposals first through the lens of local interests, localism often weakens sensitivity to national needs and interests. At worst, it drives legislators to judge the merits of environmental policies almost solely by their impact on frequently small and atypical constituencies.

Localism also whets the congressional appetite for federal distributive programs freighted with local benefits. An aroma of political pork can add appeal to an environmental program, especially if other important local issues are involved. This lesson is not lost on the environmental bureaucracies. For instance, when opposition by the powerful House Ways and Means Committee appeared to threaten defeat for the initial Superfund legislation, a program strongly supported by the EPA, the agency worked with sympathetic congressional staff members to create a list of prospective Superfund sites in each committee member's district. The committee members were then reminded of the "ticking time bombs" in their districts *and* of the potentially great financial benefits from cleanup activities—an almost irresistible double dose of localism.[20] It is not surprising that federal grants to build pollution control facilities, such as sewage treatment plants, also have instant appeal.

Even the comparatively tiny federal program for such grants to the states in the mid-1960s had great appeal. "The program was immensely popular.... Congressmen enjoyed the publicity and credit they received every time they announced another grant for another community in their district."[21] The huge $18 billion waste treatment facilities program, first authorized in 1972, is the second largest public works program in U.S. history and even more popular than the earlier construction grants. The EPA estimated that for every $1 billion spent, about 50,900 worker-years of employment would be generated in plant and sewer construction.[22]

Public works are not the only legislative bargaining chips, however. It is axiomatic that legislation often enlists congressional votes because sponsors are alert to write in diverse benefits or projects of all sorts that are attractive to important colleagues and pressure groups. Conversely, pressure groups—including environmentalists—are perpetually vigilant for opportunities to advance their agendas through legislative benefits. For example, the massive Waxman-Markey climate warming legislation approved in 2009 by the House of Representatives provoked a virtual feeding frenzy among organized groups intent on gaining a share of the benefits from provisions proposing an auction of greenhouse gas emission rights. "Every line of the text [had] billions and billions of dollars riding on it," observed economist Peter Dorman. "People will do and say anything," he asserted, to get a share of the money, including environmentalists who hope that federal revenues from the eventual auction of emissions permits will help their cause.[23]

Elections. The electoral cycle also dominates the legislative mind. The constitutionally mandated electoral cycles of the federal government—two years, four years, and six years—partition the time available for legislative deliberation into periods bounded by different elections. Within these time frames, policy decisions are continually analyzed for their electoral implications and often valued largely for electoral impacts. This affects congressional policy styles in several ways. First, the short term becomes more important than the long term when evaluating programs; legislators often attribute more importance to a program's impact on the next election than to its longer-term effects on unborn generations. Second, policies are tested continually against public opinion. Although a weak or badly divided public opinion often can be ignored, a coherent majority opinion related to an environmental issue usually wields significant influence on congressional voting, especially when legislators can associate the opinion with their own constituencies. Hazardous waste cleanup programs, for example, are hard to oppose whatever their actual merits because the "ticking time bomb" has become a durable, powerful public metaphor in practically every constituency.

Preoccupation with elections, localism, and the other aspects of congressional culture are the givens of policymaking. And congressional policymaking, as much as presidential leadership, has been responsible for creating and maintaining the entire foundation of federal environmental governance—one of Congress's greatest historical achievements. However, Congress has also become a rich source of delay, confusion, and waste in making and implementing environmental policy. These problems arise from excesses and exaggeration in the authority the constitutional framers prudently invested in Congress—a case of checks and balances gone awry. Many of these difficulties could be eliminated or mitigated by a self-imposed discipline of which Congress may be incapable.

"Ready, Fire, Aim": Crisis Decision Making. The congressional response to environmental problems is highly volatile, waxing and waning according to changing public moods, emerging environmental crises, economic circumstances, or today's front-page ecological disasters. Congress easily falls into a "pollutant of the year" mentality, mandating new programs or sudden changes in existing ones according to what environmental problems currently seem most urgent or according to the public's current mood.

The Ocean Dumping Act of 1988, for example, is the very model of crisis-inspired legislation. During summer 1988, popular bathing beaches along New York's eastern coast frequently were fouled with medical wastes, raw sewage, and other dangerous debris apparently washed ashore from New York City sewage dumped more than 100 miles offshore. Closed beaches and public revulsion at the widely publicized pollution quickly persuaded Congress to pass, without one dissenting vote, the Ocean Dumping Act, which prohibited additional ocean disposal of urban waste within a few years. Congress was unmoved by expert testimony that held the real cause of the contamination to be the continual overflow from New York City's antique sewer system, which would be hugely expensive to repair. Nor was Congress in the mood to evaluate alternatives. "There is no question," argued the chief engineer of the regional waste management agency, "that the New York City sewer system is the greatest cause of water pollution in the region. But a sewer system isn't sexy. It's expensive to fix, and nobody wants to hear about it. So people focused on what they understand ... and they understand that sewage and the sea don't seem nice together."[24] Local representative Thomas J. Manton, D-Queens, initially opposed to the act, soon capitulated to political realities. "Nobody wanted to discuss the relative risks or merits," he later explained. "It had been a bad summer, and we all wanted to be able to say we did something. So we passed a law. I tried to have a debate. And it was like I was trying to destroy the planet."[25] As a result of the act, the city of New York will have spent at least $2 billion on facilities to convert sewage into fertilizer and $300 million annually for a decade thereafter to dispose of its sludge, although many experts believe an equally effective and much cheaper solution would have been possible if Congress had not ordained that ocean dumping be eliminated entirely but, instead, had renovated the existing sewer system to remove the harmful pollutants from the affluent before ocean release.

Environmental policies are seldom so poorly conceived, but this reactive policymaking ensures an environmental agenda in which place and priority among programs depend less on scientific logic than on political circumstance. Often the losers are scientifically compelling environmental problems unblessed with political sex appeal. Moreover, once a program is legislatively attractive, it usually acquires a mandated budget that virtually ensures its survival. Most environmental scientists, for instance, consider indoor air pollution a more compelling health risk than abandoned hazardous waste sites or even some currently regulated forms of air pollution, but most of the EPA's air pollution budget is mandated for ambient air regulation, and Congress lacks enthusiasm to tackle indoor air pollution in the absence of a perceived crisis.[26]

Another result of this crisis mentality is administrative overload. The EPA and other environmental agencies have often had to implement quickly a multitude of new programs, hastily enacted without sufficient time or resources provided for the required tasks. As a result, the EPA has struggled continually and unsuccessfully to find the means to carry out all the program mandates. This crisis mentality also begets constantly mandated changes in regulatory priorities and program deadlines.

Guidance: Too Much and Too Little. Behind the facade of high purpose and ambitious action of every major environmental law probably stretches a terrain mined with muddled language, troublesome silences, and inconsistent programs. Some of this is inevitable. Mistakes in statutory design occur because federal environmental regulations address problems of great scientific and administrative complexity with which legislators have had no prior experience. Moreover, members of Congress are typically lawyers, business executives, or other nonscientific professionals who depend on the expertise of administrators to clarify and interpret the law appropriately in regard to specialized environmental programs. The constant pressure of legislative affairs discourages most members of Congress from giving considerable attention to environmental issues or from developing an adequate understanding of them. "It's tough to get Congress to focus on bills with sufficient time to develop an adequate depth of understanding," observed John A. Moore, former acting deputy director for the EPA. "You've got 1 or 2 Congressmen who truly know it; there are 400 others that are going to vote on it."[27] Even conscientious legislators can be easily intimidated when they attempt to unravel the technical complexities of environmental legislation. During congressional debate over passage of the Safe Drinking Water Act (1974), for instance, proponents argued that 12,000 contaminants existed with unknown causes. Debate raged within the EPA and Congress about whether the agency needed to regulate twenty to thirty, hundreds, or even thousands of water pollutants—even the Public Health Service's traditionally undisputed standard for selenium was made suspect. Finally, Congress had to give the EPA the final responsibility for identifying most of the appropriate pollutants for regulation.[28]

Environmental legislation is often vague and contradictory because Congress cannot or will not resolve major political conflicts entailed in the law. Instead, Congress often papers over the conflict with silence or deliberate obscurity in the statutory language. This approach results in a steady flow of political hot potatoes to the bureaucracy, which must untangle and clarify this legal language—often to the accompaniment of political conflict and legislative criticism—or leave the job to the courts. The EPA becomes enmeshed in protracted litigation and political bargaining, program regulations essential to implementing the laws often become hostage to these procedures, and Congress frequently avoids a risky political bloodletting. "Congress outsources the rulemaking to the EPA," asserts regulatory critic David Schoenbrod, "so that the legislators can claim credit for protecting health while the agency bears the inevitable blame for delays, disappointments, and costs."[29] True or not, so it often appears.

Congressional frustration with the continual delay in implementing environmental laws has led to the habitual use of extravagant, extraordinarily detailed, and inflexible language in new environmental laws; to the constant mandating of precise deadlines for completing various programs; and to prescription, in excruciating detail, of how administrators are to carry out program activities—in effect, to a cure as bad as the disease. The Clean Air Act Amendments of 1990, for instance, were packed with a multitude of new programs accompanied by hundreds of mandatory deadlines seldom carefully considered. The predictable result was that the EPA missed 198 of the 247 deadlines it was required to meet by 2000 and will miss more than half the 108 deadlines that remain to be met later.[30]

"An Odd and Intricate System of Checks and Balances." The Republican victories in the 1994 congressional elections only perpetuated the fractious relationship between the EPA and Congress. The new Republican majority in both legislative chambers at first enthusiastically assaulted the EPA's budget and regulatory authority in a comprehensive effort to severely diminish both. The Reagan administration had learned, at considerable political cost, that frontal assaults on the statutory bulwark of environmental regulation invite a public backlash. Congressional Republicans relearned the lesson between 1994 and 1998 and eventually abandoned their initial assault in favor of persistent, quieter, and less publicly risky campaigns aimed selectively at portions of various environmental laws and segments of EPA budgets vulnerable to antiregulatory strategies. Republican antipathy did slow appreciably the growth of the EPA's budget, the passage of new environmental legislation, and the revision of older laws. By the beginning of George W. Bush's administration, it seemed by a perverse political logic that friends and critics of environmental regulation had unwittingly contrived to ensure that the excessive control of the EPA, and the administrative distrust nourishing it, would be virtually institutionalized in Congress. "Pro-environment members of Congress fear that the agency will not be ardent enough in defending the environment; members more sympathetic to business concerns fear that the agency will be too ardent," concluded a comprehensive review of federal regulatory programs by Resources for the Future, an influential Washington environmental think tank. In addition,

> The pro-environment members (and the pro-business members) write detailed instructions into law; the pro-business members try to ensure that the agency will not have enough resources to fully implement the laws and that the courts will have authority to second guess any agency decisions. EPA is thus the focus of an odd and intricate system of checks-and-balances.[31]

The Legislative Bluff. Congress writes into major environmental laws a multitude of sanctions, many ostensibly severe, intended to encourage compliance with environmental regulation and to arm regulators with the power to compel it. The Clean Air Act, for instance, authorizes the EPA to impose a moratorium on the construction and operation of any new stationary source of air pollution in any urban area that fails to attain federally required air-quality standards by the mandated deadlines; this, in effect, gives the agency the authority to stop major urban economic development. The Clean Air Act also empowers the EPA to issue documents halting all federal highway construction funds and other major federal grants to any state with urban areas failing to meet deadlines for compliance with federally required air-quality standards. Tough penalties must be used selectively. Regulators need authority and opportunity to bargain about when and how penalties will be applied to regulated interests failing to comply with the laws. But a powerful sanction merely threatened will eventually become a rusty regulatory blunderbuss.

Congress has diminished the credibility of many tough sanctions written into environmental legislation by repeatedly extending compliance deadlines for regulations, thereby sidestepping the sanction problem. Consider, for example, the deadline of the Clean Air Act for the nation's metropolitan areas to meet national air-quality standards for ozone or face a moratorium on new factory construction and loss of federal highway funds. Congress first set the deadline for 1976, then extended it to 1982, then to 1987, then to late 1988, then to 1990—extensions granted to save more than sixty metropolitan areas from sanctions. Once Congress authorized the EPA to extend the deadlines, the message was clear. According to legal scholar R. Shep Melnick,

> Congress and the EPA once again showed that they would not stand behind the standards and deadlines previously announced with great seriousness. Every major participant knows that loopholes will always appear in the nick of time, thus obviating the need to impose sanctions in areas that fail to meet air quality standards.[32]

Continuing congressional setbacks in compliance deadlines have also been made for automobile emission requirements in the Clean Air Act, in water-quality standards for municipal waste treatment systems regulated under the Federal Water Pollution Control Act Amendments of 1972, and in many other programs in other environmental laws.

There are plausible reasons for this situation. Legislators may worry about the adverse economic impact of sanctions on the local and national economies or about the alleged difficulties in developing the technologies needed to meet compliance deadlines. But the congressional bluff often betrays a lack of political will to face the consequences of the commitments Congress has made to enforce the law. In effect, the toughest sanctions in environmental legislation often amount to little more than legislative make-believe.

The Bureaucracy: Power through Implementation

Federal agencies concerned with environmental affairs and closely related matters such as energy, consumer protection, and worker health have grown explosively since 1970. More than 150 major new federal laws, most concerned with the broad regulation of business and the economy in the interest of public health and safety, have been enacted since then. More than twenty new regulatory agencies have been created to implement these programs, including the EPA, the Occupational Safety and Health Administration, and the DOI's Office of Surface Mining. An understanding of such bureaucracies, and especially the more environmentally important among them, is essential to explaining the logic of federal environmental policymaking.

The Power of Discretion

The significance of the environmental agencies rests less on their size and budget than on the political realities obscured by a constitutional illusion. The Constitution appears to vest the power to formulate policy primarily in Congress, while leaving to the president and the executive branch the task of seeing that the laws are "faithfully executed." Although implemented and enforced principally in the bureaucracy, public policy actually develops in both branches of the government.

Delegated authority and administrative discretion are the wellsprings of bureaucratic power. Congress routinely invests administrators with responsibility for making a multitude of decisions it cannot or will not make itself about the implementation of policy; often this becomes legislative power delegated to the executive branch. Even when delegation is not clearly intended, administrators assume the power to make public policy when they choose how to implement policies permitting different options—hence, the existence of administrative discretion.

Congress and the president, using a variety of constitutional and statutory powers, attempt to discipline the exercise of administrative discretion. Still, this oversight holds no certain rein on administrative discretion, particularly in light of the vast number and complexity of environmental programs, the elephantine size of the bureaucracy, and competing demands on presidential and congressional time.

A commonplace example can illustrate the pervasive problem of controlling administrative discretion. In 1981, President Reagan ordered all federal administrative agencies to prepare a regulatory impact analysis— a type of benefit-cost assessment—for most of their new regulatory proposals and left to his own administrative management agency, the OMB, the responsibility of drafting guidelines for the agencies. The OMB, in turn, interpreted the president's order as requiring the responsible agencies, such as the EPA, to include in each of its assessments an evaluation of alternatives to the proposed regulation. The EPA, for its part, issued guidelines to each of its offices recommending that at least four alternatives be considered for each proposed new regulation. A review of regulatory impact analyses prepared by one EPA office in mid-1997 suggests that the intent of the original White House directive had been significantly adulterated by this trickle-down of discretionary authority from the White House to the EPA. Of the twenty-three assessments studied, six examined only one alternative to the proposed regulation. The rest compared two or more alternatives to the proposed regulation but were not always clear about how many alternatives or which types were involved. In no instance had any agency in the chain of command violated law nor was there evidence of intent to do so.[33] Still, the documents ultimately prepared by the EPA appeared to disregard in many respects the intent of the original White House directive. Whatever the interpretation, the flow of discretionary authority and its compounding influence throughout government, for good and ill, will be reality, in all seasons, for all presidents, and for all parties. The federal bureaucracy, assured of generous discretionary authority well into the future, will continue to be an independent and largely self-regulated influence in environmental policy.

Bureaucratic Competitiveness

The bureaucracy is no monolith. Its powers in environmental affairs, although collectively vast, also are dispersed and competitive. One source of this fragmentation is the federalizing of environmental administration. Many major environmental laws enacted in Washington, D.C., are administered partially or wholly through state governments; others give states an option to participate. Under the Federal Water Pollution Control Act, for instance, twenty-seven states currently administer their own water pollution permit systems; all but six states and the District of Columbia administer the Safe Drinking Water Act. The Clean Air Act permits the states to participate in several major aspects of the program, including the control of pollutants and the establishment of emission standards for stationary sources.

Another cause of fragmented administrative authority is the chronic division of and overlapping responsibility for environmental programs among federal agencies. Twenty-seven separate federal agencies share major regulatory responsibility in environmental and occupational health. Regulating even a single pollutant often necessitates what might appear to be a bureaucratic convention. Toxic substances currently are regulated under twenty different federal statutes involving five agencies. To address all the problems in human exposure to vinyl chloride, for example, would require the collaboration of all five agencies working with fifteen different laws.[34]

Dispersed authority breeds conflict and competition among agencies and their political allies over program implementation, authority, and resources—the turf wars familiar to students of bureaucracy. The story of Whitman and Norton's lunch recounted at the beginning of this chapter affirms a bureaucratic reality—collaboration is common but never dependable. And in environmental affairs, federal agencies are notoriously fitful collaborators. In this milieu of dispersed and competitive agency authority, policy implementation often becomes a continual process of collaboration and conflict between coalitions of agencies and their allies shaping and reshaping policy as the relative strengths of the conflicting alignments change. Moreover, administrative conflict crosses the institutional divisions of the federal government, spreading downward through the federal system to state and local governments and outward from government to organized private groups. Indeed, agencies failing to enlist diverse and active allies in their policy struggles may frustrate their own missions and leave their futures hostage to more politically skilled opponents.

The Environmental Protection Agency

The EPA, created by an executive order of President Nixon in 1970, is the largest federal regulatory agency in terms of budget and personnel. Its responsibilities embrace an extraordinarily large and technically complex set of programs ranging across the whole domain of environmental management. Asked if his job had been rewarding, a former administrator for the EPA replied that it was "like beating a train across a grade crossing—if you make it, it's a great rush. If you don't, you're dead."[35] An insider's guide to Washington, D.C., ranked the job of administrator for the EPA among the one hundred toughest positions in the city. Political controversy is the daily bread of the EPA's leadership. "The Administrator rarely goes to the President with good news and is more often the bearer of bad news," observed Lee Thomas, EPA administrator from 1985 to 1988. "You almost never have a decision where many people applaud it."[36] In such a politically charged setting, the EPA administrator's office has often been a revolving door through which a succession of executives pass, unwilling or unable to manage the inherited political turbulence. Such was the case during the George W. Bush administration, when Whitman, Michael O. Leavitt, and Stephan L. Johnson all occupied the administrator's office within a five-year period.

Statutory Responsibilities. The size of the EPA's regulatory burden is suggested in Box 3-1, which summarizes the EPA's current statutory responsibilities. These regulatory programs represent the major environmental legislation of the past three decades. The EPA grew steadily in staff and budget until 1981, when the Reagan administration severely reduced both budget and personnel. The agency has recovered somewhat and presently has about 18,000 employees and an annual budget exceeding $7 billion, of which less than half supports its administrative activities (most of the money underwrites water treatment and Superfund grants).[37] When adjusted for inflation, the EPA's budget at the end of the George W. Bush administration was estimated to be at 50 percent of its 1980 level.[38] The agency, whose administrator is appointed by the president, consists of a Washington, D.C., headquarters and ten regional offices, each headed by a regional administrator. Unlike most regulatory agencies, the EPA administers both regulatory and distributive programs such as the huge federal waste treatment grants, the Superfund program, and various research activities.

Notwithstanding some significant achievements, the EPA confronts a daunting array of problems in the early years of the twenty-first century: an unmanageable burden of continually growing regulatory responsibilities, a politically toxic inheritance of congressional distrust and disruptive oversight born of bitter controversies surrounding the Reagan administration

Box 3-1 Major Responsibilities of the EPA

The following are the major regulatory tasks assigned to the EPA in each important pollution control program.

Air quality
- Establishes national air quality standards.
- Sets limits on the level of air pollutants emitted from stationary sources such as power plants, municipal incinerators, factories, and chemical plants.
- Establishes emission standards for new motor vehicles.
- Sets allowable levels for toxics such as lead, benzene, and toluene in gasoline.
- Establishes emission standards for hazardous air pollutants such as beryllium, mercury, and asbestos.
- Supervises states in their development of clean air plans.

Water quality and protection
- Issues permits for the discharge of any pollutant into navigable waters.
- Develops effluent guidelines to control discharge of specific water pollutants, including radiation.
- Develops criteria that enable states to set water quality standards.
- Administers grants program to states to subsidize the cost of building sewage treatment plants.
- Regulates disposal of waste material, including sludge and low-level radioactive discards, into the oceans.
- Cooperates with the U.S. Army Corps of Engineers to issue permits for the dredging and filling of wetlands.
- Sets national drinking water standards to ensure that drinking water is safe.
- Regulates underground injection of wastes to protect purity of groundwater.
- With the U.S. Coast Guard, coordinates cleanup of oil and chemical spills into U.S. waterways.

Hazardous waste
- Maintains inventory of existing hazardous waste dump sites.
- Tracks more than five hundred hazardous compounds from point of origin to final disposal site.
- Sets standards for generators and transporters of hazardous wastes.
- Issues permits for treatment, storage, and disposal facilities for hazardous wastes.
- Assists states in developing hazardous waste control programs.
- Maintains a multibillion-dollar fund (Superfund) from industry fees and general tax revenues to provide for emergency cleanup of hazardous dumps when no responsible party can immediately be found.
- Pursues identification of parties responsible for waste sites and eventual reimbursement of the federal government for Superfund money spent cleaning up these sites.

Chemical regulation, including pesticides and radioactive waste
- Maintains inventory of chemical substances now in commercial use.
- Regulates existing chemicals considered serious hazards to people and the environment, including fluorocarbons, polychlorinated biphenyls (PCBs), and asbestos.

(continued)

Box 3-1   Major Responsibilities of the EPA (cont.)

Chemical regulation, including pesticides and radioactive waste *(cont.)*
- Issues procedures for the proper safety testing of chemicals and orders them tested when necessary.
- Requires the registration of insecticides, herbicides, or fungicides intended for sale in the United States.
- Requires pesticide manufacturers to provide scientific evidence that their products will not injure humans, livestock, crops, or wildlife when used as directed.
- Classifies pesticides for either general public use or restricted use by certified applicators.
- Sets standards for certification of applicators of restricted-use pesticides. (Individual states may certify applicators through their own programs based on the federal standards.)
- Cancels or suspends the registration of a product on the basis of actual or potential unreasonable risk to humans, animals, or the environment.
- Issues a "stop sale, use, and removal" order when a pesticide already in circulation is found to be in violation of the law.
- Requires registration of pesticide-producing establishments.
- Issues regulations concerning the labeling, storage, and disposal of pesticide containers.
- Issues permits for pesticide research.
- Monitors pesticide levels in the environment.
- Monitors and regulates the levels of radiation in drinking water, oceans, rainfall, and air.
- Conducts research on toxic substances, pesticides, air and water quality, hazardous wastes, radiation, and the causes and effects of acid rain.
- Provides overall guidance to other federal agencies on radiation protection matters that affect public health.
- Maintains inventory of chemical substances now in commercial use.

Other
- Sets acceptable noise levels for construction equipment, transportation equipment (except aircraft), all motors and engines, and electronic equipment.

---

and resurrected by the 1994 Republican congressional takeover, a chronically inadequate budget, and the administrative complexities inherent in complicated environmental regulations. The growing disparity between the EPA's administrative responsibilities and its resources has reached a point at which many observers believe the agency is, or will soon be, mired in "a pathological cycle of regulatory failure."[39]

Micromanaged and Overloaded. By the mid-1980s, it was already obvious, as the CEQ observed, that "the Environmental Protection Agency cannot possibly do all the things its various mandates tell it to do," and conditions have not improved.[40] More than two decades later, the agency is still years, or decades, behind in complying with important requirements in its ten major statutory programs, and new jobs are always ahead.

One reason for the agency's chronic compliance problems is the congressional penchant for packing legislation with a multitude of demanding deadlines, detailed management instructions, and hammer clauses that threaten dire consequences should the EPA fail to comply with various statutory deadlines. The EPA continues to experience what is probably the most relentless legislative oversight of any federal agency. (So habitually does Congress investigate the activities of the EPA that the U.S. General Accounting Office, the congressional watchdog agency, had for many years a permanent branch at EPA headquarters.) Even though EPA staff grew by approximately 18 percent during the 1990s, this growth has failed to keep pace with the accumulating new responsibilities the agency has inherited.

The cumulative result of this excessive congressional attention is written in the statistics of missed deadlines, lagging research, and impossibly distant completion dates for existing program responsibilities. The doleful litany includes the following two programs.

- The Federal Insecticide, Fungicide, and Rodenticide Act requires the EPA to evaluate more than 50,000 individual pesticide products containing more than 600 active ingredients and 900 inert ingredients. "If EPA has to prepare interim registration standards for all 600 active ingredients," the General Accounting Office concluded in 1986, "then the Agency may finish the first round reviews in about 2004."[41] In fact, by 2010 the EPA had not yet completed its first round of reviews.
- The Food Quality Protection Act (1996) requires the EPA to screen all commercial pesticides for estrogenic effects that may affect human health, to develop a screening and testing program by 1998, to implement the program by 1999, and to report to Congress on the program's accomplishments by August 2000. This requires the EPA to review data on 600 pesticides in active commerce, 1,800 inert ingredients in 20,000 pesticide products, and 75,000 industrial chemicals, plus consumer products. None of this, including the report, had been accomplished by the end of 2010.

The EPA frequently resorts to improvised strategies for deciding which programs and pollutants will get priority. Sometimes it depends on litigation initiated by private interests—most often environmental groups—to force its attention to specific programs. The agency was able to give priority to a Toxic Substances Control Act requirement that it act within one year on recommendations from its experts concerning whether a substance merited testing for carcinogenicity only because the Natural Resources Defense Council sued the EPA and obtained a judicial order for the agency to speed up the review process. Sometimes the agency ignores portions of the law to make its workload manageable. Political scientist Edward Woodhouse observes that to cope with the otherwise impossible task of screening the 60,000 chemicals presently in commercial use, as the Toxic Substances Control Act requires, the EPA "simply misinterpreted the law: the agency placed its focus exclusively on new uses of new chemicals.... EPA apparently decided (probably implicitly) that its staff and funds were inadequate to cover tens of thousands of existing chemicals."[42]

Are Integrated Programs Possible? The EPA has come to resemble a regulatory holding company, a conglomerate of offices, each focused narrowly on problems in a single environmental medium (such as air, land, or water) or on one kind of pollutant (such as toxic waste). Further, each office is responsible for numerous regulatory laws written with little attention to their compatibility. "Each program has staked out an environmental problem that it is required to 'fix,' according to the peculiar rules embodied in its statutory mandate," observed the 1985 CEQ report.[43]

The EPA originally was conceived very differently. The advisory council recommending the EPA's creation to President Nixon had argued that environmental policy had a unique character because there were "interactions and trade-offs inherent in controlling different types of pollution." The EPA was expected to be the means to "rationalize the organization of environmental efforts" and "give focus and coordination to them."[44] In short, the EPA was intended to synthesize approaches to specific environmental problems into an "integrated and holistic approach"[45]—which is precisely what the EPA has not done.

Circumstances conspired against this integrated approach from the EPA's inception. Its most grievous fault was lack of political allure. Congress and the White House, under intense public pressure to do something quickly about specific pollution problems, needed to promote what seemed the quickest solution to what appeared to be the most urgent problem of the moment. Integrated management, in contrast, seemed strange and complicated, too difficult to explain and too unpredictable in results to appeal to Congress or the public.[46] Also, the program offices concerned with air, water, and land quickly dominated the EPA and defeated most efforts to create more integrated programs; these offices had powerful constituencies, whereas the cross-media programs did not. Political scientist Barry Rabe notes,

Each environmental medium and the separate programs within each medium have attracted politically potent constituencies that are likely antagonists toward any attempt to transform—or integrate—the existing system. They include environmental professionals and agencies, representatives of business and industry, and various policy-making committees and subcommittees that operate in Congress and state legislatures.[47]

Environmental groups were usually unsympathetic, perhaps because they feared that integrated management would subvert existing programs. Moreover, environmental law usually regulates the impact of specific pollutants, such as threats to public health or groundwater quality, and legislative pressure to produce results gives regulators little incentive to take the longer time necessary to develop more holistic approaches to pollution management.

The segmented approach to pollution management embodied in the EPA's organization and most of its basic pollution control laws is often unsatisfactory because it does not deal effectively with major problems such as cross-media pollution. Consider the case of toxic metal wastes from coal-fired electricity-generating plants. These toxic wastes include a multitude of potentially dangerous chemicals, such as arsenic, selenium, lead, radioactive chromium, and barium, that scrubbers extract from coal combustion gases.[48] The resulting coal ash has been stored as solid or liquid waste on power plant sites. While the Clean Air Act guides the EPA regulation of these emission gases, the resulting waste has been treated as ordinary solid waste and regulated through the RCRA, a very different law. In December 2008, a Tennessee Valley Authority (TVA) coal ash containment pond at Kingston, Tennessee, collapsed, releasing 1.1 billion gallons of liquid ash waste—the largest industrial waste spill in U.S. history—flooding 300 acres in the small town of Harriman, Tennessee, and leaving a distillation of hazardous chemical residues. Although controversy continues among the TVA, the EPA, and Harriman's residents over the long-term human and ecological risks from this waste exposure, the spill forced national attention on the need for the EPA to classify such waste as hazardous and to limit its release into waterways. Recognizing and regulating these coal wastes as hazardous has been complicated, in large measure because these pollutants are subject to two federal laws involving different standards and EPA offices and because the EPA lacks authority to achieve the economic and regulatory efficiency that could result from treating coal combustion pollutants, or most other pollutants, from their source to their disposal as a single regulatory problem—called integrated management.

Developing an integrated approach would take considerable time at best. But integrated management has much to recommend it. It would produce regulatory methods that create significant cost reduction, and perhaps quicker results, than the segmented approaches currently applied to pollution problems. For example, removing sulfur from electric power plant air emissions usually results in toxic sludges that must then be treated by land disposal, which often creates groundwater contamination. Greater control of sulfur air emissions at their source, however, might require more costly air pollution control technologies yet result in far less overall expense and a greater reduction of health and ecological risks than regulating sulfur in the air, soil, and groundwater separately.[49]

Needed: Clear Priorities. Like the man who mounted his horse and galloped off in all directions, the EPA lacks a constant course. With responsibility for administering ten separate statutes and parts of four others, the EPA has no clearly mandated priorities and thus no way of allocating scarce resources among different statutes or among programs within a single law. Nor does the EPA have a congressional charter, common to most federal departments and agencies, defining its broad organizational mission and priorities. Although the agency has had to make informal, ad hoc decisions about program priorities to survive, these are much less satisfactory legally and politically than a clear, congressionally mandated agenda.

Congress has shown little inclination to provide the EPA with a charter or mandated priorities, in good part because the debate sure to arise on the relative merits and urgency of different environmental problems is an invitation to a political bloodletting most legislators would gladly avoid. Intense controversy over which problems to emphasize would be likely among states, partisans of different ecological issues, and regulated interests; the resulting political brawl would upset existing policy coalitions that themselves were fashioned with great difficulty. Moreover, setting priorities invites a prolonged, bitter debate over an intensely emotional issue: Should the primary objective of environmental protection be to reduce public risks associated with environmental degradation as much as seems practical, or should it be—as many environmentalists fervently believe—to eliminate all significant forms of pollution altogether? Many experts inside and outside the EPA have argued that unless Congress sets priorities enabling the agency to concentrate its resources on a relatively few, feasible, measurable objectives, the nation will be dissipating its environmental resources among a multitude of different programs and objectives with few significant results.

The Reform Struggle. The EPA's administrators have been acutely aware of the agency's managerial problems and initiated many programs throughout the 1990s to encourage greater administrative efficiency and effectiveness when opportunities arose. The difficulties involved in implementing these internal reforms arose, quite often, from conflicts among the agency's numerous stakeholders, both inside and outside the organization, whose buy-in to reform is frequently essential to its success. Even politically skilled administrators, armed with a vigorous reform agenda and administrative expertise, have struggled to overcome the divisive pluralism of interest often evident among the EPA's multiple constituencies.

A case in point is the Reinventing EPA experience. In 1995, the EPA's leadership, headed by Administrator Carol Browner, officially announced it was Reinventing EPA and launched a risky reform program to transform the fundamental legal and political character of its regulatory programs. The collective reform proposals, part of the Clinton administration's highly touted Reinventing Government initiative, were intended to make the EPA a regulatory showcase. The reinvention initiative was by far the most ambitious EPA reform agenda in two decades, and all sides agreed the proposals were aimed at the priority problems.[50]

Reinventing EPA was a well-intentioned gamble against forces over which the EPA often has little control. One problem is the agency's own organizational design and culture. The EPA's major media offices regulating air, water, and hazardous waste, especially, have been the organizational and regulatory centers of power within the agency and have not readily surrendered the significant amount of authority, budgetary resources, and technical expertise required to implement many of the reinvention initiatives. Moreover, many among the large diverse constituency of outside interests deeply concerned with the EPA's work have preferred to keep or mildly amend the agency's present structure. These stakeholders include state and local officials, scientists, regulated commercial and industrial facilities, trade organizations, and academics, frequently with strong political and professional ties to the existing programs and organizations. Many informed observers also believe that the ills that reinvention has addressed require a major rewriting of the numerous inconsistent environmental laws—a congressional job. Congress still prefers continually to amend existing laws, to tinker with the EPA's administrative structure, and to propose other marginal changes in existing arrangements instead of undertaking a rationally thorough, but politically forbidding, rewrite and reorganization of the agency's fundamental regulatory mission.

The Department of the Interior

Established as a cabinet-level department in 1845, the DOI is among the oldest and most important of all federal agencies. With a current budget of approximately $12.1 billion and 72,000 employees, the department's responsibilities leave few environmental issues untouched. These responsibilities include (1) protection and management of more than 549 million acres of public land—roughly 28 percent of the total U.S. land area—set aside by Congress for national parks, wilderness areas, forests, and other restricted uses; (2) administration of Native American lands and federal Native American programs, including authority over western tribal lands containing a large proportion of the coal, petroleum, uranium, and other largely unexploited energy resources in the western United States; (3) enforcement of federal surface mining regulations through its Office of

Surface Mining; (4) conservation and management of wetlands and estuarine areas; and (5) protection and preservation of wildlife, including endangered species. Headed by a cabinet secretary appointed by the president, the department's programs historically have been a primary concern to environmentalists. The secretary of the interior has traditionally been a westerner, a political concession to the western states, where most of the public lands are found. During the 1970s, the department secretaries appointed by Presidents Nixon and Carter, although not necessarily outspoken environmentalists or even conservationists, were at least tolerable to the growing environmentalist movement. Since the 1980s, however, the relationship between the environmental community and DOI secretaries has often been combative.

At the beginning of the Reagan administration, the DOI, and particularly Reagan's first choice of James Watt as the department's secretary, was a source of continual controversy as a result of its efforts to make sweeping changes in personnel and programs to conform with Reagan's regulatory reforms. These controversies were rooted in strong environmentalist convictions about the nature of the department that shape environmentalist organizations' responses to any departmental leadership.

The DOI has always been a battleground between interests seeking to conserve the resources in the public domain and those seeking generous access to them. The DOI's mandate to ensure "balanced use" of resources between conservation and development—a mandate that continually propels the department and its secretary into a storm of controversy concerning which use shall dominate—is a certain source of trouble for every secretary. Moreover, the department's programs serve a clientele including not only environmentalists but also the timber and cattle industries, mining companies, sports enthusiasts, a multitude of private corporations, and many other interests that expect the department to be solicitous of their viewpoints. Finally, the western states historically have maintained that they have not been given a sufficient voice in the administration of the federal properties that often constitute the vast majority of land within their boundaries. The desire of these states to assume greater control over the public domain within their jurisdictions and the resulting tensions with the federal government will outlive any administration.

Watt's strident conflict with environmentalists was unusually nasty, even for a public office rich in controversy, and he was forced to resign in October 1983 after becoming a political liability for the White House. Although Watt's successor was less publicly belligerent toward environmentalists, most environmental groups were convinced that only the leadership style had changed. The Bush administration did little to appease these critics by appointing former New Mexico representative Manuel Lujan Jr. as secretary. Lujan and his management team seemed to embrace essentially the same viewpoint as their Reagan-appointed predecessors. Congress generally frustrated the Bush administration's efforts to open vast tracts of public domain for oil exploration and commercial timbering, but Lujan continued to provoke environmentalist ire. The head of the Bureau of Mines did not improve the department's environmental image by declaring at a conference of miners, loggers, and other resource developers that environmentalists were "a bunch of nuts."[51]

Although environmentalists were generally delighted with President Clinton's selection of former Arizona governor Bruce Babbitt to be secretary of the interior, they were not so satisfied with many of Babbitt's early policy initiatives, including the scope of the department's efforts to restrict timbering and other resource development on public lands. The Clinton administration's agenda of slow and cautious environmental reform, especially grating on grassroots environmentalists who expected a bold display of environmental initiative, nurtured continuing controversy, albeit more temperate than in the 1980s, between the DOI and its environmentalist constituency. In the closing months of his administration, however, Clinton's sudden designation of vast public land tracts for national parks, refuges, wilderness, and other restricted uses enormously gratified conservationists.

Congressional Republicans were hugely annoyed by Clinton's whirlwind designations, which they considered an arrogant unconstitutional exercise of presidential discretion, and vowed unsuccessfully to undo them during President George W. Bush's term. Further complicating the department's relations with Congress was the opposition of environmentalists and most congressional Democrats to Bush's appointment of Gale Norton as the new secretary of the interior. Norton's political background inspired environmentalist criticism that she was "just Jim Watt in a skirt"[52] and awakened their apprehension about another Reagan-style assault on environmentalist legislation, which Norton's successor, former Idaho governor Kirk Kempthorne, did little to relieve. One of President Obama's earliest presidential actions, clearly intended to send a signal, was to suspend numerous DOI decisions made during the Bush administration that had opened federal lands to increased energy exploration and timber productions. Kenneth Salazar, Obama's newly appointed secretary of the interior, has been outspoken in his determination that the DOI's leadership style and agenda will be much more appealing to environmentalists and their allies. The department's mission, however, will inevitably evoke criticism and conflict among its multitude of different constituencies, regardless of which party controls Congress or the White House. Environmentalists themselves are often divided over DOI policies—for example, over the relative importance of recreation and species protection on public lands and over the volume of timber that should be harvested from the national forests.

The Nuclear Regulatory Commission

The NRC was created by Congress in 1976 to assume the regulatory responsibilities originally vested in the Atomic Energy Commission. An independent agency with five commissioners appointed by the president, the NRC regulates most nonmilitary uses of nuclear facilities and materials. The commission's major activities related to the environment include (1) the regulation of the site choice, construction, operation, and security of all civilian nuclear reactors; (2) the designation and supervision of all nuclear waste repositories; (3) the regulation of uranium mining and milling facilities; and (4) the closing of civilian nuclear facilities after they discontinue production (called decommissioning). In 2003, the NRC employed about 2,700 individuals and had a budget of approximately $510 million.

Environmental groups have been most concerned with the NRC's supervision of nuclear power plants and repositories for radioactive wastes. Although 104 nuclear plants were operating or approved for construction by 2004, the majority of these have been criticized by environmental groups for alleged deficiencies in structural safety, control of radioactive emissions, and waste storage.[53] In addition, environmental groups have often been aggressive in seeking NRC safety reviews of operating plants and personnel training procedures. The NRC has assumed a major responsibility for the review of site selection and the supervision of waste disposal at the nation's first permanent nuclear waste repository at Yucca Flats, Nevada. Environmental groups still regard the process of site construction and disposal as an issue likely to remain important for several decades.

The NRC and environmental groups have been both adversaries and allies. The environmental movement generally has supported the NRC's stricter enforcement and review of regulations for operating nuclear facilities and its increasingly rigorous standards for new facility licensing. Yet environmentalists also have criticized the NRC for allegedly siding too often with the nuclear power industry against its critics, for bureaucratic inertia and conservatism, and for ignoring technical criticism and data from sources not associated with the nuclear power industry or the commission. As with other regulatory agencies, the NRC is bound to its own clientele—the nuclear power industry—by professional associations, common technical and economic concerns, and historical sympathies; it is also committed to regulating the industry in the public interest while maintaining sufficient objectivity and disengagement from the nuclear power movement to do that job. These often conflicting responsibilities lead the NRC into controversies with environmental interests. Nonetheless, the NRC and its mission remain among the most environmentally significant elements in the executive branch.

The Department of Energy

With a current budget exceeding $26.4 billion and more than 20,000 employees, the Department of Energy (DOE) and its programs and regulatory responsibilities continually involve a great diversity of environmentally related matters. Despite its size and importance, the DOE has been a stepchild of the executive branch. Widely criticized and burdened with difficult unpopular programs throughout the 1980s, the department struggled though the 1990s with immense new problems—legal, political, economic, and technical—created by the disastrous mismanagement of the military nuclear weapons facilities under its jurisdiction since the late 1970s. These unprecedented difficulties constituted more high-profile bad news for an agency with a talent for collecting misfortune.

The DOE began George W. Bush's administration still mired in high-visibility controversy, struggling against the stigma of flagrant mismanagement and still saddled with responsibility for unpopular policies. The DOE's problems seem almost inevitable in light of its history. The department was created in 1976, when Congress combined a number of independent agencies with programs already operating in other departments to bring the federal government's sprawling energy activities within a single bureaucratic structure. Under the DOE's jurisdiction are regulatory activities and energy programs strongly affecting the environment. The more important of these include (1) promotion of civilian nuclear power activities, (2) regulation of military nuclear facilities and radioactive wastes, (3) administration of the federal government's research and development programs in energy production and conservation, (4) regulation of price controls for domestic petroleum and natural gas, and (5) administration of federal research and development grants for commercial synthetic fuels production in the United States. The DOE is the principal executive agency involved in the regulation and production of many different energy technologies with significant environmental impacts. Also, by design, it is expected to undertake a volatile agenda of frequently contradictory and inconsistent missions destined to set it at odds with itself and with the environmental community: to promote environmentally risky energy technologies and to minimize the environmental risks, to promote energy use and energy conservation, to stimulate research and development of new energy-consuming and energy-saving technologies, to control energy prices in emergencies, and to avert energy shortages and stimulate long-range energy planning.

By far the most politically and financially costly problem confronting the DOE remains the environmental contamination of the nation's nuclear weapons facilities (discussed in Chapter 8). More than 122 nuclear weapons manufacturing and laboratory sites in thirty states, the Marshall

Islands, and Puerto Rico have to be made safe. The cleanup program will probably exceed $250 billion and take perhaps a half century or more to accomplish—if it can be accomplished; no public or private agency has any experience in cleaning up radioactive contamination of such scale and complexity.[54] Spending for the cleanup of these nuclear weapons sites and for other related programs could involuntarily transform the DOE into the nation's largest environmental agency and launch it on the most expensive public works program in U.S. history.[55]

Neither a new century nor a new presidency improved political karma at the DOE. The department was anointed the lead agency for President George W. Bush's ambitious new national energy policy in 2001, intended to combat what the president proclaimed as a new national energy crisis—a situation that set the DOE on a collision course with almost all organized environmental groups that considered the new plan to be extravagantly expensive and environmentally reckless. To environmentalists, the DOE seemed to be promoting hugely accelerated fossil fuel extraction and electricity production when it should be promoting energy conservation, advocating more commercial nuclear power when it should be advocating less, and proclaiming an energy crisis when one didn't exist. Moreover, the DOE was still struggling with an apparently intractable problem of creating a permanent repository for the nation's nuclear waste. And controversy continued over the DOE's management of military nuclear waste sites.

President Obama's selection of Dr. Steven Chu, a Nobel Laureate physicist, to be secretary of the interior inaugurated what the administration expected to be a fresh ambitious agenda of environmentally benign programs. These programs emphasized energy conservation, renewable energy, federal support for innovative energy technologies, and other initiatives that environmentalists generally perceived as a welcome change from the Bush administration's apparent preference for fossil fuels and nuclear power in national energy development.

The Courts: The Role of Appraisal

Federal judges actively participate in the environmental policy process in several ways. They continually interpret environmental law, an inevitable task in light of the ambiguities and silences common to environmental legislation. This statutory interpretation often amounts to policymaking by the judicial branch. Judges also attempt to ensure that agencies discharge their mandated responsibilities under environmental legislation and otherwise comply with administrative obligations. In addition, the federal courts enforce the Administrative Procedures Act (1946), the code of administrative procedures applicable to all federal agencies. Finally, the courts ensure that environmental laws and their administrative implementation comply with constitutional standards. As the volume of environmental litigation expands relentlessly, federal judges find themselves increasingly at the pulse points of environmental policymaking. (Although critics have argued that federal judges are not prepared by a legal education for this pivotal role in adjudicating complex scientific and economic issues, the trend seems inexorable.

The Courts and Environmental Policy. The impact of the federal courts on environmental policy has changed over the decades since Earth Day 1970. In the 1970s, federal court decisions in both substantive and procedural issues generally worked to the advantage of environmental interests. During this period, environmentalists often saw the federal judiciary as the Great Equalizer, offsetting the previously enormous advantage enjoyed by regulated interests in administrative and judicial forums. Environmental organizations, aggressively exploiting the procedural advantages they had gained during the 1970s to compel federal enforcement of new regulatory programs, achieved some of their most significant judicial victories during this period. The federal courts greatly expanded opportunities for environmental groups to bring issues before the bench by a broadened definition of *standing to sue*, a legal status that authorized individuals or organizations to sue governmental agencies for failure to enforce environmental legislation. Beginning with the *Scenic Hudson* case in 1965, for instance, the federal courts broadened for more than a decade the criteria by which citizens could acquire such standing to sue federal agencies over enforcement of environmental regulations.[56]

By the late 1980s, however, the federal judiciary was no longer a predictably friendly venue for environmentalism. Business and other regulated interests began to use the federal courts far more effectively than they had previously. The increased effectiveness of business interests also exemplified the great growth in number and activity of specialized not-for-profit legal foundations representing regulated industries in environmental litigation. Reasoning that the devil should not have all the good tunes, business patterned these associations after the successful public interest legal foundations created in the 1970s to represent environmental interests. As do environmental public interest groups, these business associations maintain that they are suing the government in the public interest and enjoy tax-exempt status. However, business public interest groups are financed principally by organizations, such as the Adolph Coors Company and the Scaife Foundation, that have fought vigorously against most of the major environmental regulatory programs passed since the 1970s. The tide of judicial favor began to turn more decisively against environmental litigants in the 1990s as an increasing number of federal judges appointed by Presidents Reagan and George Bush came to the bench.[57] By the end of the 1990s, environmentalists' standing to sue was significantly limited, the rights of property owners in cases involving the Endangered Species Act and conservation restrictions on private land were enlarged to the disadvantage of environmentalist litigants, and state authority to restrict the scope of federal environmental regulations was enlarged. The benefit to business interests from this growing strength in environmental litigation does not depend solely on winning cases. Exhaustive and relentless challenges to federal regulation can delay the enforcement of environmental laws for many years and throw environmental groups on the defensive, compelling them to invest their scarce resources in protracted legal battles. Often battles are won not by the side with the best case but by the side with the most endurance.

Environmental groups anticipated that the election of George W. Bush was the prelude to another round of federal judicial appointments equally unfriendly to environmental interests. Despite its court appointments, however, the Bush administration did not fare nearly as well as predicted in the lower federal courts, where most environmental cases begin and end (the Supreme Court hears fewer than 100 cases a year; the circuit, or appellate, courts hear more than 40,000 appeals annually and often create most of the legal precedents that become the law of the land).[58] Federal judges in the Northwest, Midwest, and Far West were especially critical of the administration's efforts to open up public lands to more energy exploration, its lackluster enforcement of the Endangered Species Act, and its enthusiasm for increasing timber production on federal forests.[59]

The Supreme Court was a very different matter. The Court ended its 2009 term after a series of decisions that evoked from environmentalist legal scholars such verdicts as "the worst term ever" and "a message of extreme hostility to the goals and methods of environmental law"; in contrast, advocates of more restrained environmental regulation predictably approved what seemed to be the Court's determined direction.[60] In several high-profile cases, for example, the Court limited the ability of five conservation groups to challenge U.S. Forest Service regulations and limited the scope of business liability for Superfund cleanups. Such decisions appeared to reflect the Court's increasingly conservative outlook resulting from the gradual appointment of new justices during the Bush administration and to project a problematic future for environmentalist litigation considered by the highest federal court.

Litigation as a Political Tactic. The impact of the courts on policy, as the previous discussion suggests, arises not only from the substance of court rulings but also from the use of litigation as a tactical weapon in policy conflict—a weapon used by all sides. Most environmental litigation arises from three sources: major environmental organizations (such as the Sierra Club or the Environmental Defense Fund); business and property interests, including public interest law firms (such as the highly aggressive Western States Legal Foundation); and federal agencies (such as the EPA or the DOI) with major environmental responsibilities. Quite often the courts become another political arena in which the losers in prior policy battles fought among Congress, the bureaucracy, and the White House can launch yet another campaign. It is not surprising that environmental groups specializing in litigation, such as the Environmental Defense Fund, increased their activity during the Reagan administration in an often unsuccessful effort to counteract through the courts what they alleged to be massive regulatory resistance to their interests within the administration.

Litigation is also a stall in the policy process, a frustration to the opposition. Litigation creates a bargaining chip to be bartered for concessions from the opposition. Both environmentalists and their opposition have used the obstructive capacities of litigation to their advantage.

Many critics have pegged the NEPA's requirement of environmental impact statements as an especially productive source of lawsuits working to the advantage of environmentalists, but the data suggest otherwise. The number of lawsuits challenging agency actions under the NEPA has been diminishing steadily in number and importance. The federal courts in the 1980s were increasingly disinclined to sustain challenges as long as the judges were convinced that agencies had prepared and reviewed environmental impact statements properly. In addition, environmental impact statements are fast becoming a bureaucratic rite, meticulously observed but then substantively ignored.

When Should Judges Become Involved? The evolution of environmental politics increasingly embroils federal judges in resolving legal issues that have important policy consequences—in effect, implicating them in environmental policymaking through the courts. Moreover, many of these issues embrace highly technical or scientific disputes. Federal judges may, for instance, have to decide whether the EPA considered the proper animal tests in deciding that a chemical constituted a significant risk to human health. Judges are often reluctant participants in these affairs, so heavily weighted with policy or scientific implications. They may be compelled by law to adjudicate such matters, but are acutely aware of their limitations as technical experts. Equally important, as Supreme Court Justice Stephen Breyer observed, when the courts must substitute their judgment for an administrator's, the result is often politically unsatisfactory:

> Regulators must make "legislative-type" decisions, the merits of which depend upon finding, or prying out important general facts about the world; they work in a politically charged environment; they may need to

seek compromise solutions acceptable to warring private groups. [But judges must make decisions] the merits of which depend upon the relevant legal norm and a record ... that need not contain all relevant facts about the world.... Given these differences, a compromise solution that a regulator considers reasonable, for practical administrative reasons, might not seem practical to a judge.[61]

Both critics and defenders of existing environmental policies have frequently proposed that some alternative venue to the traditional courts be created for resolving technical and scientific controversies arising from environmental regulation. One common suggestion is the creation of a "science court" in which technical experts would resolve the scientific and technical issues involved in environmental litigation, leaving the judges free to focus on the largely legal matters. Other proposals involve creating impartial technical advisers to judges when scientific issues confront the court. These and many other alternatives discussed among environmental law activists illuminate not only the evolving impact of environmentalism on U.S. legal institutions themselves but also the larger challenge entailed in integrating the judicial branch effectively and appropriately into the whole environmental policy process.

The Political Environment of Environmental Policymaking

Governmental institutions are fated to work in a political setting that is inconstant, influential, and often fickle. Opportunities to make or change policy shift continually, often unpredictably, with changing political circumstances. At any given time, there will be differences between what policymakers want and what they can accomplish, between what they are compelled to do and what they would prefer to do, and between what is feasible and what is not. This ebb and flow of opportunity are created by different circumstances. The most important of these circumstances includes changes in the partisan control of governmental institutions, transient shifts of public mood, major economic change, and regulatory federalism. These can be called the changing seasons of policymaking.

Changing Party Majorities

The balance of party strength within Congress and between Congress and the White House powerfully shapes the substance and opportunities for environmental policymaking. In theory, opportunities to make or change policy are greatest when the White House and Congress are controlled by the same party. However, since 1970, Republicans have usually occupied the White House and Democratic majorities have usually controlled both congressional chambers. The floodtide of environmental legislation originating in Washington, D.C., during the 1970s was largely the result of a broad bipartisan environmental coalition in both chambers that strongly supported innovative environmental programs proposed or accepted by both Republican and Democratic presidents. The political climate for environmentalists darkened dramatically with Reagan's election and has remained unsettled ever since. The eight years under Reagan were marked by conflict and impasse between a president and Congress dominated by different parties and committed to radically different policy agendas.

Throughout the eight-year Reagan presidency, Republicans won, then lost, control of the Senate while Democrats retained their House majority. The result was an environmental gridlock in which the Democratic House frustrated Senate Republican efforts to pass Reagan's sweeping agenda of change in existing environmental laws.

Reagan's enormous impact on environmental policymaking in the 1980s is evidence, however, that in the hands of a politically skilled president with a clear policy agenda White House resources can be a potent policymaking instrument, with or without congressional cooperation. During the Reagan years, especially, administrators were able to obstruct and revise many environmental regulations and manipulate their agency budgets so effectively that the administration's environmental goals were at least partially achieved without any congressional cooperation.

With the exception of EPA administrator William K. Reilly, the environmentally important appointments of George Bush's administration generally went to individuals sympathetic to the Reagan-Bush regulatory reform agenda and thereby objectionable to most environmental organizations. Bush used the authority of the executive office, especially the OMB, to revise, delay, or defeat numerous environmental regulations ideologically unacceptable to the administration. The chill blowing toward the EPA from the White House was unmistakable; it became a continuing and effective obstacle to many environmental policy initiatives from Congress or the bureaucracy.

The Democrats' return to the White House with Clinton in 1992 turned out to be less the prelude to the bright future anticipated by environmentalists than a false dawn. The stunning Republican congressional victories of 1994 returned a Republican majority to both congressional chambers and elevated to its leadership a cadre of Republicans outspokenly unsympathetic to most of the major environmental legislation created by Congress in the previous two decades. The Republican leadership sponsored a multitude of new legislative proposals—part of what they called their Contract with America—that would have radically recast, and usually enfeebled, most of the major environmental laws written during the 1970s and 1980s.

These early Republican initiatives failed, mostly because public opinion polls convinced party leaders that radical antienvironmentalism would be politically disastrous for the party's 1996 congressional candidates. The immediate impact of the 1994 congressional elections was to force environmentalists again on the defensive.

Finally, in the last two years of his tenure, Clinton largely abandoned efforts at congressional collaboration to achieve his environmental objectives. Instead, he relied increasingly on his inherent powers as chief executive to achieve his policy goals. Using this authority, he was able to reserve more public land from economic development than any other president—a demonstration of White House authority (see Chapter 9) that infuriated congressional Republicans.[62]

The first six months of George W. Bush's presidency were additional confirmation that shifting congressional majorities can profoundly—and sometimes abruptly—transform the course of environmental politics. Less than six months after the 107th Congress convened, Republicans lost their tenuous Senate majority when Sen. James M. Jeffords, previously a Vermont Republican, decided to become an independent. This, in turn, delivered the Senate majority to the Democrats, whose environmental policy agenda differed substantially from that favored by President Bush and Senate Republicans. Control of the Senate's policy agenda and all its committees now belonged to the Democrats. The White House no longer had the policy initiative in the Senate, and the president's whole environmental agenda, like the rest of his legislative program, would become more difficult to promote. Although Republicans temporarily recovered their Senate majority in the 2002 elections, Democrats reclaimed control of both chambers in the startling 2006 elections, much to the satisfaction of most environmentalists, who interpreted the results as a sharp public rejection of the Bush environmental record and a mandate to the Democrats for a more environmentalist agenda. The subsequent election of Barack Obama and return of Democratic majorities to both congressional chambers in 2008 seemed to most environmentalists to imply much greater collaboration between White House and Congress in promoting environmentalist legislation.

Shifting Public Moods

"When President Nixon and his staff walked in the White House on January 20, 1969, we were totally unprepared for the tidal wave of public opinion in favor of cleaning up the nation's environment that was about to engulf us," John C. Whitaker, one of Nixon's close advisers, remembered. Congress was quicker to read the political prophecy in the polls.[63] By Earth Day 1970, recalled the same adviser, "so many politicians were on the stump that Congress was forced to close down."[64] Presidents and Congress alike always feel enormous political pressure to respond when confronted by broad public majorities demonstrating a strong interest, or apprehension, about an environmental issue.

The pressure to do something, or to *look* as if one is doing something, is almost irresistible when sudden spikes of public apprehension rise in the aftermath of a well-publicized environmental crisis. Many major environmental laws and regulations are direct responses to environmental disasters, real or threatened. The Three Mile Island nuclear reactor accident of 1979 begot new regulations from the NRC increasing the requirements for emergency planning at commercial nuclear power plants. The tragic 1984 chemical plant disaster at Bhopal, India, in which five thousand nearby residents and plant workers lost their lives, almost alone produced the community right-to-know provision of the Superfund Amendments and Reauthorization Act of 1986, which required industries using dangerous chemicals to disclose the type and amount of these chemicals to individuals living within an area likely to be affected by an accident on site. "The Bhopal train was leaving the station," observed one environmental lobbyist about Congress, "and we got the kind of legislation we could put on the train."[65] When California in early 2001 suddenly experienced rolling power blackouts and steeply rising electric power costs, President Bush and congressional spokespeople of both political parties quickly proclaimed an energy crisis and produced competing prescriptions for a new national energy plan, even while experts debated whether such a crisis really existed.

Washington's impetuous reaction to any publicly perceived environmental crisis is predictably nonpartisan. This hypersensitivity to public opinion has been criticized frequently because it sometimes results in hastily written laws that are difficult to implement. According to economists Robert W. Crandall and Paul R. Portney, "Congress bears a large share of the responsibility for the problems of environmental regulation. Congress has passed enabling statutes containing unrealistic deadlines and an unnecessary degree of specificity with respect to the standards that [agencies] must issue."[66]

Opinion can also become an obstacle to environmental policymaking when the public mood is inhospitable to action. The disappearance of gasoline and petroleum shortages in the late 1970s, and other evidence that the so-called energy crisis was passing, quickly removed energy problems from public concern and thwarted efforts by the Carter administration to pass new energy regulatory programs after mid-1978. By the time the Reagan administration finished its first term, Congress no longer felt pressure to continue mandatory plans for national fuel rationing, to require increased fuel economy standards for automobiles after 1986, or to promote solar technologies and other fuel conservation measures. Advocates of environmental issues often must wait until the opinion climate is ripe to move the White House or Congress to action. Crisis or disaster may sometimes be the only force that moves the political will.

Economic Change

In all environmental policymaking, economics is the counterpoint to ecology. The impact of environmental policies on the economy is a continual preoccupation of environmental regulators and the regulated. Economic conditions, in turn, influence environmental policymaking.

The economic impact of environmental regulations is continually an issue in all discussions of environmental policy. Concern most often focuses on whether environmental regulation will inhibit the expansion of the gross national product, how regulations will affect business investments and the market position of firms or industries, and whether regulatory costs are inflationary. Regulated interests frequently assert that specific policies will have most, or all, of these negative effects, whereas proponents of regulation usually claim no such negative effects will occur. Data wars erupt; each side summons its economists and econometrics to vindicate its position and discredit the opposition. Although the result of these conflicts is often inconclusive, the issues are vitally important. Policies that appear (or can be made to appear) to adversely affect economic growth, market positions, or business investment are likely to command greater and more critical attention from policymakers than those appearing more economically benign. In times of economic recession or depression, the economic impact of policies can become the major determinant of their survival.

Environmental regulations, in any case, do create major public and private costs. Between 1980 and 2000, about 60 percent of the cost of national pollution control was paid by the private sector.[67] In general, studies suggest that new capital spending for pollution control by the public and private sectors has not significantly deterred the growth of the gross national product or contributed much to inflation or to a rise in the Consumer Price Index. For most industries, spending for pollution control has been a gradually diminishing portion of new capital investment since 1980. In 1990, business spending on pollution control was estimated at 2.8 percent of all capital investment, but was expected to diminish to less than 2 percent by 2004, although final data are unavailable.[68]

Economic conditions affect environmental policymaking in several ways. Most important, the mix of economic activities in the United States largely determines the character and magnitude of the nation's pollution problems and the kinds of stress placed on its resource base. As the U.S.

economy moves away from heavy dependence on manufacturing, the mix of environmental stresses changes. Between 1950 and the late 1990s, employment in U.S. manufacturing declined from 50 percent of the workforce to 14 percent, while employment in service and high-technology sectors climbed to about 37 percent of the workforce. This manufacturing decline reduced the air pollution emissions from U.S. industry, but it increased the volume of solid and hazardous waste generated nationally. Since the early 1980s, the greatest stress on regional resources produced by economic growth has occurred in the South and the West.

Most theorists assume that a major economic recession, depression, or serious bout with inflation will profoundly affect environmental regulation. The United States experienced no major depression and only a few short recessions between 1970 and 2006. The serious inflation of the 1978–1983 period, intensified by rising energy prices associated with the energy crisis of the mid-1970s, did not appear to create a political climate hostile to environmental regulation. However, the economic recession beginning in 1989 and the sluggish recovery in the early 1990s affected the environmental agendas of the Bush and Clinton administrations. The economic malaise all but extinguished the Bush administration's mild enthusiasm for environmental policy innovation after 1990 and—much to the disappointment of environmentalists—inhibited the scope of environmental reforms initiated by the Clinton administration, despite the president's campaign commitment to aggressive environmentalism.

In contrast to Clinton's experience, the mild downturn of the economy at the beginning of George W. Bush's administration was congenial to Bush's environmental agenda. Like Reagan, Bush and his advisers believed that even a modest economic recession called for a relaxation of environmental regulations that allegedly inhibited economic development in the industrial sector and particularly in the energy industry—a theme that resonated well with congressional Republicans. The Bush administration seized on California's highly publicized energy problems in early 2001 as further proof that massively increased energy production had to be a national economic priority. Asserting that a national energy crisis existed, the president's early legislative agenda capitalized on the sluggish economy and California's energy ills to promote a comprehensive relaxation of environmental regulations and aggressive new energy exploration on public lands.

The severe recession crippling the national economy starting in 2006 is widely expected to have a significant impact on environmental policymaking well into the subsequent decade. Predictions include a growing public reluctance, shared by national political leaders, to support vigorous new environmental laws and regulations because they might inhibit economic recovery (a symptom of this malaise may be the growing public concern about the economic impact of environmental laws, discussed in Chapter 2). Environmental organizations have experienced a significant decline in assets leading to cutbacks in staff and programs, although many groups have responded with a greater reliance on volunteers and more efficient resource use in the most essential programs.[69]

Regulatory Federalism

Federalism disperses governmental power by fragmenting authority between national and state governments. Despite the historical enlargement of federal powers, federalism remains a sturdy constitutional buttress supporting the edifice of authority—shared, independent, and countervailing—erected for the states within the federal system. An observer has said, "It is difficult to find any government activity which does not involve all three of the so-called 'levels' of the federal system." Yet no one level monopolizes power. "There has never been a time when it was possible to put neat labels on discrete 'federal,' 'state,' and 'local' functions."[70]

Environmental programs usually are federalized, and sometimes regionalized, in their implementation, thereby introducing another political dimension into the policy process. For instance, federal air and water pollution legislation is administered through the Washington, D.C., headquarters of the EPA, its ten regional offices, and the majority of state governments, which assume the responsibility for issuing to pollution dischargers permits specifying the acceptable control technologies and emission levels. In the mid-1990s, for instance, thirty-eight states had authority to issue water permits, and forty-nine certified pesticides under federal authority. This two- and three-tiered design ensures that state and regional interests take part in the regulatory process and that, consequently, state and local governments, together with their associated interests, actively pursue their individual, often competitive objectives during program implementation. Even if the states are not formally included in the administration of federal environmental regulations, they are likely to insist on some voice in decisions affecting them. Federalism in environmental regulation guarantees voice and influence to the multitude of states involved, providing essential representation for various geographical interests affected politically and economically by federal environmental laws.

The most untiring watchdog over state environmental interests in Washington is the U.S. Senate. Anyone doubting this senatorial vigilance need only have observed the Senate committee hearing in January 2001 to approve Christine Whitman's nomination to be the new administrator of the EPA. For almost an hour and a half, before Whitman had an opportunity to speak, she had first to attend as each committee member welcomed her, congratulated her, and not coincidentally reminded her about some important local problem the EPA ought to be addressing. Sen. George V. Voinovich, R-Ohio, informed her that Ohio needed the EPA's help to burn more coal. Sen. Christopher S. Bond, R-Mo., wanted the EPA to ease its opposition to river barge traffic. Sen. Harry Reid, D-Nev., had an environmental justice problem involving Nevada's Peyote Indian tribe, and newly elected Sen. Hillary Clinton, D-N.Y., wanted the EPA to attend to Lake Onondaga. "The Army Corps of Engineers is in charge of cleaning up the lake, and currently the plan is expected to take 15 years to complete," noted Senator Clinton. "The EPA has been extremely involved in the clean-up and ... I'd like to not only bring this to your attention but to ask if the EPA under your leadership will continue this high level of involvement." Of course, she was assured, the EPA would look after Lake Onondaga.[71]

The status of the states has altered considerably since the 1970s. At the time of the first Earth Day, only a few progressive states such as California anticipated federal policymakers by initiating needed environmental regulations. Most states seemed unable or unwilling to attack vigorously their own environmental ills. In fact, a major provocation for the array of new federal environmental legislation flowing from Washington during this period was the conviction among federal policymakers that most states had neither the will nor the competence to attack grave environmental problems on their own. Today, the states have often been well ahead of Washington in developing innovative and experimental environmental management and in attacking emerging environmental problems. Aggressive state pressure often forces the EPA's policy implementation and innovation. Thus, a coalition of northeastern states, collaborating in 2006 to sue the EPA for its failure to regulate national CO_2 emissions through the Clean Air Act, eventually forced the U.S. Supreme Court to review the scientific evidence for climate warming despite the Bush administration's opposition.

Federalism can also complicate and delay program implementation. Few issues arouse state concern more than federal aid and administrative discretion for the states in program management. Federal aid comes in many forms: grants for program administration, staff training, salary supplements, program enforcement, and pollution control facilities; technical assistance in program development or enforcement; research cost sharing; and much more. In the latter 1990s, the EPA provided about $1 in every $5 spent by the states on major pollution control programs and an additional $2.5 billion in grants for the construction of waste treatment facilities. The states understandably favor generous federal cost-sharing in the administration of federally mandated environmental programs. Many proponents of environmental regulation believe that the amount of federal aid directly affects the quality of environmental protection, particularly in states lacking adequate staff and technical resources to implement programs on their own.

The amount of discretion permitted the states when interpreting and enforcing federal regulations within their own borders begets ceaseless controversy in U.S. environmental administration. In general, the states prefer the federal government to leave state administrators with enough discretion to adapt federal environmental regulations to unique local conditions and to be responsive to local economic and political interests. Assailing the federal government for imposing regulations on the states without respect for local interests is a political mantra among state officials, but the criticism grew increasingly strident as the states' competence in and resources for pollution regulation improved throughout the 1990s. States now commonly complain that federal regulations force them to conform to rules that are inappropriate, economically wasteful, or politically unfair to local interests—a mood aggravated by mounting regulatory responsibilities imposed by Washington along with diminishing financial support for their implementation.

Another fertile source of controversy in regulatory federalism is the existence of many regional conflicts deeply embedded in the nation's history. Disagreements between the western states, where most of the federal public lands reside, and Washington, D.C., over the management of the public domain west of the Mississippi—almost one-third of the nation's land area—repeatedly erupt in the course of federal environmental regulation.

A newer regional conflict appeared in the mid-1980s, when scientific evidence began to validate the existence of acid rain and the transport of acid rain precursors across national, regional, and state boundaries. It soon became apparent that much of the considerable acid deposition falling in the northeastern states originated among the extensive smokestack industries along the Ohio River Valley. Northeastern governors soon took the initiative in demanding that the EPA compel the Ohio River states to impose stricter emission controls on their smokestack industries. The offending states resisted this onslaught, thrusting the EPA into the middle of an increasingly acrimonious dispute between the Ohio River Valley states, intent on defeating new EPA emission controls on the region's fossil-fuel-burning industries, and the northeastern states, supporting the controls to limit the airborne pollution from Ohio River sources. Nine northeastern states have repeatedly sued the EPA to compel the agency first to issue and then to enforce regulations for state air pollution control permits, which, it is assumed, will accomplish the desired emission controls.

Conclusion

In an important sense, all the nation's environmental problems can be solved. There are almost no contemporary environmental problems for which a technical or scientific solution does not exist or cannot readily be found. Even when ensuring environmental quality might require social action—perhaps a major shift of consumer spending away from gas-guzzler vehicles to highly fuel-efficient cars to reduce urban smog—*what* could solve the problem is usually much easier to imagine than *how* to accomplish it. With this perspective, perhaps the greatest challenge to environmental policymaking is finding the governmental, economic, and cultural arrangements—the institutional means—to achieve the environmental ends. To most Americans, the nation's environmental challenges are epitomized by polluted air, fouled water, dangerously unregulated hazardous and toxic wastes, and a multitude of other ecological derangements. This chapter illuminates the less obvious dimension of the nation's environmental difficulties—the institutional and economic obstacles to implementing environmental policy effectively. Despite the numerous improvements in environmental quality since 1970, in many critical respects the governmental institutions on which the nation now depends to reverse its ecological degradation are struggling, and often failing, at the task.

Difficulties with environmental policymaking often originate in the fundamental constitutional design of the political system or in deeply rooted political traditions. Among these problems are excessive congressional control of the agencies implementing environmental policy, legislative reluctance to creating clear mandates and priorities within regulatory programs, the extreme fragmentation of committee control over environmental policy, and the resistance of entrenched bureaucracies to structural and policy reform. Although federalism is essential to the political architecture of any environmental regulatory program in the United States, it also complicates policy implementation by introducing competitive pluralistic interests. The institutions, moreover, must function in a volatile political climate of shifting party majorities, economic cycles, fluctuating public opinion, and contentious issues of policy implementation arising from tensions deeply embedded in a federalized regulatory process.

In essence, the quality of the nation's environmental policymaking is grounded in an institutional design that shapes and limits outcomes. To understand what policies are made, we inevitably must appreciate how they were created.

Suggested Readings

Kamieniecki, Sheldon, and Michael E. Kraft. *Business and Environmental Policy: Corporate Interests in the American System.* Cambridge, Mass.: MIT Press, 2007.

Keller, Ann Campbell. *Science in Environmental Policy: The Politics of Objective Advice.* Cambridge, Mass.: MIT Press, 2009

Lindstrom, Matthew J., and Zachary A. Smith. *The National Environmental Policy Act: Judicial Misconstruction, Legislative Indifference, and Executive Neglect.* College Station: Texas A & M Press, 2001.

National Academy of Public Administration. *Setting Priorities, Getting Results: A New Direction for the U.S. Environmental Protection Agency.* Washington, D.C.: National Academy of Public Administration, 1995.

Scheberle, Denise. *Federalism and Environmental Policy: Trust and the Politics of Implementation.* Washington, D.C.: Georgetown University Press, 2004.

Notes

1. Quoted in Annie Youderian, "Yellowstone Snowmobile Case Is Moot, Court Rules," *Courthouse News Service*, December 3, 2009, available at: http://www.courthousenews.com/2009/12/03/Yellowstone_Snowmobile_Case_Is_Moot_Court_Rules.htm (accessed February 10, 2010).
2. For this EPA story, see Katherine Q. Seelye, "EPA Surprises Its Leader and Interior Chief on Snowmobiles," *New York Times,* May 2, 2003, A5.
3. T. R. Reid, "For Snowmobiles, an Uncertain Fate; Future in Parks May Hinge on Election," *Washington Post,* March 15, 2004, A23.
4. Felicity Barringa, "Judge's Ruling on Yellowstone Keeps It Open to Snowmobiles," *New York Times,* October 16, 2004, A9.
5. Felicity Barringa, "Secretary Tours Yellowstone on Snowmobile," *New York Times,* February 17, 2005, A18.
6. Bettina Boxall, "Bush's Grade on Environment Falls," *Los Angeles Times,* August 4, 2006, A1.
7. Jack Welch, "Blue Ribbon Coalition Responds to Yellowstone Debate," August 7, 2009, available at: http://cs.amsnow.com/snocs/blogs/news/archive/2009/08/07/blue-ribbon-coalition-responds-to-yellowstone-debate.aspx (accessed October 20, 2009).
8. Ibid.
9. Quoted by Nancy Pelosi, speaker of the House of Representatives, in Ken Root, "Agriculture Still Has Clout with Politicians," *High Plains Journal,* March 21, 2007, B12.
10. Useful illustrations of presidential activism in environmental policymaking are found in Dennis L. Soden, ed., *The Environmental Presidency* (Albany: SUNY Press, 1999); Norman J. Vig, "Presidential Leadership and the Environment," in *Environmental Policy: New Directions for the Twenty-First Century,* ed. Norman J. Vig and Michael E. Kraft (Washington, D.C.: CQ Press, 2003), 103–125.
11. A useful summary of the EOP's development can be found in Harold C. Relyea, "The Executive Office of the President: An Historical Overview," Congressional Research Report to Congress, Order Code 98-606 GOV, Washington, D.C., November 26, 2008.
12. OMB Watch, "Comments on President Obama's Memorandum on Scientific Integrity," May 13, 2009, available at: www.ombwatch.org/files/regs/PDFs/OMB_Watch_comments_on_scientific_integrity.pdf.
13. National Environmental Policy Act, Title II, 42 U.S.C. § 4321 et seq. (1970).
14. Quoted in Russel E. Train, "The Environmental Record of the Nixon Administration," *Presidential Studies Quarterly* 26, no. 1 (1996), 191.

15. Henry M. Jackson Foundation, "Facing the Future: Recommendations on the White House Council on Environmental Quality: A Report to the President Elect," Tulane Institute on Water Resources, Law, and Policy, Tulane Law School, New Orleans, October 2008, 4.

16. Christopher Schroeder, "The Evolution of Federal Regulation of Toxic Substances," in *Government and Environmental Politics: Essays on Historical Development since World War II,* ed. Michael J. Lacey (Lanham, Md.: University Press of America, 1990), 118.

17. Ralph Huitt, "Political Feasibility," in *Policy Analysis in Political Science,* ed. Ira Sharkansky (Chicago: Markham, 1970), 414.

18. Barry G. Rabe, *Fragmentation and Integration in State Environmental Management* (Washington, D.C.: Conservation Foundation, 1986), 16–17. See also Michael E. Kraft, "Congress and Environmental Policy," in *Environmental Politics and Policy: Theories and Evidence,* ed. James P. Lester (Durham, N.C.: Duke University Press, 1989), 179–211.

19. "Mississippi 'Pork' Ranking," Official Trent Lott Press Release, May 2, 2002, available at: www.lott.senate.gov/news/2000/502.pork.html (accessed February 8, 2004).

20. Mark J. Landy and Mary Hague, "The Coalition for Waste: Private Interests and Superfund," in *Environmental Politics: Public Costs, Private Rewards,* ed. Michael S. Grave (New York: Praeger, 1992), 72.

21. R. Douglas Arnold, *Congress and the Bureaucracy* (New Haven, Conn.: Yale University Press, 1979), 133.

22. Lawrence Mosher, "Clean Water Requirements Will Remain Even if the Federal Spigot Is Closed," *National Journal,* May 16, 1981, 874–878.

23. Quoted in Marcia Clemmitt, "Energy and Climate Change: Should Carbon-Based Fuels Be Phased Out?" *CQ Researcher,* July 24, 2009, available at: http://library.cqpress.com/cqresearcher/search.php?PHPSESSID=207p8d3i1ek2nbscahp1j5iad3&fulltext=climate+change&action=newsearch&sort=custom%3Asorthitsrank%2Cd&x=15&y=12 (accessed November 14, 2009).

24. Quoted in *New York Times,* March 22, 1993, B8.

25. Quoted in ibid.

26. U.S. General Accounting Office (GAO), "Indoor Air Pollution: Federal Efforts Are Not Effectively Addressing a Growing Problem," Report No. GAO/RCED 92-8, Washington, D.C., October 1991, 6.

27. Quoted in Margaret E. Kriz, "Pesticidal Pressures," *National Journal,* December 12, 1988, 125.

28. Jared N. Day, "Safe Drinking Water-Safe Sites: Interaction between the Safe Drinking Water Act and Superfund, 1968–1995," in *Improving Regulation: Cases in Environment, Health, and Safety,* ed. Paul S. Fischbeck and R. Scott Farrow (Washington, D.C.: Resources for the Future, 2000).

29. David Schoenbrod, "The EPA's Faustian Bargain," *Regulation* (fall 2006): 41.

30. GAO, "Implementation of the Clean Air Act Amendments of 1990: Statement of David G. Wood, Associate Director, Environmental Protection Issues," Report no. GAO/T-RCED 00-183, Washington, D.C., February 10, 1990, 9.

31. Clarence Davies and Jan Mazurek, *Regulating Pollution: Does the U.S. System Work?* (Washington, D.C.: Resources for the Future, 1997), 6–7.

32. R. Shep Melnick, "Pollution Deadlines and the Coalition of Failure," *Public Interest* 75 (spring 1984): 125.

33. GAO, "Improving EPA's Regulatory Impact Analysis," Report no. GAO/RCED 97-38, Washington, D.C., April 1997.

34. David D. Doniger, *The Law and Policy of Toxic Substances Control* (Baltimore: Johns Hopkins University Press, 1978), 3.

35. Quoted in John H. Trattner, *The Prune Book: The 100 Toughest Management and Policy-Making Jobs in Washington* (Lanham, Md.: Madison Books, 1988), 250.
36. Quoted in ibid., 249.
37. U.S. Environmental Protection Agency (EPA), Office of the Chief Financial Officer, "FY 2008: Budget in Brief," Publication no. EPA-205-S-07-001, Washington, D.C., February 2007, v.
38. Cited in J. Clarence Davies Jr., *Nanotechnology Oversight: An Agenda for the New Administration* (Washington, D.C.: Woodrow Wilson Center, 2008), 10.
39. Richard J. Lazarus, "The Tragedy of Distrust in the Implementation of Federal Environmental Law," *Law and Contemporary Problems* 54 (autumn 1991): 334. See also Marc K. Landy, Marc J. Roberts, and Stephen R. Thomas, *The Environmental Protection Agency: Asking the Wrong Questions* (New York: Oxford University Press, 1990); Paul R. Portney, ed., *Public Policies for Environmental Protection* (Washington, D.C.: Resources for the Future, 1990), chaps. 1, 8.
40. Council on Environmental Quality (CEQ), *Environmental Quality, 1985* (Washington, D.C.: Council on Environmental Quality, 1986), 14. See also Walter A. Rosenbaum, "Into the Nineties at EPA: Searching for the Clenched Fist and the Open Hand," in *Environmental Policy in the 1990s*, 2nd ed., ed. Norman J. Vig and Michael E. Kraft (Washington, D.C.: CQ Press, 1994), 121–143.
41. GAO, "Pesticides: EPA's Formidable Task to Assess and Regulate Their Risks," Report No. GAO/RCED 86–125, Washington, D.C., April 1986, 35.
42. Edward J. Woodhouse, "External Influences on Productivity: EPA's Implementation of TSCA," *Policy Studies Review* 4 (February 1985): 500.
43. CEQ, *Environmental Quality,* 1985, 12–13.
44. Richard Harris and Sidney Milkis, *The Politics of Regulatory Change: A Tale of Two Agencies* (New York: Oxford University Press, 1989), 228.
45. EPA, "Ash Council and Creation of EPA," September 21, 2007, available at: http://www.epa.gov/history/publications/costle/04.htm (accessed January 19, 2009).
46. Peter W. House and Roger D. Shull, *Regulatory Reform: Politics and the Environment* (Lanham, Md.: University Press of America, 1985), esp. 106.
47. Rabe, *Fragmentation and Integration,* 126.
48. EPA, Office of Solid Waste, "Human and Ecological Risk Assessment of Coal Combustion Waste," RTI, Research Triangle Park, N.C., August 6, 2007, available at: www.earthjustice.org/news/press/007/coal-ash-pollution-contaminates-groundwater-increases-cancer-risks.html.
49. Conservation Foundation, *State of the Environment: An Assessment at Mid-Decade* (Washington, D.C.: Conservation Foundation, 1984), Chap. 9.
50. Walter A. Rosenbaum, "Still Reforming after All These Years," in *Environmental Policy: New Directions for the Twenty-First Century,* ed. Norman J. Vig and Michael E. Kraft (Washington, D.C.: CQ Press, 2003), 175–200.
51. Quoted in *New York Times,* March 23, 1991, 6.
52. Zachary Coile, "Interior Chief Gale Norton to Step Down," *San Francisco Chronicle,* March 11, 2006, A1.
53. Michelle Adato, James Mackenzie, Robert Pollard, and Ellyn Weiss, *Safety Second: The NRC and America's Nuclear Power Plants* (Bloomington: Indiana University Press, 1987), esp. chaps. 1, 5.
54. GAO, "Department of Energy: Cleaning Up Inactive Facilities Will Be Difficult," Report no. GAO/RCED 92–149, Washington, D.C., June 1993; see also GAO, "Much Work Remains to Accelerate Facility Cleanups," Report no. GAO/RCED 93-15, Washington, D.C., January 1993.

55. See Christopher Madison, "The Energy Department at Three—Still Trying to Establish Itself," *National Journal,* October 4, 1980, 16–19.

56. *Scenic Hudson Preservation Conference v. Federal Power Commission,* 354 F.2d 608 (2d Cir. 1965).

57. Lettie M. Wenner, "Environmental Policy in the Courts," in *Environmental Policy in the 1990s,* 2nd ed., ed. Norman J. Vig and Michael E. Kraft (Washington, D.C.: CQ Press, 1994), 156.

58. Werner J. Grunbaum, *Judicial Policy Making: The Supreme Court and Environmental Quality* (Morristown, N.J.: General Learning Press, 1976), 31. See also Lettie McSpadden Wenner, "The Courts and Environmental Policy," in *Environmental Politics and Policy: Theories and Evidence,* ed. James P. Lester (Durham, N.C.: Duke University Press, 1989), 261–288.

59. Barton H. Thompson Jr., "Conservative Environmental Thought: The Bush Administration and Environmental Policy," *Ecology Law Quarterly* 37 (2005): 307–348; John D. Graham, Paul R. Noe, and Elizabeth L. Branch, "Managing the Regulatory State: The Experience of the Bush Administration," *Fordham Urban Law Journal* 33 (2006): 903–953. Blaine Harden, "Bush Policy Irks Judges in West; Rulings Criticize Agencies for Not Protecting the Environment," *Washington Post,* October 6, 2006, A3.

60. Jennifer Koons, "Supreme Court: A Rough Term for Environmentalists," *Environment and Energy Daily,* June 25, 2009, available at: www.eenews.net/public/ Greenwire/2009/06/25/3; Adam Liptak, "Environmental Groups Find Less Support in Court," *New York Times,* July 3, 2009, A10.

61. Stephen Breyer, *Breaking the Vicious Circle: Toward Effective Risk Regulation* (Cambridge, Mass.: Harvard University Press, 1993), 59.

62. See Douglas Jehl, "Road Ban Set for One-Third of U.S. Forests," *New York Times,* January 5, 2001, A5; Eric Pianin, "Ban Protects 58.5 Million Acres," *Washington Post,* January 5, 2001, 1.

63. John C. Whitaker, "Earth Day Recollections: What It Was Like When the Movement Took Off," *EPA Journal* 14 (July–August 1988): 14.

64. Ibid.

65. Quoted in Margaret Kriz, "Fuming over Fumes," *National Journal,* November 26, 1988, 3008.

66. Robert W. Crandall and Paul R. Portney, "Environmental Policy," in *Natural Resources and the Environment: The Reagan Approach,* ed. Paul Portney (Washington, D.C.: Urban Institute Press, 1984), 14.

67. U.S. Department of Commerce, Bureau of the Census, *Statistical Abstract of the United States, 1992* (Washington, D.C.: Government Printing Office, 1993), 217. Figures are given in 1982 dollar values, corrected for inflation.

68. EPA, "Environmental Investments: The Cost of a Clean Environment: A Summary," Washington, D.C., 1990, vi.

69. W. K. Kellog Foundation, *The Quiet Crisis: The Impact of the Economic Downturn on the Nonprofit Sector* (Washington, D.C.: Kellog Foundation, March 2009).

70. Morton Grodzins, "The Federal System," in *American Federalism in Perspective,* ed. Aaron Wildavsky (Boston: Little, Brown, 1967), 257.

71. U.S. Congress, Senate Committee on Environment and Public Works, "Confirmation Hearing for Administrator of the Environmental Protection Agency," January 17, 2001, 107th Cong., 1st sess., 27.

Chapter 4

Common Policy Challenges
Risk Assessment and Environmental Justice

> [The EPA] will need to ensure that it allocates resources to needed research on emerging issues, such as the relative toxicity of particulate matter components, and to assessing which sources of uncertainty have the greatest influence on benefit estimates. While EPA officials said they expect to reduce the uncertainties associated with the health benefit estimates in the final particulate matter analysis, a robust uncertainty analysis of the remaining uncertainties will nonetheless be important for decision makers and the public to understand the likelihood of attaining the estimated health benefits.
>
> U.S. Government Accountability Office, 2006[1]

> Risk assessment means never having to say you're certain.
> —Humor among professional risk assessors

Until 1998, few Americans knew about phthalates nor cared about them. In November 1998, however, the environmental organization Greenpeace International released the first of its many reports demanding that the toy industry worldwide immediately abandon the use of the chemical DINP (diisononyl phthalate), an ingredient in vinyl, the material widely used throughout the industry in producing thousands of children's products as varied as pacifiers, rubber ducks, teddy bears, dolls, rattles, and teething rings. The report was another sortie in the organization's militant campaign against a large class of chemicals called phthalates, or plasticizers, which bond with vinyl molecules to make plastic products more flexible. In the United States, the announcement unleashed a publicly alarming, escalating controversy that quickly assumed a pattern common to the contemporary politics of environmental risk assessment.

A Toxic Nightmare from Toyland?

First came a dramatic public condemnation of an important industrial chemical. Greenpeace International asserted that the Aristech Chemical Corporation of Pittsburgh, Pennsylvania, a subsidiary of the Mitsubishi Corporation, used the chemical DINP to manufacture products that children might chew, such as pacifiers and rattles, even though a similar compound caused liver damage in laboratory rats.[2] The accusation and accompanying information, quickly disseminated worldwide by the media, was alarming not only to the chemical producers and to parents whose children might be exposed to the products but also to the hundreds of manufacturers and consumers of other products using plasticizers—products such as medical equipment, food containers, consumer goods, packaging material, and much more—because plasticizers are a global commodity. Within weeks, two major U.S. medical advocacy groups, Health Care Without Harm and the American Nursing Association, issued a "health alert" warning that intravenous bags and tubing made of vinyl chloride contained a chemical very similar to DINP that previously had been removed from toy products because of suspected toxicity. A story on the popular ABC news program *20/20* in early 1998 repeated many of the Greenpeace International allegations, thus ensuring a huge domestic audience for the controversy. Within a few weeks, the plasticizer debate was a media event.[3]

Next, an acrimonious, highly technical dispute erupted in the public media, abetted by technical publications and professional spokespeople caught up in the controversy, over the extent of the health risks resulting from exposure to the plasticizers. At the same time, the controversy became quickly politicized. Organized groups representing environmentalists, consumers, public health interests, the chemical and toy manufacturers, governmental agencies, parents, political think tanks, and many others rapidly aligned on disputing sides of the issue. Conflict approached the surreal, as exquisitely technical and publicly confounding arguments raged over baby bottle nipples, animal fetuses, Teletubbies, squeeze toys, liver biopsies, monkey testicles, and other exotica. Even Barbie and Dr. C. Everett Koop, the former U.S. surgeon general, appeared. At stake were possibly a billion dollars in worldwide product sales, the ethical and economic stature of the chlorine chemical industry, markets for hundreds of manufacturers using the embattled chemicals, and perhaps the health of uncounted children worldwide.

The Political Front

Within a week of the Greenpeace International announcement, twelve consumer, environmental, and religious groups demanded that the U.S.

Consumer Product Safety Commission (CPSC), the federal regulatory agency responsible for ensuring the safety of children's products sold in the United States, ban vinyl toys for small children. Shortly thereafter, twenty-eight members of Congress addressed President Bill Clinton with a letter urging him to ensure that the Department of Commerce was not pressuring European countries to keep their markets open to children's vinyl products. The National Environmental Trust, a coalition of environmental organizations, urged the U.S. government to ban all vinyl baby products. In November 1998, the CPSC also stated that it was uncertain about the risks to babies from DINP but nonetheless advised parents to throw away nipples and pacifiers made with vinyl and asked manufacturers not to use DINP in products children might put in their mouths.

Meanwhile, the manufacturer of DINP and many industrial consumers were rising to DINP's defense. Major toy manufacturers such as Mattel; large toy retailers, including Toys R Us; and the industry's trade association, the Toy Manufacturers of America, all publicly defended the safety of the plasticizers used for decades in children's products. Defenders of DINP were enormously gratified when a nonprofit organization of distinguished scientific experts represented by Dr. Koop asserted that it stood "firmly behind the conclusions drawn from the weight of the scientific evidence [that] consumers can be confident that vinyl medical devices and toys are safe."[4]

A Scientific Enigma

The actual risk to children from exposure to plasticizers seemed anything but clear. One problem was the absence of a standard procedure to determine how much of the suspect chemical a child could realistically be expected to absorb. For example, how much DINP could a child be expected to consume by chewing a toy? In addition, toy components vary considerably in their plasticizer content. For instance, high levels of DINP were found in the arms of the Rugrats Tommy Pickles Ice Cream Face doll and in the shoes of the Cabbage Patch Kids Starr Rosie doll but not elsewhere on either doll.

Another major problem involved the reliability of the animal tests indicating that DINP and its predecessor could cause liver damage in humans. Critics of these tests noted that similar damage did not occur in other experimental animals including guinea pigs, hamsters, and monkeys. Also, the age of the test animals might matter. Other disagreements arose over the relative importance to be given to toxic effects observed in different organs of experimental animals. Nonhuman primates, for example, were likely to be resistant to the testicular cancers that might appear in other kinds of animals exposed to the plasticizers, and critics argued that such primate experiments should be ignored in certain kinds of risk assessment.[5]

Finally, there was the unsettling enigma about how long it could take before any health problems might appear among children exposed to plasticizers. Health professionals noted that the damaging effects of such exposure might be latent for many years and that, as a consequence, the current incidence of any suspected damage might greatly underestimate the long-term damage to humans. Thus, it might seem prudent to ban the plasticizers even in the absence of convincing current evidence of their danger.

Barbie Gets a Green Makeover

With the controversy public, the Toy Manufacturers of America reluctantly advised its members to voluntarily eliminate DINP-based vinyl products even while it maintained their safety. "Greenpeace has a clear agenda," the association asserted. "It's not looking for a compromise. It's looking for the elimination of a chlorine-based product."[6] Aristech; the Chlorine Chemistry Council, representing the users of all chlorine-based products; and toy manufacturers continued to defend DINP. The industry's capitulation was ensured when Mattel, the world's largest toy manufacturer, announced in December 1999 that it would substitute plant- and vegetable-based plastics for chlorine-based vinyls. Barbie was destined for a complete chemical makeover, along with a multitude of other familiar toys and products from other manufacturers, among them Teletubbies, Pony Luv, and Clear and Soft pacifiers and nipples.

And the Winner Is …

In 2003, to the considerable satisfaction of the Chlorine Chemistry Council and toy manufacturers, the CPSC voted unanimously to deny the petition to ban phthalates from products for children under five years old because there appeared to be "no demonstrable health risk."[7] The CPSC also knew how to defend itself. This decision, it noted, was supported by numerous scientific studies including a meticulous inquiry concerning "mouthing habits" among infants. The "average daily mouthing time" of soft plastic toys for children 12–24 months of age was 1.9 minutes, considerably less than the 75 minutes per day determined to be the risk threshold.[8] Average daily mouthing time, however, was not the science that satisfied most public health and environmental advocates, who continued to advocate the elimination of phthalates from toys.

By 2006, phthalate opponents had rearmed with a new wave of highly publicized scientific studies once again implying that phthalates *might* be a human toxic. One university study suggested that mothers exposed during pregnancy to high levels of phthalates found in cosmetics, plastics, and detergents might have "less masculine" boys; another investigation noted that plastic food containers might "contribute" to breast cancer.[9] The Cosmetic, Toiletry and Fragrance Association protested that "an extensive body of science research" proved the safety of cosmetics, but public health and environmental advocates persisted, determined to skewer high-profile industries, such as nail polish manufacturers, with apparently damning scientific research.

Public health and environmental organizations also exploited opportunities to bring pressure on the federal government from other political venues. As early as 2002, the California legislature passed legislation prohibiting baby toys containing phthalates. In December 2006, San Francisco became the first U.S. city to prohibit sale, manufacture, and distribution of products with high phthalate concentrations.[10] A powerful political blow against phthalates was struck by the European Union (EU), which in late 2006 passed a law regulating the manufacture and use of 30,000 toxic substances, including phthalates, thus creating enormous pressure on U.S. industry to do the same.

By 2010, continuing scientific evidence raised such substantial doubt about phthalate safety that parents and other consumers of phthalate-containing products were no longer left to decide which side—if any—should be trusted. A 2008 report from a committee of the National Academy of Sciences voiced considerable concern about phthalate safety and urged Congress and the EPA to promote new studies about the effects of cumulative human exposure to *all* phthalates.[11] This report, fortified by other accumulating research, created a receptive setting for new regulatory legislation. In September 2008, Congress passed the Consumer Product Safety Reform Act (CPSRA) mandating, among other important provisions, that the CPSC impose progressively more stringent limits on lead in children's products, prohibit DINP and certain other phthalates in children's toys and care products, and require manufacturers of children's products to test their safety and certify it.

An unusual aspect of the new legislation was its adoption of the precautionary principle as a risk assessment standard. Traditionally, risk assessments required by federal environmental laws thrust on government regulators the responsibility to establish that a chemical or an activity is dangerous to human health or the environment before it can be regulated. In contrast, the precautionary principle shifts the burden of proof to a chemical's creators or proponents to demonstrate the safety of a product when scientific uncertainty prevails. In essence, the precautionary principle is the regulatory equivalent of "better safe than sorry."

The American Chemistry Council, a major organizational voice of the chemical industry, predictably expressed the industry's dissatisfaction with the CPSRA, arguing that "after all this study and review, no reliable scientific evidence has found phthalates to cause adverse human health effects." This seemed to imply a forthcoming round of new litigation challenging the law.

Although the appearance of the CPSRA's precautionary principle is an important innovation in federal environmental risk assessment (to be considered shortly), in most respects the decade-long phthalate controversy, richly endowed with protracted litigation, sustained political infighting, and disputed science, still followed a policymaking pathway common to most environmental risk assessments required by federal environmental regulation and likely to endure.

Risk Assessment and the Limits of Science

In recent years the EPA alone has written more than 7,500 risk assessments annually in various forms to carry out its regulatory responsibilities.[12] In 1993, President Clinton further elevated the importance of risk assessment by requiring in Executive Order 12866 that all regulatory agencies, not only environmental ones, "consider, to the extent reasonable, the degree and nature of risks posed by various substances or activities within its jurisdiction" and mandating that each proposed regulatory action explain how the action will reduce risks "as well as how the magnitude of risk addressed by the action relates to other risks within the jurisdiction of the agency."[13]

Traditional risk assessment associated with environmental regulation creates a flow of decisions that start, as Figure 4-1 indicates, when the EPA or another regulatory agency is required to determine whether a substance—a commercial chemical, for example—constitutes a sufficient hazard to humans or to the environment to require regulation under one of many current environmental regulatory laws. The process begins with research that assembles currently available information about the possible adverse health or environmental effects of a suspected hazard, such as a chemical. If the research suggests possibly adverse effects to humans or the environment, the regulatory agency proceeds to risk assessment, during which additional information is obtained or experiments are conducted concerning the current levels of exposure to a suspected chemical and an estimate is made of the likely adverse consequences. If this risk assessment indicates that a chemical is sufficiently hazardous to meet the requirements for regulation, the agency proceeds to risk management, during which regulators consider alternative strategies for the chemical's regulation and then propose a regulatory plan. Note that, although Figure 4-1 may imply that this is a dependably neat, deliberate, and timely sequence

Figure 4-1 The Risk Assessment Process

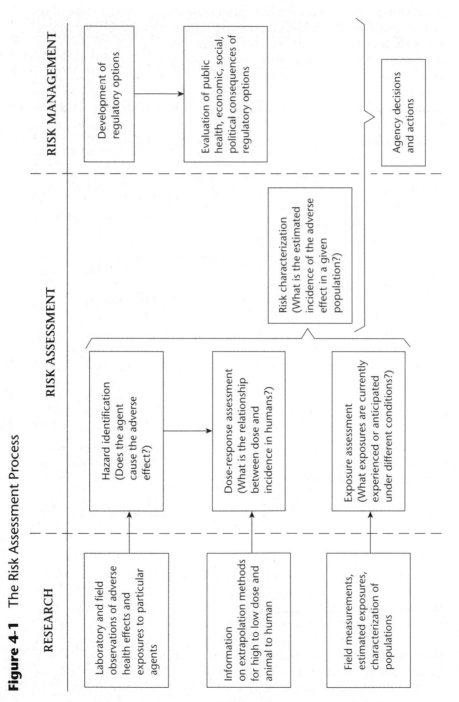

Source: National Research Council, *Risk Assessment in the Federal Government: Managing the Process* (Washington, D.C.: National Academy Press, 1983), 21. Reprinted with permission from the National Academies Press, Washington, D.C.

of decisions, the reality is often more episodic, with many decisions contested and an elapsed time in years or even decades.

Risk assessment has grown increasingly controversial until it now incites the impassioned conflicts once confined to such holy wars as the benefit-cost debate. A major reason for the controversy is that risk assessment lies in the treacherous zone between science and politics, where practically all environmental policies reside and where collaboration between public officials and scientists is both essential and difficult. What public officials and scientists involved in policymaking want from each other is often unobtainable. Public officials seek from scientists information that is accurate enough to indicate precisely where they should establish environmental standards and credible enough to defend in the inevitable conflicts to follow. Scientists want government to act quickly and forcefully on ecological issues they believe to be critical.[14] Yet science often cannot produce technical information in the form and within the time desired by public officials. Indeed, science often cannot provide the information at all, leaving officials to make crucial decisions from fragmentary and disputable information.

In short, risk assessment frequently compels public officials to make scientific judgments and scientists to resolve policy issues for which neither may be trained. The almost inevitable need to resolve scientific questions through the political process and the problems that arise in making scientific and political judgments compatible are two of the most troublesome characteristics of environmental politics.

Derelict Data and Embattled Expertise

Controversy among experts commonly arises in environmental policymaking. Contending battalions of experts—garlanded with degrees and publications and primed to dispute each other's judgment—populate congressional and administrative hearings about risk assessment. Policymakers are often left to judge not only the wisdom of policies but also the quality of the science supporting the policies.

Missing Data. Why is controversy so predictable? Frequently there is a void of useful data about the distribution and severity of environmental problems or possible pollutants. Many problems are so recent that public and private agencies have only just begun to study them. Many pollutants—hazardous chemicals, for instance—have existed for only a few decades; their ecological impacts cannot yet be measured reliably. The EPA alone receives about 1,500 petitions annually requesting the approval of new chemicals or new uses of existing chemicals for which tests may be required.[15] Quite often the result is that nobody has

the information "somebody should have." For instance, the EPA and
the U.S. Department of Health and Human Services together have data
reporting the degree of exposure among the general population for less
than 7 percent of more than 1,400 chemicals considered to pose a threat
to human health.[16] Lacking high-quality data, experts often extrapolate
answers from fragmentary information, and plausible disputes over the
reliability of such procedures are inevitable.

Late and Latent Effects. Disagreement over the severity of environmental problems also arises because the effects of many substances
thought to be hazardous to humans or the environment may not become
evident for decades or generations. The latency and diffusion of these
impacts also may make it difficult to establish causality between the suspected substances, or events, and the consequences. Asbestos, a hazardous
chemical whose malignancy has been documented since 1979, illustrates
these problems.[17] Since World War II, approximately 8–11 million U.S.
workers have been exposed to asbestos, a mineral fiber with more than
two thousand uses; its heat resistance, electrical properties, immunity to
chemical deterioration, and other characteristics made it appear to be
ideal to a multitude of major industries. In the past, it was used widely
to manufacture brake and clutch linings, plastics, plumbing, roofing tile,
wall insulation, paint, paper, and much else. Asbestos is highly carcinogenic. Among those exposed to significant levels of asbestos, 20–25
percent died of lung cancer, 7–10 percent perished from mesothelioma
(cancer of the chest lining or stomach), and another 8–9 percent died
from gastrointestinal cancer.[18] The toxicity of asbestos became apparent
only decades after workers were exposed because the cancers associated
with it do not become clinically evident until fifteen to forty years after
exposure and severe illness may appear two to fifty years after the cancers first appear in humans. Added to the incalculable cost of human
suffering is the immense economic impact of these delayed effects. More
than two thousand new cases of incurable asbestos-related cancer now
appear each year in the United States. Presently, 300,000 lawsuits arising
from human exposure to asbestos are pending in the nation's courts, and
20,000–50,000 lawsuits are predicted annually for several decades. U.S.
corporations and insurers have spent more than $30 billion to defend
and settle asbestos lawsuits. The total cost of these suits, according to
several professional estimates, may exceed $200 billion.[19]

Many other substances used in U.S. commerce, science, and domestic life are suspected of producing adverse impacts on humans or the
environment. Yet conclusive evidence might not appear for decades,
whereas government officials must decide whether to regulate these
substances now. Difficult as such decisions are, a failure to act, as in

the case of asbestos, eventually may prove so costly in human suffering and economic loss that many scientists may be reluctant to wait for conclusive data even though others may argue the evidence is inconclusive. These issues are illustrated vividly by the federal government's continuing problems with the chemical dioxin.

The Case of Dioxin. Early in the 1990s, the EPA was persuaded by growing scientific evidence to initiate a searching reevaluation of its twenty-year-old exposure standards for the chemical dioxin, which it had characterized earlier as one of the most lethal substances on Earth.[20] The most dangerous among the seventy-five varieties of dioxin was thought to be 2,3,7,8-tetrachlorodibenzodioxin (TCCD), considered so harmful that the EPA's maximum exposure standards had limited human ingestion of TCCD to 0.006 trillionth of a gram per day for every kilogram (2.2 pounds) of body weight over an average lifetime—in other words, an average-size man was limited daily to an amount equal to a grain of sand sliced 1 billion times.

The EPA's original exposure standard for dioxin, as with most risk assessments made by federal agencies, was extrapolated largely from animal experiments. In the late 1970s, the EPA ordered an end to the production of the weed killer 2,4,5-T, also a dioxin, on the basis of its own earlier studies and additional, if circumstantial, evidence of great harm to individuals exposed to high concentrations of the herbicide. When concentrations of dioxin far exceeding levels considered safe were discovered during 1981 in the soil of Times Beach, Missouri—the result of illegal toxic waste disposals—the EPA decided that public safety required the permanent evacuation of the entire Missouri community. All 2,240 residents were removed to new residences and reimbursed for their property at a cost exceeding $37 million, while an additional $100 million was spent to clean up other nearby contaminated sites. During the 1980s, hundreds of lawsuits were filed against the federal government by Vietnam War veterans for alleged health impairment from exposure to dioxin in the defoliant Agent Orange. Meanwhile, the EPA's strict standards were expected to cost the paper and pulp industry about $2 billion for pollution control.

But a growing number of scientific experts questioned not only the EPA's exposure standards for dioxin but also the reliability of all the animal studies for determining the safe levels of human exposure to hazardous substances.[21] A particularly damning public indictment of the EPA's own standard appeared in 1991 when the federal scientist who had ordered the evacuation of Times Beach admitted to a congressional committee that he made the wrong decision. "Given what we know now about this chemical's toxicity," then–assistant surgeon general Vernon N. Houk stated, "it looks as if the evacuation was unnecessary."[22] In 1991, the World Health Organization declared its support for a new standard increasing the permissible human exposure by 1,600 percent above the EPA's limits.

Additional complications arose in 1992 when a panel of experts convened by the EPA concluded that, although dioxin was a significant cancer threat to people only when they were exposed to unusually high levels in chemical factories, it wreaked biological havoc among fish, birds, and other wild animals even in minute doses.[23] In early 1993, another blow against dioxin regulation was delivered by the director of the National Institute of Environmental Health Sciences, the agency supervising all federal animal studies used in toxics regulation. The agency's director released portions of a report from a panel of leading toxicologists that concluded that many of the assumptions driving the animal research "did not appear to be valid."[24] Animal studies alone, concluded most of the experts, were not reliable for judging the exposure risks to human beings in toxics research. Environmental organizations resisted any relaxation of the EPA's current dioxin standard. Scientific experts speaking for these organizations asserted that the new evidence created no compelling case for a new standard. Nonetheless, the Clinton administration and EPA officials were extremely uneasy with the existing exposure standards, and a thorough restudy of the issue was ordered.

In mid-2000, the EPA released the results of its long-awaited restudy. To the surprise of the White House and most EPA officials, the agency for the first time concluded that dioxin TCCD was a "human carcinogen" and that one hundred related chemicals were "likely" human carcinogens. The result was all the more startling because domestic emissions of dioxin had declined by 87 percent since 1984. However, TCCDs can accumulate in human body fat from repeated exposures, and thus, the report asserted, dioxin was a significant health risk to humans who ingested it through a normal diet.[25] For the small proportion of the population with extremely high-fat diets, the odds of developing cancer were estimated to be as high as 1 in 100, or ten times the EPA's previous estimate. Low-grade exposure could create other health problems, the report concluded, including hormonal and developmental defects in babies and children. Some environmental organizations then deduced from the EPA's risk estimates that about 100 of the 1,400 cancer deaths occurring in the United States daily were attributable to dioxin. The EPA knew full well what to expect, warning its senior officials to anticipate that when the report became public "many stakeholders [will] take dramatic action" and "pressure from other interests" would grow. Predictably, the EPA's decision was assailed from both sides of the controversy. The Chlorine Chemistry Council, which represented the major chemical producers involved, asserted the EPA was "out of sync" with dioxin regulation in the rest of the world and the report was "counterintuitive to what the facts are." The U.S. Chamber of Commerce suggested the decision wasn't based on "sound science." Greenpeace International, like some other environmental groups, lacerated the EPA for failing to control aggressively the remaining dioxin emissions; "That suggests that [EPA] can't walk and chew gum at the same time," it sniffed.[26]

Still the dioxin controversy would not go away. After another review that continued until mid-2003, the EPA sent its dioxin assessment to an Interagency Working Group to be reviewed by other relevant federal agencies. Congress then passed legislation requiring the working group to request that the National Research Council, a part of the National Academy of Sciences, perform a complete review of the assessment document—a cascade of reviews that environmentalists claimed was a tactic by the George W. Bush administration to stall the implementation of new dioxin regulations indefinitely.[27] In July 2006, the National Academy of Sciences review concluded that the agency "did not sufficiently quantify the uncertainties and variables associated with risks [of dioxin exposure]" and recommended that the EPA reassess the risks of dioxin exposure— especially exposure to very low dioxin doses—and issue a revised risk assessment explaining more clearly "how it selects both the data upon which the reassessment is based and the methods used to analyse them."[28] Meanwhile, the existing EPA risk standards would be enforced. In December 2009, the EPA, in accord with new administrator Lisa Jackson's promise to accelerate its dioxin review, issued a draft preliminary report containing revised dioxin exposure standards and pledged to complete a comprehensive final report by the end of 2010.[29]

Animal and Epidemiological Experiments. As the dioxin controversy illustrates, estimates of the health risks from suspected toxics are a source of much controversy. But, having rejected most controlled human studies as ethically repugnant, scientists are left with no certain alternatives in arriving at risk estimates. They may attempt to characterize a substance's danger based on existing knowledge of how chemical carcinogens affect human cells, but little knowledge exists about the precise way in which these chemicals alter the structure and chemistry of cells. The common alternative is controlled animal experiments in which test animals are exposed to substances, the effects are monitored, and the risks to human beings are extrapolated from the findings.

These animal studies are particularly controversial when used to estimate the effects of low levels of chemical exposure on humans—for instance, a dose of a few parts per million or billion of a pesticide or heavy metal in drinking water over thirty years. The human risks of cancer or other serious illnesses will be small, but how small?[30] And how reliable is the estimate? Animal studies do not and cannot use enough animals to eliminate all possibilities of error in estimating the effects of low-level exposure on humans. To demonstrate conclusively with 95 percent confidence that a certain low-level dose of one substance causes fewer than one case of cancer per million individuals would require a "megamouse" experiment involving 6 million animals.[31] Instead, researchers use high doses of a substance with relatively few animals and then extrapolate through statistical models the effect on humans from low-level exposure to the tested substance. But these models can differ by a factor of as much as 100,000 in estimating the size of the dose that could produce one cancer per million individuals. A litany of other problems are associated with small animal studies. Failure to observe any response to a substance among a small group of animals does not mean a substance is safe. Moreover, various animals differ greatly in their sensitivity to substances; dioxin is five thousand times more toxic to guinea pigs than to hamsters, for example.[32]

Epidemiological studies depend on surveys recording the relationship between known human exposure to suspected hazardous substances and the known effects. Such after-the-fact studies have been used to establish the cancer risks of exposure to cigarette smoke and asbestos, for example. The lack of scientific controls is a serious deficiency in almost all epidemiological studies.

The Limited Neutrality of Scientific Judgment

Perhaps fifty opportunities exist in a normal risk assessment procedure for scientists to make discretionary judgments. Although scientists are presumed to bring to this task an expertise untainted by social values to bias their judgments, they are not immune to social prejudice, especially when their expertise is embroiled in a public controversy. According to physicist Harvey Brooks, a veteran of many public controversies,

> The more an issue is in the public eye, the more expert judgments are likely to be influenced unconsciously by pre-existing policy preferences or by supposedly unrelated factors such as media presentations, the opinions of colleagues or friends, or even the emotional overtones of certain words used in the debate.[33]

Scientific judgment on environmental issues can be influenced by one's beliefs about how government should regulate the economy, by one's institutional affiliation, or by other social and political attributes.[34] Another study of several hundred risk professionals involved in federal environmental policymaking suggests that, once risk professionals become involved in policymaking, there is "a weakening of disciplinary perspectives and a strengthening of viewpoints based on politics and ideology."[35] In general, the study concludes that risk professionals working for corporations or trade associations differ from those working for government or academic institutions in their technical judgments about how risk should be determined and when substances should be regulated, as well as in broader attitudes about governmental regulation.

Social or political bias can be particularly pernicious when not recognized or admitted by the experts. It is now evident that many technical controversies in policymaking may not be resolvable by resort to scientific evidence and argument because scientific solutions will be permeated with social, political, or economic bias. Indeed, political controversy often subverts scientific integrity. Experts can be readily, even unintentionally, caught up in the emotionally and politically polarizing atmosphere of such disputes, their judgment compromised so badly that, as political scientist Dorothy Nelkin remarks, their expertise "is reduced to one more weapon in a political arsenal."[36] Yet no barrier can be contrived to wholly insulate science from the contagion of social or economic bias. This is a strong argument for keeping scientific and technical determinations open to examination and challenge by other experts and laypersons.

What Risks Are Acceptable?

Risk assessment for environmental policymaking is also difficult because no clear and consistent definition of *acceptable risk* exists in federal law. *Acceptable risk* is usually defined in environmental regulation by statutory criteria—that is, by standards written into law to guide regulators in determining when to regulate a substance. Despite repeated congressional efforts at clarification, the only consistency in these statutory standards is their inconsistency.[37]

The EPA, uneasy with the enormous scientific uncertainties inherent in determining acceptable risk, frequently has shrouded its discretionary decisions in a fog of verbal mystification. Nonetheless, determining acceptable risk remains an intensely discretionary—and often political—affair, however much the language of the law may try to conceal it.

A Multitude of Risk Criteria

A multitude of different congressional standards guide regulatory agencies in making determinations of acceptable risk. Different substances often are regulated according to different standards. The same agency may have to use as many as six or seven standards, depending on which substances, or which laws, are involved. The same substance may be subject to one regulatory standard when dumped into a river and another when mixed into processed food. Statutory risk standards are commonly vague and sometimes confusing; congressional intent may be muddled, often deliberately.

In general, regulatory agencies encounter one or more of the following statutory formulas in determining the permissible exposure levels to various substances.[38] The examples are drawn from existing legislation.

- *Health-based criteria.* Regulatory agencies are to set standards based on risks to human health from exposure to a hazard. These standards are usually "cost oblivious" because they seldom permit agencies to use the cost of regulation as a consideration in standard setting. Health-based criteria, however, can involve different levels of acceptable health risk. The Clean Air Act mandates that national primary ambient air quality standards "shall be ... in the judgment of the Administrator, based on [air quality] criteria and allowing an adequate margin of safety ... requisite to protect human health" (Clean Air Act [1970]). The EPA is also left to determine the magnitude of this "margin of safety" and to whom it applies.[39]

- *Technology-based criteria.* The EPA is instructed to ensure that pollution sources will use the best available or the maximum achievable technology, or some other specified technology criteria, to control their hazardous emissions. The Safe Drinking Water Act (1974) and the Federal Water Pollution Control Act (1956) use technology-based standards. In effect, acceptable risks are defined by whatever residual risks to public health may exist after the prescribed control technologies are applied to a pollution source. From the EPA's perspective, the regulatory task is eased somewhat because the agency does not have to assess the actual public health risks from exposure to a specific pollutant. Instead, it has to ensure that the prescribed technology is applied to the pollution source.

- *Balancing criteria.* Congress mandates that an agency consider, to varying extents, the costs of regulation, or the magnitude of threat to human health, alongside the benefits in setting a standard for human or environmental exposure. Or Congress may permit cost considerations to be among other criteria that an agency may consider. These statutes define how various considerations, such as cost and risk, are to be balanced in determining acceptable risk. For instance, a law may *permit* an agency to balance the benefits for a given regulatory standard (which may include health as well as monetary benefits) against the costs of its enforcement. In contrast, another law may *require* agencies to balance the benefits against the economic costs in setting standards for exposure to a substance.

A close reading of these guidelines reveals the enormous discretion customarily left to regulatory agencies in determining how to balance the various statutory criteria. Limited by its lack of scientific expertise yet reluctant to leave agencies with too much discretion in determining acceptable risk, Congress often packs regulatory laws with so many criteria for risk determination—lest any important consideration be ignored—that regulatory decisions become enormously complicated. Consider, for instance, the criteria the EPA was ordered to use under the Toxic Substances Control Act (TSCA) of 1976 when deciding whether the risks from exposure to a substance are unreasonable:

> The type of effect (chronic or acute, reversible or irreversible); degree of risk; characteristics and number of humans, plants and animals, or ecosystems, at risk; amount of knowledge about the effects; available or alternative substances and their expected effects; magnitude of the social and economic costs and benefits of possible control actions; and appropriateness and effectiveness of TSCA as the legal instrument for controlling the risk.[40]

Agencies spend considerable time working out detailed internal regulations to translate these complexities into workable procedures. They may attempt to reach understandings concerning how criteria will be balanced, with interest groups active in the regulatory process. But agencies often face imperious deadlines for making regulatory decisions, fragmentary information relevant to many criteria for standard setting, and disputes among interest groups concerning the validity of information and the priorities for criteria in policymaking. In the first years of a new regulatory program, an agency can expect virtually every major decision to be challenged through litigation, usually by an interest alleging the agency has failed to interpret its statutory responsibilities properly. An agency sometimes invites litigation. By interpreting the manner in which risk determinations should be made by agencies, judges often dissipate the fog of uncertainty about congressional intent and provide agencies with firm guidelines for future determinations.

Missing data and muddled laws often promote waffling when agencies struggle to define acceptable risk. This is why the EPA's encounter with TSCA's murky risk criteria seems like an adventure in regulatory wonderland. In 1991, the U.S. General Accounting Office (GAO; later the General Accountability Office) asked the EPA why it had never used its authority under TSCA to require the testing of several chemicals whose toxicity was strongly suspected. The responsible EPA office replied that the chemicals did not pose the "significant risk to human health or the environment" that TSCA required for regulation. "In explaining why EPA has never used [its] authorities in the chemical testing program," commented the investigators, the agency stated that it "uses a 'high threshold' of risk in assessing whether a chemical imposes significant or unreasonable risks." However, noted the GAO, "the EPA has never defined the meaning of 'significant' or 'unreasonable' for the purpose of implementing TSCA."[41] In light of TSCA's confounding definitions of acceptable risk, the EPA's behavior might be considered preordained.

The Disappearing Threshold

One of the most politically controversial aspects of determining acceptable risk remains the problem of the disappearing threshold, a largely unanticipated result of three tendencies among Congress and the agencies concerned with environmental regulation. First, in writing and enforcing most environmental legislation during the 1970s, officials remained risk averse in dealing with potential hazards; risk reduction was preferred to risk tolerance. Second, Congress generally assumed that with many, or most, regulated substances, some threshold of exposure would exist below which the risks to humans or the ecosystem were negligible. Congress certainly did not anticipate removing *all* traces of human or ecological hazards. Third, legislators, who were largely indifferent to regulatory costs, compared to health criteria, in setting regulatory standards, discouraged agencies from using cost-benefit analyses when determining acceptable risks.

Economics and technology now present regulation writers with some difficult decisions as a result of these circumstances. Extremely sophisticated technologies enable scientists to detect hazardous substances in increasingly small concentrations, currently as small as parts per billion or trillion. It is usually impossible to assert scientifically that such low concentrations are wholly innocent of adverse risk, however slight, to humans or the environment. In addition, the cost of controlling hazardous substances often rises steeply as progressively higher standards are enforced; for instance, after reducing 85 percent of a substance in a waterway, it may cost half as much or more to remove an additional 5–10 percent. In effect, the risk threshold once presumed by policymakers has vanished; no measurable concentration of a substance apparently can be assumed innocent of potential harm to humans or the environment. To eliminate conclusively *any* probable risks from such substances, regulators would have to require the total elimination of the substance—an extraordinarily expensive undertaking. The threshold problem thus is created. Should a trade-off be made between the costs and benefits of risk prevention, and, if so, what criteria should govern the choice?

Critics assert that regulators should err in this trade-off on the side of caution by insisting on extremely high standards for controlling risks out of all proportion to the benefits to society or the environment and without sensitivity to the economic burden imposed on regulated interests.[42] This may leave the public with unrealistic expectations about the benefits, which in most cases will be extremely small if not undiscoverable when regulators insist on eliminating even minuscule risks from hazardous substances.[43] Advocates of strict risk management, however, usually respond that the full extent of risk is unknown or may be greater than currently estimated; they also may dispute the accuracy of opposing data. Often they are indignant at the suggestion that human lives may be endangered if the cost of protection is deemed excessive—an assertion, skillfully delivered, that implies that officials are venal or inhumane for imperiling lives to save money for a regulated interest. Elected officials are understandably wary when dealing with these publicly sensitive issues, especially when the advocates of strict regulation may cast them as the villains. It is easy to make tolerance for even small risks appear to be cruel gambling with the destinies of innocent people, even though risk assessment deals in probabilities, not certainties, of accident, death, or disease. And environmental groups are typically unyielding in opposition to any relaxation of existing health standards.

Risk Assessment Reconsidered: The Precautionary Principle

The CPSRA—the 2008 legislation that Congress intended to resolve the phthalate controversy mentioned at the beginning of this chapter—incorporated the precautionary principle, rare in national environmental legislation but vigorously promoted by many environmentalists, together with related scientists and policy professionals, as being more environmentally protective than traditional risk assessment procedures. The precautionary principle, in one widely accepted interpretation, declares, "when an activity raises threats of harm to human health or the environment, precautionary measures should be taken even if some cause and effect relationships are not fully established scientifically."[44]

The principle has been widely adopted and implemented throughout EU environmental legislation and in such important international environmental agreements as the Montreal Protocol on Ozone (1987), the Rio Declaration (1992), and the EU Stockholm Protocol on Persistent Organic Pollutants. It is the premise undergirding the global movement to control greenhouse gas emissions. Proponents of the precautionary principle assert that it has several advantages over traditional risk assessment:

- It mandates preventive action in the face of uncertainty rather than waiting for the determination of acceptable risk and the resolution of all the many scientific controversies often involved in regulating possible hazards.

- It shifts the burden of proof to the proponents of an activity or chemical, who assume the obligation to establish the safety or acceptability of the suspected hazard.
- It promotes the exploration of a wide range of alternatives to possibly harmful actions, including the possibility of not creating the potential hazard.
- It encourages public participation in decision making by requiring transparency and stakeholder participation.[45]

Proponents of the precautionary principle would contend, for example, that if these principles had been invoked in the regulation of dioxin much of the previously described political controversy, enormous consumption of time, seemingly interminable litigation, and unresolved (and perhaps unsolvable) scientific disputes about acceptable risk could have been avoided while the human and environmental danger from dioxin exposure would have been more rapidly reduced. In effect, the precautionary approach insists that, even if errors may occur, is it is better to err on the side of caution when deciding how to manage a suspected hazard.

The precautionary principle, however, also entails potentially significant risks that prompt others to caution against its widespread adoption. Perhaps the most fundamental concern, as one regulatory expert asserts, is that "it seeks to stop innovation before it starts."[46] The precautionary principle may stifle important commercial, scientific, or economic initiatives whose possibly substantial benefits will be lost—what economists call the opportunity costs—because real or suspected hazards may also be involved. In addition, some urgent problems may be unsolvable without significant real or anticipated risk. The continually growing volume of radioactive wastes from commercial nuclear electric utilities is sometimes cited as an example. These wastes must be isolated and stored indefinitely as securely as possible even though the containment may itself entail calculated human or environmental risks. Moreover, failure to assume the risks arising from developing and regulating a substance or technology may deliver these into the hands of irresponsible, perhaps dangerous, interests prepared to ignore risks and regulation—an argument sometimes proposed to justify the controversial proposal that the federal government undertake research on human cloning.

The appearance of the precautionary principle in the CPSRA, in any event, may be a prelude to its further adoption in future regulatory laws concurrently with the continued implementation of traditional risk assessment methods in others. If so, it will be important for future policymakers to know how to use the different procedures selectively. The precautionary principle, at the very least, will require policymakers and regulators to learn an unfamiliar way of thinking about risk management. "Teaching ourselves and our leaders a persistent precautionary approach," observes one scientist, "is like learning to tie shoes by following instructions. It's hard to do at first and may require justification, repetition and reassurance."[47]

The Value of Science in Environmental Policymaking

Despite the scientific disputes attending environmental policymaking, it remains important to recognize how often science provides useful and highly reliable guidance to policymakers. Often the scientific data relevant to an issue clearly point to the adverse effects of substances and define the magnitude of their risks. This was certainly evident in the data leading to the federal government's decision to ban most domestic agricultural uses of the pesticides dichlorodiphenyltrichloroethane (DDT), aldrin, and dieldrin, for instance. Furthermore, even when one set of data does not alone provide definitive evidence of human risks from exposure to chemicals, numerous studies pointing to the same conclusion taken together can provide almost irrefutable evidence; such was the case in the epidemiological evidence indicting asbestos as a human carcinogen. Often the reliability of data will be routinely challenged by those opposed to the regulation of some substance, regardless of the ultimate merit—or lack thereof—of their case. In the end, public officials must make decisions on the basis of the best evidence available. For all their limitations, scientific data often enable officials to define more carefully and clearly the range of options, risks, and benefits involved in regulating a substance, even when the data cannot answer all the questions of risk conclusively.

Even if indisputable data were available on the risks of human exposure to all levels of a substance, controversy over the acceptable level would continue. It is asserted sometimes that science should be responsible for determining the magnitudes of risk from exposure to chemicals and that government should define the acceptability. In other words, defining *acceptable risk* is largely a political matter. Such a division of labor is rarely possible. Scientists, too, are often drawn into the nettlesome problem of determining what levels of exposure to substances ultimately will be acceptable.

Risk and Discrimination: The Problem of Environmental Justice

In October 1997, a jury in New Orleans in a landmark decision awarded $3.4 billion in damages to eight thousand people who had been evacuated a decade previously from their community near a major train route after a tank car filled with the chemical butadiene had caught fire. This award was the largest liability ever assessed in federal court on the basis of environmental discrimination. The fact that most of the plaintiffs lived in a poor, underprivileged neighborhood, and thus were exposed to "environmental racism," appeared to have been a major consideration in the jury's generous damage award, even though their attorneys had only alluded to such racism during the trial. "No one said this is racism," explained one of the lawyers for the neighborhood, "but the facts were such that any commonsense appraisal would tell you that the poorer, underprivileged neighborhood was discriminated against."[48]

It is testimony to the present political potency of the environmental justice movement in the United States that merely a decade previously the idea of environmental racism was virtually unknown in public discourse and in the language of the courts, let alone as a cause for civil damage claims. Now, issues of environmental justice—or environmental equity— are raised in so many different political and judicial venues that the language has become almost a staple in political discussions involving minorities and health risks. One of new EPA administrator Lisa Jackson's earliest administrative decisions was to declare environmental justice an agency priority. "I want to see a full-scale revitalization of what we do and how we think about environmental justice," she asserted. "This is not an issue we can afford to relegate to the margins. It has to be part of our thinking in every decision we make."[49]

What Is Environmental Justice?

No consensus exists in law or political debate on the meaning of *environmental justice* or about *environmental equity* and *environmental racism*—two terms often used interchangeably with *environmental justice*. After considerable difficulty, the EPA in 1994 decided that *environmental justice* should be taken to mean "the fair treatment and meaningful involvement of all people regardless of race, color, national origin, or income with respect to the development, implementation or enforcement of environmental laws, regulations, and policies."[50] In contrast, Robert D. Bullard, an environmental justice scholar and leading national advocate for the environmental justice movement, equates environmental justice with the elimination of environmental inequity, which he suggests has at least three implications:[51]

- *Procedural inequity.* The extent to which governing rules, regulations, and evaluation criteria are not applied uniformly. Examples of procedural inequity are holding hearings in remote locations to minimize public participation, stacking boards and commissions with pro-business interests, and using English-only material to communicate to non-English-speaking communities.

- *Geographical inequity.* A situation in which the direct benefits, such as jobs and tax revenues, from industrial production are received by some neighborhoods, communities, and regions , but the costs, such as the burdens of waste disposal, are fixed elsewhere. For example, communities hosting waste-disposal facilities receive fewer economic benefits than the communities generating the waste.
- *Social inequity.* The extent to which environmental decisions mirror the power arrangements of the larger society and reflect the still-existing racial bias in the United States. Institutional racism, for instance, influences the siting of noxious facilities, placing many black communities in so-called sacrifice zones.

Whether or not it is also linked with equity or racism, the concept of environmental justice is commonly evoked in situations in which identifiable minorities have been exposed, deliberately or not, to disproportionate health or safety risks from a known hazard such as a chemical waste dump or an environment-polluting industrial site. Still, practically every definition of *environmental justice* or related terms abounds in ambiguities—what, for instance, constitutes a disproportionate health risk and how is a *minority* defined?

As these definitions demonstrate, the advocates of environmental justice now use the term, or its close relations, to embrace an enormous diversity of political and economic practices far surpassing the human health and safety issues traditionally associated with environmental risk. It has been left to the courts, legislators, advocacy groups, and scholars to render order from this definitional confusion as they struggle to translate such abstractions into law and political practice. More important than its precise definition, however, is the concept's social impact. From an inauspicious beginning in the mid-1980s, the movement has gradually become a potent political force. Its most important impacts have been to compel government attention at all levels to issues of environmental discrimination, to motivate grassroots political movements nationwide that mobilize minorities against apparent environmental discrimination, and to bring environmental discrimination within the scope of judicial concern and remedy.

A Growing Movement

The environmental justice movement achieved major national attention in 1991 when six hundred delegates met in Washington, D.C., at the first National People of Color Environmental Leadership Summit. From its inception, the movement's relationship to mainstream environmental advocacy groups has been ambivalent. "For the most part," observes historian Martin V. Melosi, "the movement found strength at the grass-roots, especially among low-income people of color who faced serious environmental threats from toxics and hazardous wastes."[52] Thus, the movement assumes a very different social and economic aspect from the predominantly middle-class, white, and relatively affluent organizations dominating U.S. environmental politics. Moreover, the movement's agenda focuses primarily on local communities, toxic and hazardous waste sites, and new organizational identities. At the same time, environmental justice generates a political gravity that can draw minority advocates into a closer political orbit with organized environmentalism. Mainstream environmental organizations have been quick to recognize that environmental justice offers an opportunity to attract economic and racial minorities to the environmental movement and to overcome persistent criticism that environmentalism is, or appears to be, a "white thing." The Sierra Club's national Environmental Justice and Community Partnerships and the National Resources Defense Council's Environmental Justice Web site are two among many illustrations of this strategy. Environmental justice organizations, for their part, often create strategic partnerships with mainstream environmental advocacy groups when this works to their political advantage, yet the movement insists on maintaining an identity apart from mainstream environmentalism.

The movement's fundamental conviction that cultural, racial, and ethnic minorities have been exposed disproportionately to health and safety risks throughout the United States has inspired an aggressive campaign to identify and mobilize these minorities, to demand various forms of compensation for those afflicted by such discrimination, and to demand that governmental policymaking be redesigned to weigh issues of environmental equity in environmental policymaking. The movement has been aided powerfully by active support from numerous social action organizations affiliated with many of the nation's major religious denominations. The movement has also been alert to the environmental justice implications of the global climate change issue, and in mid-2000, a new climate justice movement emerged from the organizational base. "Climate change is the most significant social and political challenge of the 21st Century," a leadership manifesto declares, "and the time to act is now." This new climate agenda "must be just, fair, sustainable, and equitable" and should, among other goals:

- Establish a zero carbon economy and achieve this by limiting and reducing greenhouse gas emissions in accordance with the levels advocated by the scientific community.

- Protect all of America's people—regardless of race, gender, nationality, or socioeconomic status—and their communities equally from the environmental, health, and social impacts of climate change.
- Ensure that carbon reduction strategies do not negatively impact public health and do not further exacerbate existing health disparities among communities.
- Require those most responsible for creating the impacts that arise from climate change to bear the proportionate cost of responding to the resulting economic, social, and environmental crisis.[53]

The environmental justice movement has grown in size, organizational skill, and political influence. In 2000, the movement was estimated to include approximately four hundred organizations. By 2010, one directory listed more than eight hundred groups (many of these may be very small and transitory, however).[54]

The movement's impact has been magnified enormously in recent years as the result of an enlarging, increasingly skillful network of collaborating local, state, and national organizations. The Internet has provided a highly congenial, and virtually costless, venue for network development. These numerous organizations include academically based groups such as the Clark Atlanta University's Environmental Justice Resource Center; the University of Michigan's Environmental Justice Program and Multicultural Environmental Leadership Development Initiative; the Energy Justice Network; advocacy specialists in the American Bar Association, the Environmental Law Institute, and other professional legal associations; and a multitude of independent legal and paralegal entities at all government levels. The EPA maintains a very substantial environmental justice Web site. Another Web site can create an environmental justice scorecard for communities, based on federal toxic emissions reports, that "profiles environmental burdens in every community in the U.S., identifying which groups experience disproportionate toxic chemical releases, cancer risks from hazardous air pollutants, or proximity to Superfund sites and polluting facilities emitting smog and particulates."[55] Joining these organizations are numerous locally based environmental justice groups such as New York's Environmental Justice Alliance. In addition, specialized environmental justice media are increasing, such as the Inner City Press's *Environmental Justice Reporter*. The movement's leadership now embraces virtually all people of color and all the economically disadvantaged within its mission, so that Native Americans, Latinos, and Asians, among other important domestic minorities, are being recruited.

This growing coalition committed to social equity in environmental regulation illustrates why the creation and solution of environmental risks are often inherently a political issue. In early 1994, President Clinton issued Executive Order 12898 instructing all federal agencies to develop strategies to ensure that their programs "do not unfairly inflict environmental harm on the poor and minorities." The executive order, applicable to all federal agencies and to any program "that substantially affects human health or the environment," was the first comprehensive effort by the federal government to address a problem long implicit in environmental policymaking and only reluctantly acknowledged by past administrations.[56] The EPA became one of the first federal agencies to recognize the importance of the environmental justice movement by creating its own Office of Environmental Justice as early as 1992. Since then, numerous state and local governments have also declared a commitment to environmental justice by law or executive order. In early 2004, for example, New Jersey's governor issued an executive order that mandated the state's Departments of Environmental Protection and Transportation to develop a strategy to reduce pollution exposure in minority and low-income neighborhoods.

Administrative Challenges

Administering laws that mandate environmental justice has been labored and controversial from its inception. Stakeholders may agree on its necessity, yet translating *environmental justice* into public policy—like implementing other public laws—can manufacture formidable obstacles between the word and the deed.

One major obstacle has been the frequent lack of resources and (sometimes) resolve among federal agencies to implement aggressively their environmental justice mandates. The EPA, in particular, has constantly struggled with impediments—not all of its own creation—in enforcing its own environmental justice regulations and Executive Order 12898. These problems promoted Administrator Lisa Jackson's promise of "a full-scale revitalization" of the environmental justice program.[57] Some of these problems arise from White House failures to fund generously the agency's environmental justice activists and from the meager data sometimes available to characterize environmental justice conditions. Often, however, pressure by environmental justice organizations is required to compel careful attention to these matters from the EPA and other federal agencies.

Scientific data relevant to environmental justice problems has been improving significantly since the mid-1990s, but almost all discourse about environmental justice—whatever the venue—is still likely to ignite controversy over the scientific basis of claims to environmental injustice.[58] Fragmentary evidence accumulating for decades and more deliberate studies in recent years often seem to demonstrate that minorities and poor individuals are disproportionately exposed to health risks from environmental pollutants.[59] The economically disadvantaged may also be more likely than others to have a hazardous waste site for a neighbor. Several studies have suggested as much; for example, one Detroit, Michigan, survey, cited by sociologists Paul Mohai and Bunyan Bryant, indicated that "minority residents in the metropolitan area are four times more likely than white residents to live within a mile of a commercial hazardous waste facility."[60]

For environmental justice advocates, the evidence seems convincing if not overwhelming. For example, a policy paper by one major advocacy group begins, "Although communities of color, tribes and indigenous peoples, and the poor have been heavily and disproportionately affected by noxious risk producing environmental practices for decades," as if stating common knowledge.[61] At the other extreme, Christopher H. Foreman Jr. of the Brookings Institution completed an extensive study of claims made by environmental justice advocates and concluded,

> [W]hen you clear away all the smoke blown over risk and racism in recent years, there turns out to be remarkably little good evidence indicating that low-income and minority citizens regularly bear a disproportionate share of society's environmental risk, much less that they develop pollution-related illnesses more often than other citizens.[62]

The controversy feeds on several refractory problems. One problem is the frequent difficulty of obtaining information about population exposures to environmental risks that is sufficiently rich in detail and covering a long-enough period to satisfy the requirements of common risk assessment methods. Rebecca A. Head, an environmental justice advocate and public health official, explains:

> Current health assessment models may also fail to be capable of using all the possible variables, and therefore can be unreliable in predicting and proving potential disease or injury due to environmental contamination. Risks or dangers associated with exposures to chemicals are especially problematic in communities housing multiple facilities that may be, albeit legally, emitting various chemicals into the air, water or soil. The chances are increased that residents will be exposed to many different chemicals simultaneously.[63]

Especially when there is a possibility of population exposure to multiple environmental hazards—a situation quite common in minority communities—the appropriate scientific protocols for estimating individual or population exposure have seldom existed, and almost never existed before 2000 for regulatory decision making by government.

Another difficulty is that, with the exception of lead exposure, little reliable evidence exists about the specific relationship of race or class to environmental health measures. Until recently, census information and other comprehensive social data seldom permitted comparisons between economic or social groups in terms of exposure to various environmental hazards. In addition, any estimates of selective exposure to environmental risk must take into account complex genetic, racial, and hereditary differences among populations.

An additional obstacle is demonstrating that economic or racial minorities have been exposed deliberately to disproportionate environmental risks or that risk exposures were assumed involuntarily. For example, it may be demonstrated convincingly that populations living for decades near a known environmental hazard (such as a petrochemical plant) are largely poor racial minorities and that they are more heavily exposed to environmental pollutants than non–racial minorities in the same community. Yet it may be argued in political debate and courtrooms that such individuals often moved to their residences deliberately and with knowledge of the environmental risks, so that the environmental exposures were voluntary.

Finally, difficulties arise over the appropriate strategies for identifying how risks may be distributed unfairly in environmental regulation and how this inequity can be solved. Over how long a period, for example, should risk estimates be made? Which populations qualify as disadvantaged? To what extent should the ability of individuals to protect themselves from such risk be taken into account? What sort of environmental risks should be included? How can such issues be introduced early enough in the regulatory decision-making process to influence the outcomes?

Surveying these difficulties, critics have argued that the environmental justice agenda is ultimately a means to much broader political ends. The movement's political potency, so the argument runs, is grounded less on scientific credibility than on the capacity of its grassroots organizers to mobilize minorities and to articulate deeply rooted historical social grievances for which environmental issues are often symbolic. "It effectively speaks to the fear and anger among local communities feeling overwhelmed by forces beyond their control, and outraged by what they perceive to be assaults on their collective quality of life," Foreman concludes.[64] To the movement's leadership, such assertions are likely to appear to be an effort to deflect attention from the evidence of environmental injustice by implicitly attacking the integrity of its leadership.

In any case, the environmental justice movement now claims a salience on the agenda of national environmental policy that is unlikely to decline in the near future. For the nation's governments, one of the most daunting challenges is to find a way to effectively translate lofty goals such as environmental equity or environmental justice into specific policy procedures and specific governmental actions. How do we bring environmental justice to the desktop and conference table of routine governmental regulation? It seems evident that a successful policy translation will require, at least, the rapid development of a science base, which means acquiring and disseminating information about the exposure of minority populations to specific environmental hazards and developing reliable methodologies for estimating individual and population risks from such exposure. Administrative law and procedure must be modified in detail and depth so that considerations of inequitable environmental risk can be considered in a timely and explicit manner in regulatory decision making. Converting prescription into practice will be arduous, however, in light of the current disagreement on appropriate metrics for measuring discrimination and equity and on the degree of difference among populations that constitutes inequity.

Conclusion

The complex new problems of risk assessment in environmental regulation confirm that we live in a historically unique era of technocratic power. U.S. science and industry, in common with those of other advanced industrial nations, now possess the capacity to alter in profound but often unpredictable ways the biochemical basis of future human life and thus to change future ecosystems radically. In its extreme form, represented by nuclear weapons, modern technology has the power to eradicate human society, if not humanity itself. But modern technologies also can alter the future ecosphere in a multitude of less dramatic but significant ways: through the deliberate redesign of genetic materials in human reproduction, through the depletion of irreplaceable energy resources such as petroleum or natural gas, through the multiplication of long-lived hazardous substances whose biological impacts on humans and the ecosystem may magnify through hundreds of years, and many more. We are practically the first generation in the world's history with the certain technical capacity to alter and even to destroy the fundamental biochemical and geophysical conditions for societies living centuries after ours. It is, as one social prophet noted, a power that people of the Middle Ages did not even credit to devils.

With this new technocratic power comes the ability to develop technologies, to manufacture new substances, and to deplete finite resources so that the benefits are largely distributed in the present and the risks for the most part are displaced into the future. Future societies may inherit most of the burden to create the social, economic, and political institutions necessary for managing the risks inherent in this generational cost transfer.

Such technical capacity can become an exercise of power undisciplined by responsibility for the consequences.

The status of nuclear wastes in many ways provides a paradigm for this problem. Because the wastes from civilian nuclear reactors currently cannot be recycled, as was assumed when the nuclear power industry began in the United States during the 1950s, the federal government now must find a safe and reliable way to dispose of the growing amount of nuclear wastes from these facilities.

Among the most dangerous of these substances are high-level wastes—those highly toxic to humans for long periods—found in the spent fuel rods from civilian reactors. Strontium-90 and cesium-137, for instance, must be isolated from human exposure for at least six hundred years; other high-level wastes must be isolated for perhaps a thousand years. Equally dangerous and much more persistent are the transuranic wastes forming over long periods from the decay of the original materials in the spent fuel rods after they are removed from the reactors. Plutonium-239 remains dangerous to most species for at least 24,000 years, perhaps for as long as 500,000 years. This plutonium, noted one commentator generally sympathetic to the nuclear power industry, "will remain a source of radioactive emissions as far in the future as one can meaningfully contemplate."[65] Other transuranics include americum-241 (dangerous for more than 400 years) and iodine-129 (dangerous for perhaps 210,000 years).

Practically speaking, such figures mean that hazardous wastes must be prevented from invading the ecosystem for periods ranging from centuries to hundreds of millennia. Not only must they be securely isolated physically, but also human institutions must survive with sufficient continuity to ensure their responsible administration throughout these eons. Many other chemicals created in the past few decades, including widely used pesticides such as DDT, 2,3,5-T, and dieldrin are not biodegradable and may persist throughout the world ecosystem indefinitely. Although less dangerous than nuclear wastes, these and other substances also represent a displacement of risks to human health and to the ecosystem well into the future.

This transfer of risk raises fundamental ethical and social questions for government. Should public institutions be compelled in some formal and explicit way to exercise regard for the future impact of decisions concerning environmental management today? And if so, how much regard? When deciding whether to develop dangerous technologies, should government be forced, if necessary, to consider not only the future ecological implications of these technologies but also the ability of future societies to create institutions capable of controlling them?

This issue is significant because government and economic institutions have a tendency to discount the future impacts of new technologies or newly developed chemicals when compared with the immediate impacts. In economic terms, this is done in formal cost-benefit analysis by discounting future benefits and costs rather substantially. In political terms, it amounts to adopting a strategy that favors taking environmental actions on the basis of short-term political advantage rather than long-term consequences. (Elected officials, especially, often treat as gospel the legendary advice of a former House Speaker to a new colleague: "Remember that when it comes time to vote, most folks want to know 'what have you done for me lately?'") It is particularly difficult for public officials to develop a sensitive regard for the distant future when there are no apparent political rewards for doing so. At some time, the political cynic in practically all public officials whispers, "What has posterity done for you lately?"

Suggested Readings

Bryant, Bunyan. *Environmental Justice: Issues, Policies, and Solutions.* Washington, D.C.: Island Press, 1995.

Davies, J. Clarence, ed. *Comparing Environmental Risks: Tools for Setting Governmental Priorities.* Washington, D.C.: Resources for the Future, 1996.

Foreman, Christopher H. *The Promise and Peril of Environmental Justice.* Washington, D.C.: Brookings Institution Press, 1998.

Keller, Ann Campbell. *Science in Environmental Policy: The Politics of Objective Advice.* Cambridge, Mass.: MIT Press, 2009.

Margolis, Howard. *Dealing with Risk: Why the Public and the Experts Disagree on Environmental Issues.* Chicago: University of Chicago Press, 1997.

Mitchell, Sandra D. *Unsimple Truths: Science, Complexity, and Policy.* Chicago: University of Chicago Press, 2009.

National Research Council. *Science and Decisions: Advancing Risk Assessment.* Washington, D.C.: National Academies Press, 2009.

Notes

1. U.S. Government Accountability Office (GAO), "Particulate Matter: EPA Needs to Make More Progress in Addressing the National Academies' Recommendations on Estimating Health Benefits," Report no. GAO-06-992T, Washington, D.C., July 19, 2006, 8.
2. Matthew L. Wald, "Chemical Element of Vinyl Toys Causes Liver Damage in Lab Rats," *New York Times,* November 13, 1998, A20.
3. Matthew L. Wald, "Citing Possible Dangers, Groups Seek Ban on Vinyl Toys," *New York Times,* November 20, 1998, A24; Scott Allen, "IV Bag Hazards Are Alleged; Trace Toxins Found, Interest Groups Say," *Boston Globe,* February 22, 1999, A3.
4. Holcomb B. Noble, "A Debate over Safety of Softeners for Plastic," *New York Times,* September 28, 1999, B10.
5. Andrea Foster and Peter Fairley, "Phthalates Pay the Price for Uncertainty," *Chemical Week,* February 17, 1999, 54.
6. Ibid.
7. David Kohn, "New Questions about Common Chemicals," *Newsday,* March 3, 2003, available at: www.ourstolenfuture.org/Commentary/News/2003/2003-0304-Newsday-phthalates.htm.

8. Steven Milloy, "A Toy Story," *Tech Central Station*, February 25, 2003, available at: www.techcentralstation.com/022503C.html (accessed February 28, 2004).
9. Seth Borenstein, "Study Links Chemical to Changes in the Womb," *Albany Times-Union*, May 27, 2005, A1; "Plastics," *Houston Chronicle*, June 3, 2005, B10.
10. Jane Kay, "San Francisco Prepares to Ban Certain Chemicals in Products for Tots, but Enforcement Will Be Tough—and Toymakers Question Necessity," *San Francisco Examiner*, November 19, 2006, Al.
11. National Academy of Sciences, Committee on Health Risks, *Phthalates and Cumulative Risk Assessment: The Task Ahead, Report in Brief* (Washington, D.C.: National Academy Press, 2008).
12. National Academy of Public Administration, *Setting Priorities, Getting Results: A New Direction for EPA* (Washington, D.C.: National Academy of Public Administration, 1995), Chap. 3.
13. "Executive Order 12866—Regulatory Planning and Review," *Federal Register*, October 4, 1993.
14. For a general discussion of the political and administrative setting of risk assessment, see Committee on Risk Assessment of Hazardous Air Pollutants, National Research Council, *Science and Judgment in Risk Assessment* (Washington, D.C.: National Academies Press, 1994), Chap. 2.
15. GAO, "Chemical Risk Assessment: Selected Federal Agencies' Procedures, Assumptions and Policies," Report no. GAO-01-810, Washington, D.C., August 2001, 14.
16. Ibid.
17. See Council on Environmental Quality, *Environmental Quality, 1979* (Washington, D.C.: Council on Environmental Quality, 1980), esp. 194.
18. Ibid.
19. Gregory Zuckerman, "Specter of Costly Asbestos Litigation Haunts Old Economy Companies," *Wall Street Journal*, December 27, 2000, A3; Alex Berenson, "A Surge of Asbestos Suits, Many by Healthy Plaintiffs," *New York Times*, April 10, 2002, A1.
20. On the history of the controversy over dioxin, see John A. Moore, Renate D. Kimbrough, and Michael Gough, "The Dioxin TCDD: A Selective Study of Science and Policy Interaction," in *Keeping Pace with Science and Engineering: Case Studies in Environmental Regulation*, ed. Myron F. Ulman (Washington, D.C.: National Academies Press, 1993), 221–242.
21. Ibid.
22. Quoted in Keith Schneider, "Times Beach Warning: Regrets a Decade Later," *New York Times*, August 15, 1991, D23.
23. Keith Schneider, "Panel of Scientists Finds Dioxin Does Not Pose Widespread Cancer Threat," *New York Times*, September 26, 1992, D20.
24. Joel Brinkley, "Many Say Lab-Animal Tests Fail to Measure Human Risk," *New York Times*, March 23, 1993, D20.
25. Cindy Skrzycki and Joby Warrick, "EPA Links Dioxin to Cancer; Risk Estimate Raised Tenfold," *Washington Post*, May 17, 2000, A1.
26. Ibid.
27. U.S. Environmental Protection Agency (EPA), National Center for Environmental Assessment, "Draft Dioxin Assessment," October 2003, available at: http://cfpub.epa.gov/ncea/cfm (accessed March 4, 2004).
28. National Research Council, *Health Risks from Dioxin and Related Compounds: Evaluation of the EPA Assessment* (Washington, D.C.: National Academies Press, 2006). See also "EPA Assessment of Dioxin Understates Uncertainty about Health Risks and May Overstate Human Cancer Risk," *National Academies News*, July 11, 2006, available at: www.nationalacademies.org/onpinews/newsitem.aspx?RecordID=11688 February 20, 2007.

29. "EPA Administrator Pledges Strong Federal Cleanup Presence at Dow Dioxin Site in Michigan and Accelerated Assessment of Dioxins' Human Health Impacts," May 26, 2009, available at: http://yosemite.epa.gov/opa/admpress.nsf/6fa790d452bcd7f58525750100565efa/3ffa6e8e70763f28852575c20064b26b!OpenDocument.

30. On the general problems of animal experiments, see David D. Doniger, *The Law and Policy of Toxic Substances Control* (Baltimore, Md.: Johns Hopkins University Press, 1978), Pt. I.

31. Animal data are cited in Philip M. Boffey, "The Debate over Dioxin," *New York Times,* June 25, 1983, A10.

32. Ibid.

33. Harvey Brooks, "The Resolution of Technically Intensive Public Policy Disputes," *Science, Technology, and Human Values* 9 (winter 1984): 40. For estimates of discretionary judgments in risk assessment, see National Research Council, Commission on Life Sciences, Committee on the Institutional Means for Assessment of Risks to Public Health, *Risk Assessment in the Federal Government: Managing the Process* (Washington, D.C.: National Academies Press, 1983), Chap. 1.

34. Frances M. Lynn, "The Interplay of Science and Values in Assessing and Regulating Environmental Risks," *Science, Technology, and Human Values* 11 (spring 1986): 40–50.

35. Thomas M. Dietz and Robert W. Rycroft, *The Risk Professionals* (New York: Russell Sage, 1987), 111.

36. Dorothy Nelkin, ed., *Controversy: The Politics of Technical Decisions* (Beverly Hills, Calif.: Sage, 1984), 17.

37. A comprehensive review of the various statutory standards for risk in federal law is found in John J. Cohrssen and Vincent T. Covello, *Risk Analysis: A Guide to Principles and Methods for Analyzing Health and Environmental Risks* (Washington, D.C.: Council on Environmental Quality, 1989), 14–15; see also Walter A. Rosenbaum, "Regulation at Risk: The Controversial Politics and Science of Comparative Risk Assessment," in *Flashpoints in Environmental Policymaking: Controversies in Achieving Sustainability,* ed. Sheldon Kamieniecki, George A. Gonzalez, and Robert O. Vos (Albany, N.Y.: SUNY Press, 1997), 31–62.

38. This analysis is based on National Academy of Public Administration, *Setting Priorities, Getting Results,* Chap. 3.

39. In contrast, the Food Quality Protection Act (1996) requires, very precisely, that the EPA must set the standard to protect infants and children from allowable pesticide residues in food at ten times the safety factor for adults unless reliable data show that a different factor would be safe.

40. Council on Environmental Quality, *Environmental Quality, 1979,* 218.

41. GAO, "EPA's Chemical Testing Program Has Not Resolved Safety Concerns," Report no. GAO/RCED 91-136, Washington, D.C., June 1991, 14.

42. A sampling of this literature may be found in the collection of articles by Peter Lewin, Gerald L. Sauer, Bernard L. Cohen, Richard N. Langlois, and Aaron Wildavsky in *Cato Symposium on Pollution,* special issue of *Cato Journal* 2 (spring 1982).

43. Ibid.

44. Science and Environmental Health Network, "Wingspread Conference on the Precautionary Principle," January 26, 1998, available at: www.sehn.org/wing.html.

45. Stephen G. Wood, Stephen Q. Wood, and Rachel A. Wood, "Whither the Precautionary Principle? An American Assessment from an Administrative Law Perspective," *American Journal of Comparative Law* 54, Suppl. (fall 2006): 581–610.

46. Ronald Bailey, "Precautionary Tale," *Reason Magazine,* April 1999, available at: http://reason.com/archives/1999/04/01/precautionary-tale (accessed April 20, 2010).

47. Nancy Myers, "Introduction," in *Precautionary Tools for Reshaping Environmental Policy*, ed. Nancy Myers and Carolyn Raffensperger (Cambridge, Mass.: MIT Press, 2004), 12.

48. Quoted in *Wall Street Journal*, October 29, 1997, B3.

49. Lisa P. Jackson, "Remarks to the National Environmental Justice Advisory Council, As Prepared 07/21/2009," available at: http://yosemite.epa.gov/opa/admpress.nsf/dff15a5d 01abdfb1852573590040b7f7/313ec9a2bc80d677852575fa007b3c42!OpenDocument.

50. EPA, "Environmental Justice," February 10, 2004, available at: www.epa.gov/compliance/ environmentaljustice (accessed March 4, 2004).

51. Robert D. Bullard, "Waste and Racism: A Stacked Deck?" *Forum for Applied Research and Public Policy* 8 (spring 1993): 29–35. On the general problems of defining environmental justice, see Evan J. Rinquist, "Environmental Justice: Normative Concerns and Empirical Evidence," in *Environmental Policy in the 1990s*, 3rd ed., ed. Norman J. Vig and Michael E. Kraft (Washington, D.C.: CQ Press, 1997), 231–254; EPA, Office of Policy, Planning, and Evaluation, *Environmental Equity: Reducing Risk for All Communities, Vol. 1: Workgroup Report to the Administrator* (Washington, D.C.: U.S. Environmental Protection Agency, June 1992), 1.

52. Martin V. Melosi, "Environmental Justice, Political Agenda Setting, and the Myths of History," *Journal of Policy History* (January 2002): 44.

53. Environmental Justice Leadership Forum on Climate Change, "Principles of Climate Justice," November 2009, available at: www.weact.org/Coalitions/EJLeadershipForum onClimateChange/tabid/331/Default.aspx.

54. Environmental Justice Resource Center, "People of Color in the United States and Puerto Rico," *People of Color Environmental Groups Directory* (Flint, Mich.: C. W. Mott Foundation, 2000), Chap. 4; Multicultural Environmental Leadership Development Initiative, "Directory of Environmental Justice Organizations," available at: http://meldi.snre.umich.edu/ej_orgs.

55. Scorecard, the Pollution Information Site, http://scorecard.org/ (accessed April 21, 2010).

56. "Executive Order 12898—Federal Actions to Address Environmental Justice in Minority Populations and Low-Income Populations," *Federal Register*, February 11, 1994.

57. See, for example, GAO, "Environmental Justice: EPA Should Devote More Attention to Environmental Justice When Developing Clean Air Rules," Report no. GAO 05-289, Washington, D.C., July 5, 2005, 10.

58. See, for example, Anita Milman, "Geographic Pollution Mapping of Power Plant Emissions to Inform Ex-Ante Environmental Justice Analyses," *Journal of Environmental Planning and Management* 49 (July 2006): 587–604; Paul Mohai and Robin Saha, "Reassessing Racial and Socioeconomic Disparities in Environmental Justice Research," *Demography* 43 (May 2006): 383–399.

59. Ivette Perfecto and Baldemar Valazquez, "Farm Workers: Among the Least Protected," *EPA Journal* 18 (March–April 1992): 13–14; Dee R. Wernette and Leslie A. Nieves, "Breathing Polluted Air," *EPA Journal* 18 (March–April 1992): 16–17.

60. Paul Mohai and Bunyan Bryant, "Race, Poverty, and the Environment," *EPA Journal* 18 (March–April 1992): 8.

61. Eileen Gauna, Sheila Foster, Carmen Gonzalez, Lisa Heinzerling, Catherine O'Neill, Clifford Rechtschaffen, and Robert R. M. Verchick, "CPR Perspective: Environmental Justice at Stake," Center for Progressive Reform, available at: www.progressiveregula- tion.org/perspectives/environjustice.cfm (accessed March 3, 2004).

62. Christopher H. Foreman Jr., "The Clash of Purposes: Environmental Justice and Risk Assessment," Brookings Institution: Social Policy, March 20, 1988, available at: www .brookings.edu/views/articles/foreman/1998RPP.htm (accessed March 5, 2004).

63. Rebecca A. Head, "Health-Based Standards: What Role in Environmental Justice?" in *Environmental Justice: Issues, Policies, and Solutions,* ed. Bunyan Bryant (Washington, D.C.: Island Press, 1995), 29.
64. Foreman, "Clash of Purposes."
65. Phil Gailey, "Evacuation Issue Threatening Nuclear Plants," *New York Times,* May 12, 1983, A1.

Chapter 5

More Choice
The Battle over Regulatory Economics

Benefit-cost analysis has a solid methodological footing and provides a valuable performance measure for an important governmental function, improving the well-being of society. However, benefit-cost analysis requires analytical judgments which, if done poorly, can obfuscate an issue or worse, provide a refuge for scoundrels in the policy debate.

—Scott Farrow and Michael Toman,
*Using Environmental Benefit-Cost Analysis to
Improve Governmental Performance*, 1998

GAO's recent reviews of four Corps civil works projects and actions found that the planning studies conducted by the Corps to support these activities were fraught with errors, mistakes, and miscalculations, and used invalid assumptions and outdated data. Generally, GAO found that the Corps' studies understated costs and overstated benefits, and therefore did not provide a reasonable basis for decision-making.

—Government Accountability Office,
*Corps of Engineers: Observations on Planning and Project
Management Processes for the Civil Works Program*, March 2006

Controversy over the economic rationality of environmental regulation has not ceased since the first Earth Day. Critics assert that both the process and the objectives of environmental regulation are flawed by economic inefficiency, irrationality, and contradiction. Spokespeople for the business sector, state and local governments, and other regulated interests often join many economists in advocating fundamental changes in the criteria used in formulating environmental regulations and in the methods used to secure compliance with them. Environmentalists and many economists, among others, believe that economic arguments are often inappropriate, if not deliberately deceptive, when used by critics to evaluate environmental policies.

Although some environmental regulatory programs are very costly, the total public and private cost of regulation to the United States appears reasonable. Currently the United States invests an estimated 1.5–2.5 percent of its gross domestic product in environmental protection—which most economists consider to be an acceptable amount and which is comparable with that of other industrialized nations. Spending for environmental regulation represents about 1.5 percent of recent federal budgets, a modest figure when compared with other social programs such as Medicare or Social Security, which account for about 12 and 22 percent, respectively, of recent spending.[1] Moreover, the collective benefit from all this spending, by most estimates, far exceeds the costs. The U.S. Environmental Protection Agency (EPA) has calculated, for instance, that the economic benefits from the Clean Air Act (CAA) alone are four times greater than the cost.[2]

Still, troubling problems arise. Could the same or better results—perhaps far better—be achieved much less expensively? Could regulated business also save considerable money and invest it in more socially productive activities? Might better results be had by switching to a different form of regulation? Is the average consumer paying too much for environmental protection? As regulatory costs and dissatisfaction over regulatory achievements mount, even the environmental movement, traditionally hostile to proposals for economic reform, has felt compelled to examine critically the economic basis of current environmental laws. The debate can whirl into mind-numbing complexity that only an economist could love, but the answers may powerfully shape future environmental regulation, and the major issues, at least, are clear.

Controversy has traditionally focused on two issues: the use of benefit-cost analysis (BCA) as a major criterion in writing environmental regulations and the effectiveness of marketplace incentives rather than the current command-and-control methods for securing compliance with environmental standards. This chapter looks at these issues, beginning with a discussion of the BCA controversy, followed by a brief description of the command-and-control approach to regulation and a comparison with some proposed alternatives.

The Benefit-Cost Debate

In theory, BCA seems simple and straightforward. Essentially, it is a process by which federal agencies (usually regulators such as the EPA)

BCA compare the net benefits and costs of a proposed action—usually a regulatory law—to determine whether the benefits exceed the costs. Using this procedure, they can also compare alternative proposals to determine which is the more economically desirable. BCA is a constant issue in environmental regulation because a common complaint about almost all environmental regulations written since 1970 is that the congressionally mandated procedures for setting environmental standards are too often insensitive to costs. "Cost-oblivious" laws, such as portions the CAA or the Occupational Safety and Health Act, in which benefit-cost considerations are explicitly forbidden as regulatory criteria, are cited as examples of legislatively ordained disregard for the economic consequences of regulation. Other laws, such as the Resource Conservation and Recovery Act (RCRA), have been criticized for failing to require specifically that regulatory agencies consider costs among other factors in setting environmental standards. In the view of critics, this mandated indifference toward BCA breeds a carelessness about costs among regulators that inflicts economic penalties on regulated interests. Even when Congress has permitted or required some kind of BCA in regulatory decision making, critics assert that too often agencies can ignore the results or treat them as a formality.[3]

A Long and Contentious History

The conflict over BCA resonates throughout U.S. regulatory history. Every administration since John F. Kennedy's has attempted to use some institutional arrangement to promote sensitivity to economic costs and benefits in regulatory policymaking by federal agencies. Toward the end of the 1970s, the White House and Congress began to pressure federal agencies through executive action and legislative mandates to give economic considerations greater attention in environmental regulation. Jimmy Carter, the most avowed environmentalist of all recent presidents, nonetheless established a White House review entity with the pugnacious acronym RARG (Regulatory Analysis Review Group), whose mission included reducing the cost of federal environmental regulations. The mildly controversial RARG annoyed environmentalists; what replaced it infuriated them.[4]

The Battle over Regulatory Impact Analyses. Ronald Reagan, whose administration was viewed by environmentalists with nearly unanimous disfavor, initiated the most aggressive effort to promote BCA in environmental policymaking with Executive Order 12291. The executive order, issued practically the day Reagan was inaugurated, required all federal agencies to prepare a type of BCA, called a regulatory impact analysis (RIA), for any major new regulatory proposals to demonstrate that the benefit of such proposals would exceed the anticipated costs. Reagan's order unleashed a prolonged bitter conflict among ideological supporters of Reagan's so-called regulatory reform in Congress, the executive agencies, and the business community on one side and environmentalists, most congressional members, and other White House critics on the other. Proponents of the executive order believed it was long overdue, a sensible remedy to excessively numerous and expensive federal regulatory laws, and a blow to increasingly costly governmental interference in economic life. Critics were convinced that Reagan's order was a covert attack on environmental regulation, virtually a subversion of congressionally mandated environmental programs, and that the enforcement of it by the Office of Management and Budget (OMB) an illegal, if not unconstitutional, presidential encroachment on the regulatory process. Contention over Executive Order 12291 became a running theme during the Reagan years, dissipating only when George Bush's administration found the contention too politically costly and quietly backed away from Reagan's aggressive enforcement policies.

Bill Clinton's administration appeared to put the BCA controversy to rest, at least temporarily, when Clinton issued Executive Order 12866 in September 1993, significantly relaxing the requirements for the preparation and review of RIAs in federal agencies and greatly diminishing the OMB's role in the process, much to the satisfaction of environmentalists. Nonetheless, the new order still required federal agencies to prepare and review BCAs frequently, insisting that they remain a formal part of regulatory procedure.

The Second Generation of Benefit-Cost Analysis. When George W. Bush entered the White House in 2001, Congress had already attempted to push BCA well beyond what Clinton or even Reagan had accomplished. Congressional Republicans had unleashed a fusillade of new BCA legislative proposals during the 1990s intended to make regulatory BCA ever more rigorous and, although these measures were (sometimes barely) defeated, the legislative mood was obvious to federal agencies—a Republican Congress would vigorously press BCA on regulatory agencies whenever possible and make economics a major consideration in regulatory policy debate.[5]

By the time of George W. Bush's inauguration, BCA in the form of RIAs had come to stay in environmental regulation. The White House and Congress now accepted the idea that RIAs (or another form of BCA) should be considered frequently, if not routinely, when the EPA or other regulatory agencies propose new environmental regulations. As Cass Sunstein notes, the second-generation debate raises

> difficult questions about how (not whether) to engage in cost-benefit analysis—how to value life and health, how to deal with the interests of future generations, how to generate rules of thumb to simplify complex inquiries ... how and when to diverge from the conclusion recommended by cost-benefit analysis.... [6]

In his second term, George W. Bush refueled the BCA controversy with Executive Order 13422, which mandated the most substantial and (critics claimed) most aggressive benefit-cost assault on environmental regulations since Ronald Reagan ordained RIAs. Among other major provisions, Executive Order 13422 required all executive agencies writing RIAs to (1) identify in writing the specific market failure or problem that warrants a new regulation, (2) designate a presidential appointee within the agency as a "regulatory policy officer" who can control upcoming rulemaking activity in that agency, and (3) provide their best estimates of the cumulative regulatory costs and benefits of rules they expect to publish in the coming year—in short, to embed BCA more deeply and pervasively throughout regulatory rulemaking.[7] An additional provision expanded OMB's authority to issue "guidance documents" and other instructions to regulatory agencies. Environmentalists charged that all this amounted to a White House power grab at environmental regulation. The new RIA makeover, however, gained little traction because the Obama administration quickly nullified its impact with the new Executive Order 13422 in February 2009, largely restoring the earlier Clinton rules and mandating another review of the RIA process.

Many Varieties of Benefit-Cost Analysis. If calculate they must, what kind of BCA should environmental agencies use? Every federal environmental law currently requires, or permits, a somewhat different approach to BCA. The one certainty is that no current federal law *compels* the EPA or any other environmental regulator to adopt or reject a proposed regulation solely on the basis of a benefit-cost calculation (although such proposals now routinely appear in Congress). One federal law, the CAA, *prohibits* the EPA from basing any air quality standard on a consideration of cost. Some federal laws, such as the Safe Drinking Water Act (1974), require the EPA to "consider" benefits and costs when contemplating new regulations; other statutes, such as the Occupational Safety and Health Act, may instruct regulators to consider only regulations that are "economically feasible"; and still others may allow the regulatory agency to consider benefits and costs among other factors when writing regulations, without specifying how much importance the economic considerations ought to assume.[8] Presidential requirements that agencies create an RIA apply only when an agency is not instructed to perform an economic analysis in some other manner by a particular law. It is hardly surprising, then, that environmental regulatory agencies approach BCA in different ways. Sometimes the same agency must use a different approach to BCA depending on which law it is enforcing. Most economists and other regulatory experts believe that, at the very least, the current jumble of procedures for BCA requires radical simplification.

Despite all the differences, a few important common issues arise in virtually all approaches to BCA. These issues concern the general merits of BCA and the procedures by which benefits and costs are calculated.

The Case for Benefit-Cost Analysis

A number of advantages are claimed for BCA. Many regulatory experts believe that BCA can greatly assist Congress and regulatory agencies in setting priorities for pollution control by identifying which regulations are the most economically desirable. "By drawing attention to costs and benefits," argues Sunstein, "it should be possible to spur the most obviously desirable regulations, to deter the most obviously undesirable ones, to encourage a broader view of consequences, and to promote a search for least-cost methods of achieving regulatory goals."[9]

Economists point to transparency as another advantage of BCA in the sense that "the results of a well-executed BCA analysis can be clearly linked to the assumptions, theory, methods and procedures used in it. This transparency can add to the accountability of public decisions by indicating where the decisions are at variance with the analysis."[10] Thus, an argument over the economic impact of a proposed environmental regulation would presumably be clarified considerably because a competent BCA would enable all sides to understand what went into the economic evaluation and to examine the validity of the components of that valuation. In addition, proponents believe that a competent BCA can reveal where important information is lacking about the costs of and benefits from a policy—what has been called ignorance revelation. Moreover, it is also argued, BCA gives policymakers a common metric for comparing policies and choosing among them.[11]

Proponents of BCA argue that, at the very least, it can point decision makers to the most economically desirable, or cost-effective, policies for achieving a regulatory goal. "Even if one objects ... to basing environmental policy on benefit-cost analysis," argues economist A. Myrick Freeman III, "it still makes good sense to be in favor of cost-effective environmental policies. Cost-effectiveness means controlling pollution to achieve the stated environmental quality standards at the lowest possible total cost."[12] Moreover, proponents add, critics of BCA are really objecting to *incompetent* analysis, especially when created deliberately to produce a desired outcome. Competent BCA sometimes can identify policies that are both economically and environmentally wiser than those currently implemented. According to Freeman, a well-conceived BCA would probably have revealed better alternatives to many federally financed water resource developments such as dams, stream channelization, and flood-control projects that were justified originally by questionable BCAs. Freeman notes that these analyses used techniques that systematically overstated the benefits of water resource development, understated the economic costs, and ignored environmental costs. The result was the construction of a number of economically wasteful and environmentally damaging projects as well as serious consideration of misguided proposals such as the one to build a dam in the Grand Canyon.[13]

When all the regulated sectors of the U.S. economy are considered, the critics reason, a huge inflationary diversion of capital from more economically desirable uses results. Critics frequently allege that excessive regulatory costs will drive some firms out of business or out of the country. Spokespeople for major national business associations, such as the Business Roundtable and the U.S. Chamber of Commerce, have alleged that excessive regulatory costs have depressed significantly the growth rate of the gross national product.

Few proponents of BCA argue, however, that it should be the sole criterion for regulatory strategies. Still, they believe that the routine use of the procedure would make regulators more sensitive to the costs of their regulatory decisions and more likely to select regulatory procedures with net benefits or with the least cost among alternatives. Many supporters also believe that BCA leads to a better quality of decision making. As economist Paul Johnson observes, "The value is that it injects rational calculation into a highly emotional subject.... It offers you a range of alternatives. Without stringent analysis, nobody knows whether costs imposed by regulatory programs are money well spent."[14] And, although it is seldom admitted, many advocates hope the publicity given to regulatory costs, especially when net benefits are lacking, will deter agencies from choosing such regulations.

The Case against Benefit-Cost Analysis

Environmentalists traditionally have opposed the routine use of BCA in setting environmental standards. Some still regard it a categorical evil, wholly inappropriate for the selection of environmental regulations. Others recognize that economic considerations may sometimes merit attention in writing environmental laws but believe benefit-cost calculations are easily distorted to the advantage of regulated interests. Most environmentalists regard BCA as nothing less than a covert assault on environmental regulation whenever it is used. Environmentalists assert that BCA often distorts economic reality by exaggerating the regulatory costs and underestimating the benefits. Regulated interests, the argument continues, often deliberately magnify their compliance costs; it is difficult, in any case, to obtain accurate economic data from them. In addition, regulated interests give little attention to the economic "learning curve," which often yields a substantial savings over the full period of regulation as they gain experience and expertise in controlling their pollutants. Benefits from regulation, in contrast, are often underestimated because they are not easily calculated. For instance, how are the health benefits from significantly cleaner air over the next several decades to be calculated? What value is to be placed on rivers, streams, and lakes made fishable and swimmable again? What is the dollars-and-cents value of an irreplaceable old-growth forest conserved for another generation?

Some benefits almost defy monetizing. For instance, an agency may consider regulatory alternatives involving different levels of risk to populations from exposure to hazardous or toxic substances. What is the appropriate value to be placed on a life saved? A variation of BCA sometimes advocated in such a situation is to compare the costs of regulation with estimates of the lives saved from the different strategies. Such a comparison implicitly requires regulators to decide how much an individual human life is worth.

As a practical example, in 2006 a BCA study conducted by the EPA examined the impact of reducing its recommended air quality threshold for soot from 15 micrograms per cubic meter to 14 micrograms. This apparently minor reduction would create an estimated $1.9 billion in additional annual control costs among the regulated industries but would also prevent an estimated 24,000 premature deaths. "It's pretty darn obvious," asserted the president of the environmental advocacy group Clean Air Watch, "that better standards would mean fewer premature deaths."[15] Not all experts agree with this regulatory arithmetic. But a metric that measures lives against dollars spent on pollution controls appears to confront decision makers with a choice that will seem arbitrary, if not morally repugnant: saving dollars or lives.

Critics note, moreover, that BCA traditionally ignores equity considerations—an increasingly potent argument as the environmental justice movement expands (see Chapter 4). In a sense, this is correct; common BCA lacks a social conscience because it is unconcerned with the social distribution of benefits and costs—that is, with which groups are winners and losers in the distribution.[16] "It is often argued," explains economists

Raymond J. Kopp, Alan J. Krupnick, and Michael A. Toman, "that [BCA] takes the existing distribution of income as given and does not consider the equity implications of the policies it seeks to evaluate. This criticism points to the anonymous manner in which the welfare changes of individuals are aggregated."[17] It is possible, however, to factor at least some equity considerations into BCA, but such an exercise is uncommon and fraught with difficulties for regulatory agencies that must decide whose equities are to be considered and how to compare equity among different groups.

Perhaps the most persuasive reason for resisting BCA, in the environmentalist's view, is that reducing an environmental value such as clean air or water to a monetary figure makes it appear to be just another commodity that can be priced, bought, and sold. According to Stephen Kelman,

> Many environmentalists fear that subjecting decisions about clean air or water to the cost-benefit tests that determine the general run of decisions removes those matters from the realm of specially valued things.... The very statement that something is not for sale enhances and protects the thing's value in a number of ways.... [It] is a way of showing that a thing is valued for its own sake, whereas selling a thing for money demonstrates that it was valued only instrumentally.[18]

Environmentalists often believe they stand apart from regulated business through a profound ethical disagreement over the intrinsic worth of wild places, uncontaminated air and water, and other environmental amenities. This conviction of moral purpose imparts to the movement much of its passion and persistence. It also elevates arguments over BCA to the level of ethical principles, making compromise especially difficult.

Reality and Rhetoric

In practice, BCA has often proven to be more paper tiger than bulldog in regulatory affairs. Reagan's BCA initiative never achieved the epic impact that its proponents wished because its implementation was badly flawed. Several major environmental programs, such as the CAA and the Occupational Safety and Health Act, prohibited BCA or severely limited its application in the regulations implementing them (although the EPA spent $2 million preparing an unused BCA for an air-quality standard anyway).[19] Many other regulatory proposals escaped Executive Order 12291 because their impacts did not exceed $100 million. Currently, agencies often prepare BCAs but, lacking confidence in the results, turn to other criteria in writing regulations. Sometimes—perhaps often—agencies do not, despite formal requirements, diligently explore alternatives to their proposed regulations. At the end of a comprehensive independent 2008 survey of RIA writing at EPA, Richard Morgenstern, a former high-level EPA economist, concluded:

> One of the things that we found in actually reviewing specific regulations was that despite the mandate that exists and the guidelines that agencies consider alternatives ... in many instances they do not consider alternatives. So if you think about it, what's the point of doing what's probably a million dollar study in looking into a lot of aspects of regulation if you're not going to give serious consideration to an alternative?[20]

And agencies showed little consistency in how they prepared their analyses, notwithstanding OMB guidelines. Experience demonstrated at the EPA, as in many other agencies, the severe limitations and inherent bias implicit in data deficiencies.[21]

In some instances, however, the White House has used—or has attempted to use—BCA to stifle environmental regulations objectionable to the president. This was perhaps the most potent impact of Reagan's RIAs. The Reagan administration's use of BCA, in the end, created a pervasive bias against environmental regulation that embittered environmentalists against RIAs and engendered continuing suspicion of the OMB's role in regulatory review.[22] The OMB's review of regulatory agency RIAs, however, was far less aggressive under Reagan's successor, George Bush. Although environmentalist criticism of the OMB's role in regulatory RIAs subsided during the Clinton years, the controversy flared continually through George W. Bush's administration and into the Obama years.

The Controversial Office of Information and Regulatory Affairs. Since George W. Bush's inauguration, a continual flashpoint of cost-benefit conflict has been the OMB's Office of Information and Regulatory Affairs (OIRA), which is responsible for oversight of the RIA process throughout the executive branch. In following Bush's Executive Order 13422, OIRA not only reviewed the RIAs produced by the EPA and related agencies but also examined critically the scientific studies used to justify environmental regulations and their related BCAs. "Once staffed mainly by economists and policy analysts," writes science policy specialist Charles W. Schmidt, "OIRA also employed a variety of health and environmental scientists," which has provoked criticism from environmentalists and others that "OIRA is overstepping its legislative mandate because health and environmental expertise should be concentrated in the agencies that draft legislation."[23] Critics suspected the OIRA was using its newly acquired scientific resources to delay or reject regulatory proposals by challenging the scientific accuracy or credibility of the data supporting the regulations instead of confining itself to examining the relevant BCAs. For example, they asserted, OIRA sometimes attempted to discredit proposed regulations by questioning the qualifications of peer reviewers for the science studies used by the EPA to justify the regulations. Proponents of OIRA's new approach, however, asserted that scientific reviews would improve the quality of the science on which environmental regulations are based and that scientific studies often must be reviewed to determine how RIAs were constructed. Environmentalists, regarding the OIRA's new approach as additional evidence of pervasive White House political interference with the conduct of science, anticipated a major change in OIRA's behavior with the election of Barack Obama, an outspoken proponent of OIRA reform. Not anticipated was Obama's choice of Cass Sunstein, a well-known Harvard scholar and proponent of CBA, as OIRA's new director. Sunstein's appointment left environmentalists uncertain, and many confused if not disillusioned, about the expected OIRA reforms.

Benefit-Cost Analysis's Continuing Problem. By now, thousands of regulatory economic analyses have been prepared by federal administrators—more than 1,200 by the EPA alone. Yet federal agencies continue to struggle when attempting to estimate realistically the benefits or costs of the regulatory programs they implement. Whatever the reason— incompetence, inexperience, creative bookkeeping, or something else— regulatory cost estimates frequently prove to be inaccurate. For example, the EPA's Superfund cost estimates have been unreliably low, and the situation is no better for hazardous waste site remediation required by the RCRA.[24] Often, EPA officials, like other regulatory officials, appear nonchalant about guidelines—or perhaps confounded by them—even when guidance is explicit. For instance, the Clean Air Act Amendments of 1990 required the EPA to produce a BCA for any proposed regulations to implement the amendments. Congress specifically required that the EPA describe the key economic assumptions, the extent to which benefits and costs were quantified, and the extent to which alternatives were considered in the BCA procedure. When the GAO evaluated twenty-three RIAs written under these guidelines, it discovered considerable disparities. Eight RIAs did not identify key economic assumptions such as the value placed on human life. Analyses explicit about economic assumptions were often silent about the reasons for those chosen. All the RIAs assigned dollar values to the estimated costs of proposed regulations, but only eleven assigned dollar values to the benefits.[25]

Regulatory officials, environmental or otherwise, still frequently discount their own agency analyses when making regulatory decisions. This is not necessarily administrative malfeasance—federal agencies are usually required only to consider the benefits and costs in the course of policy-making—but the situation bespeaks the considerable practical difficulty in using RIAs and the substantial official uneasiness about the situation. Nonetheless, estimates about policy benefits and costs, some perhaps grievously flawed, continue to pack policy debates.[26]

At least one agency, the U.S. Army Corps of Engineers, seems almost incapable of conquering a historical addiction to "cooked" BCAs.[27] Environmentalists are especially critical of these dubious BCAs because of the Corps's enormous impact on the nation's environmental management. The Corps's budget annually exceeds $4 billion for "civil works"—local public works such as levees, dams, and drainage canals, dear to all congressional members even though these projects often become environmental disasters. For almost a century, these projects have frequently been justified by dubious BCAs, which Congress uncritically accepts because doing so works to the advantage of local constituencies. Every president from Jimmy Carter to George W. Bush has vigorously opposed these questionable projects, with mixed success. "On Capitol Hill," writes a veteran political reporter, "it is still considered almost bad form to oppose a water project in another member's district.... Corps authorizations have long been viewed as congressional prerogatives, nearly as automatic as the franking privilege or special license plates."[28] Despite repeated promises to swear off "cooked" economics, the Corps still invites suspicion of its BCA math. Few verdicts about the Corps's BCA process have been as blistering as the GAO evaluation toward the end of the George W. Bush administration, which had virtually nothing good to conclude. "The cost and benefit analyses performed by the Corps to support decisions on Civil Works projects or actions were generally inadequate to provide a reasonable basis for deciding whether to proceed with the project or action," stated the GAO. For example, for the Delaware Deepening Project, GAO found credible support for only about $13.3 million per year in project benefits compared with the $40.1 million per year claimed in the Corps's analysis; and for the Oregon Inlet Jetty Project, the GAO analysis determined that if the Corps had incorporated more current data into its analysis, the reported benefits would have been reduced by about 90 percent.[29]

In reality, the Corps's resolve to improve its BCAs has often been smothered by the incessant congressional pressure to justify coveted projects. Consider, for example, Louisiana's congressional delegation, the undisputed national champion at harvesting Corps projects, commendable and otherwise. During George W. Bush's first administration, before Hurricane Katrina, Louisiana reaped $1.6 billion in Corps-funded projects and, in the years following Katrina, an additional $14 billion, mostly to reconstruct the New Orleans levees. "We live and die by what the Corps of Engineers does or doesn't do, literally," observed John Breaux,

Louisiana's Democratic U.S. senator for eighteen years, "The Corps are us."[30] Louisiana's congressional delegation, nonetheless, is distinguished only by its proficiency in collecting Corps projects. Few congressional delegations can long resist the temptation to press the Corps for benefit-cost calculations that justify attractive local projects.[31]

BCA is not, however, necessarily an administrative charade. Impressive examples of improved economic efficiency and substantial savings due to BCA at the EPA, for instance, exist. Nonetheless, and despite confidence among many economists that BCA quality and influence are improving among regulatory agencies, the evidence still is not convincing. More persuasive is the conclusion from a meticulous study of forty-eight major federal health, safety, and environmental regulations between 1996 and 1999: "We find that economic analyses prepared by regulatory agencies do not provide enough information to make decisions that will maximize the efficiency and effectiveness of a rule." Moreover, the findings "strongly suggest that agencies failed to comply with the executive order and adhere to the OMB guidelines."[32]

Some Lessons

Much can yet be learned from the experiences since 1980. The blizzard of econometric data normally accompanying arguments over the cost of regulation should be at least initially considered suspect—by all sides. Willfully or not, regulated businesses will often overestimate the costs of regulation and the proponents of regulation will often underestimate them. Also, as experience with the Reagan and George W. Bush administrations illustrates, BCA is so vulnerable to partisan manipulation that it is often discounted by officials even when they are *allowed* to consider the economics of regulation. A former adviser to President Richard Nixon recalls, "In executive branch meetings, the EPA staff repeatedly seemed to minimize pollution costs, while other agencies weighed in with high costs to meet the identical pollution standard. Often, we halved the difference...."[33] Many regulatory decisions made on the basis of political, administrative, or other considerations are sanctified later by economics for the sake of credibility. Sometimes, costs are inflated grossly not so much by individual regulations as by the multiplicity and unpredictability of regulatory procedures.

This discussion should clarify at least a few aspects of the benefit-cost controversy. First, there is no substantial evidence that regulatory costs have become so excessive that BCA must be routinely imposed on *all* environmental regulation programs. Second, there are doubtless instances, perhaps a substantial number of them, in which BCA might suggest better solutions to environmental regulation than would otherwise be selected.

For this reason, such analysis should not be excluded categorically from consideration unless Congress specifically mandates an exclusion. Third, it matters a great deal who does the calculating. All BCAs should be open to review and challenge during administrative deliberations. Fourth, Congress should indicate explicitly in the text of environmental legislation or in the accompanying legislative history how it expects regulatory agencies to weight economic criteria alongside other statutory guidelines to be observed in writing regulations to implement such legislation. Fifth, regulatory costs might be diminished significantly not by using BCA but by using economic incentives in securing the compliance of regulated interests with environmental programs.

The Emerging Problem of Environmental Valuation

The BCA controversy illuminates an especially vexing problem inherent to most debates about environmental policy: How can environmental amenities be valued accurately if some metric must be devised? This issue is at the core of traditional economic theory because it raises profound questions about the assumptions implicit in placing value on nonmarket goods, such as clean air or pristine wilderness. In recent years, this problem has stimulated considerable debate among economists and others concerned with environmental valuation, which has led to several significant proposals for a radical change in the way environmental amenities are evaluated and, as a consequence, in how environmental policymaking transpires.

Environmental Accounting. Many economists, recognizing that the continuing development of environmental policymaking increasingly confronts policymakers with problems of environmental valuation not addressed by traditional economics, propose the development of environmental accounting as an alternative. In effect, environmental accounting attempts to broaden enormously the scope of environmental amenities to which society attaches significant value and to devise a metric appropriate for comparing these values with other, usually monetary, values involved in policy evaluation. In this perspective, environmental amenities with obvious and immediate human benefits would be valued—clean air and water, for instance—but so would habitats essential to the preservation or proliferation of species, ecological sites essential for biosphere preservation or improvement, environments of unusual beauty, flora and fauna of biological significance, or other aspects of the human environment important for ecological reasons. Identifying these distinctively valued ecological elements will be difficult and challenging but no less so than assigning an appropriate value to them.

Environmental accounting is especially difficult because it requires both economists and ecologists to work at the intellectual margins of their disciplines, where theory and evidence are often tenuous. Ecologists, for instance, may strongly suspect that the eradication of certain species will create a long-term economic disruption of human environments—without being able to prove it or to estimate the scope of the disturbance. Because many environmental amenities are neither bought nor sold in markets, economists would have to construct shadow prices—best estimates of real market value—by a tortuous, inevitably contentious logic. "Demand and supply curves must be constructed," explains economist Roefie Hueting; however, "constructing a complete demand curve is difficult because the intensity of individual preferences for environmental functions cannot be expressed in market behavior or translated into market terms. This is further complicated by the fact that the consequences of today's actions will often only be manifest in future damage."[34]

Many economists assert, in rebuttal, that a procedure called revealed preferences is a reasonable substitute for a market in valuing environmental amenities. Economists Kopp, Krupnick, and Toman offer an example:

> It would be wrong ... to think of economic values as dollar-denominated values in one's brain to be downloaded when a person is asked the worth of a beautiful sunset; rather, such a value might be inferred from the things that one gives up to see the sunset (e.g., the cost of travel to the ocean).... To economists ... the importance of things (tangible or intangible) is revealed by what a person will give to obtain them.... If the thing given up was money, the value can be expressed in monetary units; otherwise, it is expressed in the natural units of the thing given.[35]

Contingent Valuation. One profound consequence of environmentalism's political ascendancy in the United States has been to compel a sustained rethinking of traditional economic and ecological theories to come to terms with the problems of environmental valuation implicit in contemporary environmental regulation. One approach to environmental valuation currently proposed for federal policymakers is a methodology called contingent valuation, meaning that a monetary value is to be assigned to an environmental amenity whose use or destruction would deprive others of its future availability. Contingent valuation could be used, for example, to estimate the monetary cost to the public created by haze over the Grand Canyon, by widespread pollution of Alaskan waters caused by oil tanker spills, or by any other event that deprives the public of the passive value in an environmental amenity. In a typical case, a representative segment of the relevant public would be asked how much it would be willing to pay to prevent haze over a national park, to avoid an oil spill, or to preclude some other environmental problem.

Through statistical procedures, a monetary value would then be assigned to an environmental amenity based on these public valuations. Alaska's state government used contingent valuation in the early 1990s to discover what value Americans who might never visit Prince William Sound would assign to preventing a catastrophic oil spill there—a strategy used to estimate the monetary damages for which the Exxon Corporation would be held liable for the devastating oil spill by the tanker *Exxon Valdez* in 1989. Based on an average response of $30 per person, Alaskan officials estimated that Americans would collectively pay $2.8 billion to avoid such a disaster.[36] In 1989, the federal courts, apparently influenced by an endorsement of contingent valuation by a panel of distinguished U.S. economists, ordered the Department of the Interior to take into account the losses to people not directly affected by environmental problems when estimating the cost of CAA and Superfund violations in facilities under its jurisdiction.

Contingent valuation remains controversial among economists and other policymakers. Many economists dismiss the methodology as "junk economics" because, they assert, the public cannot accurately assess the value in the passive use of an environmental amenity. Critics argue that the public is overly generous with hypothetical statements about personal outlays, tends to exaggerate the value of an amenity, and is often influenced by the wording of questions. To support these contentions, critics cite studies showing enormous variability in public environmental valuations: saving an old-growth forest in the Pacific Northwest was valued between $119 billion and $359 billion and sparing the whooping crane from extinction was valued between $51 billion and $715 billion.[37] Understandably, some of the most aggressive opponents of contingent valuation in federal policymaking are corporations, such as Exxon, which feel at considerable financial risk. Neither Bill Clinton nor George W. Bush were willing to issue an executive order explicitly permitting, or encouraging, contingent valuation. Whatever federal agency may adopt the methodology on its own can expect to defend it before a federal judge because it is certain to be challenged legally and, thus, unlikely to be implemented for several years at least.

Environmental Risk. An alternative approach to environmental valuation might be to substitute risk for dollars, thereby avoiding the problem of monetizing environmental amenities. Such an approach might, for instance, compare the risks of losing an environmental amenity with those of preserving it, assuming that a satisfactory risk metric can be created. Or, in another variation, the monetary benefits in altering an amenity might be compared with the risks in losing it. Suppose, for example, that federal regulators must decide whether to open a large portion of wilderness area, the habitat of a rare or endangered species, to oil and gas exploration. The benefits of exploration could be calculated in terms of the potential governmental royalties, new employment, regional economic development, corporate taxes, or other monetized considerations. These might be compared with the expected number of species endangered or lost, the extent of land made unusable for other purposes, the amount of air and water pollution generated, and the special resources affected (such as historic sites, national parks, and recreation areas). These strategies require a comparison of dollars to risks, or risks to risks, each with its own difficulties. Nonetheless, environmental officials often do make such comparisons implicitly or informally in arriving at regulatory decisions, and formalizing the procedure would at least force the comparisons to become explicit and reviewable.

Regulation Strategies: Command and Control versus the Marketplace

The CAA was the first in a long succession of federal environmental laws based on the command-and-control approach to environmental regulation (see next section). Chapters 6 and 7 illustrate well how this approach has been translated into specific statutes to control air and water pollution, toxic and abandoned waste, drinking water quality, and practically every other environmental hazard currently regulated by Washington, D.C. Many economists, regulatory scholars, and policy practitioners, including some environmental leaders, now consider command-and-control regulations to be a statutory antique, too economically flawed and administratively clumsy to cope effectively with many current environmental problems. At the very least, they suggest, command-and-control laws often require refitting with newer economic approaches. The most commonly proposed reform for the command-and-control approach is to substitute or add market-based approaches that rely fundamentally on economic incentives and markets to accomplish the environmental improvements intended.

Market-based regulation, in fact, has become a fundamental standard by which critics judge almost all aspects of command-and-control regulation. Thus, it is helpful to compare briefly the philosophy of command-and-control with market-based regulation before discussing current environmental regulations in greater detail.

Command-and-Control Regulation

The foundation of federal pollution regulation is the command-and-control approach, also called standards and enforcement. The structure and philosophy of this approach create many of the characteristic processes and problems familiar from current governmental management of the environment. Regulatory horror stories abound, convincing believers that a better approach lies in less direct governmental involvement and more economic incentives to encourage pollution abatement. In fact, both approaches have virtues and liabilities, and a combination of both approaches often seems more effective than one alone.[38] The command-and-control approach can best be understood as a set of five phases through which pollution policy evolves: goals, criteria, quality standards, emission standards, and enforcement.

Goals. In theory, the first step in pollution abatement begins with a determination by Congress of the ultimate objectives to be accomplished through pollution regulation. In practice, these goals are often broadly and vaguely worded. Sometimes, as when Congress decides to "press technology" by setting pollution standards that it hopes will force industry to develop control technologies not currently available, the goals are deliberately made extremely ambitious as an incentive for vigorous regulatory measures by regulated interests. The principal goals of the CAA are, for example, to protect public health and safety. Vague goals are not as important in defining the operational character of a regulatory program as are the more detailed specifications for the setting of pollution standards, emission controls, and enforcement—the real cutting edges of regulation. Statements of goals, however, may be politically significant as signals to the interests involved in regulation about which pollutants and sources will be given priority and how vigorously Congress intends to implement programs. The CAA goal of establishing national air-quality standards for major pollutants, for instance, was an unmistakable signal that Congress would no longer tolerate the continual delays in controlling air pollution caused by past legislative willingness to let the states create their own air-quality standards. It was also evidence that regulated interests had lost their once dominant position in the formation of air pollution policy.

Criteria. Criteria are the technical data, commonly provided by research scientists, indicating which pollutants are associated with environmental damage and how such pollutants, in varying combinations, affect the environment. Criteria are essential to give public officials some idea of what pollutant levels they must achieve to ensure various standards of air and water quality. If regulators intend to protect public health from the effects of air pollution, they must know what levels of pollution—sulfur oxides, for instance—create public health risks. In a similar vein, restoring game fish to a dying lake requires information about the levels of organic waste such fish can tolerate. Criteria must be established for each regulated pollutant and sometimes for combinations of pollutants.

Obtaining criteria frequently is difficult because data on the environmental effects of many pollutants still may be fragmentary or absent. Even when data are available, there is often as much art as science in specifying relationships between specific levels of a pollutant and its environmental effects because precise correlations may not be obtainable from the information. The reliability of criteria data also may vary depending on whether they are obtained from animal studies, epidemiological statistics, or human studies. Criteria are likely to be controversial, especially to those convinced that a set of data works to their disadvantage. Given the limitations in the criteria data, regulatory agencies often have had to set pollution standards with information that was open to scientific criticism but was still the best available.

Quality Standards. Goals and criteria are preludes to the critical business of establishing air-quality and water-quality standards—the maximum levels of various pollutants to be permitted in air, soil, workplaces, or other locations. As a practical matter, defining standards is equivalent to declaring what the public, acting through governmental regulators, will consider to be "pollution." An adequate set of quality standards should specify which contaminants will be regulated and what variation in levels and combinations will be accepted in different pollutant categories.

Creating quality standards—in effect, another way of defining acceptable risk—is ultimately a political decision. Criteria documents rarely provide public officials with a single number that defines unambiguously what specific concentration of a pollutant produces precisely what effects. A rather broad range of possible figures associated more or less closely with predictable effects is available; which one is accepted may be the result of prolonged struggle and negotiation among the interests involved in regulation. This battle over numbers is a matter of economics as much as science or philosophy. The difference between two possible pollution standards, only a few units apart, may seem trivial to a layperson. But the higher standard may involve millions or billions of additional dollars in pollution-control technologies for the regulated interests and possibly many additional years before standards are achieved. Sometimes Congress establishes a standard based on a number's political "sex appeal." The original requirements in the CAA that automobile emissions of hydrocarbons and carbon monoxide be reduced by 90 percent of the 1970 levels by no later than 1975 were accepted largely because the 90 percent figure sounded strict and spurred the auto industry into action. In practical terms, the figure might have been set at 88 percent

Table 5-1 *National Ambient Air Quality Standards*

Pollutant	Standard value[a]		Standard type[b]
Carbon monoxide (CO)			
8-hour average	9 ppm	10 mg/m³	Primary
1-hour average	35 ppm	40 mg/m³	Primary
Nitrogen dioxide (NO₂)			
Annual arithmetic mean	0.053 ppm	100 µg/m³	Primary and secondary
Ozone (O₃)			
1-hour average	0.12 ppm	235 µg/m³	Primary and secondary
8-hour average[b]	0.08 ppm	157 µg/m³	Primary and secondary
Lead (Pb)			
Quarterly average		1.5 µg/m³	Primary and secondary
Particulate (PM₁₀) *Particles with diameters of 10 µm or less*			
Annual arithmetic mean		50 µg/m³	Primary and secondary
24-hour average		150 µg/m³	Primary and secondary
Particulate (PM₂.₅) *Particles with diameters of 2.5 µm or less*			
Annual arithmetic mean[b]		15 µg/m³	Primary and secondary
24-hour average[b]		65 µg/m³	Primary and secondary
Sulfur dioxide (SO₂)			
Annual arithmetic mean	0.03 ppm	80 µg/m³	Primary
24-hour average	0.14 ppm	365 µg/m³	Primary
3-hour average	0.50 ppm	1,300 µg/m³	Secondary

Source: U.S. Environmental Protection Agency, Office of Air Quality Planning and Standards, http://www.epa.gov/air/criteria.html.

[a]The two values are approximately equivalent concentrations.
[b]The ozone 8-hour standard and the PM₂.₅ standards are included for information only. A 1999 federal court ruling blocked implementation of these standards, which the EPA proposed in 1997.

or 85 percent, or some other number in this range, with about the same results. Air-quality standards created by the EPA for the major criteria pollutants—that is, pollutants that the CAA specifically designates for regulation because of their well-known pervasive threat to public health—are identified in Table 5-1.

Emission Standards. Standards for clean air or water are only aspirations unless emission standards exist to prescribe the acceptable pollutant discharges from important sources of air or water contamination. If emission standards are to be effective, they must indicate clearly the acceptable emission levels from all important pollution sources and should be related to the pollution-control standards established by policymakers.

Congress has used two different methods of determining how emission standards should be set. In regulating existing air pollution sources under the CAA, Congress requires that emissions be limited to the extent necessary to meet the relevant air-quality standards; determining what emission controls are necessary depends on where the quality standards are set. In controlling new air pollution sources, and most water polluters, the emission controls are based on the available technologies. This technology-based approach sets the emission levels largely according to the performance of available technologies. A direct and critical relationship exists between air-quality standards and emission controls. For example, once the EPA declares national ambient air-quality standards, each state is required in its State Implementation Plan to calculate the total emissions of that pollutant within an airshed and then to assign emission controls to each source of that pollutant sufficient to ensure that total emissions will meet air-quality standards. In effect, this approach calls for the states to decide how much of the total pollution "load" within an airshed is the responsibility of each polluter and how much emission control the polluter must achieve. This process has become bitterly controversial. Experts often have difficulty in determining precisely how much of a pollution load within a given body of water or air can be attributed to a specific source; this difficulty compounds the problem of assigning responsibility for pollution abatement equitably among a large number of polluters.[39]

Regulated interests, aware of the relationship between air-quality standards and emission controls, will attack both standards and controls in an effort to avoid or relax their assigned emission controls. Regulated industries also chronically complain that insufficient attention is given to the cost of emission controls when government regulators prescribe the acceptable technology. Polluters often balk at installing the specific control technologies prescribed by governmental regulators. The scrubber wars between electric utilities and regulatory authorities, for instance, continued for more than two decades. Alleging that the scrubbers— complex and expensive technologies that remove toxic gases from power plant air emissions—prescribed by the government are inefficient and unreliable, coal-fired utilities fiercely resisted installing the scrubbers until compelled to do so. The battle ended only when the 1990 amendments to the CAA permitted other control alternatives.

The backlash against emission controls often falls on state government officials who, under existing federal law, usually are responsible for setting specific emission levels, prescribing the proper technologies, and enforcing emission restraints on specific sources. Enforcing emission controls is accomplished largely through issuing a permit to individual dischargers specifying the permissible emission levels and technological controls for their facilities. Despite several decades of experience and substantial financial assistance from the federal government, some state regulatory authorities remain understaffed and undertrained. In the late 1990s, however, most state regulatory agencies had become highly professional to the point where failures in state environmental regulation could no longer be routinely attributed to incompetence. The political and economic influence of regulated interests, nonetheless, is often far more formidable in state capitals than in Washington, D.C., and state regulators often feel especially vulnerable to these local pressures.

Enforcement. A great diversity of enforcement procedures might be used to ensure that pollution standards are achieved; adequate enforcement must carry enough force to command the respect of those subject to regulation. Satisfactory enforcement schemes have several characteristics: they enable public officials to act with reasonable speed (very rapidly in the case of emergencies) to curb pollution, they carry sufficient penalties to encourage compliance, and they do not enable officials to evade a responsibility to act against violations when action is essential. It is desirable that officials have a range of enforcement options that might extend from gentle prodding to secure compliance at one end all the way to litigation and criminal penalties for severe, chronic, or reckless violations at the other. In reality, when it comes to enforcement, administrative authority is often the power to "make a deal." Armed with a flexible variety of enforcement options, administrators are in a position to bargain with polluters that are not in compliance with the law, selecting those enforcement options they believe will best achieve their purposes. This bargaining, a common occurrence in environmental regulation, illustrates how political pressure and administrative discretion concurrently shape environmental policy (enforcement is examined in greater detail in the next section). In the end, an effective pollution abatement program depends largely on voluntary compliance by regulated interests. No regulatory agency has enough personnel, money, and time to engage in continual litigation or other actions to force compliance with pollution standards. Furthermore, litigation usually remains among the slowest, most inflexible, and inefficient means of achieving environmental protection. Administrative agencies prefer to negotiate and maneuver to avoid litigation as a primary regulatory device whenever possible.

What's Wrong with the Command-and-Control Approach? Economists have been the most outspoken critics of command-and-control regulation. However, they are now joined by an increasing number of other critics, including some leading environmental organizations such as Environmental Defense, whose experience with command-and control regulation since 1970 has demonstrated that it has some severe deficiencies. First, they assert, it offers regulated interests few economic incentives to comply rapidly and efficiently with mandated pollution standards. In the economist's perspective, the standards-and-enforcement approach lacks an appeal to the economic self-interest of the regulated. Even severe penalties for noncompliance with the law often fail to motivate polluters to meet required pollution control deadlines. Penalties are often not assessed or are severely weakened by negotiation with regulatory agencies. Some firms find it more profitable to pay penalties and to continue polluting in violation of the law than to assume the often far steeper costs of compliance. In addition, polluters have no economic incentive to reduce their emissions below the regulatory requirements.

Second, traditional regulatory approaches require the federal government to specify the appropriate technologies and methods for their use in practically every instance in which pollutants are technologically controlled. Highly complicated, exquisitely detailed specifications that make poor scientific or economic sense for particular industries or firms can result. One reason for this situation is that neither Congress nor administrators may have sufficient scientific training or experience to make correct judgments about the appropriate technologies for pollution abatement in a specific firm or industry. Also, regulators sometimes lack sufficient information about the economics of firms or industries to know which technologies are economically efficient—that is, which achieve the desired control standards the least expensively. In general, according to economists Allen V. Kneese and Charles L. Schultze,

> Problems such as environmental control ... involve extremely complicated economic and social relationships. Policies that may appear straightforward—for example, requiring everyone to reduce pollution by the technologically feasible limit—will often have ramifications or side effects that are quite different from those intended. Second, given the complexity of these relationships, relying on a central regulatory bureaucracy to carry out social policy simply will not work: there are too many actors, too much technical knowledge, too many different circumstances to be grasped by a regulatory agency.[40]

Examples of costly mistakes in specifying technological controls are not hard to find. Instances occurred in the writing of the regulations to implement the Surface Mining Control and Reclamation Act of 1977. For example, International Inc., a General Electric subsidiary, complained that the EPA and the Office of Surface Mining in the Department of the Interior required that all runoff from areas disturbed by surface mining must pass through a sedimentation pond, although other management practices, such as the use of straw dikes and vegetative cover, would achieve substantially the same results. The company had to build at its Trapper Mine near Craig, Colorado, a $335,000 sedimentation pond when alternative methods could have achieved the same results at 10 percent of the cost.[41] In another example, the Conoco Company complained that Consolidated Coal, its subsidiary, unnecessarily spent $160 million annually to meet engineering standards imposed on surface mines by the federal government. The National Academy of Sciences, speaking through its National Research Council, had recommended a different, less expensive, and apparently equally effective approach.[42]

Third, proponents assert that incentive approaches can be simply and economically administered. As a National Academy of Public Administration report notes,

> Incentive-based systems are administratively simple because ... they require much of the regulatory energy to be expended up front in the design state of the regulatory program. If the design is correct, less burdensome administration may be facilitated. Further, once the program is in place, regulators can rely on the energies of the private sector to drive pollution downward.[43]

The alternative seems to require bureaucratic legions toiling endlessly in the regulatory vineyards. "Command-and-control regulation," continues the report, "may impose a never-ending requirement on regulators to develop new and more stringent industry-specific regulations on smaller and smaller discharge points."[44]

Fourth, proponents point out that a market incentive approach is easier for the public to understand and presumably easier to approve. Economic incentives focus on a pollution-reduction goal that the public would presumably find much more comprehensible—hence, easier for government to defend politically—than technology specifications with all the mystifying technical disputation about their appropriateness and efficiency.

Regulation Goes to the Market

Economic incentives are not new to U.S. environmental management. Many familiar forms of environmental control, such as sewage treatment charges, taxes on leaded gasoline, and deposit-refund systems for disposable beer and soft drink containers, use the pulling power of economic incentives to encourage pollution control. Table 5-2 provides a brief summary of the different methods used in the United States.

Not until a decade after Earth Day 1970 did the EPA first experiment warily with economic regulatory incentives. This set in motion a succession of additional economic innovations at the EPA, culminating in the current emissions trading program in the CAA.

Table 5-2 *Economic Incentives Used in Environmental Regulation*

Incentives	Examples	Pros and cons
Pollution charges and taxes	Emission charges Effluent charges Solid waste charges Sewage charges	*Pros:* Stimulates new technology; useful when damage per unit of pollution varies little with the quantity of pollution *Cons:* Potentially large distributional effects; uncertain environmental effects; generally requires monitoring data
Input or output taxes and charges	Leaded gasoline tax Carbon tax Fertilizer tax Pesticide tax Virgin material tax Water user charges Chlorofluorocarbon taxes	*Pros:* Administratively simple; does not require monitoring data; raises revenue; effective when sources are numerous and damage per unit of pollution varies little with the quantity of pollution *Cons:* Often weak link to pollution; uncertain environmental effects
Subsidies	Municipal sewage plants Land use by farmers Industrial pollution	*Pros:* Politically popular; targets specific activities *Cons:* Financial impact on government budgets; may stimulate too much activity; uncertain effects
Deposit-refund systems	Lead-acid batteries Beverage containers Automobile bodies	*Pros:* Deters littering; stimulates recycling *Cons:* Potentially high transaction costs; product must be reusable or recyclable
Marketable permits	Emissions Effluents Fisheries access	*Pros:* Provides limits to pollution; effective when damage per unit of pollution varies with the amount of pollution; provides stimulus to technological change *Cons:* Potentially high transaction costs; requires variation in marginal control costs
Reporting requirements	Proposition 65 Superfund Amendments and Reauthorization Act	*Pros:* Flexible, low cost *Cons:* Impacts may be hard to predict; applicable only when damage per unit of pollution does not depend on the quantity of pollution
Liability	Natural resource damage assessment Nuisance, trespass	*Pros:* Provides strong incentive *Cons:* Assessment and litigation costs can be high; burden of proof large; few applications
Voluntary programs	Project XL 33/50 Energy Star	*Pros:* Low cost; flexible; many possible applications; way to test new approaches *Cons:* Uncertain participation

is it this based on regulation?

Source: U.S. Environmental Protection Agency, Office of Policy, Economics, and Innovation, "The United States Experience with Economic Incentives for Protecting the Environment," Document no. EPA-240-R-01-001, Washington, D.C., January 2001, ix.

Bubbles, Nets, and Offsets. In 1979, the EPA moved away from the traditional standards-and-enforcement approach to air pollution by introducing its "bubble policy" for controlling emissions from existing air pollution sources. This policy assumed "that an imaginary enclosure, or bubble, is placed over an industrial plant. From this enclosure, or bubble, a maximum allowable level of emissions is permitted. A firm in this bubble would be free to use more cost-effective pollution controls than are usually allowed."[45] For example, a firm with three smokestacks emitting pollution might find it least costly to cut back severely on the emissions from one stack while leaving the others only slightly controlled. If the total emissions leaving the imaginary bubble over the plant did not violate air-quality standards, the firm would be free to decide how best to comply with the law. Advocates of the approach assumed that the result would be a substantial cost savings for the firm and quicker compliance with pollution standards because the firm would be free to choose the solution that best suited its economic self-interest. With bubbling, the EPA also allowed emissions banking, which permitted a regulated firm to earn credits for keeping pollutants below the required level. Firms could apply these credits against their own future emission-control requirements, sell them to other firms, or save them.

The results have been inconclusive since air pollutants have been netted, offset, bubbled, and banked. Estimates suggest that the aggregate cost savings for firms have been modest. By the mid-1980s the 132 federal- and state-sanctioned "bubbles" had saved firms an estimated $435 million, netting about $4 billion, both relatively small sums when compared with the total compliance costs for firms regulated by the CAA.[46] Some experts believe that the savings from emissions trading have been exaggerated by the private sector. Others argue that the rules have not been vigorously enforced. In any case, few firms seized the opportunity to start emissions trading. Then came Title IV of the 1990 amendments to the CAA, initially permitting many of the nation's biggest fossil-fuel-burning electric utilities to create what could potentially be a huge market for emissions trading. Title IV also allows smaller utilities to join the "big dirties" (the most polluting industries) within a few additional years, thereby expanding the prospective marketplace in emissions. Title IV creates by far the most significant test of market-based regulation since the inception of the environmental era in 1970. Title IV's acceptance by influential spokespeople for mainstream environmentalism—albeit with fingers crossed—betrays a recognition that market-based reform is probably inevitable and perhaps overdue.

Cap and Trade: The Gamble on Sulfur Dioxide Emissions Trading.

The most innovative provision of the 1990 amendments to the CAA is the emissions trading scheme created by Title IV. These provisions, some-times called the Acid Rain Program, aim specifically at emissions of sulfur oxides associated with human health risks, environmental degradation, and especially acid precipitation. The regulatory approach, known as cap and trade, is intended to reduce by the year 2010 the nation's total emis-sions of sulfur dioxide to 8.5 million tons below the level of 1980 emis-sions. To accomplish this overall goal, a mandatory cap is established on the total sulfur dioxide emissions annually from the nation's utilities. The program is implemented in two phases.

Phase I began in 1995 and regulated 110 of the nation's electric utili-ties with the largest sulfur dioxide emissions, primarily coal-burning facilities, and 182 smaller units, all in the East and Midwest.

- A mandatory cap is set on the total sulfur dioxide emissions permit-ted annually from these sources.
- Each source is granted by the EPA an annual allowance—each allowance equals 1 ton of sulfur dioxide emissions—based on its current emission levels and the overall emission cap.
- At the end of each year, each source must have allowances equal to its emissions for that year.
- Each utility is permitted to bank, sell, or carry over to the following year any emission allowances in excess of its actual emissions.
- Each utility must carefully measure and report its annual emissions and submit to an annual EPA emission audit.
- Each utility is free to select whatever method it chooses to control its emissions and to meet its annual emission cap.

Phase II began in 2000 and regulated electric utilities and other sources of sulfur dioxide emissions nationally. Altogether, more than two thou-sand units were affected by this phase by the beginning of 2001. All units are regulated in the same manner as in Phase I.

The early results of cap and trade were keenly scrutinized. The critical tests: Would a market in tradable emission permits develop among the regulated utilities, and would it produce the economic and environmental benefits predicted by its proponents?

By early 1994 the Chicago Board of Trade had created a national emis-sions trading market for Title IV, and modest trading had occurred there, and in California (which has its own version of emissions trading), between some utilities. Several important issues were evident immedi-ately. First, environmental groups in the Northeast expressed a concern that midwestern utilities would purchase permits from other areas and stockpile them, thus permitting themselves to continue emissions at unac-ceptably high levels. Proponents of Title IV, however, believe that other utilities will not have enough emission permits to sell to the advantage of the midwestern facilities. A second concern among environmentalists is that some of the big dirties will abandon their plans to replace existing plants with new, less polluting facilities and will, instead, stockpile emission permits for older, dirtier facilities. Midwestern utilities and their supporters, in contrast, have been concerned that the emission limits will inhibit economic growth in the economically depressed Ohio River Valley and adjacent areas. Utilities elsewhere have been concerned also with the effect of emission levels on economic growth. Most utilities remain apprehensive about the impact of the new scheme on their own market share and economic future.

Most economists believe it is too early for confident judgments about the impact of emissions trading, but early evidence suggests what the EPA has called "impressive environmental and economic results." During the first four years of Phase I, "power plants reduced their sulfur dioxide emissions far below the level that was legally allowable under all the provisions of the program," the EPA concluded.

> Furthermore, in response to the economic dynamics created ... these plants released substantially less pollution relative to the more stringent level of "base" allowable emissions established by Congress. At the same time, the [sulfur dioxide] emissions trading market has done what markets do best: drive down costs.[47]

Other studies have indicated that the pollution control costs experienced by the electric utilities were substantially less than had been anticipated at the outset of the program.[48] These economic benefits have also been associated with substantial reductions in ambient sulfur dioxide originating from utility emissions.[49] Economist Robert N. Stavins, an expert on emissions trading and Title IV, believes there have been other, less tangible but equally important benefits as well. The Title IV experience has demonstrated to both sides of the debate that emissions trading can be implemented without a multitude of lawsuits, argues Stavins, and proves as well that the system can be administered with relative simplicity. Stavins suggests that environmentalists should take the credit for a valuable lesson learned from experience with Title IV.[50]

Moreover, the big dirties did not buy up additional permits to increase their allowable sulfur dioxide emissions, as many environmentalists had feared would happen. "While in their youth," write economic historians Hugh Gorman and Barry D. Solomon about emissions trading programs, they are "now a legitimate policy tool, and a regulatory infrastructure and culture is emerging that allows regulators to use this tool."[51]

But important questions remain. Many of the largest utilities have yet to initiate major plant expansions long planned for the future. Once expansion begins, will they begin to buy additional permits to increase their allowable emissions, as critics have predicted? As Phase II begins, thousands of additional emission sources of all kinds will become regulated. Will the system work as well in this very different emissions market? Will regulated utilities and other sulfur dioxide emission sources find permit trading as attractive if they must also bear additional costs from anticipated new controls on other air emissions, such as nitrogen oxides? Many economists and other experts on emissions trading have also warned against using the limited experience with Title IV as a justification for prescribing a similar approach to controlling global greenhouse gases. Although Congress may be tempted to take this one-size-fits-all approach to controlling air pollution emissions internationally, most experts feel much more domestic experience with emissions trading is still necessary.

Conclusion

To most Americans, the nation's environmental troubles are epitomized by polluted air, fouled water, dangerously unregulated hazardous and toxic wastes, and a multitude of other ecological derangements. This chapter illuminates a less obvious dimension of the environmental crisis that is equally dangerous in its ecological implications—the economic problems in implementing environmental policy effectively. In many critical respects, the institutions and policies the nation now depends on to reverse its ecological degradation are failing, sometimes badly. Equally as imperative as new technological solutions to ecological ills are new economic and institutional solutions. Finding these solutions will require critical difficult debate within the environmental movement and among public policymakers at all governmental levels concerned with ecological restoration.

These problems are especially refractory because they often originate in the fundamental constitutional design of the political system or in deeply rooted political traditions. Among these is a historical dependence on traditional policy approaches to environmental problems, particularly the command-and-control method of regulation and the single-media approach to controlling specific pollutants. Although other approaches often seem more appropriate, and in some cases have been tried experimentally, they are strongly resisted by a multitude of institutional, professional, and economic interests with a stake in the status quo. Often the environmental movement itself has been excessively conservative in resisting policy innovation.

Among the significant economic problems arising from environmental regulation, none is debated more often than the high cost of environmental regulation. As costs continually rise well above expectations, the need to find cost-effective, cost-saving approaches to policymaking grows more apparent. Although BCA is sometimes a useful strategy for reducing regulatory costs, its serious political and economic deficiencies suggest that other approaches, involving more economic incentives for pollution abatement in the private sector, are likely to be more broadly effective. None of the problems now associated with regulatory incapacity is likely to be solved easily or quickly.

Suggested Readings

Ackerman, Frank, and Lisa Heinzerling. *Priceless: On Knowing the Price of Everything and the Value of Nothing.* New York: The New Press, 2004.

Harrington, Winston, Richard D. Morgenstern, and Thomas Sterner, eds. *Choosing Environmental Policy: Comparing Instruments and Outcomes in the United States and Europe.* Washington, D.C.: Resources for the Future, 2004.

Heal, Geoffrey. *Nature and the Marketplace: Capturing the Value of Ecosystem Services.* Washington, D.C.: Island Press, 2001.

Portney, Paul R., and Robert N. Stavins, eds. *Public Policies for Environmental Protection.* 2nd ed. Washington, D.C.: Resources for the Future, 2000.

Revesz, Richard, and Paul Livermore. *Retaking Rationality: How Cost Benefit Analysis Can Better Protect the Environment and Our Health.* New York: Cambridge University Press, 2008.

Tietenberg, Tom, and Lynne Lewis. *Environmental Economics and Policy.* 6th ed. Upper Saddle River, N.J.: Prentice-Hall, 2009.

Notes

1. U.S. Environmental Protection Agency (EPA), National Center for Environmental Economics, "Environmental Protection: Is It Bad for the Economy?" February 13, 2001, available at: www.epa.gov/economics.

2. EPA, Office of Policy and Office of Air and Radiation, "The Benefits and Costs of the Clean Air Act, 1990 to 2010: EPA Report to Congress," Report no. EPA-410-R-99-01, Washington, D.C., November 1999.

3. The arguments for considering costs in environmental regulation are usefully summarized in Allen V. Kneese and Charles L. Schultze, *Pollution, Prices and Public Policy* (Washington, D.C.: Brookings Institution Press, 1975). See also A. Myrick Freeman III, "Economics, Incentives, and Environmental Regulation," in *Environmental Policy in the 1990s,* 2nd ed., ed. Norman J. Vig and Michael E. Kraft (Washington, D.C.: CQ Press, 1997), 189–208.

4. On the history of BCA, see Richard A. Liroff, "Cost-Benefit Analysis in Federal Environmental Programs," in *Cost-Benefit Analysis and Environmental Regulations: Politics, Ethics, and Methods,* ed. Daniel Swartzman, Richard A. Liroff, and Kevin G. Croke (Washington, D.C.: Conservation Foundation, 1982), 35–52; Richard N. L. Andrews, "Cost-Benefit Analysis as Regulatory Reform," in *Cost-Benefit Analysis and Environmental Regulations: Politics, Ethics, and Methods,* ed. Daniel Swartzman, Richard A. Liroff, and Kevin G. Croke (Washington, D.C.: Conservation Foundation, 1982), 107–136; Norman J. Vig, "Presidential Leadership and the Environment: From Reagan to Clinton," in *Environmental Policy in the 1990s,* 2nd ed., ed. Norman J. Vig and Michael E. Kraft (Washington, D.C.: CQ Press, 1997), 98–118.

5. For a summary of the issues involved, see Walter A. Rosenbaum, "Regulation at Risk: The Controversial Politics and Science of Comparative Risk Assessment," in *Flashpoints in Environmental Policymaking: Controversies in Achieving Sustainability,* ed. Sheldon Kamieniecki, George A. Gonzalez, and Robert O. Vos (Albany: SUNY Press, 1997), 31–62.

6. Cass Sunstein, "Cost-Benefit Default Principles," AEI-Brookings Joint Center Working Paper no. 00-07/University of Chicago, Law and Economics Working Paper no. 104, Washington, D.C., October 2000, 5, available at: http://papers.ssrn.com/sol3/papers .cfm?abstract_id=247884 (accessed April 23, 2010); see also John D. Graham, Paul R. Noe, and Elizabeth L. Branch, "Managing the Regulatory State: The Experience of the Bush Administration," *Fordham Urban Law Journal* 33 (May 1, 2006): 953–1001.

7. Curtis W. Copeland, "Changes to the OMB Regulatory Review Process by Executive Order 13422," *CRS Report to Congress, February 5, 2007* (Washington, D.C.: Congressional Research Service).

8. Ibid., 10–14.

9. Quoted in ibid., 10.

10. Raymond J. Kopp, Alan J. Krupnick, and Michael A. Toman, "Cost-Benefit Analysis and Regulatory Reform: An Assessment of the Science and Art," Discussion Paper no. 97-19, Resources for the Future, Washington, D.C., 1997, 14.

11. Ibid.

12. Freeman, "Economics, Incentives, and Environmental Regulation," 150, 153.

13. Ibid.

14. Paul Johnson, "The Perils of Risk Avoidance," *Regulation* (May–June 1980): 17.

15. Brian Hansen, "New Soot Rules to Cost Power Sector $400 Million Annually, EPA Reckons," *Inside Energy,* October 16, 2006, 6.

16. Kopp, Krupnick, and Toman, "Cost-Benefit Analysis and Regulatory Reform."

17. Ibid.

18. Stephen Kelman, "Cost-Benefit Analysis: An Ethical Critique," *Regulation* (January–February 1981): 39.

19. U.S. General Accounting Office (GAO), "Cost-Benefit Analysis Can Be Useful in Assessing Regulations, Despite Limitations," Report no. GAO/RCED 84-62, Washington, D.C., April 1984, iii.

20. E&E News PM, "RFF's Morgenstern Discusses Cost-Benefit Analysis Reform," E&ETV's OnPoint Vol. 10 No. 9, April 2, 2009, available at: www.eenews.net/tv/tran script/969.

21. Ibid.

22. On the history of the OMB's use of BCA under the Reagan administration, see W. Norton Grubb, Dale Whittington, and Michael Humphries, "The Ambiguities of Cost-Benefit Analysis: An Evaluation of Regulatory Impact Analysis under Executive Order 12,291," in *Environmental Policy under Reagan's Executive Order,* ed. V. Kerry Smith (Chapel Hill: University of North Carolina Press, 1984), 121–166; GAO, "Cost-Benefit Analysis Can Be Useful," 7; Edward Paul Fuchs, *Presidents, Managers, and Regulation* (Englewood Cliffs, N.J.: Prentice-Hall, 1988), esp. 124; Joseph Cooper and William F. West, "Presidential Power and Republican Government: The Theory and Practice of OMB Review," *Journal of Politics* 50 (November 1988): 864–895.

23. Charles W. Schmidt, "Subjective Science: Environmental Cost-Benefit Analysis," *Environmental Health Perspectives* (August 2003): A530.

24. GAO, "Much Work Remains to Accelerate Facility Cleanups," Report no. GAO/RCED 93-15, Washington, D.C., January 1993, 17.

25. GAO, "Improving EPA's Regulatory Impact Analyses," Report no. GAO/RCED 97-38, Washington, D.C., 1997, 2.

26. Traci Watson, "Clean Air: EPA Report Hails Law as Success," *USA Today,* October 21, 1997.
27. The Corps is not required to use an RIA, but it must still produce a BCA for proposed projects.
28. Michael Grunwald, "An Agency of Unchecked Clout: Water Projects Roll Past Economics, Environmental Concerns," *Washington Post,* September 10, 2000, available at: www.washingtonpost.com/wp-dyn/content/article/2006/05/12/AR200605120 1550.html (accessed April 23, 2010).
29. GAO, "Corps of Engineers: Observations on Planning and Project Management Processes for the Civil Works Program," Report no. GAO 06-529T, Washington, D.C., March 15, 2006, 1.
30. Quoted in Gerard Shields, "Congress and the Corps—Politics, Provincialism, Sometimes Interfere with Priorities, Plans," (Baton Rouge) *Advocate,* November 9, 2008, A01
31. See, for example, the comprehensive report National Academy of Public Administration, "Background: Adapting to Changing Missions and Demands," *Prioritizing America's Water Resources: Budget Reform for Civil Works Construction Projects at the U.S. Army Corps of Engineers* (Washington, D.C.: National Academy of Public Administration, 2007), Chap. 2.
32. Robert W. Hahn, Jason K. Burnett, and Yee-Ho I. Chan, "Assessing the Quality of Regulatory Impact Analyses," Working Paper no. 001, AEI–Brookings Joint Center for Regulatory Studies, Washington, D.C., January 2000, executive summary. For similar conclusions, see also Winston Harrington, Richard D. Morgenstern, and Peter Nelson, "On the Accuracy of Regulatory Cost Estimates," Working Paper no. 99-18, Resources for the Future, Washington, D.C., January 1999.
33. John C. Whitaker, "Earth Day Recollections: What It Was Like When the Movement Took Off," *EPA Journal* 14 (July–August 1988): 11.
34. Roefie Hueting, "Correcting National Income for Environmental Losses: A Practical Solution for a Theoretical Dilemma," in *A Survey of Ecological Economics,* ed. Rajaram Krishnan, Jonathan M. Harris, and Neva R. Goodwin (Washington, D.C.: Island Press, 1995), 248.
35. Kopp, Krupnick, and Toman, "Cost-Benefit Analysis and Regulatory Reform," 30.
36. *New York Times,* September 6, 1993.
37. Ibid.
38. Winston Harrington, Richard D. Morgenstern, and Thomas Sterner, eds., "Overview," in *Choosing Environmental Policy: Comparing Instruments and Outcomes in the United States and Europe* (Washington, D.C.: Resouces for the Future, 2004), 1–22; National Academy of Public Administration, *The Environment Goes to Market* (Washington, D.C.: National Academy of Public Administration, 1994), Chap. 1; Paul R. Portney, ed., *Current Issues in U.S. Environmental Policy* (Baltimore: Johns Hopkins University Press, 1978), esp. Chap. 1; Erica L. Dolgin and Thomas G. P. Guilbert, eds., *Federal Environmental Law* (St. Paul, Minn.: West Publishing, 1974), esp. the articles by Robert Zener, "The Federal Law of Water Pollution Control," 682–791, and Thomas Jorling, "The Federal Law of Air Pollution Control," 1058–1148.
39. On the problem generally, see Kneese and Schulze, *Pollution, Prices, and Public Policy,* Chap. 2.
40. Ibid., 116.
41. *National Journal,* May 30, 1981, 971–973.
42. Ibid.
43. National Academy of Public Administration, *Environment Goes to Market,* 12.
44. Ibid.
45. Robert W. Hahn and Gordon L. Hester, "EPA's Market for Bads," *Regulation* (December 1987): 48–53.

46. Ibid.
47. EPA, Office of Air and Radiation, "Progress Report on the EPA Acid Rain Program," Report no. EPA-430-R-99-011, Washington, D.C., November 1999. See also EPA, Office of Policy, Economics and Innovation, Office of the Administrator, "The United States Experience with Economic Incentives for Protecting the Environment," Report no. EPA-240-R-01-001, Washington, D.C., January 2001.
48. Ibid.
49. Douglas R. Bohi and Dallas Burtraw, "SO$_2$ Allowance Trading: How Experience and Expectations Measure Up," Discussion Paper 97-24, Resources for the Future, Washington, D.C., February 1997.
50. Robert N. Stavins, "What Can We Learn from the Grand Policy Experiment? Positive and Normative Lessons from SO$_2$ Allowance Trading," *Journal of Economic Perspectives* 12 (1998): 69–88.
51. Hugh Gorman and Barry D. Solomon, "The Origins and Practice of Emissions Trading," *Journal of Policy History* (September 2000): 315.

Chapter 6

Command and Control in Action
Air and Water Pollution Regulation

In environmental history, the twentieth century qualifies as a peculiar century because of the screeching acceleration of so many of the processes that bring ecological change.

—J. R. McNeill,
Something New under the Sun:
An Environmental History of the Twentieth Century (2001)

Clean air and clean water are powerful public images. Leaders of the environmental movement regard the Clean Air Act (CAA) of 1970 and the Federal Water Pollution Control Act Amendments (FWPCAA) of 1972 as the foundations of the environmental era. Public opinion polls show that Americans universally recognize the nation's degraded air and waters as major ecological problems. This means that clean air and water have acquired political chic. Politicians so routinely assure constituents of their unceasing regard for clean air and clean water that both have become clichés instead of realities.

After four decades of sustained effort by government and the private sector to eliminate air and water pollution, with a cumulative public expenditure since 2000 of $80 billion and an additional $27 billion spent annually by industry, the nation's air and water remain seriously polluted.[1] Some dramatic achievements, many lesser but impressive gains, and a multitude of marginal improvements make up the veneer that brightens reports about implementation of the CAA and the FWPCAA with cosmetic success. But air and water quality remain seriously degraded throughout much of the United States. By 2009, the EPA estimated that more than 158.5 million Americans, mostly urbanites, lived in counties where pollution levels exceed at least one national air-quality standard.[2] The water quality in almost two-thirds of the nation's river miles has never been

195

assessed because of deficient state monitoring resources.[3] The water quality in approximately one-third of the nation's surveyed lakes, estuaries, and streams is still considered by the EPA to be significantly impaired.[4]

Why aren't there truly impressive results from so massive a national investment? Many difficulties arise from inexperience in implementing wholly new regulatory programs. To many observers (as noted in the discussion of market approaches to regulation in Chapter 5), the problem is the policy itself, the command-and-control logic so firmly embedded in the two earliest, and most important, national pollution laws of the first environmental era. Other difficulties result from new or unexpected scientific discoveries that complicate pollution control. But all these difficulties are compounded by a failure of political will: a reluctance to invest the enormous resources and make the politically difficult decisions needed to deal effectively with air and water pollution on a national scale. These and other significant influences shaping current air and water pollution regulation will become apparent as this chapter examines the implementation of the CAA and the FWPCAA since the 1980s.

The Political Anatomy of Command-and-Control Regulation

The language and logic of command-and-control regulation is politically innocent. Formally, as observed in Chapter 5, environmental regulators are supposed to follow a legislatively prescribed pathway to pollution control by now built into virtually every federal environmental law: (1) regulate toward the *goals* identified by Congress, (2) identify the *criteria* for setting pollution standards, (3) set the *quality standards* for each regulated pollutant, (4) create the *emission standards* for regulated pollutants, and (5) see to *enforcement* of quality and emission standards. In reality, each command-and-control element is a distinctive decision-making arena rich with political implications—often unintended—lurking behind the statutory language and shaping the impact of regulation as much as the formal language of the law.

The technicality of pollution regulation, however, frequently creates a language and style of action that conceals, sometimes deliberately, the extent to which these political forces are operating behind the façade of prescribed regulatory procedures. Nonetheless, regulation is fundamentally a political enterprise. A number of characteristic political processes and issues arise regardless of the specific pollution program involved. Basically, political pressure and conflict flow to wherever administrative discretion exists in the regulatory process. Such administrative discretion ordinarily is found at several characteristic points in pollution regulation:

- *When words, phrases, or policy objectives are unclear.* Congress may deliberately shift responsibility to administrators for settling disputes between interests that are in conflict over how a law should be phrased. Tossing this political hot potato to administrators ensures that partisans on all sides of an issue with something to gain or lose by the law's interpretation will scramble to influence whatever officials or bureaucracies resolve such obscurities. Sometimes this lack of legislative clarity results less from deliberation than from congressional confusion or ignorance. In any case, regulators usually find themselves caught between competing group pressures to interpret statutes or regulations in different ways. Such pressures, in fact, should be considered routine in the regulatory process.
- *When technical standards must be created or revised.* Existing legislation regulating air pollution, water pollution, and hazardous substances ordinarily requires the EPA to define the standards and prescribe the appropriate control technologies necessary to meet mandated standards. Often regulatory agencies also are required by such legislation to review periodically and, if appropriate, revise such standards or technology requirements. Legitimate disagreement often exists (as noted in Chapter 5) over the technical and economic justifications for most regulatory standards. In the presence of expert dissension about such issues, a large measure of discretion rests with regulatory agencies for resolving such disputes. This discretion, and the conflict it invites, will reappear whenever agencies review regulatory standards. In fact, virtually all major technical determinations by regulatory agencies are politicized by the activity of pressure groups, Congress, competing governmental agencies, and other interests seeking to shape discretionary decisions to their respective advantage.
- *When compliance deadlines are flexible.* Pollution legislation may bristle with explicit compliance deadlines, but administrators almost always have authority to extend them. Legislation is particularly generous in granting administrators authority to extend compliance deadlines when, in their opinion, economic hardship or other inequities may result from strict enforcement. Thus, the CAA instructs the EPA to set emission standards for new air pollution sources by considering, among other things, "the degree of emission limitation achievable through the application of the best system of emission reduction which (taking into account the cost of achieving such reduction) the administrator determines has been adequately demonstrated." Such a fistful of discretionary authority in effect permits the EPA to extend compliance deadlines for specific air pollution sources by increasing the time allowed to search

for pollution controls meeting these multiple criteria. In many cases a compliance deadline also may be relaxed if an agency determines that it is beyond the technical ability of a polluter to install the proper controls in the required time. Agencies sometimes can achieve a backdoor extension of compliance deadlines by deliberately delaying the establishment of a standard long enough to permit the regulated interests to make adjustments to the anticipated standard.

Beyond Public View

The implementation of most environmental regulatory programs does not routinely involve the public, or public opinion, in the process. Unlike the White House and Congress, the federal bureaucracy is neither highly visible nor readily understood by the public; regulation operates, in the words of political scientist Francis E. Rourke, behind an "opaque exterior"[5] that the public seldom cares to penetrate. This dearth of dependable public interest means that the constellation of political forces and actors involved in regulatory politics ordinarily is confined to organized interests, governmental officials, scientists, technicians, and other insiders. Given the complexity and technicality of environmental issues, this situation is not surprising. But it emphasizes the extent to which regulatory politics tends to involve a process that is highly specialized and commonly closed to public involvement.

When Enforcement Is Discretionary

Few provisions in current pollution legislation compel federal officials to stop a polluting activity. Most often enforcement actions are discretionary, as in Section 111 of the CAA, which instructs the EPA administrator to regulate any pollutant from a stationary source when, in the judgment of the administrator, it may cause or contribute to "air pollution which may reasonably be anticipated to endanger public health or welfare." Even when enforcement action is initiated, officials are usually given optional methods for securing compliance.

Typically, air and water pollution laws are enforced through state or local agencies with considerable discretion to decide what level of emission controls will be required of an air or water polluter and when emission controls must be achieved. These become conditions for the permit that all air- and water-polluting firms must obtain from state, federal, and local authorities to operate. In air pollution regulation, for instance, this discretion can arise from the regulator's authority under the CAA to decide which emission controls are technically and economically feasible and to issue variances that temporarily waive emissions-control deadlines or technology specifications.[6] Regulators seek voluntary compliance.

They want to avoid imposing penalties as a means of ensuring compliance if possible because they know that resorting to administrative or judicial tribunals very likely will involve a protracted inflexible process with no assurances that the polluter will be compelled to control emissions speedily and efficiently at the conclusion. In fact, polluters often provoke such action, hoping to avoid emission controls indefinitely by exploiting the complexities of the administrative or judicial procedures involved.

Regulated firms often balk at a regulatory agency's initial specification of acceptable control technologies and deadline dates for compliance with emission standards. The usual solution is bargaining between regulator and regulated, particularly when regulatory agencies confront an economically and politically influential firm or group of firms that is capable of creating political pressures on the regulatory agency to reach some accommodation over required control technologies or compliance deadlines. Regulatory agencies typically will make some concession to firms concerning the required control technologies or compliance deadlines. One form of these concessions is the frequently used variance that allows a firm some delay in achieving emission controls that are otherwise required under the law. A firm often is able to negotiate a variance permitting it to discharge on an interim basis at its existing emission levels and to obtain several additional variances that can delay significantly the achievement of required emission controls.

Agencies also depend heavily on firms to monitor and report their own pollution emissions, in part because of the sheer volume of regulated entities. Under the CAA, for instance, more than 3,400 major sources and 45,600 minor sources of wastewater discharge must be controlled. The 1990 amendments to the CAA increased the regulated sources to more than 35,000 major and 350,000 minor facilities.[7]

Most regulatory agencies still lack the personnel and other resources to inspect routinely and monitor all emission controls within their jurisdictions. Voluntary compliance is almost a necessity in regulation. Quite often, regulatory agencies monitor only the larger sources of pollution emissions within their jurisdiction, leaving smaller sources to report their own compliance with permit conditions under all but exceptional circumstances. Even monitoring the largest pollution sources does not necessarily ensure that air or water pollutants are satisfactorily regulated. For example, in 2009 the EPA reported that although it was able to assure that most dischargers of large volume water pollutants complied with their discharge permits, the compliance of numerous smaller volume polluters could not be assured because the agency's resources supporting the oversight of compliance and enforcement with the Clean Water Act had progressively diminished since the early 2000s.[8] The EPA has encountered similar problems when monitoring compliance with the CAA's stationary source emission permits. Confronted with a daunting challenge compounded with relentlessly multiplying regulatory responsibilities and insufficient resources, and burdened by episodic White House antipathy, the EPA's efforts to enforce its regulatory duties has been a constant struggle.[9]

Although administrative discretion, limited resources, and political pressure clearly limit the vigor and strictness in enforcement of environmental regulations, these constraints can sometimes be inevitable, even prudent. Often the use of administrative discretion to "make a deal" over pollution allows a regulatory agency to achieve more pollution abatement than would be the case if it insisted on extremely stringent emission standards in full and immediate compliance with the law. This is true particularly when the regulated firm either is unable to comply fully and immediately with a strict interpretation of the law or is willing to fight indefinitely in the courts or administrative hearing rooms to prevent any regulation. Many regulatory agencies, limited by staff and funding that are inadequate for their mandated responsibilities, have no practical alternative to relying on voluntary compliance and accommodation. Finally, regulatory agencies often confront regulated interests—including other governmental agencies subject to pollution control—that are too politically or economically powerful to be compelled to comply fully and immediately with the law. Although this should be no excuse for exemption from full compliance with environmental regulation, it is often an immutable political reality with which regulatory agencies must make peace. In such circumstances, agencies may logically conclude that it is better to bargain with the regulated interests in the hope of achieving some limited goals than to adopt what may well become an ultimately futile strategy of insisting on stringent compliance with the law in spite of massive resistance from the polluter.

Discretion in the enforcement of pollution regulation, however inevitable, also means that this discretion at times will be abused. Discretion sometimes leads agencies to yield needlessly and negligently to political pressures that prevent enforcement of essential pollution controls. It is unfortunate that these are among the unavoidable risks inherent in the exercise of discretionary authority, without which environmental administration would be impossible.

Regulating Air Quality

Since Earth Day 1970, the federal government has continually monitored a variety of environmental indicators and has published current assessments of environmental quality using these indicators. These data provide a useful baseline for observing changes in national environmental quality since the major federal environmental programs began in the early 1970s. They are also an essential standard for judging the impact of the CAA and other federal legislation. The CAA, together with its important 1977 and 1990 amendments, constitutes one of the longest, most complex, and most technically detailed federal regulatory programs ever enacted. The CAA creates a standards-and-enforcement program in which the federal government establishes national ambient air-quality standards for major pollutants, the states and local government agencies assume primary responsibility for implementing the program within federal guidelines, and the various levels of government share enforcement responsibilities. However, the states may enact more stringent standards for airsheds in their jurisdictions.

Overall, national air quality has undoubtedly improved—in a few instances, dramatically—since the CAA's enactment in 1970. By 2006, the EPA was regulating more than two hundred air pollutants—most of them toxic air pollutants identified by Congress in 1990. However, the most important of these pollutants in terms of public health and political significance are the so-called criteria pollutants—carbon monoxide, nitrogen oxides, ozone, particulate matter, sulfur dioxide, and lead—whose regulation was mandated in 1970 by the original CAA and whose health effects are summarized in Box 6-1. After 2006, the EPA regulated only so-called small particulates (those smaller than 2.5 microns, $PM_{2.5}$). As Table 6-1 illustrates, the improvement in both air quality and pollution emissions associated with these six pollutants between 1980 and 2008 has been in most cases significant and, in the case of lead, dramatic. Airborne lead, which is especially hazardous to children, has been virtually eliminated through the abolition of leaded automobile fuels. Since 1980, sulfur dioxide emissions decreased by more than 63 percent and carbon monoxide emissions by almost 70 percent. America's urban environment has improved significantly. The data understate the significance of these achievements because they do not estimate what pollution emissions would have been in the absence of regulation, during a period (1970–2008) when the U.S. population increased by 42 percent and vehicle miles traveled increased by 178 percent. Improvements in air quality have been especially significant since the mid-1980s when the cumulative effect of earlier regulation began to appear. Additional improvement is predicted as new regulatory programs are implemented. For example:

- New EPA diesel regulations for trucks are expected to remove 90 percent of the soot from present diesel motor emissions.
- The new EPA 2006 Clean Air Mercury Rule is expected to significantly reduce mercury emissions from coal-fired power plants—the largest remaining sources of mercury emissions in the country—from 48 to 15 tons per year, a reduction of nearly 70 percent.

Box 6–1 *Human Health and Environmental Effects of Common Air Pollutants*

Ozone (ground-level ozone is the principal component of smog)
- *Source.* Ozone is produced by a chemical reaction involving volatile organic compounds (VOCs) and nitrogen oxides.
- *Health effects.* Ozone causes breathing problems, reduced lung function, asthma, irritated eyes, stuffy nose, and reduced resistance to colds and other infections and may speed up aging of lung tissue.
- *Environmental effects.* Ozone can damage plants and trees; smog can cause reduced visibility.
- *Property damage.* Ozone damages rubber, fabrics, and other materials.

Volatile organic compounds (smog-formers)[a]
- *Source.* VOCs are released from burning fuel (for example, gasoline, oil, wood, coal, and natural gas) and from solvents, paints, glues, and other products used at work or at home. Cars are a common source of VOCs. VOCs include chemicals such as benzene, toluene, methylene chloride, and methyl chloroform.
- *Health effects.* In addition to ozone (smog) effects, many VOCs can cause serious health problems such as cancer.
- *Environmental effects.* In addition to ozone (smog) effects, some VOCs such as formaldehyde and ethylene may harm plants.

Nitrogen dioxide (one of the nitrogen oxides; smog-forming chemical)
- *Source.* Nitrogen dioxide is produced in the burning of gasoline, natural gas, coal, oil, and other fuels. Cars are a common source of nitrogen dioxide.
- *Health effects.* Nitrogen dioxide causes lung damage and illnesses of the breathing passages and lungs (the respiratory system).
- *Environmental effects.* Nitrogen dioxide is an ingredient of acid rain (acid aerosols), which can damage trees and lakes. Acid aerosols reduce visibility.
- *Property damage.* Acid aerosols can eat away stone used in buildings, statues, and monuments.

Carbon monoxide
- *Source.* Carbon monoxide is produced in the burning of gasoline, natural gas, coal, oil, and other fuels.
- *Health effects.* Carbon monoxide reduces the ability of blood to bring oxygen to body cells and tissues; the cells and tissues need oxygen to work. Carbon monoxide may be particularly hazardous to people who have heart or circulatory (blood vessel) problems and to people who have damaged lungs or breathing passages.

Particulate matter (dust, smoke, soot)
- *Source.* Particulate matter is produced in the burning of wood, diesel, and other fuels; by industrial plants; through agriculture (for example, plowing and burning off fields); and from driving on unpaved roads.

---

[a] All VOCs contain carbon, the basic chemical element found in living things. Carbon-containing chemicals are called organic. Volatile chemicals escape into the air easily. Many VOCs are also hazardous air pollutants, which can cause serious illnesses. The EPA does not list VOCs as criteria air pollutants, but they are included here because efforts to control smog also target VOCs for reduction.

(continued)

Box 6–1   *(cont.)*

- *Health effects.* Particulate matter causes nose and throat irritation, lung damage, bronchitis, and early death.
- *Environmental effects.* Particulate matter is the main source of haze that reduces visibility.
- *Property damage.* Ash, soot, smoke, and dust can dirty and discolor structures and other property, including clothes and furniture.

Sulfur dioxide
- *Source.* Sulfur dioxide is produced in the burning of coal and oil (especially high-sulfur coal from the eastern United States), and through industrial processes (for example, those involving paper and metal).
- *Health effects.* Sulfur dioxide causes breathing problems and may cause permanent damage to lungs.
- *Environmental effects.* Sulfur dioxide is an ingredient in acid rain (acid aerosols), which can damage trees and lakes. Acid aerosols reduce visibility.
- *Property damage.* Acid aerosols can eat away stone used in buildings, statues, and monuments.

Lead
- *Source.* Lead is found in leaded gasoline (being phased out), paint (used, for example, on houses and cars), and smelters (metal refineries); it is used in the manufacture of lead storage batteries.
- *Health effects.* Lead causes brain and other nervous system damage; children are especially at risk. Some lead-containing chemicals cause cancer in animals. Lead causes digestive and other health problems.
- *Environmental effects.* Lead can harm wildlife.

Source: Adapted from Environmental Protection Agency, Office of Air Quality Planning and Standards, *The Plain English Guide to the Clean Air Act,* available at: www.epa.gov/oar/oaqps/pcg_caa/pegcaa11 .html (accessed March 6, 2001).

Despite this improvement, the nation's air remains seriously degraded in several respects. First, ground-level ozone, a primary component of urban smog, remains a pervasive problem. This low-level ozone poses significant human health risks and produces more than $1 billion in agricultural crop damage annually. Currently, more than 144 million Americans, mostly urbanites, live in areas that are not in compliance with the ozone standard. Second, emissions of nitrogen oxides, a precursor of acid precipitation and a greenhouse gas contributing to urban smog, have increased since 1970. Third, U.S. releases of greenhouse gases, especially carbon dioxide (CO_2), is predicted to increase by more than 42 percent between 2000 and 2020 under present U.S. air quality policies—a surge in climate-warming emissions that is considered highly undesirable by most climate scientists, unacceptable by environmentalists, and threatening internationally (as discussed fully in Chapter 10).[10] In addition, the

Table 6-1 Changes in Air Quality, 1980–2008

	Percentage change in air quality	
	Change 1980–2008[a]	Change 1990–2008[a]
Carbon monoxide (CO)	−79	−68
Ozone (O_3) (8-hour)	−25	−14
Lead (Pb)	−92	−78
Nitrogen dioxide (NO_2)	−46	−35
PM_{10} (24-hour)	—	−31
$PM_{2.5}$ (annual)[b]	—	−19
$PM_{2.5}$ (24-hour)[b]	—	−20
Sulfur dioxide (SO_2)	−71	−59

	Percentage change in emissions	
	Change 1980–2008[c]	Change 1990–2008[c]
Carbon monoxide (CO)	−56	−46
Lead (Pb)	−99	−79
Nitrogen oxides (NO_x)	−40	−35
Volatile organic compounds (VOCs)	−47	−31
Direct PM_{10}	−68[d]	−39
Direct $PM_{2.5}$	—	−58
Sulfur dioxide (SO_2)	−56	−51

Source: U.S. Environmental Protection Agency, *Air Quality Trends,* available at: http://www.epa.gov/airtrends/aqtrends.html (accessed January 25, 2010).

Notes: "—" indicates trend data not available. PM = particulate matter.

[a]Negative numbers indicate improvements in air quality.
[b]$PM_{2.5}$ air quality based on data since 2000.
[c]Negative numbers indicate reductions in emissions.
[d]Direct PM_{10} emissions for 1980 are based on data since 1985.

control of small particulates, identified as an important public health problem in the early 1990s, has just begun. Fourth, air toxics have yet to be adequately regulated. The 1990 amendments to the CAA required the EPA to regulate 188 air toxics, including well-known health threats such as dioxins, benzene, arsenic, beryllium, mercury, and vinyl chloride. To date, the EPA has established emission standards for only ninety-nine of these pollutants.

Improved air quality, like other environmental gains in recent decades, is fragile and highly vulnerable to technological change, economic cycles, and other social impacts. A case in point is the rapidly growing consumer demand for light trucks, minivans, pickups, and other sports vehicles. The EPA estimates that light trucks will be the fastest growing source of greenhouse gases in the first decade of the twenty-first century, exceeding the combined emissions of all domestic industrial sources. Sport utility vehicles (SUVs), essentially a passenger vehicle mounted on a light truck platform, form the fastest growing segment of the domestic automotive market. But environmentally they have had little to recommend them. SUVs emit 30–70 percent more smog-producing pollutants than standard passenger cars. And they are much less fuel efficient. Nevertheless, consumers have loved them; Americans bought almost 2 million SUVs annually in recent years, accounting for almost 19 percent of annual passenger vehicle sales.[11]

Equally important, SUVs paralyze the political will. Federal officials, aware of the vehicles' popularity, have been loath to propose more stringent emission controls for this environmentally hazardous technology. Light truck regulation, especially, has become a "third rail" political issue. "Detroit is giving people what they want," noted one observer. "Americans—even ones who fancy themselves as environmentalists—have fallen in love with trucks."[12]

The Clean Air Act and the 1977 Amendments

In broad outline, the CAA, including the 1977 amendments, mandates the following programs:

1. *National air-quality standards.* The act directed the EPA to determine the maximum permissible ambient air concentrations for pollutants that it found to be harmful to human health or the environment. The EPA was instructed to establish such standards for at least seven pollutants: carbon monoxide, hydrocarbons, lead, nitrogen oxide, particulates, ozone, and sulfur oxides. The agency was to set two types of national ambient air-quality standards without considering the cost of compliance:
   a. *Primary standards.* Primary standards were supposed to protect human health with an adequate margin of safety for particularly vulnerable segments of the population, such as the elderly and infants. Originally, all air-quality control regions in the United States were required to meet primary standards by 1982; this deadline was extended several times and still remains unenforced.
   b. *Secondary standards.* Secondary standards were intended to maintain visibility and to protect buildings, crops, and water. The EPA is required by the 1977 amendments to the CAA to review all criteria for ambient air quality every five years after 1981.

2. *Stationary source regulations.* The EPA was to set maximum emission standards for new stationary sources, called new source performance standards. The following procedures were to be followed:

    a. Standards were to be set on an industry-by-industry basis; the states then were to enforce the standards.

    b. In setting new source performance standards, the EPA was required to take into account the costs, energy requirements, and environmental effects of its guidelines.

    c. For existing sources (those dischargers active at the time the act was passed), the EPA was to issue control-technique guidelines for the states' use.

3. *State implementation plans.* Each state was required to create a plan indicating how it would achieve federal standards and guidelines to implement the act fully by 1982. The state implementation plans, which the EPA was to approve no later than 1979, were to contain information relating to several important elements:

    a. The nation was divided into 247 air-quality control regions for which states were made responsible. The regions were classified as either attainment or nonattainment regions for each of the regulated pollutants.

    b. States were also made responsible for enforcing special air-quality standards in areas with especially clean air. These regions were called prevention of significant deterioration (PSD) regions.

    c. States were required to order existing factories in nonattainment areas to retrofit their plants with control technologies representing "reasonably available control technology." Companies wanting to expand or build new plants in nonattainment areas had to install control equipment that limited pollutants to the least amount emitted by any similar factory anywhere in the United States. This technology was to be specified by the states without regard to cost.

    d. New factories in nonattainment areas also were required to purchase offsets from existing air polluters.

    e. States in nonattainment areas were given until 1987 to meet carbon monoxide and ozone standards if the states required an annual automobile inspection and maintenance on catalytic converters on newer automobiles. In 1987, Congress extended the deadline for compliance in nonattainment areas to 1988.

    f. In PSD areas, all new stationary emission sources were required to install the best available control technology.

4. *Mobile source emission standards (for automobiles and trucks).*
Title II of the CAA created a detailed but flexible timetable for
achieving auto and truck emission controls.
   a. For autos there was to be a 90 percent reduction in hydrocarbon
   and carbon monoxide emissions by 1975 and a 90 percent
   reduction in nitrogen oxide emissions by 1976, when measured
   against 1970 emission levels.
   b. The administrator of the EPA was authorized to grant extensions
   of these deadlines for approximately one year. Considerable
   extensions were repeatedly granted by the EPA and others were
   authorized by Congress.
       i. In 1977, compliance deadlines for all emissions were extended
       for two more years, to be followed by stricter standards for
       hydrocarbons and carbon monoxide in 1980 and further
       tightening of the hydrocarbon standard in 1981, together with
       higher nitrogen oxide standards.
       ii. Beginning in 1982, Congress repeatedly waived compliance
       deadlines for auto emission controls until 1990. The Clean
       Air Act Amendments of 1990 set new, and greatly reduced,
       tailpipe standards for cars. Emission standards for hydro-
       carbons, carbon monoxide, and nitrogen oxides were greatly
       reduced, and all new cars were required to comply with the
       standards by 1996.

By 1990 the original CAA and its massive 1977 amendments apparently had achieved significant reductions in several ambient air pollutants,
particularly suspended large particulates, lead, and carbon monoxide, as
Table 6-1 indicates. With the exception of lead, however, reductions in
other pollutants still seemed unsatisfactorily slow, and urban air pollution—
especially concentrations of nitrogen oxide, ozone, and volatile organic
compounds—continued to be a major concern. After almost a decade of
bitter impasse, the White House, environmentalists, and Congress collaborated to rewrite comprehensively the 1970 legislation by passing the
Clean Air Act Amendments of 1990, the most important and imaginative
regulatory reform in more than a decade.

The Clean Air Act Amendments of 1990

The new amendments are a curious melange of hammer clauses, multi-
tudinous deadlines, and other tread-worn approaches combined with a
timely sensitivity to emerging problems and an aggressive new approach
to global climate protection based on an innovative market-inspired

scheme for emissions trading. This mix of tradition, invention, and desperation represents what may be the last, best hope for fortifying the original CAA sufficiently to achieve its purpose. The 1990 amendments added to the original act's two titles concerning acid precipitation and ozone protection and substantially amended most of the remaining provisions while keeping the basic command-and-control approach of the original legislation. The major features are outlined in the sections that follow.[13]

Title I: Nonattainment Areas. The amendments established a new classification of areas that failed to meet national air-quality standards for ozone, carbon monoxide, and particulates and created deadlines of from three to twenty years for attaining these standards. They also created a graded set of regulatory requirements for each area, depending on the severity of the pollution. An example of the new regulatory regime is the requirement that urban areas meet two regulatory standards depending on their degree of ozone and carbon monoxide pollution. Unlike the original act, which required only that cities make "reasonable further progress" in meeting air-quality standards, the new amendments set specific air-quality goals and deadlines.

Title II: Mobile Sources. The new amendments set more than ninety new emission standards for autos and trucks. The most important emission requirements were:

- Tailpipe emissions of hydrocarbons were to be reduced by 35 percent, and nitrogen oxides were to be reduced by 60 percent for all new cars by the 1996 model year.
- Beginning in 1998, all new cars were required to have pollution control devices with a ten-year, 100,000-mile warranty.
- Auto manufacturers were required to produce by 1996 a fleet of experimental cars available in southern California that met emission standards that were more stringent than the 1996 levels already required by the amendments.
- Petroleum companies were required to produce cleaner-burning fuel to be used in the most polluted areas by 1992 and in all areas with ozone problems by 1996.

Title III: Hazardous Air Pollutants. The amendments required the EPA to create national emission standards for hazardous air pollutants for all major sources of hazardous or toxic air pollutants and specified 189 chemicals to be regulated immediately. They established a multitude of specific deadlines by which the EPA was ordered to list categories of industrial processes that emit dangerous air pollutants, to establish health-based standards for each hazardous chemical emission, and to ensure that sources of hazardous emission have established safety controls at their facilities.

Title IV: Control of Acid Deposition. The amendments created a new emissions trading program for sulfur oxides, a major precursor of acid precipitation. Under this new approach, the EPA was "to allocate to each major coal-fired power plant an allowance for each ton of emission permitted; sources cannot release emissions beyond the number of allowances they are given. Allowances may be traded, bought, or sold among allowance holders.... The EPA [was] required to create an additional pool of allowances to permit construction of new sources or expansion of existing ones."[14] Title IV required that national sulfur oxide emissions be reduced by half by the year 2000—a reduction of 10 million tons annually from the 1980 levels. The 110 largest sulfur oxide sources in the utility industry were required to meet stricter emission standards. In addition, emissions of nitrogen oxides were to be reduced by 2 million tons annually, compared with 1980 levels, through more traditional regulatory methods.

Title VI: Stratospheric Ozone Protection. Title VI listed specific ozone-depleting chemicals and created a schedule for phasing out their production or use. It also pledged the United States to an accelerated phase-out of ozone-depleting chemicals that exceeded the schedule to which the United States had agreed in the 1987 Montreal Protocol on Substances That Deplete the Ozone Layer.

Current Controversies in Air Quality Regulation

The CAA is the nation's longest, most complex regulatory law. Its legal and technical intricacy seems to ensure employment for a generation of lawyers and judges unborn and unrelenting partisan debate about its wisdom and implications among politicians and economists. At the same time, it is among the most revolutionary and ambitious environmental laws in U.S. history, the foundation of U.S. environmental regulation. Thus the issues and their embedded controversies have profound implications for the future of the U.S. environment. One of these important matters (discussed in Chapter 5) is emissions trading. Other major issues involved with the CAA concern the impact of federalism, regulatory science, and partisan change in the presidency. Current controversies over urban smog, small particulate regulation, and controls for new air pollution sources illustrate these issues.

Combative Federalism: The Smog Wars. Regulating urban smog has been difficult because so many varied sources contribute to its creation. Large stationary sources, such as fossil-fuel-burning utilities, factories, mineral smelters, and chemical manufacturers, are major contributors. But thousands of small sources, most previously unregulated and many until recently unrecognized—including paint manufacturers, dry cleaners, and gasoline stations—collectively make a major contribution. The automobile stubbornly remains a chronic polluter despite the advent of efficient emission-control technologies. One reason is that pre-1970 vehicles, the worst auto polluters because they lack emission controls, are not being replaced as quickly as predicted. And at least one-fourth of the pollution-control devices on new cars are "disabled" (in the EPA's illusive phrase), that is, deliberately destroyed.[15] In addition, as noted earlier, the ever-growing fleet of new, highly polluting light trucks and other sports vehicles continues to capture a large proportion of the domestic new-vehicle market. Many state and local governments also have failed to enforce their own implementation plans, especially requirements for annual auto emission inspections, proposals to limit auto access to urban areas, and other arrangements annoying to the public and costly to businesses. Even the best available technologies may be insufficient to control adequately all important emissions. Emission controls now remove 96 percent of the pollutants emitted before controls were instituted in 1972.[16] Many experts believe existing auto emission controls have reached "the knife edge of technological feasibility" and that additional emission reductions are unlikely unless a great many states require motorists to switch from conventional to new, more expensive reformulated fuels or hybrid motor vehicles.

In a forceful, politically risky move to reduce urban air pollution further, the EPA in 1997 promulgated new ambient air-quality standards for ozone and particulates, two primary causes of smog, but it did so only after a ferocious political fight that laid bare the tensions between state and federal governments inherent in regulatory federalism. The EPA's review of these standards had been long overdue, according to the requirements of the CAA, and was compelled only through a lawsuit sponsored by the American Lung Association. The new standards, finally proposed in early 1996, were considerably tougher than the existing ones. Experts predicted that the new regulations would increase the number of counties (virtually all urban) out of compliance with particulate standards from 41 to 150 and those violating the ozone standard from 189 to 332—in short, a huge increase in the number, and thus the political weight, of the counties affected. Massive opposition from organized business developed quickly. As a 1997 Congressional Research Service report observed:

Industry and business interests, led by the National Association of Manufacturers and the American Petroleum Institute, have urged that the ... standards not be tightened, claiming excessive costs, lack of significant demonstrable benefits, loss of competitiveness, and technical infeasibility. An industry-business Air Quality Standards Coalition has been formed to contest the stronger rules, and has picked up support from the small business community, farm groups, and the U.S. Conference of Mayors. At the same time, health and environmental stakeholders have either supported the proposals or proposed tightening them further.[17]

The EPA defended its decision by citing the strong support from its own scientific advisory panels and by asserting that the new rules would avert 15,000 premature deaths, 350,000 cases of aggravated asthma, and 1 million cases of decreased lung function in children.

Congress—the second front in all political battles between the states—was immediately embroiled in the affair. Eleven different congressional committees collectively held more than a month of hearings on the revised standards. More than 250 senators and representatives wrote to the EPA and congressional committees about the matter. Congressional alignments generally reflected the ongoing battle over smog between the northeastern and midwestern states. Northeastern states believed the new regulations would diminish cross-border air pollution originating in the Midwest and would compel midwestern utilities to assume more responsibility for reducing those emissions. The midwestern states, generally in compliance with existing air-quality standards, anticipated having to enact economically costly, politically distasteful new air emission controls, especially on utilities, some of which would have to reduce existing emissions by 85 percent. Bill Clinton's administration wavered for months in the political heat despite outspoken support for the proposals by EPA administrator Carol Browner; the president's own congressional party was deeply divided on the matter. Finally, in July 1997, President Clinton approved the regulations, to the surprise of many environmentalists who had been convinced that the president would never accept the political risks. Several months later, even as the EPA proposed stringent new emission controls on utilities to implement the new air-quality standards, the northeastern states renewed the geographical struggle. Asserting that the EPA's newly proposed emission controls would take too long to implement, they sued the EPA for failing to order emission reductions in forty midwestern power plants in accordance with other provisions of the CAA. Although the federal courts refused to mandate that the EPA issue such orders, the agency indicated that it might revise its proposed emission standards anyway and, in any case, that it intended to issue its final version sometime in 2001. When this final version was issued, the regulated utilities promptly, and unsuccessfully, sued the agency in an effort to prevent the implementation of the new standards.

The advent of the George W. Bush administration provoked additional confrontations between the EPA and the northeastern states. Complaining that mideastern air pollution made the northeast "the tailpipe of America," nine northeastern states sued the EPA in 2002 to prevent the enactment of new rules delaying the installation of new pollution control technologies on older midwestern utilities (see the section "Politics and Regulatory Change: New Source Review" later in the chapter) and in 2005 initiated additional suits against the Bush administration's proposed new standards for power plant mercury emissions. The Northeast's sustained legal and political pressure on the EPA produced a truce of sorts by 2007. The battle over New Source Review had stalled in the courts, and the Bush administration announced in 2005 a new Clean Air Interstate Rule (CAIR) that was intended to reduce power plant emissions of nitrogen and sulfur oxides by more than 60 percent within a decade. The EPA estimated that the CAIR, the centerpiece of the Bush administration's air pollution policies, would prevent 17,000 deaths annually by 2015 and appeared to be another regulatory pathway to cleaner northeastern air that environmentalists generally supported. Meanwhile, the New Source Review battle languished in the judiciary.

Like virtually all major environmental regulations, however, the CAIR was also quickly embattled in the federal courts. Dissatisfied environmentalists, state officials, and some regulated industries launched the CAIR on a convoluted judicial journey that appeared to end in July 2008 when the federal district court, supporting environmentalist critics of CAIR, declared that CAIR was "contrary to law and unsupported adequately by reasoned decision-making" and ordered the EPA to reconsider the regulation's new emission standards. But it was soon apparent that the court's ruling assured a regulatory muddle that all contending factions wished to avoid. "In anticipation of CAIR's adoption, some utility companies have already invested significantly in pollution controls for their power plants that might be too costly to operate if the tighter policies do not end up taking effect," explains one analyst. Moreover,

> State officials are also in a bind. They face deadlines for other longstanding air quality standards.... Without the now-vacated Bush policies, the affected states probably won't hit their deadlines, and could face penalties as a result. The Bush rules would have given power plants a financial incentive to reduce pollution. With those incentives off the table, plants may back out of contracts for new pollution control equipment or run the equipment less. That will put pressure on states to find new ways to cut pollution and meet the deadlines.[18]

In December 2008, federal judges, responding to further initiatives from virtually all major interests involved in the CAIR, reversed themselves and agreed to permit the EPA to enforce the CAIR rules temporarily, thus assuring sufficient predictability of the new regulations while the Obama administration considered further rule revisions. The Obama administration, however, is unlikely to end such a tooth-and-claw sectional brawl quickly because the conflict feeds on deeply nested political tensions in the federalist system: sectional competition for political and economic power, conflicts over the interpretation of the Constitution's federalist language, corporate conflicts over state market regulation, and others. Still, the contention is a virtual primer on U.S. environmental regulation. It involves both separated federal institutions and state governments, pluralistic private and public interests, congressional advocacy of state and regional viewpoints, scientific contention about environmental standards, judicial intervention in regulation, the resort to litigation as a political weapon, and much more that is fundamental to U.S. environmental policymaking. In broadest perspective, it is politics American-style.

Science and Regulatory Change: Small Particulates. Regulation strives for predictability, consistency in interpreting and applying the law, and stability in established norms for decision making. Science breeds discovery, embraces change, promotes experimentation, and challenges tradition. Science is troublesome to regulatory order. Since 1970, the CAA has regulated airborne particulates as one of the original criteria pollutants. But the continuing enrichment of the scientific base for regulation since 1970 is forcing a change in our understanding of which substances should be regulated and which levels can be tolerated. New scientific evidence poses for the EPA difficult and disruptive new choices about particulate regulation.

In 1971, the EPA issued air-quality standards for particulates without distinction regarding size. Particulates (extremely small solid particles of matter found in the air and produced by dust, smoke, fuel combustion, agriculture, and forest cultivation, among other sources) have been known for many decades to pose health hazards. Initially, however, the EPA's standards on particulates assumed that size was not a significant factor in the health risks posed. By 1987, accumulating scientific research had demonstrated conclusively that small particulates, those smaller than 10 microns (1 micron, or micrometer, equals 1/25,000 inch), are especially hazardous to humans because they can be inhaled into lung tissue, unlike larger particulates, which are caught in the air passages to the lungs.[19] These smaller particulates are commonly found in cigarette smoke, diesel engine emissions, windblown dust, and many other sources. They are also dangerous because they can carry carcinogenic chemicals into the lungs. In 1987, the EPA issued new air-quality standards for small particulates. However, existing emission controls for particulates were not designed specifically to control small particulates, and many sources of small particulates were not regulated at all.

About 250 air-quality control regions failed the new ambient air-quality standards for fine particulates. In the West, a major problem was wind-blown dust, not easily controlled by any existing technology. The EPA established tailpipe standards for emissions from diesel trucks and buses, beginning with the 1988 model year, that became increasingly stringent for models beginning in 1991. But monitoring data about the origin and distribution of fine particulates were inadequate, and states were slow to identify the magnitude of their problems and the sources to be regulated. Control technologies for stationary sources of small particulates were not well tested, and the control costs were not accurately known. In effect, small particulates had become a separate emission-control problem, and the states spent much of the 1990s acquiring a capability to regulate them. The EPA's most recent particulate standards, enacted concurrently with the 1997 revised smog rules, created new regulations specifically for particulates smaller than 2.5 microns because scientific research had demonstrated that these posed a distinct human health risk. Automobile manufacturers, fossil-fuel-burning facilities, and the trucking industry were predictably concerned about the additional compliance costs to meet the proposed standards. And they were angered by this regulatory ratcheting—the appearance of new, progressively more stringent regulatory rules with which they must comply—creating the third different particulate standard within a decade. Proponents of the new standards argued that they were protecting the elderly, children, and people with chronic lung disease from a new, scientifically verified health risk. For regulated interests, the real problem seemed to be the potent, economically disruptive impact of regulatory science on environmental management.

Predictably, the disaffected truckers, utilities, and other regulated industries took their case to court—all the way to the Supreme Court—challenging the EPA's authority to promulgate the new regulatory rules in what turned out to be perhaps the most significant environmental regulatory cases since the 1970s. Essentially, the dissidents challenged the EPA's discretionary authority, granted by Congress in the CAA, to set ambient air-quality standards solely on the basis of public health considerations. The EPA, they argued, had interpreted this authority too broadly, and Congress had been negligent in permitting the agency too much discretion in interpreting such authority. Had the Supreme Court agreed with this argument, the logic could well have overturned a huge array of other environmental regulations across the whole domain of federal environmental regulation and left a chaos of regulatory confusion. The Supreme Court, however, rejected the assault on the EPA's congressionally delegated authority and in a landmark ruling (*Whitman v. American Trucking Associations*, 531 U.S. 457) affirmed in 2001 both the delegated authority and the EPA's latitude in interpreting that authority.

What followed was a consummate example of EPA decision making driven by the judicial lash. With Supreme Court approval, the EPA began to issue regulations in 2002 to implement its small particulate standards. But the agency was sued again in 2002, this time by environmental groups for failing to review its standards for small and large particulates by a 2002 deadline set by the CAA (which required an EPA review of all air-quality standards every five years). After further negotiation, the EPA reached a settlement with the environmental groups in which it agreed to review again its particulate standards. In 2006, the EPA decided to implement its new small particulate standard and also to abandon its earlier standard for large particulates—another instance of regulatory ratcheting driven by ongoing scientific research. Meanwhile, the EPA estimated in 2005 that at least 129 counties with more than 68 million people appeared to exceed the standard for small particulates established in 1997 and that almost 400 additional counties with a population exceeding 91 million people had provided insufficient data to even determine whether they had met particulate standards.[20] Thus, a substantial proportion of the national population, most of them urban dwellers, appeared to be living in areas that might be subjected in the near future to increasingly stringent air pollution controls that could significantly affect economic development.

Critics of the new standard accused the Office of Information and Regulatory Affairs (OIRA), the White House entity so often censured for improper intervention in the EPA's regulation writing (see Chapter 5), of more interference in EPA rulemaking. The critics asserted that, during the 2006 revision of the fine particulate standard, the OIRA had pressured the EPA to ignore the advice of its scientific advisers who had recommended an even lower standard than was proposed. The rulemaking also disclosed that OIRA had edited the text of the final rule, removing a sentence that said reducing fine particulate exposure "may have substantial impact on the life expectancy of the U.S. population."[21] In November 2009, EPA administrator Lisa Jackson announced that the EPA would begin reviewing, and if necessary revising, existing standards for particulates and all criteria pollutants regulated by the CAA.

Politics and Regulatory Change: New Source Review. In mid-2002, the EPA brought to a full boil a controversy simmering since the CAA's creation in 1970. By then, the conflict had escalated into a major confrontation between the George W. Bush administration and environmentalists. All this resulted from a volatile combination of circumstances that repeatedly transformed environmental rulemaking into partisan political warfare: large regulatory costs and environmental risks, a major economic sector, vague legislation, and (especially in this instance) a new presidency. The outcome, moreover, was likely to profoundly affect air quality for a generation or more.

The controversy began with an arcane section of the CAA concerned with "new source performance standards." The original CAA of 1970 required all major stationary sources of air pollution built after 1975 to install pollution control technologies but exempted existing pollution sources. Many of these existing operations, especially major pollution sources, such as coal-burning electric-power plants, continued to operate older facilities with occasional modification instead of building new plants with the required expensive pollution control technologies. This situation, in effect, perpetuated thousands of major air-polluting facilities well beyond their normal lifetime and prompted Congress to amend the law.

The Clean Air Act Amendments of 1977 added to the original legislation a new source review (NSR) provision that required older air-polluting facilities to install the best available control technologies whenever they underwent "major modification," a strategy meant to discourage the continued existence of the older pollution sources. At the same time, however, the act still permitted companies to carry out "routine maintenance" of existing facilities without replacing them. Thus, a crucial issue arose: When did "routine maintenance" become a "major modification"? As one legal analyst explained,

> The wording of the NSR was vague enough to allow companies to fight regulators over the definition of major modification.... [The companies] could try to define almost all construction on existing plants as minor or routine. The grandfather clause exempting old plants, combined with uncertainty about what, exactly, was routine maintenance, permitted companies not only to keep old, heavily polluting plants running, but to use those plants to boost output in a way that escaped Clean Air Act emission requirements.[22]

Companies—especially the electricity utilities—fought the EPA over the NSR standards. Throughout the 1980s and most of the 1990s, the federal and state governments struggled with the definition of *major modification*, and few companies were compelled to upgrade their existing facilities by the NSR provisions.

This stalemate ended in the late 1990s. New York, on behalf of other northeastern states downwind of air pollution originating from midwestern power plants, sued several large midwestern utilities in 1999 for failure to comply with the NSR standards that required new pollution controls. The Clinton administration also sued fifty-one large coal-fired electricity utilities for similar reasons. The stakes were enormous. The court rulings would affect 17,000 power plants nationally, involve several billion dollars in potential new pollution control costs for the utilities, and possibly determine the breadth and quality of national air pollution control for decades. The new litigation was vigorously opposed by the coal-fired electricity utilities and their trade associations, the petroleum and mining industries, major manufacturing corporations, and virtually every other economic interest at risk if the NSR provisions were aggressively enforced as interpreted by the Clinton administration's EPA. Corporations with facilities at risk argued that the EPA's standards for defining *major modification* were unclear and that, in any case, there were more economically and technically efficient ways of achieving the purposes of the NSR than an inflexible requirement that new facilities must install the best new pollution controls.

This litigation was still before the courts when the 2000 presidential elections brought a sea change to environmental regulation in Washington. The new Bush administration strongly identified with the nation's energy producers and their regulatory viewpoint while opposing the EPA's general command-and-control approach to air pollution regulation during the Clinton era. In addition, the first National Energy Plan proposed by the Bush administration tilted heavily in the direction of new energy production and called for, among other increased production measures, the building of 1,300–1,900 new electric-power plants by 2020. Bush preferred to terminate the Clinton administration's lawsuits against the electricity utilities and, instead, to encourage expansion of the electric-power industry by relaxing the NSR standards and creating a market for emissions trading as an alternative to technological controls for all new electric-power plants. Congressional Democrats generally regarded the Bush proposals as a reincarnation of Reagan's antienvironmentalism, and debate over reforming the NSR tended to divide along party lines. In late 2003, the EPA proposed revising the NSR regulations by generously increasing the opportunities for companies to enlarge their existing pollution sources without installing the pollution control technologies that the NSR seemed to require.[23] A coalition of environmental, public health, and state regulatory agencies promptly initiated a lawsuit challenging the EPA's new proposal. The coalition charged that the proposal would drastically increase the volume of future air pollution and further discourage the replacement of older, polluting facilities with newer, environmentally cleaner ones, and a federal court agreed.[24]

The EPA was now under court order to rewrite its NSR standard again. In late 2005, the EPA proposed—to the satisfaction of most

environmental groups—a new NSR standard creating nationwide consistency in how states implemented the program for electricity-generating units. The proposed changes would standardize the emissions tests
used in NSR to determine whether a physical or operational change at
a power plant would cause an emission increase that would require the
plant to install additional pollution controls. By the end of 2006, a
series of additional federal court decisions had largely eliminated the
NSR standards supported by the Bush administration. The new, tougher
NSR standards were, for the moment, in place and would, if implemented, affect 800 electric-power plants and 17,000 factories nationally. The EPA , however, initiated no new enforcement actions until the
Obama administration took office; then, as major electricity utilities
expected (and regretted), the EPA declared its intention to enforce
aggressively the new NSR standards.

Urban smog, airborne toxics, and small particulates are a few among
many ambient air problems challenging the nation's ability to realize the
ambitious goals set by the CAA in 1970. These problems test the nation's
technological skill and economic resiliency. They will challenge the political determination of its officials and the public's commitment to the
environmental protection that the majority professes to support. These
problems are also reminders of how incrementally slow the implementation and how modest the achievements of the CAA have been. The
nation's experience with regulating water pollution has been much the
same.

Regulating Water Quality

The nation's aquatic inheritance is not just water but different water
systems, each essential to modern U.S. society and each currently threatened,
or already severely polluted, by different combinations of pollutants.

Surface Water

The nation's surface waters—streams, rivers, lakes, wetlands, and
coastal areas—are the nation's most visible water resource. Almost 99
percent of the population lives within 50 miles of a publicly owned lake.
Streams, rivers, and lakes account for a high proportion of all recreational
activities, commercial fishing grounds, and industrial water resources.
Because surface waters are so intensively used and so highly visible, their
rapidly accelerating degradation became the most immediate cause for
congressional action in the 1960s and 1970s; arresting water pollution
and restoring the nation's once high water quality became a focal point
for environmental legislation. Most of the fragmentary data available on

national water quality since 1970 come from monitoring surface-water conditions. But surprisingly little reliable information exists about the quality of most U.S. surface waters.

Even after the turn of the twenty-first century, estimates of surface-water quality continue to be ambiguous and uncertain, largely because comprehensive reliable monitoring data remain unavailable. Federal agencies such as the EPA and the Council on Environmental Quality have traditionally based their surface-water-quality indexes on only six pollutants, excluding common sources of water degradation such as heavy metals, synthetic organic compounds, and dissolved solids. In general, surface-water quality seems, despite some spectacular achievements, to have remained in about the same condition since the late 1980s. It is often difficult, in any case, to know what significance to impute to available statistics because EPA assessments cover only about one-third of all U.S. surface-water area. This translates into an assessment of approximately 19 percent of river miles, 43 percent of lake acres, and 36 percent of estuary square miles. Wetlands are still largely terra incognita; only 8 percent of wetlands acreage has been evaluated for water quality.

The states' haphazard water-quality monitoring creates massive information deficiencies that frustrate accurate national assessment. Just how problematic is state monitoring is suggested by a GAO description of the evaluated data used by many states. "Evaluated data," explains the GAO report, "include site-specific monitoring data more than 5 years old and information that serves as an indicator of water quality conditions, such as anecdotal evidence or reports on wildlife or habitat conditions"[25]—in short, sophisticated guesswork.

But evidence of a major long-term improvement in the overall quality of the nation's surface waters is, as noted earlier, quite elusive. Considering the nation's population growth and economic expansion since 1980, the stability of water quality must be considered an achievement of sorts—it could have been much worse. Nevertheless, the quality of the nation's surface water apparently is not greatly improved, and the goals of the FWPCAA still seem decades from achievement. Existing information is often inconsistent. And so things will remain as long as the dull but essential task of data collection remains politically unattractive and underfunded.

The leading causes of surface-water pollution, along with the data limitations, can be identified readily (see Figure 6-1). By far the largest contributors to this pollution are agricultural runoff, urban runoff, and other sources of nonpoint pollution (that is, pollution arising from diffuse, multiple sources rather than from a pipe or other point source); these are the most technologically and politically formidable pollutants yet to be controlled.

Figure 6-1   Major Sources of Impairment in Assessed Rivers and Streams

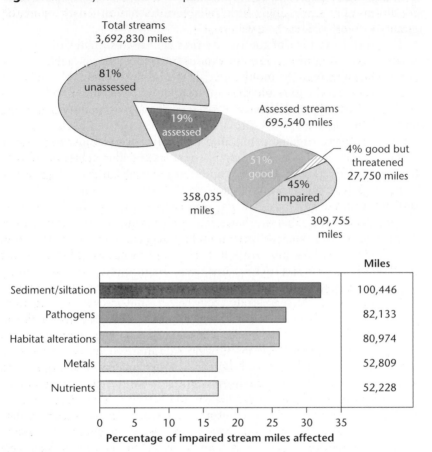

Source: U.S. Environmental Protection Agency, Office of Water, "National Water Quality Inventory and Report to Congress, 2002 Reporting Cycle," Report no. EPA-841-R-07-001, Washington, D.C., 2007, 8.

Note: Percentages do not add to 100% because more than one cause or source may impair a water body.

The Federal Water Pollution Control Amendments. The federal government's major water pollution regulatory program is embodied in the FWPCAA of 1972, which concerns primarily surface-water quality. The 1972 legislation amended the Water Pollution Control Act of 1948. These 1972 amendments completely changed the substance of the earlier legislation and established the regulatory framework that has prevailed ever since. The 1972 legislation was strengthened greatly by new amendments passed in 1987 as the Water Quality Act. In more than 120 pages of fine print, the FWPCAA mandates the following regulatory program for the nation's surface waters:

1. *Goals.* The amendments established two broad goals whose achievement, if possible, assumed an unprecedented regulatory structure and unusually rapid technological innovation:
   a. That "the discharge of pollutants into navigable waters of the United States be eliminated by 1985."
   b. That "wherever attainable, an interim goal of water quality which provides for the protection and propagation of fish, shellfish and wildlife and provides for recreation in and on the water be achieved by 1 July 1983."
2. *Regulatory provisions for existing dischargers.* The legislation required that all direct dischargers into navigable waterways satisfy two different standards: one relating to water quality and the other to effluent limits. The water-quality standards, established by the states according to guidelines issued by the EPA, were to identify the use for a body of water into which a polluter was discharging (such as recreation, fishing, boating, waste disposal, or irrigation) and to establish limits on discharges to ensure that use. Effluent standards, established by the EPA, were to identify what technologies any discharger had to use to control its effluents. In meeting these dual requirements, the polluter was required to achieve whichever standard was stricter. A different set of standards was established for municipal wastewater treatment facilities.
   a. *Effluent limits for existing nonmunicipal sources.* Except for city waste treatment plants, all existing dischargers were required to have technological controls, prescribed by the EPA, which were to meet the following criteria:
      i. The "best practicable control technology currently available" by July 1, 1979.
      ii. The "best available technology economically achievable" by July 1983.
   b. *Effluent limits for municipal treatment plants.* All treatment plants in existence on July 1, 1977, were required to have "secondary-treatment" levels. All facilities, regardless of age, were required to have "the best practicable treatment technology" by July 1, 1983.
   c. *Effluent limits for new nonmunicipal sources.* All new sources of discharge, except municipal treatment plants, were required to use control technologies based on "the best available demonstrated control technology, operating methods or other alternatives."

    d. *Toxic effluent standards.* The EPA was required to establish special standards for any discharge determined to be toxic.

3. *Regulatory provisions for indirect dischargers.* Many pollutants, including chemical toxics, are released into municipal wastewater systems by industrial and commercial sources and later enter waterways through city sewage-treatment plants that are unable to eliminate them. The law required the EPA to establish pretreatment standards, which were to prevent the discharge of any pollutant through a public sewer that "interferes with, passes through or otherwise is incompatible with such works." The purpose of this provision was to compel such indirect dischargers to treat their effluent before it reached the city system.

4. *Federal and state enforcement.* The EPA was authorized to delegate responsibility for enforcing most regulatory provisions to qualified states, which would issue permits to all polluters specifying the conditions for their effluent discharges.

5. *Waste treatment grants.* The act authorized the expenditure of $18 billion between 1973 and 1975 to assist local communities in building necessary wastewater treatment facilities. The federal government assumed 75 percent of the capital cost for constructing the facilities.

6. *Nonpoint pollution regulation.* Amendments added in 1987 required each state to have a plan approved by the EPA for controlling pollution from nonpoint sources. Such plans must include "best management practices," but states are permitted to decide whether to require owners and managers to use such practices or to make their use voluntary.

    The 1972 legislation was written by a Congress unchastened by the political, economic, and technological obstacles to pressing technology in pollution regulation. The legislation, as originally written, was the purest example of "technology forcing" in the federal regulatory code. The use of effluent standards in addition to water-quality standards for dischargers was based on the premise that "all pollution was undesirable and should be reduced to the maximum extent that technology will permit."[26] Compliance deadlines were almost imperiously ordained for the total elimination of water pollution in a decade. Nonetheless, the administrative and technical complexities of making the legislation work seemed surmountable. The original legislation serves as an enduring monument to the U.S. politicians' belief in the possibilities of social engineering and to the political muscle of the environmental movement in the early 1970s.

    Even the most ardent advocates of the legislation, however, recognized that the rigorous compliance deadlines for effluent treatment and wastewater facility construction would not be attained. They were convinced that pressing technology ultimately worked—eliminating all pollutants from the nation's waters hardly seemed impossible to a people who could launch a satellite carrying their language a billion light-years into space. Acknowledging the likelihood of short-term failures, advocates of the legislation were nonetheless convinced that only by pressing technology relentlessly for rapid compliance with regulations could they sustain the sense of urgency and bring sufficient weight of federal authority to bear on polluters to obtain their long-term objectives.

The Political Setting. The political struggle over implementation of the FWPCAA has been shaped by several factors. First, the implementation of the legislation is federalized. The 1972 amendments made concessions to the states that Congress had been unwilling to make in the CAA of 1970 and that environmentalists generally opposed. The 1972 amendments permitted the states to decide on the designated use for a body of water. In general, state regulatory agencies are more vulnerable than Washington, D.C., to pressure from local water polluters to designate uses for bodies of water that will permit moderate to heavy pollution. This propensity of local regulatory agencies to accommodate regulated interests also extends to enforcement of designated water uses and the associated emission controls. Regulated interests often are likely to press vigorously for a major state role in the administration and enforcement of water-quality standards, believing that this works to their advantage more than implementation through the EPA's regional and national offices. State enforcement of pollution controls on major dischargers improved significantly in the 1990s, but many violators still go undetected or unpunished. In the mid-1990s, the GAO calculated that as many as one in every six of the nation's major dischargers regularly violated their permits, but the EPA estimated the number to be twice that.

Thirty-five states have assumed major implementation responsibilities, such as issuing and enforcing permits for effluent dischargers, initiating requests for federal grants to build new local waste treatment facilities, and supervising the administration of the grant programs in their jurisdictions. The states thus exercise considerable influence on program implementation directly through their own participation—and the pursuit of their own interests in the program—and through their congressional delegations, which remain ever vigilant in protecting the interests of the folks back home. Moreover, conflict arising from differing state and federal viewpoints on program implementation becomes interjected immediately into the daily administrative implementation of the law. Control standards vary greatly among the states for the same pollutant, often provoking states with strict standards to complain that more lenient states enjoy an unfair advantage in the competition for new business. Among six major states, for instance, the same five toxic pollutants were treated very differently:

In some states, the permitting authorities consistently established numeric limits on the discharges, while in other states, the authorities consistently required monitoring. In some states, no controls were imposed. In addition, the numeric discharge limits for specific pollutants differed from state to state and even within the same state for facilities of similar capacity.[27]

The political character of the program also depends on the enormous administrative discretion left to the EPA in prescribing the multitude of technologies that must be used by effluent dischargers to meet the many different standards established in the law. In 1972, when the Clean Water Act was amended, for instance, about 20,000 industrial dischargers were pouring pollutants into more than 2,500 municipal waste treatment facilities. The EPA was charged with identifying the pretreatment standards to be used by each major class of industrial discharger. This might eventually require standards for several hundred different classes and modified standards for subclasses. The final standards issued by the EPA in 1976 for industries producing "canned and preserved fruits and vegetables" alone contained specifications for fifty-one subcategories. Administrators also are limited by the state of the art in treatment technologies and by dependence on the regulated interests for information concerning the character of the discharger's production processes and technical capacities. We already have noted that administrative discretion invites political pressure and conflict. The technical determinations required in setting effluent standards also invite controversy and litigation.

Finally, the program's implementation has been affected continually by the active, if not always welcome, intervention of the White House, Congress, and the federal courts in the program's development. Federal and state regulatory agencies have had to conduct the program in a highly political environment, in which all major actions have been subject to continual scrutiny, debate, and assessment by elective public officials and judges. This is hardly surprising for a program involving so many billions of dollars and so many politically and economically sensitive interests. But, as we observe later in this chapter, the economic and environmental costs of such politicized administration are high.

A Stubborn Problem: Nonpoint Pollution. The most common source of surface-water pollution has remained virtually uncontrolled in every state since the 1972 passage of the FWPCAA. Nonpoint pollution is estimated to be the major cause of pollution in 65 percent of the stream-miles not meeting state standards for their designated use.[28] Overall, more than one-third of the stream-miles in the United States appear to be affected by nonpoint pollution. Nonpoint pollution also

Figure 6-2   Point and Nonpoint Sources of Nitrogen in Watersheds of
Continental United States

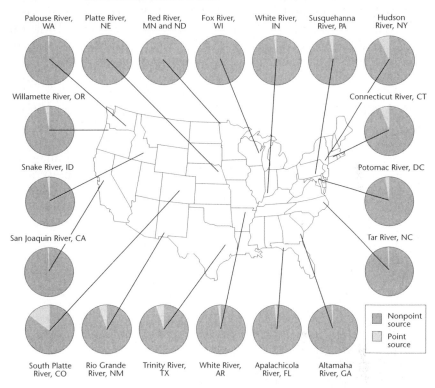

Proportions of nonpoint and point sources of nitrogen vary in watersheds across the continental United States. Commercial fertilizer and manure typically constitute the major sources of nitrogen to the first NAWQA study units. Atmospheric nitrogen is significant in most study units except in the far West and the Northern Great Plains. Point sources are an important source of nutrients to watersheds near large urban areas, such as Denver in the South Platte River Basin and Hartford in the Connecticut, Housatonic, and Thames River Basins.

Source: U.S. Department of the Interior, U.S. Geological Survey, "The Quality of Our Nation's Water—Nutrients and Pesticides," Circular No. 1225 (November 2000), 29.

affects ground-water quality. Earlier we noted that nonpoint pollution is the leading cause of water-quality impairment. Figure 6-2, which portrays the proportion of nitrogen in major streams across the United States originating from nonpoint sources, illustrates the geographical breadth of nonpoint pollution.

This pollution is especially troublesome for several reasons. Its origin is often elusive. Almost all states lack enough information to identify most of the nonpoint sources polluting their surface waters.[29] It is not easily controlled technically or economically. Many different sources require many different control strategies. The largest source of nonpoint pollution is agriculture; crop lands, pasture, and range lands together pollute about one-third of the nation's stream-miles with metabolic wastes from animals, sediment, fertilizers, pesticides, dissolved solids, and other materials. Agricultural runoff and urban storm water runoff are the major causes of the eutrophication of lakes, whereby dissolved organic substances create such a high level of oxygen demand in the waters that higher forms of plants and animals die from oxygen deprivation. Eutrophication eventually leaves most lakes lifeless.

Reducing agricultural pollution requires several difficult strategies because technological solutions are rarely available. Most often, production practices must be altered. Farmers might be encouraged, or required, to reduce the volume of fertilizer, pesticides, and other chemicals used in crop production. Animal populations might be limited or dispersed. New crop and land management techniques might reduce soil runoff. In many instances, land-use planning might be used to prevent, or reduce, agricultural activities. But powerful agricultural groups and members of Congress for whom they are a major constituency believe such strategies will have adverse economic impacts and have opposed most measures intended to reduce agricultural runoff by most of these methods. Many state governments, fearful of damaging a major component of the state economy, are reluctant to do more than encourage farmers to voluntarily seek ways to limit their pollution runoff.

The current strategy for controlling nonpoint pollution has set regulators on a collision course not only with agricultural organizations but also with the commercial timber industry, the commercial and residential construction industry, meat packers and shippers, coal mining firms, and a multitude of trades and professions associated with each. Since the early 1990s, the EPA has required states to identify all their waters that fail water-quality standards and, for each impaired water, to identify the amount by which each nonpoint pollutant must be reduced to meet these water-quality standards. Specifically, each state is required to specify for each nonpoint pollutant a total maximum daily load (TMDL), that is, the maximum amount of each pollutant permitted in each water body over a twenty-four-hour period. This calculation has proven to be enormously difficult and controversial. The scale of the undertaking is staggering. The National Academy of Sciences reported in 2000:

Given the most recent lists of impaired waters submitted by EPA, there are about 21,000 polluted river segments, lakes, and estuaries making up over 300,000 river and shore miles and 5 million lake acres. The number of TMDLs required for these impaired waters is greater than 40,000 [and] most states are required to meet an 8- to 13-year deadline for completion of the TMDLs.[30]

Nonetheless, most states have created some TMDLs or have attempted to do so. Perhaps the most nationally visible conflict over these calculations has arisen from efforts by the state of Florida and the federal government to create TMDLs for dissolved phosphorous in runoff degrading the Everglades from the vast sugar-growing region north of Lake Okachobee. In this instance, as in most others involving the creation of TMDLs, scientific and legal controversy abounds and litigation proliferates. The TMDL calculation remains inherently problematic, and state regulators complain that the process is so adversarial that TMDL should mean "too many damn lawyers."

"This State's Gone Hog Wild": The Battle over Concentrated Animal Farms. In mid-1997, corporate animal farms for the first time made national news—and in the worst possible way. In eastern North Carolina, one corporate hog farm, home to 12,000 pigs, was flooded by runoff from heavy rain. The swirling runoff flushed 25 million gallons of feces and urine from the farm's 8-acre waste lagoon into a knee-deep tide that inundated surrounding cotton and tobacco fields and then poured into the New River. The spill killed 10 million fish along a 17-mile stretch of the river between Richlands and Jacksonville, closed 364,000 acres of wetlands to shellfishing for months, and prompted Rep. Charlie Rose, D-N.C., to demand that the EPA declare a moratorium on new factory farms until their environmental contamination could be controlled. The following year, North Carolina's largely corporate hog farms produced more than 16 million hogs—the nation's second largest state hog production. "This state's gone hog wild," Rose complained. "We have a wonderful quality of life here, but a greedy, unregulated hog industry will ruin it overnight if we're not careful."[31]

The North Carolina spectacle was among the first of an increasing number of highly publicized incidents to thrust the problem of concentrated animal farming into national visibility and frame an ongoing political struggle in almost every agricultural state. Concentrated animal feeding operations (CAFOs) are a textbook example of the vexing regulatory challenge posed by a rapidly evolving environmental problem accompanied by meager relevant information and fragmented regulatory laws. CAFOs are the collision point between the rapidly accelerating vertical integration in U.S. food production and the tired pace of regulatory reform—another instance of regulation racing to catch up with economic and technological innovation. Moreover, the issue is a tangle of surface water, groundwater, and drinking water regulatory problems falling between the margins of state and federal water pollution laws and provoking the jurisdictional problems common to regulatory federalism.

CAFOs are quickly transforming virtually all sectors of major animal production in the United States—cattle, hogs, poultry, turkeys, and dairy. The EPA describes these farms as

> facilities that confine animal feeding activities, thereby concentrating animal populations, animal manure, and animal mortality. AFO [animal feeding operation] activities can cause a range of environmental and public health problems, including oxygen depletion and disease transmission in surface water, pathogens and nutrient contamination in surface and ground water, methane emissions to the air, and excessive buildup of toxins, metals, and nutrients in soil.[32]

CAFO farming has expanded rapidly until, currently, more than 77 percent of the beef cattle and 72 percent of hogs and (egg-)layers in the United States are raised and managed on large farms. CAFOs also produce prodigious quantities of waste that must be managed. A large farm with 800,000 hogs, for example, produces over 1.6 million tons of manure per year, which is one and a half times more than the annual sanitary waste produced by the city of Philadelphia, Pennsylvania (about 1 million tons), with a population of almost 1.5 million people.[33]

The production of small, family-owned AFOs is diminishing rapidly in the wake of increasing CAFOs. For example:

- "The structure of the pork industry has also changed dramatically during the past three decades. The number of hog producers in the United States was more than 1 million in the 1960s but fell to about 67,000 by 2005.... Although the total inventory of hogs has changed little over the years, the structural shift toward concentration has been dramatic with the 110 largest hog operations in the country, each of which has over 50,000 hogs, now constituting 55% of the total national inventory (USDA 2005)."[34]
- "The number of farms in Iowa raising hogs decreased from 64,000 in 1980 to 10,500 in 2000—an 84% decrease—while the average number of hogs per farm increased from 250 to 1,430 over this same period.... Farms with more than 500 hogs now account for 65% of the statewide inventory and 75% of the U.S. inventory."[35]

More than seven thousand very large CAFOs currently operate in the United States, most owned by large food production corporations and housing from 1,000 to more than 100,000 animals each. Currently, ten corporations produce 92 percent of all domestic poultry, and fifty pork farms account for almost half the nation's pork production.

In Oklahoma, North Carolina, Missouri, Georgia, Colorado, Texas, and Utah—to cite but a few examples—corporate animal production has become a major agricultural industry and the provocation for bitter political conflict. The EPA estimates that groundwater in seventeen states has been impaired by fecal streptococci and fecal coliform bacteria originating on animal feedlots. In these states, CAFOs are more than an environmentalist matter; they set smaller family farmers against corporate farms, rural legislators against urban ones, and economic boomers against proponents of slow growth.

At least four major laws, including the Clean Water Act and the CAA, provide the EPA with authority to regulate some aspect of CAFO waste, but no single federal law currently creates an integrated regulatory approach.[36.] The states vary enormously in the extent to which their existing water pollution laws control CAFOs. Intense disputes have become common concerning how strictly CAFOs should be regulated and whether their continued proliferation should be encouraged. Congressional members from every state experiencing a growth surge in large CAFOs have introduced legislation calling for a comprehensive federal regulatory program affecting all states and thereby eliminating the possibility that some states might create so-called pollution havens for large CAFOs. Although President Clinton called for newer, more stringent regulations in his 1998 Clean Water Action Plan, neither Congress nor the responsible federal regulatory agencies initiated tougher comprehensive measures, an impasse due largely to conflicts between Washington and the states over their respective roles in a new regulatory regime and to disagreement among major corporate animal producers over acceptable regulations.

By 2008, CAFOs so dominated commercial animal production that the EPA, despite growing state action, initiated a needed national regulatory strategy to address the environmental issues. From its inception, the initiative has been limited by the EPA's lack of relevant data and limited resources for implementation. As a 2008 GAO report noted:

> For example, with regard to water quality, EPA officials acknowledged that the potential human health and environmental impacts of some CAFO water pollutants, such as nitrogen, phosphorus, and pathogens, are well known. However, they also stated that EPA does not have data on the number and location of CAFOs nationwide and the amount of discharges from these operations. Without this information and data on how pollutant

concentrations vary by type of operation, it is difficult to estimate the actual discharges occurring and to assess the extent to which CAFOs may be contributing to water pollution.[37]

The EPA expects to have relevant data available in about 2012. The CAFO wastes also create a variety of potentially hazardous and unregulated air emissions because the human and environmental health effects have not been characterized sufficiently to determine their relevance to the CAA. Among these emissions are methane, nitrous oxide, hydrogen sulfide, ammonia, and possibly the products from decomposition of animal manure and urea, as well as particulate matter from dry manure, bedding and feed materials, biological matter (animal dander and feathers), and unpaved dirt lots.[38]

Groundwater

During the 1980s the nation's groundwater became a major concern. Lying below Earth's upper porous surface and a lower layer of impermeable rock, groundwater percolates through the upper layer and collects until it eventually saturates subsurface soil and rock. Much of this water flows slowly to the sea through permeable layers of sand or gravel called aquifers. These aquifers sustain the life and vitality of communities throughout much of the United States. Groundwater is as essential as surface water to the nation's existence, and it is far more abundant—the annual flow of groundwater is fifty times the volume of surface flows, and most lies within one-half mile of Earth's surface. Almost 50 percent of the U.S. population and 95 percent of its rural residents depend on groundwater for domestic uses. More than 40 percent of all agricultural irrigation originates from groundwater. Because groundwater filters slowly through many levels of fine soil as it percolates downward and flows onward through the aquifers, it traditionally has been virtually free of harmful pollutants. Today, however, groundwater is seriously degraded in many areas of the United States.

Almost every state has one or more sources of serious groundwater contamination. The U.S. Office of Technology Assessment first reported the good news in 1984 that only 1–2 percent of the nation's available groundwater was known to be contaminated and then delivered the bad news that "this may be an underestimate because monitoring for contamination has focused on public water supplies ... while the release of substances known to contaminate ground water is undoubtedly widespread."[39] Although groundwater monitoring has improved since then, the complexity of groundwater systems and the expense of monitoring have convinced the EPA that "we may never have a complete

picture of the nature and extent of the problem."[40] But the EPA has identified an enormous number of actual or potential sources of groundwater
contamination:

- About 13,000 hazardous waste sites that are now potential candi-
  dates for the Superfund National Priority List (an inventory of the
  most dangerous sites)
- Millions of septic systems
- More than 180,000 surface impoundments, such as pits, ponds, and
  lagoons
- An estimated 500 hazardous waste land disposal facilities and about
  16,000 municipal and other landfills
- Millions of underground storage tanks
- Thousands of underground injection wells, used to dispose of hazardous and solid wastes by flushing them into deep aquifers
- Millions of tons of pesticides and fertilizers spread on the ground,
  mostly in rural areas

Many Programs, Many Governments, Many Agencies. The 1977 discovery of massive groundwater contamination caused by the abandoned
hazardous waste site at New York's Love Canal became the nation's first
groundwater crisis. Groundwater contamination has been a crisis-driven
issue, thrust on governmental agendas by waves of public apprehension following revelations of widespread groundwater contamination
from hazardous waste dumps, agricultural chemicals, and industrial and
governmental chemical accidents. Improved monitoring also has added
urgency to the groundwater issue by revealing previously unknown
chemical contamination (although often in only trace amounts). But
monitoring has just begun, and the quality of most underground waters
remains unknown.

Traditionally, groundwater management has been considered a state
and local governmental responsibility. Although the federal government
has no comprehensive groundwater management program, approximately
forty-five different federal programs affect groundwater in some manner.[41] The primary federal responsibility for implementing many of the
major programs affecting groundwater rests with the EPA. In addition to
the FWPCAA, other important legislation affecting groundwater quality
includes the Marine Protection, Research and Sanctuaries Act (1972); the
Safe Drinking Water Act (SDWA; 1974) and its 1986 amendments; the
Resource Conservation and Recovery Act (RCRA; 1976); and the Superfund legislation (1980) together with its 1984 amendments. However,
many other agencies and programs are also involved. The melange of
federal agencies and programs involved in groundwater management

ensures incoherence, inconsistency, and competing authority in the federal government's approach to groundwater problems.

The states' considerable responsibility for groundwater management has been acquired through federal legislation and their own initiative. Forty-one states currently have their own groundwater-quality standards, although little consistency exists among them. The number of ground water contaminants regulated varies from 14 in one state to 190 in another. In addition, almost all states have assumed responsibility for implementing federal drinking water standards established under the SDWA.

Controlling subsurface pollution is troublesome because groundwater filters very slowly as it flows. An aquifer may move no more than 10–100 feet annually. In any case, many toxic contaminants are not captured or neutralized by filtering. Moreover, the extent of groundwater pollution may be impossible to estimate adequately because the pollution plume radiating outward through an aquifer from a pollution source can take a number of unpredictable directions. Often, plumes will contaminate millions or billions of gallons of water.

Moreover, many sources of groundwater contamination are still being identified. The nation's estimated 1.2 million abandoned oil and gas wells, of which perhaps 200,000 are not properly plugged, are examples. Abandoned wells, often drilled to a depth of more than 1 mile, can contaminate groundwater with brine, which is four times more saline than seawater and contains heavy metals, radioactivity, and other possible toxic substances (toxics). In Texas, perhaps 40,000 to 50,000 abandoned wells may pose pollution problems, and an estimated 386,000 wells have never been registered. According to one Texas health official, "We've found leaking wells from the old days that were rock-plugged, bucket-plugged, tree-stump plugged and even one plugged with nothing more than a glass jug." In Louisiana, almost 1,500 unplugged wells are uncontrolled because money is lacking.[42]

Continuing Chemical Contamination. The many substances known or suspected to contaminate groundwater defy concise enumeration. One survey indicated that the states collectively have set standards for approximately 35 inorganic compounds, 39 volatile organic compounds, 125 nonvolatile organic compounds, and 56 pesticides, among other substances.[43] These chemicals represent only a small portion of those used in the U.S. economy and found in groundwater. These contaminants originate from many sources. The states are just beginning to regulate many of these sources, such as underground storage tanks, underground injection wells, and abandoned waste sites. Although most states have at least some standards for groundwater quality, it is unclear how well the standards are enforced. Among groundwater contaminants, synthetic chemicals and nutrients, particularly nitrates and phosphates, remain especially difficult to regulate because of their great number and wide diffusion in the ecosystem. Most states set standards for and monitor only a fraction of the chemicals likely to be present in groundwater. Almost all states identify toxics as a major source of water-quality problems. These toxics can originate in thousands of abandoned and poorly regulated hazardous waste sites or from agricultural activity, injection wells, municipal landfills, and sludges. Sludges (the semisolid wastes produced in many air and water pollution control activities) often contain many hazardous or toxic chemicals. Municipal waste treatment plants in the United States annually produce more than 7.7 million dry metric tons of hazardous sludge, and this figure more than doubled by the year 2000. In addition, the dangerous chemicals removed from water as sludge frequently infiltrate the ecosystem again when they migrate to surface and underground water. Many states as yet have no regulatory program to manage this cross-media pollution migration.[44]

During the 1990s, federal and state regulators made three chemical groundwater contaminants a priority: nutrients, pesticides, and underground storage tanks (USTs). Nutrients, such as nitrates, are found most often in groundwater affected by agricultural production, including both crops and livestock. Recent estimates indicate that nitrate concentrations exceeding federal standards are found in about 12 percent of domestic water supply wells; trace amounts, not considered dangerous, are more often found in wells near agriculture activity.[45]

Nitrate infiltration is not now considered a major national problem, but pesticides and USTs are more troublesome. In the 1990s, at least 143 pesticides and 21 of their transformation products were detected in the groundwater of forty-three states. These pesticide concentrations usually do not exceed state water-quality standards for agricultural areas. However, pesticides may be a more serious problem in nonagricultural areas, particularly around golf courses, commercial and residential areas, rights-of-way, timber production and processing areas, and public gardens. In any case, pesticides are ubiquitous in all U.S. waters. The U.S. Geological Survey reported that more than 90 percent of the water and fish samples from all streams contained one or several pesticides, and half the wells sampled contained pesticides—all evidence that pesticides have seriously infiltrated U.S. groundwater.

A major concern is the limited information available about the health effects associated with exposure to most pesticides, even in trace amounts. Federal groundwater standards, called maximum contaminant limits (MCLs), have yet to be established for most of these pesticides. Existing MCLs are often based on incomplete information. In 1995, the U.S. Geological Survey cautioned,

Existing criteria may be revised as more is learned about the toxicity of these compounds.... MCLs and other criteria are currently based on individual pesticides and do not account for possible cumulative effects if several different pesticides are present in the same well. Finally, many pesticides and most transformation products have not been widely sampled for in ground water and very little sampling has been done in urban and suburban areas, where pesticide use is often high.[46]

Governmental concern about USTs grew steadily through the 1990s with the increasing number of discovered sites. Five to six million tanks, most used for retail gasoline or petroleum storage, are buried throughout the United States. Of the 1.7 million USTs currently regulated, at least 300,000 are known to be leaking.[47] These leaks contaminate the groundwater, damage sewer lines and buried cables, poison crops, and ignite fires and explosions. More than 80 percent of the tanks in use were constructed of bare steel, are easily corroded, and had to be replaced or severely modified to meet new federal standards mandated in the mid-1990s. Unfortunately, many of these USTs have been abandoned and long forgotten. Often located under active or abandoned gasoline stations, airports, large trucking firms, farms, golf courses, and manufacturing plants, many leaking sites may never be discovered.

Federal law required all known USTs to comply with stringent new control standards by December 1998. As a result, 1.3 million substandard USTs have been closed, and about 760,500 have been registered under the new standards with regulators. However, discovering and controlling the remaining USTs will be a formidable matter. Among those yet to be controlled, half of the abandoned USTs known to regulators have been orphaned (that is, no identifiable owner can be found), and perhaps as many as half of the remaining abandoned USTs (an estimated 76,000) may never be located.[48]

Drinking Water

We need look no further than the kitchen tap for an emerging groundwater concern. All ecosystems are intricately and subtly interrelated. The negligent dumping of contaminants into surface water and groundwater eventually follows a circle of causality, delivering the danger back to its source. So it is in the United States.

The average American uses 100 gallons of water daily (most of it to water lawns and wash motor vehicles). More than 80 percent of the nation's community water systems depend on groundwater for domestic use, and the remainder use surface water to provide Americans with the 1 billion glasses of drinking water consumed daily. Recognizing that community drinking water was threatened by the rising volume of pollutants entering surface and groundwater, Congress passed the SDWA in 1974 to ensure that public water supplies achieved minimum health standards. In 1977, the EPA, following the SDWA's mandate, began to set national primary drinking water standards that established maximum levels in drinking water for microbiological contaminants, turbidity, and chemical agents, and by 1985, standards existed for approximately thirty substances. Standard setting lagged badly at the EPA, however, and in another demonstration of excessive congressional control, the 1986 amendments to the SDWA required the EPA to adopt standards for sixty-one more contaminants by mid-1989, create twenty-five more standards from a new list by 1991, and set standards for twenty-five additional chemicals every three years thereafter. Once standards are established, the states are given primary responsibility for enforcing them, and other provisions of the act, on more than 79,000 public water systems. Since the 1986 amendments were written, the number of regulated contaminants has expanded to 72 and is expected to reach 120 by 2010.

By 1996, it was apparent that this excursion into legislative micromanagement was ill-conceived, and in an enlightened moment rare to its oversight of the EPA, Congress relaxed its grip on the EPA's regulatory process with the 1996 amendments to the SDWA. The amendments instructed the EPA to focus its efforts on the highest-risk drinking water contaminants, with special attention to those particularly dangerous to the elderly and children—a more manageable and productive task. Equally important, the 1996 amendments contained right-to-know provisions that required all community drinking water systems to provide consumers with periodic information about the quality of their drinking water, about compliance with existing federal and state quality controls, and about opportunities for public involvement in local drinking water regulation. The states welcomed other provisions of the amendments that offered federal financial assistance to upgrade local water systems because a great many states lacked the financial, technical, and staff resources to enforce even the SDWA's minimum standards and many small and large water systems were virtually ignored.

In many respects, the SDWA has been a success. By the end of the 2005, about 90 percent of the U.S. population was served by community water systems with no reported violations of existing health-based standards, and almost one hundred contaminants were regulated under the act.[49] Unfortunately, many water systems, including some of the largest, are still infiltrated by dangerous concentrations of chemical and biological contaminants—many of which have no set standards and, as a consequence, have no regulatory controls. In many cases, existing treatment technologies cannot fully remove many microbial and chemical contaminants, including synthetic organic compounds and pesticides.

Injection wells appear to be a major source of drinking water con-tamination. More than 253,000 active or abandoned injection wells exist in the United States. About one-half of all liquid hazardous waste gener-ated in the United States is pumped into these injection wells, the largest portion from oil and gas production and refining facilities. Although liquid hazardous wastes are subject to federal regulation, no detailed national standards exist for the solid waste eliminated through the injec-tion wells. Rural water supplies seem especially vulnerable to contami-nation from injection wells and abandoned hazardous waste sites. A 1984 EPA assessment of rural water quality reported unsafe levels of cadmium in about one-sixth of the nation's rural wells, mercury concentrations above safe levels in about one-quarter of the wells, and lead at dangerous levels in one-tenth of these wells.

Conclusion

Air and water are the primary issues on the environmental agenda. They are the first, most essential, most politically visible, and most impor-tant tasks of environmental restoration and regulation. The condition of the nation's air and water has been examined in considerable detail in this chapter to emphasize the daunting scope and complexity of the challenge of ecological restoration and to illustrate how short a distance the United States has traveled toward that goal since environmentalism emerged as a major political force in the country in the 1970s.

This chapter illustrates that the difficulties encountered in cleaning up the nation's air and water cannot be blamed solely on political incompe-tence, policy deficiencies, administrative failures, or scientific bungling. Rather, scientific and technological development continually poses new challenges to regulation by creating new chemicals and new technologies with unanticipated environmental effects. In addition, scientific research continually redefines and elaborates the nature of environmental degrada-tion and its consequences—as shown in the study of airborne particulates and toxics, for instance—forcing continual rethinking of and change in regulatory strategies. And even so unexciting and obscure an activity as environmental monitoring leads to new definitions of environmental deg-radation, as the study of groundwater contamination reveals. The United States, as with all other nations now committed to environmental restora-tion, must suffer a learning curve. It must acquire experience in a policy domain with which no government on Earth was involved a scant few decades ago. Those who govern can learn, but it takes time.

This review of the nation's current air and water pollution control pro-grams is a sobering reminder that it will take a very long time, and require an enormous amount of money, scientific resources, and administrative skill, to give us back the healthful air and water we once had and hope to have again. So formidable a goal will not be easily realized. It may not happen in the lifetime of any American living today.

Suggested Readings

Bryner, Gary C. *Blue Skies, Green Politics: The Clean Air Act and Its Implementation.* 2nd ed. Washington, D.C.: CQ Press, 1995.

Cohen, Richard E. *Washington at Work: Back Rooms and Clean Air.* New York: Macmillan, 1992.

Morag-Levine, Noga. *Chasing the Wind: Regulating Air Pollution in the Common Law State.* Princeton, N.J.: Princeton University Press, 2003.

Rogers, Peter. *America's Water: Federal Role and Responsibilities.* Cambridge, Mass.: MIT Press, 1999.

Sharpstein, Bill. *Dirty Water: One Man's Fight to Clean Up One of the World's Most Polluted Bays.* Berkeley: University of California Press, 2010.

Thornton, Joe. *Pandora's Poison: Chlorine, Health, and a New Environmental Strategy.* Cambridge, Mass.: MIT Press, 2000.

Notes

1. Industry estimates based on U.S. Department of Commerce, *Pollution Abatement Costs and Expenditures, 2005* (Washington, D.C.: Government Printing Office, 2008), v; public spending based on "Budget of the United States Government: Historical Tables Fiscal Year 2009," Table 3.2: "Outlays by Function and Subfunction, 1962–2013," Government Printing Office, available at: http://www.gpoaccess.gov/usbudget/fy09/hist.html.

2. U.S. Environmental Protection Agency (EPA), "National Air Quality Standards and Trends: Highlights," 2008, available at: www.epa.gov/air/airtrends/2008 (accessed January 20, 2010).

3. U.S. General Accounting Office (GAO), "EPA: Major Performance and Accountability Challenges," Report no. GAO-01-257, Washington, D.C., January 2001, 16.

4. EPA, Office of Water, "Water Quality Conditions in the United States: A Profile from the 1998 National Water Quality Inventory Report to Congress," Report no. EPA-841-F-00-006, Washington, D.C., June 2000, 1.

5. Francis E. Rourke, *Bureaucracy, Politics, and Public Policy* (Boston: Little, Brown, 1969), 103.

6. Paul B. Downing and James N. Kimball, "Enforcing Pollution Laws in the U.S.," *Policy Studies Journal* 11 (September 1982): 55–65.

7. GAO, "EPA Cannot Ensure the Accuracy of Self-Reported Compliance Monitoring Data," Report no. GAO/RCED 93-21, Washington, D.C., March 1993, 4; GAO, "Air Pollution: Difficulties in Implementing a National Air Permit Program," Report no. GAO/RCED 93-59, Washington, D.C., February 1993, 2.

8. GAO, "Clean Water Act: Longstanding Issues Impact EPA's and States' Enforcement Efforts," Report no. GAO 10-165T, Washington, D.C., October 15, 2009.

9. GAO, "Environmental Protection Agency: Major Management Challenges," Report no. GAO 09-434, Washington, D.C., March 4, 2009.

10. EPA, "Climate Change-Greenhouse Gas Emissions," March 12, 2007, available at: www.epa.gov/climatechange/emissions/index.html#proj, based on data from U.S. Department of State, "U.S. Climate Action Report-2002," Washington, D.C., 2002.

For other U.S. projections, see EPA, "Inventory of U.S. Greenhouse Gas Emissions and Sinks: 1990–2004," Report no. USEPA-430-R-06-002, Washington, D.C., April 2006; Juliet Eilperin, "Ex-EPA Chiefs Agree on Greenhouse Gas Lid," *Washington Post,* January 19, 2006, A04.

11. Brent D. Yacobucci, "Sport Utility Vehicles, Mini-Vans, and Light Trucks: An Overview of Fuel Economy and Emissions Standards," Congressional Research Service, Report no. RS 20298, Washington, D.C., January 16, 2001.

12. Keith Bradsher, "Study Says Height Makes S.U.V.'s Dangerous in Collisions," *New York Times,* May 16, 2001, C4.

13. These summaries are adapted from Gary C. Bryner, *Blue Skies, Green Politics: The Clean Air Act of 1990 and Its Implementation,* 2nd ed. (Washington, D.C.: CQ Press, 1995), Chap. 4.

14. Ibid., 126.

15. "States Faulted on Inspections," *New York Times,* March 11, 1989, B6.

16. *New York Times,* March 29, 1989.

17. James E. McCarthy, "Clean Air Act Issues," Issue Brief 97007, Congressional Research Service, Washington, D.C., October 8, 1997.

18. Rebecca Adams, "Clean Air Policy Gets a Little Murkey," *CQ Weekly—In Focus,* August 4, 2008, available at: http://www.cqpolitics.com/wmspage.cfm?docID=weekly report-000002933551&cpage=1 (accessed May 4, 2010).

19. EPA, Office of Air and Radiation, "1995 National Air Quality Trends Brochure: Particulate Matter (PM-10)," Washington, D.C., 1997.

20. EPA, "Air Trends," available at: www.epa.gov/air/airtrends/sixpoll.html (accessed March 1, 2007).

21. "EPA to Overhaul Air Pollution Standards," OMB Watch, November 10, 2009, available at: http://www.ombwatch.org/node/10550 (accessed January 25, 2010).

22. Environmental Literacy Council, "New Clean Air Regulations," May 5, 2003, available at: www.enviroliteracy.org/article.php/537.html (accessed March 20, 2004).

23. The details of this controversy are described by Katherine Q. Seelye, "Regulators Urge Easing U.S. Rules on Air Pollution," *New York Times,* January 8, 2002, A10; Christopher Drew and Richard Oppel Jr., "Remaking Energy Policy: How Power Lobby Won Battle of Pollution Control at E.P.A.," *New York Times,* March 6, 2004, A10.

24. For details, see "Lawsuit Challenges Gutting of Crucial Clean Air Act Program," Earth Justice, October 27, 2003, available at: www.earthjustice.org/news/print.html?ID=705 (accessed March 20, 2004).

25. GAO, "Water Quality: Identification and Remediation of Polluted Waters Impeded by Data Gaps," Report no. GAO/T-RCED 00-88, Washington, D.C., February 2000, 5. See also GAO, "The Nation's Waters: Key Unanswered Questions about the Quality of Rivers and Streams," Report no. GAO/PEMD 86-6, Washington, D.C., September 1986, 3.

26. Robert Zener, "The Federal Law of Water Pollution Control," in *Federal Environmental Law,* ed. Erica L. Dolgin and Thomas G. P. Guilbert (St. Paul, Minn.: West, 1974), 694.

27. GAO, "Drinking Water Quality," Report no. GAO/RCED 97-123, Washington, D.C., July 29, 1997, 3–4.

28. EPA, "Environmental Progress and Challenges: EPA's Update," Washington, D.C., 1996, 49.

29. GAO, "National Water Quality Inventory Does Not Accurately Represent Water Quality Conditions Nationwide," Report no. GAO/RCED 00-54, Washington, D.C., March 22, 2000, 27.

30. National Academy of Sciences, Commission on Geosciences, Environment and Resources, *Assessing the TMDL Approach to Water Quality Management: Executive Summary* (Washington, D.C.: National Academies Press, 2000), 2.

31. Quoted in Michael Satchell, "Hog Heaven—and Hell," *U.S. News & World Report,* January 22, 1996, 55, 57–59. See also Natural Resources Defense Council, "America's Animal Factories: How States Fail to Prevent Pollution from Livestock Waste," December 1998, available at: www.nrdc.org/water/pollution/factor/aafinx.asp (accessed March 30, 2004).

32. EPA, "Concentrated Animal Feeding Operations (CAFO)-Final Rule," available at: http://cfpub.epa.gov/npdes/afo/cafofinalrule. cfm?program_id=7 (accessed February 6, 2007).

33. GAO, "Concentrated Animal Feeding Operations: EPA Needs More Information and a Clearly Defined Strategy to More Effectively Protect Air and Water Quality," Report no. GAO 08-1177T, Washington, D.C., September 24, 2008, 14.

34. Kelley J. Donham, Steven Wing, David Osterberg, Jan L. Flora, Carol Hodne, Kendall M. Thul, and Peter S. Thorne, "Community Health and Socioeconomic Issues Surrounding Concentrated Animal Feeding Operations," *Environmental Health Perspectives* (November 14, 2006): 1.

35. Peter S. Thorne, "Environmental Health Impacts of Concentrated Animal Feeding Operations: Anticipating Hazards—Searching for Solutions," *Environmental Health Perspectives* 115, no. 2 (2007): 297 (accessed February 2007).

36. Ibid., "Summary."

37. GAO, "Concentrated Animal Feeding Operations," "Highlights."

38. National Academy of Sciences, "Air Emissions from Animal Feeding Operations: Current Knowledge, Future Need," Washington, D.C., 2003.

39. U.S. Office of Technology Assessment, "Groundwater Protection in the United States," 1984, available at: www.purdue.edu/envirosoft/groundwater/src/overview.htm (accessed May 7, 2010).

40. EPA, "Environmental Progress and Challenges," 52.

41. GAO, "Groundwater Quality: State Activities to Guard against Contaminants," Report no. GAO/PEMD 88-5, Washington, D.C., February 1988, 13.

42. Thomas C. Hayes, "Making a Difference; Taking On Big Oil," *New York Times,* April 12, 1992, 3, 14.

43. GAO, "Groundwater Quality," 38–39.

44. GAO, "Water Pollution: Serious Problems Confront Emerging Municipal Management Program," Report no. GAO/RCED 90-57, Washington, D.C., March 1990, 3.

45. David K. Mueller and Donald R. Helsel, "Nutrients in the Nation's Waters—Too Much of a Good Thing?" U.S. Geological Survey Circular 1136, Washington, D.C., 1996.

46. U.S. Geological Survey, "Pesticides in Ground Water," USGS Fact Sheet FS-255-95, Washington, D.C., 1995.

47. EPA, "Securing Our Legacy," Washington, D.C., 1988; EPA, "Environmental Progress and Challenges," 102–103.

48. EPA, Office of Underground Storage Tanks, "The UST Corrective Action Program," Washington, D.C., 1997. See also EPA, Office of Underground Storage Tanks, "Report to Congress on a Compliance Plan for the Underground Storage Tank Program," Report no. EPA-510-R-00-001, Washington, D.C., June 2000.

49. EPA, Office of Water, "Drinking Water: Past, Present, and Future," Report no. EPA-816-F-00-002, Washington, D.C., February 2000.

Chapter 7

A Regulatory Thicket
Toxic and Hazardous Substances

> *National Journal: Dioxin, a chemical that EPA has recognized as a likely human carcinogen, has been in the assessment process for almost two decades. Why is it taking so long to assess dioxin?*
>
> *Stephenson: It's hard to tell. You've got to think the end result of these assessments is that someone's going to have to do something, going to clean it up, and it's going to cost a lot of money. So there's a lot of care and attention being given to just how risky is this chemical; what would we need if we put a chemical control designation on it; what would it cost to clean it up? The Department of Defense uses many of these chemicals, and so they would be tasked with cleaning up. Should there be a standard or regulation for a chemical? And there's a legitimate concern about the scientific research. There's generally research that's contradicting on both sides of the argument. And they have to sift through all that research. But we think better planning and shortening the process in general should be feasible for all chemicals.*
>
> —John Stephenson, director, Natural Resources Division,
> U.S. General Accountability Office, 2009[1]

If legal historians should choose a Top Ten in Toxic Litigation, a place surely will be reserved for the small community of Glen Avon, California. There, in early 1993, a legal spectacle began that demanded superlatives. "It's got to be among the top five civil cases in the history of American jurisprudence," one defense lawyer burbled as the proceedings began. Indeed, everything seemed dramatically oversized, like a production from some Hollywood of Hazardous Waste.[2] After eight years of planning and the screening of 2,000 jurors, the trial began with 3,700 plaintiffs (all Glen Avon residents); 13 defendants, including the state of

California and major corporations such as Rockwell International, Northrop, McDonnell Douglas, and Montrose Chemicals; and injury claims exceeding $800 million. At issue was liability for injuries alleged to have been inflicted on Glen Avon residents from exposure to more than two hundred chemicals in 34 million gallons of waste dumped into the Stringfellow Canyon between 1956 and 1972.

By the time the trial began, Glen Avon residents had already received more than $50 million in damages from one hundred companies that had used the site for dumping, but $22 million had been spent to initiate the new trial. The thirty lawyers and twenty-four jurors would eventually review more than 300,000 pages of court documents and 13,000 defense and 3,600 plaintiff exhibits for the initial proceeding. By then, the Stringfellow site had graduated from top billing on the EPA National Priority List of the nation's worst abandoned waste sites to "one of the most contaminated sites on the planet."[3]

The trial has been held in installments. The first trial, involving seventeen plaintiffs, ended on September 17, 1993, when the jury found the state of California responsible for allowing toxic releases from the Stringfellow site but awarded the plaintiffs only $159,000 of the $3.1 million they had claimed in damages. The second trial, which began in September 1994, involved plaintiffs claiming much more serious injuries. In 1994, most of the plaintiffs settled out of court and the number of plaintiffs was reduced to only 763. The next year, the federal court ruled that the state of California was liable for all the site cleanup costs. After three more years of litigation, California agreed to assume the cleanup costs if seventeen private plaintiffs dropped their demands for $90 million in reimbursement for their own cleanup costs.

In early 2000, another federal judge determined that only 135 of the 763 remaining plaintiffs still had standing-to-sue status (see Chapter 3). This litigation will continue, by conservative estimate, through 2010. Estimates also suggest that the site may require four hundred years of remediation at a cost of $740 million. In 2000, California also initiated lawsuits against thirty-five of its own insurers for refusing to compensate the state for the Stringfellow cleanup costs. In early 2005, sixteen insurers finally settled with the state for $93 million in cleanup costs (which made the list of "The 100 Top Insurance Verdicts of 2005" in one legal publication).[4] Trials began in 2006 for the first of the remaining nineteen insurers. Meanwhile, California was spending more than $10 million annually to clean up and monitor the waste site. In March 2009, the California Supreme Court, hearing final appeals on cases involving the last four of the nineteen insurers contesting the state's claims, ruled in favor of California's claims on the companies.

The box score: more than 37 years from site closure to latest litigation, $150 million spent on cleanup, $96 million in current settlement costs, 17 acres of contaminated ground, and 34 million gallons of toxic waste for which to account.[5] Considering the magnitude of the site contamination and the cleanup so far accomplished, the EPA impetuously claimed Stringfellow a "success story."[6] But new pollution still appears. In 2002, plumes of the chemical perchlorate were discovered contaminating drinking water wells near the site. After an EPA investigation revealed perchlorate diffusion into the site itself, a remedial study was initiated in December 2008 and the EPA, collaborating with state environmental agencies, will be conducting pilot tests as part of the design of a new pretreatment plant to be constructed and operational by 2012.

It may also take decades before the emotional pain associated with the Stringfellow site dissipates from Glen Avon's civic life. The local school board voted in 2003 to name a new $60 million school Glen Avon High School only by a narrow three-to-two majority and only after months of bitter contention within the community. Opponents of the new name contended that it helps to perpetuate the Stringfellow stigma and inhibits civic growth. "Glen Avon," explained one civic activist, suggests to many people a community that is "nothing but white trash, toxic waste and toothless women."[7]

The Stringfellow Canyon site is considered among the worst toxic site cleanups ever attempted. Even so, many legal experts believe that the Stringfellow litigation is a signpost along an upward road to ever more expansive and expensive future litigation as hazardous waste regulations multiply and government seeks more aggressively to satisfy public apprehension about toxic and hazardous substances.

An ironic counterpoint to this growing litigation with its burgeoning liability awards has been the mounting disagreement among scientific experts about the extent of public risk from exposure to manufactured, stored, and abandoned chemical substances. Indeed, in no other area of environmental regulation has scientific uncertainty about the extent of the risk and identity of hazardous substances been greater or more public.

This chapter is about the ambitious and extraordinarily difficult task of regulating the creation, use, and disposal of the nation's hazardous and toxic wastes. It focuses on four complex federal laws. Congress once predicted that three of these laws—the Toxic Substances Control Act (TSCA; 1976), the Resource Conservation and Recovery Act (RCRA; 1976), and the Comprehensive Environmental Response, Cleanup and Liability Act (known as "Superfund"; 1980)—would amount to cradle-to-grave regulation of toxic and hazardous substances. The fourth law, the Food Quality Protection Act (1996), is an effort to improve this regulation as a result of new concerns about public exposure to hazardous and toxic substances arising since the earlier laws were enacted. Implementing these laws has proved enormously challenging not only because the scope and expense of regulation were vastly underestimated but also because new scientific controversies arise concerning the extent to which existing hazardous and toxic substances—or others continually being created—constitute significant risks to humans or to the environment. To illustrate why these conflicts defy satisfactory resolution, the chapter describes the ongoing scientific and political controversies associated with efforts to regulate the well-known group of chemicals called dioxins and another class of chemicals called endocrine disruptors, which many critics argue are more political fiction than scientific reality.

In short, cradle-to-grave regulation is not a reality, although progress has been made. After many decades of massive public investment in a multitude of regulatory programs aimed at almost every aspect of toxic and hazardous substances, accomplishments seldom satisfy either program proponents or critics—even though (or maybe because) altogether the EPA enforces thirteen major laws affecting hazardous substance use and disposal in the United States. Most of these laws are burdened by the daunting variety of materials to be regulated, by inadequate data on the distribution and effect of these substances on humans and the environment, by political and administrative impediments to implementation, and by widespread public criticism and distrust. These chronic problems gravely debilitate the nation's waste management laws.

An Ambiguous Inheritance

The environmentalists' hell is a firmament of compacted pesticide awash in toxic sludge. Environmentalists are not alone in attributing to chemicals a special malevolence. Most Americans apparently believe that the air, water, and earth are suffused with real or potential toxic menaces. The Gallup Organization polled a sample of Americans in mid-2009 concerning which environmental risks they "personally worry about" and discovered that Americans worried most about (1) drinking-water pollution; (2) river, lake, and reservoir pollution; (3) contamination of soil and water by toxic waste; and (4) air pollution—all more or less associated with chemical substances.[8]

Americans are often misinformed about the extent of environmental risks and frequently exaggerate the danger from the environmental pollutants they most fear. But widespread media coverage of hazardous chemical spills, newly discovered abandoned toxic waste sites, and other real or alleged crises involving dangerous substances have forced attention on toxic and hazardous substances and imparted a sense of urgency to resolving the problems. Moreover, mounting evidence about the pervasiveness of potentially dangerous chemicals throughout the United States and uncertainty about the risks they pose to society and the environment increase public apprehension and provoke demands that the government do something to control public exposure to these substances. Toxic and hazardous substances have progressed rapidly from secondary importance in the environmental agenda in the early 1970s to a primary concern in the early years of the twenty-first century.

Chemicals

Most toxic and hazardous substances are an inheritance of the world-wide chemical revolution following World War II. The creation of synthetic chemicals continued at such a prolific pace after 1945 that by the mid-1960s the American Chemical Society had registered more than 4 million chemicals, an increasing proportion of which were synthetics created by U.S. chemists since 1945. Today, about 35,000 chemicals are used daily in U.S. industry; between 500 and 1,000 new chemicals are created annually. Currently the EPA has more than 10,000 new chemicals pending review, as required by TSCA.[9]

About 98 percent of chemical substances used commercially in the United States (most of them polymers) are considered harmless to humans and the ecosystem. However, about 120,000 establishments in the United States create and distribute chemicals, and the industry's capacity to produce and distribute still more new substances is growing. TSCA does not require chemical companies to test the approximately seven hundred new chemicals introduced into commerce each year for toxicity, and companies generally do not voluntarily perform such testing.[10] As new chemicals proliferate and the long-term risks associated with older chemicals are better understood, the need to protect humans and the environment from the relatively small but enormously diverse set of toxic and hazardous substances grows more imperative.

Toxic and Hazardous Chemicals

Although many chemicals have been tested to determine their hazardousness—it is often relatively easy to decide if a chemical is corrosive, ignitable, or otherwise clearly dangerous when handled or abandoned in the environment—few have been tested rigorously to determine their toxicity or risk to human or environmental health. Testing is particularly difficult and expensive when the long-term effects of a chemical are being investigated. Studies may require decades. The lack of data about the human health effects of possibly dangerous chemicals is illustrated in Table 7-1, based on a U.S. General Accounting Office (GAO; later General Accountability Office) survey of potentially harmful chemicals identified by several federal agencies.[11]

Cancer is the gravest and most widely feared of all toxic impacts from hazardous substances. By 2007, perhaps 1,500–2,000 of all chemical substances, a small proportion of all suspected carcinogenic chemicals

Table 7-1 *Availability of Human Exposure Data for Potentially Harmful Chemicals through the EPA and the Department of Health and Human Services*

Priority chemicals	Chemicals measured or being measured		
Description of list	Number in list	N	Percentage
Chemicals found most often at the national Superfund sites and of most potential threat to human health	275	62	23
EPA's list of toxics of concern in air	168	27	16
Chemicals harmful because of their persistence in the environment, tendency to bioaccumulate in plant or animal tissues, and toxicity	368	52	14
Pesticides of potential concern as listed by EPA's Office of Pesticide Programs and the U.S. Department of Agriculture's Pesticide Data Program	243	32	13
Chemicals that are reported in the Toxics Release Inventory; are considered toxic; and are used, manufactured, treated, transported, or released into the environment	579	50	9
Chemicals most in need of testing under the Toxic Substances Control Act (Master Testing List)	476	10	2

Source: U.S. General Accounting Office, "Environmental Information: EPA Needs Better Information to Manage Risks and Measure Results," Report no. GAO-01-97T, Washington, D.C., October 3, 2000, 4.

produced in the United States, had been tested sufficiently to determine their carcinogenicity. Among those tested, more than three hundred showed substantial evidence of carcinogenicity.[12]

The list of chemicals convincingly associated with acute or chronic human cancer is growing slowly. However, persuasive scientific evidence that *environmental* pollutants are causing widespread cancer is still largely unavailable. For example, the National Cancer Institute and the U.S. Centers for Disease Control and Prevention reported a lack of confirmed evidence that such pollutants were associated with cancer epidemics. The National Cancer Institute estimated that perhaps 1–3 percent of all annual U.S. cancer deaths resulted from exposure to environmental pollution.[13] The elusiveness of data, in turn, seems to the critics of current regulation like a confirmation that existing toxics legislation is scientifically, as well as economically, flawed.

Currently, more than twenty-four federal laws and a dozen federal agencies are concerned with regulating the manufacture, distribution, and disposal of carcinogenic substances. Their work is impeded seriously not only by disagreements over the health risks posed by the many chemicals under their jurisdiction but also by a lack of accurate current information about the variety and composition of those chemicals.

Pesticides are a large component of toxic and hazardous waste. More than 20,700 pesticides are currently used in the United States. The United States produces more than 1.2 billion pounds of pesticides annually, with more than 890 active ingredients.[14] Pesticides are so widely and routinely used in U.S. agriculture that many farmers believe productivity cannot be sustained without them.

Common foods are treated with dozens of possible carcinogens used widely in commercial agriculture; for example, twenty-five are used for corn, twenty-four for apples, twenty-three for tomatoes, and twenty-one for peaches.[15] Consider the chemical bath in which the dinner-table onion was probably raised:

- *Fungicides:* chlorothalonil (Bravo), 2 pints per acre, seven to ten times a year; maneb (Manex), 1–3 pounds per acre, seven to ten times a year; metalaxyl (Ridomil), 1.5–2 pounds per acre, once a year
- *Insecticides:* Parathion, 0.5 pint per acre, or azinphos methyl (Guthion), 1–1.5 pounds per acre, two or three times a season; chlorpyrifos (Lorsban), placed in furrow at planting and sprayed twice to control onion maggots
- *Herbicide:* Oxyfluorfen (Goal), 0.25 ounces per acre, one application a season
- *Sprout inhibitor:* Maleic hydrazide, 2 pounds per acre before harvest to prevent onions from sprouting before they reach market[16]

The EPA has prohibited or restricted the manufacture of more than five hundred commercial chemicals, including many proven carcinogens such as dioxin, asbestos, PCBs, and the pesticide DDT. Even if a substance is restricted or prohibited, the EPA often lacks the resources to implement controls quickly. For example, although the EPA estimates that more than half a million office buildings, apartment houses, stores, and other public or commercial buildings presently contain potentially dangerous loose asbestos, the agency decided as early as 1988 to take no action because the federal government, the states, and the private sector lacked the money and personnel to remove safely the deteriorating asbestos.[17]

Chemical Testing

Chemical testing of any sort is time-consuming and costly, but when the long-term effects of a chemical are investigated, studies may require decades. Moreover, substances currently suspected of having toxic effects often have not existed long enough for long-term impacts to be apparent. Today's American, middle-age, blue-collar workers may be the first generation of U.S. laborers to reveal the chronic effects of workplace exposure to chemicals introduced in U.S. industry during World War II. If testing deals with chronic effects of exposure to small quantities of chemicals—doses as small as parts per billion or trillion—difficulties in identifying the presence of the substance and the rate of exposure among affected populations may be formidable. Thus, a major problem in regulating dangerous substances has been to obtain the essential test data on which determinations of risk depend.

Pesticides illustrate the test burden confronting the EPA. Most of the 50,000 pesticide products used in the United States since 1947 were registered before their long-term effects were understood. Amendments in 1972 to the Federal Insecticide, Fungicide, and Rodenticide Act required the EPA to reevaluate all existing pesticides in light of new information about their effects on humans and the environment. In addition, more than 3 billion pounds of pesticides are used annually in the United States. These pesticides contain about six hundred active ingredients that must be reviewed by the EPA. The EPA has prohibited, or limited severely, the use of many pesticides, including DDT, aldrin, dieldrin, toxaphene, and ethylene dibromide, and as a result, the levels of persistent pesticides in human fatty tissue had declined from about 8 parts per million in 1970 to slightly more than 2 parts per million by the mid-1980s. However, the EPA is decades behind in reviewing all the active ingredients and the pesticide compounds made from these ingredients.

Toxics

In the 1990s, airborne toxics received major federal attention for the first time, adding another large category of substances to the EPA's regulatory responsibilities. The Superfund Amendments and Reauthorization Act (SARA) of 1986 required the EPA to create the first national inventory of toxic releases into the environment from industries in the United States. Almost all these chemicals are among the 188 specifically destined for regulation under the Clean Air Act Amendments of 1990. Taking a broader perspective, the latest Toxics Release Inventory (TRI), issued by the EPA in mid-2009, disclosed that discharges of 650 toxic wastes from all reporting sources totaled about 4.1 billion pounds in 2007, a decrease of 45 percent since the TRI was created.[18] Figure 7-1 indicates the reported methods of toxic disposal.

One significant aspect of the 2007 TRI data is the decrease in the total volume of toxic releases by industries consistently reporting since the TRI's creation; between 1988 (the first reporting year) and 2007, the volume decreased by 57 percent.[19] (See Figure 7-1.) However, data from

Figure 7-1   Toxics Release Inventory: Total Reported Releases, 2007

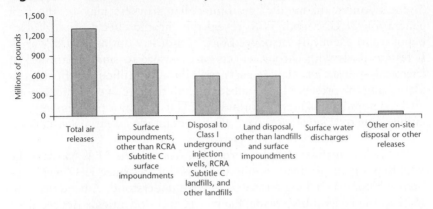

Source: U.S. Environmental Protection Agency, "Toxics Release Inventory: Summary of Key Findings, 2007," 4, available at: http://www.epa.gov/triinter/tridata/tri07/index.htm.

specific industries can be highly variable (for example, toxic metal discharges from mining and underground disposal of toxics increased between 2001 and 2007). Thus, TRI figures for specific industries and toxics may reveal important trends hidden by aggregate data. What the TRI clearly demonstrates is the scale on which the toxic release problem affects every state and territory (Table 7-2). The TRI has also become an especially effective psychological weapon for environmentalists because the average American now can readily identify the nature and source of toxic releases at home or work.

Abandoned Wastes

The discovery in 1978 of a huge abandoned toxic waste site near Niagara Falls, New York, made the site—called Love Canal—a national synonym for chemical contamination. The debacle of Love Canal escalated rapidly into a national media event dramatizing to Americans the apparent danger of abandoned toxic wastes within the United States. A flood tide of further media revelations about abandoned chemical wastes throughout the country followed, together with intense environmentalist lobbying and growing public pressure for a congressional response. In the crisis-driven style characteristic of the 1970s, Congress reacted by passing in 1980 the Superfund legislation, which included an appropriation of $1.6 billion to clean up the nation's worst abandoned toxic and hazardous waste sites. By the latter 1990s, however, it was evident that the magnitude of the abandoned waste problem and the cost to clean up

Table 7-2 *Hazardous Waste Sites on the National Priority List by State and*
  Outlying Area, 2008

State and outlying area	Total sites	Rank	Percentage distribution	Federal	Nonfederal
Alabama	15	26	1.2	3	12
Alaska	5	45	0.4	5	—
Arizona	9	39	0.7	2	7
Arkansas	9	40	0.7	—	9
California	97	2	7.8	24	73
Colorado	20	20	1.6	3	17
Connecticut	15	24	1.2	1	14
Delaware	14	27	1.1	1	13
District of Columbia	1	(X)	0.1	1	—
Florida	52	6	4.2	6	46
Georgia	16	23	1.3	2	14
Hawaii	3	46	0.2	2	1
Idaho	9	41	0.7	2	7
Illinois	49	7	3.9	5	44
Indiana	31	14	2.5	—	31
Iowa	12	33	1.0	1	11
Kansas	12	34	1.0	1	11
Kentucky	14	28	1.1	1	13
Louisiana	13	31	1.0	1	12
Maine	12	35	1.0	3	9
Maryland	19	21	1.5	10	9
Massachusetts	32	12	2.6	6	26
Michigan	67	5	5.4	1	66
Minnesota	25	18	2.0	2	23
Mississippi	6	44	0.5	—	6
Missouri	29	16	2.3	3	26
Montana	15	25	1.2	—	15
Nebraska	13	32	1.0	1	12
Nevada	1	49	0.1	—	1
New Hampshire	21	19	1.7	1	20
New Jersey	116	1	9.3	8	108
New Mexico	14	29	1.1	1	13
New York	86	4	6.9	4	82
North Carolina	32	13	2.6	2	30
North Dakota	—	50	0.0	—	—
Ohio	40	10	3.2	5	35
Oklahoma	9	42	0.7	1	8
Oregon	12	36	1.0	2	10
Pennsylvania	96	3	7.7	6	90
Rhode Island	12	37	1.0	2	10
South Carolina	26	17	2.1	2	24
South Dakota	2	47	0.2	1	1

(continued)

Table 7-2 *Hazardous Waste Sites on the National Priority List by State and Outlying Area, 2008 (cont.)*

State and outlying area	Total sites	Rank	Percentage distribution	Federal	Nonfederal
Tennessee	14	30	1.1	4	10
Texas	49	8	3.9	4	45
Utah	19	22	1.5	4	15
Vermont	11	38	0.9	—	11
Virginia	30	15	2.4	11	19
Washington	48	9	3.8	13	35
West Virginia	9	43	0.7	2	7
Wisconsin	38	11	3.0	—	38
Wyoming	2	48	0.2	1	1
Guam	2	(X)	(X)	1	1
Puerto Rico	13	(X)	(X)	1	12
Virgin Islands	2	(X)	(X)	—	2
Total	1,318	(X)	(X)	163	1,155
Total United States	1,301	(X)	(X)	161	1,140

Source: U. S. Department of Commerce, *Statistical Abstract of the United States* (Washington, D.C.: U.S. Government Printing Office, 2009).

Notes: "—" indicates zero; (X) indicates not applicable. Data are as of December 31, 2008. They include both proposed and final sites listed on the National Priorities List for the Superfund program as authorized by the Comprehensive Environmental Response, Compensation, and Liability Act (CERCLA) of 1980 and the Superfund Amendments and Reauthorization Act (SARA) of 1986.

the worst abandoned waste sites far exceeded original expectations. Moreover, Superfund's implementation proceeds glacially. The Superfund legislation required the EPA to create a list of the nation's most dangerous hazardous waste sites, called the National Priority List (NPL); to rank the sites according to human health and environmental risks; and to initiate action to clean up the sites according to their ranking. Begun in 1980, in 2002 the NPL included 1,291 sites (Table 7-2). By 2004, almost nine hundred of the NPL sites had been cleaned up substantially and removed from the NPL list, but new sites are added as these are removed.[20] Moreover, the agency estimates that there are at least 50,000 eligible sites, and many experts believe the actual number may exceed this estimate by at least 20,000.[21] Thus, even though the pace of Superfund site cleanup improved significantly in the 1990s, the program still confronts a huge backlog of contaminated sites while contending with massive cost overruns, technical complexities, political squabbles, and endless litigation. Moreover, the rate of NPL site cleanup appeared likely to diminish because the pace at which new sites have been added to the NPL declined to approximately half between the end of Bill Clinton's administration and the end of 2004.[22] Now in its third decade, the Superfund lumbers toward a future certain only in political controversy.

Despite the enormous publicity attending Superfund, most of the waste produced each year in the United States is not dangerous when it is disposed of properly. But a ton (literally) of hazardous waste is created annually for every American in the United States. Among the more than 14,000 regulated producers of waste, the overwhelming majority are chemical manufacturers or allied industries that produce almost 80 percent of the nation's hazardous waste. Other significant sources include mining and milling, municipal household and commercial waste, and the processing of radioactive materials. America's chemical junkyards are increasing in volume by an estimated 3–10 percent annually.

More than half of the nation's liquid waste is flushed into deep underground cavities or water systems by many industries and municipalities, where it is presumed to disperse too deeply to contaminate water or soil used by humans. However, such disposal is seldom carefully monitored or regulated. Experts suspect that many hazardous materials buried in this way will migrate through subsurface water flows until they contaminate drinking water wells and aquifers used for irrigation, lakes, rivers, or soil. For these reasons, the National Academy of Sciences has recommended that the federal government promote incineration, chemical processing, or other more modern procedures for waste disposal. Although federal and state water quality regulators have succeeded in diminishing underground disposal, more than 12 million gallons of waste materials are still injected underground annually.[23]

The Rush to Regulate

Considering all the difficulties involved in regulating toxic and hazardous substances, Congress and environmentalists expected too much of science by requiring in TSCA that all new chemicals be screened before being brought to market to determine their toxicity. It is difficult, perhaps impossible, to know in advance how a chemical will be used, in what quantities, and where, even though manufacturers are required to provide an estimate in their Premanufacture Notice to the EPA.[24]

The Risk Problem

The risk assessment problems discussed in Chapter 4 abound with toxic and hazardous chemical regulation, as illustrated by the continuing controversy over the effects of toxic chemicals on the neighborhood adjacent to the Love Canal dump site. In late 1982, the EPA released the results of a massive inquiry it had made, along with the U.S. Public

Health Service, into the health effects of the Love Canal site. Contrary to earlier studies by New York state, the EPA asserted that it had found the neighborhood near Love Canal no less safe for residents than any other part of Niagara Falls, New York. The evidence seemed formidable. More than 6,000 samples of human and environmental materials near the site were collected and subjected to 150,000 analytical measurements to determine what contaminants they contained. This evidence suggested that only a ring of houses a block from the waste site or closer had been affected significantly. But the study was challenged immediately because 90 percent of the samples were free of *any* chemicals. This result, asserted experts, could mean either an absence of chemicals or insufficient sensitivity in the measuring procedures. Although the assistant secretary for health and the deputy EPA administrator for New York testified to congressional committees that they were confident the undetected chemicals could not be present in more than minute quantities, the Environmental Defense Fund's own scientific expert asserted that so much variance existed in the competence of the many laboratories conducting the tests and that so many sources of error could exist in some tests that chemicals could indeed have been present. Officials at the National Bureau of Standards also questioned the sensitivity of the test procedures. That same year, the federal Centers for Disease Control released its own study of former Love Canal area residents, indicating that they were no more likely to suffer chromosomal damage than residents elsewhere in Niagara Falls. Even if such damage were present, noted the study, it was impossible to know if it was linked to the later occurrence of illnesses.[25]

Uncertainties about risk are almost a constant in regulating hazardous substances, and as a consequence, errors of judgment leading to excessively strict regulation or perhaps to dangerously negligent control of chemical substances are probably inevitable. In general, Congress and the regulatory agencies implementing congressional hazardous waste programs have been risk averse, preferring to err, if err they must, in the direction of stricter control and more willingness to accept pessimistic estimates of risk from toxic substances. Beginning with the later years of Jimmy Carter's administration, however, federal agencies have moved toward greater attention to costs and regulatory complexity in setting standards of exposure and control.

Costs and Complexity

It is doubtful that either friend or foe of the federal regulatory programs enacted in the mid-1970s realistically understood the enormous expense that would be involved in the new hazardous substance legislation. New regulatory agencies had to be created or existing ones expanded. An inventory of many thousands of chemicals had to be created, existing literature on the health effects of chemicals searched, new research initiated, new regulations promulgated, litigation involving the legality of new regulatory standards conducted, and so forth. Only as regulatory agencies began the first tentative steps in assembling data on the human and environmental effects of chemical substances did the vast vacuum of relevant information become obvious. A major reason for the protracted delays in implementing the new laws has been the tedious but essential work of building a foundation of necessary technical data on which regulatory standards could be erected. The collective costs to the 14,000 regulated chemical manufacturers will add billions of dollars to the regulatory total.

A small sample of the direct and indirect costs associated with recent hazardous substance legislation can only suggest the scale on which such regulatory programs must operate:

> The average priority abandoned waste site cleaned up by the EPA under Superfund legislation has cost $2.1 million and will cost far more in the future; the aggregate expense for eliminating all the nation's worst abandoned waste sites is expected to be many times the initial Superfund authorization of $1.6 billion.[26]

> The EPA's regulations for disposal of hazardous waste on land sites exceeded 500 pages in the Federal Register. EPA officials say the costs of compliance for the affected industries will exceed $1 billion yearly.[27]

When the massive costs are projected against the fragmentary scientific data on the effects of many chemicals and the often tenuous evidence relating chronic impacts to extremely low levels of exposure, arguments over the acceptability of the costs in light of the benefits inevitably arise. Critics of federal environmental programs have asserted that most impose not only unacceptable costs for the regulation of acknowledged hazards but also staggering costs for the stringent control of substances with unproven effects. Some critics, including leaders in the administrations of Ronald Reagan and George Bush, argued that costs and benefits should become a routinely important—although not necessarily the most important—factor in determining whether a substance should be regulated.

Criticism of regulatory costs often feeds on the disparity between the timing and character of the costs and the timing and character of the benefits from regulation. The costs tend to be tangible, immediate, and massive: dollars must be spent, agencies created, rules promulgated, and other expensive actions initiated. In contrast, years or decades may pass before any apparent benefits accrue. The benefits may be intangibles—deaths and illnesses prevented, public costs of future regulation avoided, or public safety enhanced—that tend to be discounted by those who must pay for regulation in the present. Examples exist that show the future benefits of regulation can be enormous. The number of U.S. deaths from exposure to asbestos as much as forty years ago will grow to between eight and ten thousand annually. More than 200,000 claims outstanding against major asbestos manufacturers at the beginning of the twenty-first century must be settled. The current value of these future claims has been estimated conservatively at $40 billion.[28]

A Continuing Controversy: Endocrine Disruptors

The list of worrisome chemicals lengthened in the latter 1990s when scientific and governmental attention turned suddenly to a potentially huge inventory of chemicals called endocrine disruptors. Scientific research has suggested that certain externally produced chemicals, especially many human-made synthetic compounds, may sometimes mimic naturally produced hormones in humans and animals and may interfere, perhaps disastrously, with the normal functioning of the endocrine system. Many of these disruptors, according to some scientific theories, gain their potency from the bioaccumulation of extremely small doses in human and animal tissue over long periods of time. The possible human health effects could include cancers of the reproductive system, reduced sperm counts in males, abnormalities of fetal development leading to learning and behavioral disorders, and many other pathologies associated with hormonal malfunctions. Some scientists believe that disruptors have been responsible for sexual abnormalities and deformities in gulls, terns, eagles, and fish.[29]

If endocrine disruptors exist, apprehension seems prudent. "The number of substances which have been suggested as possibly contributing to perturbation of the endocrine system ... is vast," explained one careful study of the issue.

> Man-made or generated substances include broad classes of chlorinated and non-chlorinated compounds and heavy metals widely used in industrial and household products such as paints, detergents, lubricants, cosmetics, textiles, pesticides, and plastics, as well as byproducts of sewage treatment and waste incineration and other forms of combustion. Many pharmaceutical products, including contraceptives, have hormonal activity. There are also large amounts of plant hormones (mainly phytoestrogens) commonly ingested in human (and animal) diets—especially vegetarian products.... [30]

In short, there is something to unnerve everybody. Yet the disruptor issue emerges from a fog of enormous uncertainty and scientific controversy. The effect of disruptors on humans and animals, the identity of truly dangerous substances, the results of long- and short-term exposures, the relative dangers to adults and fetuses, and much more are largely unknown. Scientists themselves disagree about the danger. "Even though sound scientific evidence can be found on both sides ... simple cause and effect data are not available," explained one expert review of the evidence. "But even without certain scientific evidence, the potential health, social and economic effects are forcing government, organizations and the general public to take notice."[31]

The public history of endocrine disruptors is the very model of how environmental issues acquire political clout. Expert meetings held in the United States in 1991 and 1993 first called major scientific attention to the possible danger of endocrine disruptors. However, the issue's political momentum began to mount when in 1993 the BBC broadcast the documentary *Assault on the Male*, which suggested that human and animal reproductive problems might arise from endocrine disruptors. The issue rose to national attention with the publication in 1996 of *Our Stolen Future*, written by a team of U.S. scientific interpreters, who vividly described the menace presumably posed by disruptors:

> Hormone-disrupting chemicals are not classical poisons or typical carcinogens. They play by different rules. They defy the linear logic of current testing protocols built on the assumption that higher doses do more damage. For this reason, contrary to our long-held assumptions, screening chemicals for cancer risk has not always protected us from other kinds of harm. Some hormonally active chemicals appear to pose little if any risk of cancer.... [S]uch chemicals are typically not poisons in the normal sense. Until we recognize this, we will be looking in the wrong places, asking the wrong questions.[32]

This aura of mystery, dread, and imminence proved to be a powerful political catalyst, creating additional media attention, provoking public concern, and compelling a response from government officials. In 1996, Congress passed the Food Quality Protection Act, which amended several major federal environmental and public health laws to require that the EPA create and then implement within three years an endocrine disruptor screening program for chemicals, and—as if to prove beyond refutation its environmental vigilance—Congress further mandated the EPA to add an additional tenfold safety factor to protect infants and children when setting standards for allowable pesticide residues in food, unless reliable data showed that a different factor would be safe. The EPA appointed a scientific advisory committee on endocrine disruptors in 1996, and two years later, it reported that, although the available data were insufficient to verify the magnitude of risk or the variety of chemicals associated with endocrine disruption, enough evidence existed to justify more intensive research and more public information about the potential problems arising from suspected endocrine disruption.

Although Congress mandated that the EPA craft an endocrine disruptor screening program and implement it by 1999, administrative and scientific difficulties have frustrated both objectives—additional testimony to the impotence of congressional micromanagement. Also, preliminary estimates suggest that the necessary testing protocols will probably be extremely expensive, perhaps approaching $1 million for each chemical tested, and that tests would be required for many hundreds of chemicals and their compounds. The chemical industry believes that insufficient evidence exists to justify the imposition of such an expensive testing regimen, and scientists themselves disagree about the magnitude of the endocrine disruptor problem. "Every policy paper, every study gets embroiled in scientific disputes over the EPA's assumptions on everything from children's dietary habits to the amount of roach killer an average family is likely to use," observed one progress report.[33] Although the issue predictably attracts public attention, environmental advocates have yet to discover the political leverage to shake the program from its glacial pace.

Chemical Threat or Chemiphobia?

Endocrine disruptors raise anew the recurring controversy about whether the public and its governments have become chemiphobic, exaggerating the health risks posed by chemicals and becoming intolerant of even reasonable risks. The controversy grows with the relentless increase in the cost and complexity of regulation. Although experts agree that the public should be concerned about the health risks associated with exposure to chemical substances and chemical wastes, they cannot easily determine *which* kinds of exposure and *how much* exposure are unacceptably risky. A related issue is that the elimination of *all* risk from exposure to toxic and hazardous substances is often impossible or unacceptably expensive, yet federal regulations such as the Superfund legislation do not clearly define how much cleanup is enough. The problem, as two informed critics observed, is "how clean is 'clean,'" and the solution is not apparent. According to political scientists Marc Landy and Mary Hague,

> In principle, one would want to clean until [an abandoned hazardous waste] site is called perfectly "safe." However ... there is no scientifically identifiable point at which an "unsafe" site becomes "safe." No matter how much cleanup has been performed at a site, it can always be argued that more cleanup would reduce risk even further.[34]

A second issue involves political chemistry. When public fear about hazardous substances blends with official eagerness to appear tough on pollution, the resulting risk-averse political climate often spawns hasty severe regulatory policies. A political synergy between public fear and governmental overreaction often results, as we have observed previously, in targeting for greatest attention those pollutants exciting the greatest public apprehension rather than those posing the most scientifically documented health risks. Risk-averse regulation can result in a regulatory intolerance for even minimal health risks, mistaken environmental priorities, and excessive regulatory costs.

Finally, regulatory costs have been especially controversial in toxic and hazardous substance regulation because of the rapid and severe escalation in the number of regulations and the growing recognition that future regulations will cost enormously more. Federal regulations, for instance, require all municipal landfills to be built with plastic and clay liners, liquid collectors, and treatment systems to prevent leaking toxic waste. These regulations have drastically raised the cost of opening a new municipal landfill and forced most of the country's existing 6,500 landfills to close when retrofitting became too expensive. And future landfill costs may be far greater still as the variety of waste-dump toxics and their health risks are better documented.[35]

To many critics, all these problems are justification for chemiphobia while impelling governmental regulators to appease public opinion through excessively harsh chemical controls at enormous economic, scientific, and political cost to the nation. To many conservative critics, these regulations are too often "animated by a quasi-religious mind-set that combines an aversion to even minimal risks with a strong preference for governmental intervention in markets and a fierce hostility toward corporations."[36] Even the many experts who disagree with these conclusions often recognize, as subsequent discussion reveals, that toxic and hazardous substance regulation is the most difficult, least satisfactory domain of contemporary environmental policymaking.

Federal Law: Regulation from the Cradle to the Grave?

Among the two dozen federal laws relating to toxic and hazardous substances, four federal laws, three passed in the 1970s, define the fundamental framework for regulating the disposal of these substances: the Toxic Substances Control Act (TSCA; 1976), the Resource Conservation and Recovery Act (RCRA; 1976), the Superfund legislation (1980), and the Food Quality Protection Act (1996). These laws represent a congressional effort to create a comprehensive regulatory program for all chemical substances from their initial development to final disposal—the cradle-to-grave control that seemed essential to achieving, for the first time, the responsible public management of chemical products. Few laws, even by the standard of recent environmental legislation, mandate a more complex and technically formidable administrative process than do these programs. A brief review of their major provisions suggests the immense regulatory tasks involved.

The Toxic Substances Control Act: Regulating Chemical Manufacture and Distribution

The major purpose of TSCA and its 1986 amendments (the Asbestos Hazard Emergency Response Act) is to regulate the creation, manufacture, and distribution of chemical substances so that substances hazardous to humans and the environment can be identified early and then controlled properly before they become fugitive throughout the ecosystem. TSCA and its amendments require the EPA to achieve five broad objectives.

1. *Information gathering.* The EPA is required to issue rules asking chemical manufacturers and processors to submit to the administrator information about their newly developed chemicals. The information is to include the chemical's name, formula, and uses; estimates of production levels; a description of byproducts; data on adverse health and environmental effects; and the number of workers exposed to the chemical. In achieving these goals the administrator also is to
   a. publish a list of all existing chemicals.
   b. see that all people manufacturing, processing, or distributing chemicals in commerce keep records on adverse health reactions, submit to the EPA-required health and safety studies, and report to the EPA information suggesting that a chemical represents a previously undetected significant risk to health or the environment.
2. *Screening of new chemicals.* Manufacturers of new chemicals are to notify the EPA at least ninety days before producing the new chemical commercially. Information similar to that required for existing chemicals is also required for new chemicals. The EPA is allowed to suspend temporarily the manufacture of any new chemical in the absence of adequate information as required under the law and to suspend production of a new chemical permanently if it finds a "reasonable basis to conclude that the chemical presents or will present an unreasonable risk of injury to health or the environment."[37]

3. *Chemical testing.* The EPA is given the authority to require manufacturers or processors of potentially harmful chemicals to test them. The Interagency Testing Committee, composed of representatives from eight federal agencies, was created to recommend to the EPA priorities for chemical testing. As many as fifty chemicals can be recommended for testing within one year.

4. *Control of chemicals.* The EPA is required to take action against chemical substances or mixtures for which a reasonable basis exists to conclude that their manufacture, processing, distribution, use, or disposal presents an unreasonable risk of injury to health or the environment. Permitted actions range from a labeling requirement to a complete ban. The control requirements are not to "place an undue burden on industry," yet at the same time they are to provide an adequate margin of protection against unreasonable risk. TSCA specifically required the regulation and eventual elimination of PCBs.

5. *Control of asbestos.* The EPA is required to develop a strategy for implementing the congressional mandate that all schools be inspected for asbestos-containing material and to develop and implement plans to control the threat of any asbestos discovered.

The Resource Conservation and Recovery Act: Regulating Solid Waste

The major purposes of RCRA and its 1980 and 1984 amendments are to control solid waste management practices that could endanger public health or the environment and to promote resource conservation and recovery. Solid wastes are defined in the act to include waste solids, sludges, liquids, and contained gases—all forms in which discarded toxic and hazardous substances might be found. In addition to providing federal assistance to state and local governments in developing comprehensive solid waste management programs, RCRA also mandates the following:

1. *Criteria for environmentally safe disposal sites.* The EPA is required to issue regulations defining the minimum criteria for solid waste disposal sites considered environmentally safe. It is also required to publish an inventory of all U.S. facilities failing to meet these criteria.

2. *Regulation of hazardous waste.* The EPA is required to develop criteria for identifying hazardous waste, to publish the characteristics of hazardous wastes and lists of particular hazardous wastes, and to create a manifest system that tracks hazardous wastes from their

points of origin to their final disposal sites. The EPA also is to create a permit system that would require all individuals or industries generating hazardous waste to obtain a permit before managing such waste. Permits would be issued only to waste managers meeting the safe disposal criteria created by the EPA.

3. *Resource recovery and waste reduction.* The act requires the Commerce Department to promote the commercialization of waste recovery, to encourage markets for recovered wastes, and to promote waste recovery technologies and research into waste conservation.

4. *State implementation.* The act provides for state implementation of regulations affecting solid waste management and disposal if state programs meet federal standards. The EPA will enforce these provisions in states that do not, or cannot, comply with federal regulations for the program's enforcement.

5. *Mandated deadlines and waste-by-waste review.* The 1984 RCRA amendments create deadlines for the EPA to set standards for the disposal of specific wastes. If the EPA fails to do so, congressionally mandated standards will be applied. The EPA is also ordered to evaluate nineteen specific substances, and deadlines are established for the agency to regulate new kinds of waste disposal activity.

The 1984 amendments—bristling with mandated deadlines and meticulously detailed instructions—bespeak a profound congressional distrust of the EPA's commitment to enforcing RCRA during the first Reagan administration. The amendments were conceived in an atmosphere strident with congressional censure of the EPA. Sen. George J. Mitchell, D-Maine, captured the mood of the majority:

> Strong congressional expression of disapproval of EPA's slow and timid implementation of the existing law is necessary, as well as a clear congressional direction mandating certain bold, preventive actions by EPA which will not be taken otherwise.... The Agency has missed deadlines, proposed inadequate regulations, and even exacerbated the hazardous waste problem by suspending certain regulations.[38]

Congress was determined to drive the EPA hard. It instructed the EPA in exquisite detail concerning how to implement virtually every aspect of RCRA, from the allowable permeability of liners for surface impoundments to the concentrations at which many different chemical wastes must be banned from land disposal. Twenty-nine different deadlines for specific program activities were listed, for example, a ban on land disposal of bulk liquid in landfills within six months, new regulations for small-quantity waste generators within seventeen months, and interim construction standards for underground storage tanks within four months.[39]

Superfund

When the first Superfund legislation was enacted, the' nation's abandoned and uncontrolled hazardous waste dumps were largely an uncharted wasteland. The nation's governments knew little about the location or composition of many waste sites, some abandoned longer than memory of their existence. The law seldom clearly placed financial responsibility for the management or removal of these wastes with their creators; liability for damage or injury to individuals or communities from such wastes often was difficult, or impossible, to assign or to enforce. Often, procedures for cleaning up waste sites were unknown, or local officials were ignorant of accepted procedures. The financial burden on state and local governments to control or remove these wastes seemed overwhelming. Because a comprehensive, collaborative program among the nation's governments seemed essential, Congress attempted to address these and other major abandoned waste problems through four major Superfund programs.

1. *Information gathering and analysis.* Owners of hazardous waste sites were required to notify the EPA by June 1981 about the character of buried wastes. Using this information, the EPA would create a list of national sites.
2. *Federal response to emergencies.* The act authorized the EPA to respond to hazardous substance emergencies and to clean up leaking chemical dump sites if the responsible parties failed to take appropriate action or could not be located.
3. *The Hazardous Substance Response Fund.* The act created an initial trust fund of $1.6 billion to finance the removal, cleanup, or remedy of hazardous waste sites. About 86 percent of the fund was to be financed from a tax on manufacturers of petrochemical feedstocks and organic chemicals and on crude oil importers. The remainder was to come from general federal revenues.
4. *Liability for cleanup.* The act placed liability for cleaning up waste sites and for other restitution on those responsible for release of the hazardous substances.

By the mid-1980s, it was obvious that the number of abandoned sites needing immediate cleanup and the costs involved had been grossly underestimated. The 1984 chemical disaster at Bhopal, India, had drawn congressional attention to the lack of community planning for chemical emergencies in the United States. And Congress was increasingly critical of the slow pace of Superfund site cleanups. In 1986, Congress passed the Superfund amendments, known as SARA, which changed the original legislation significantly in the following ways:

1. *Greatly increased spending.* The new amendments authorize an additional $8.5 billion for NPL site cleanups and an additional $500 million specifically to clean up pollution created by abandoned underground liquid storage tanks.
2. *New cleanup standards.* The standards mandated for all sites are to be permanent remedies to the maximum extent practicable, using the best-available technologies. State standards for cleanup are to be followed when they are more stringent than federal standards. People who live near the sites are to be informed about all phases of the process and are to be involved in the cleanup planning process.
3. *The Emergency Planning and Community Right-to-Know Act.* Title III of SARA authorizes communities to get detailed information about chemicals made by, stored in, and emitted from local businesses. It requires the formation of state and local planning committees to draw up chemical emergency response plans for every community in the nation.

The intent of Congress was to make the creators of hazardous waste sites bear as much financial responsibility as possible for ensuring the safety of the sites.

With Superfund and SARA, Congress finished its attempt to craft, within less than a decade, the first truly comprehensive federal regulation of virtually all hazardous or toxic materials in the United States. With TSCA, RCRA, and Superfund, Congress in effect ordered the federal government, in collaboration with state and local authorities, to become the primary manager of all dangerous chemical substances currently used or planned for production.

The Food Quality Protection Act: Improved Pesticide Regulation

Somewhere on the learning curve for environmental policymaking belongs the Food Quality Protection Act, a constructive congressional effort to eliminate the regulatory muddle created by fifty years of different statutory standards for pesticide residues on food. The act simplified regulatory standards for an extremely widespread, diverse, and politically contentious group of chemicals. It also represented a thoughtful congressional effort to create a consistent and reasonable risk standard to replace the multitude of standards previously existing for pesticide residues. Equally important, it abolished the zero-tolerance provisions for pesticide residues required by the Delaney clause of the Federal Food, Drug and Cosmetic Act (1949), which had become widely regarded as unreasonably stringent scientifically and economically. The most important provisions of the act include the following:

1. *A single, health-based standard.* All pesticide residues must demonstrate "a reasonable certainty of no harm" if they are to be permitted in food products.
2. *Tightened risk standards.* Risk calculations must consider all nonoccupational sources of exposure, including drinking water, and exposure to other pesticides with a common mechanism of toxicity when setting tolerances. This provision allows regulators to consider not only the effect of the residue itself but also the impact of other kinds of exposure to the same, or similar pesticides, outside a workplace.
3. *Provisions for children.* This provision requires an explicit determination of safe exposures for children and, if necessary, a tenfold increase in the adult safety standards to be used for children when the relevant children's data are uncertain.
4. *Endocrine testing.* The EPA is required to establish a comprehensive screening program for chemical endocrine effects on humans, to implement the program, and to report on its progress to Congress.
5. *Consumer right-to-know.* This provision requires distribution of brochures in grocery stores on the health effects of pesticides, how to avoid risks, and which foods have tolerances for pesticide residues based on benefit considerations.

Leading national environmental advocacy groups generally accepted the new legislation warily, recognizing reluctantly that zero tolerance for pesticide residues probably had become an indefensible cancer-exposure standard economically and even scientifically. Still, many environmental leaders feared the new legislation might have breached irreparably a high wall of resistance to cancer risk they had legally erected over fifty years, inviting a flood of other legislation eroding the zero-tolerance standard for other ingredients in food.

The Regulatory Thicket

TSCA, RCRA, and the Superfund regulatory programs described in the preceding sections, each a morass of administrative and technical complexity, were passed in less than four years. The EPA and other responsible governmental agencies were confronted with an avalanche of new regulatory mandates, bristling with insistent compliance deadlines, for which they were expected to be rapidly prepared. It is doubtful that the agencies could have discharged these responsibilities satisfactorily under the most benign circumstances. From their inception, the programs were afflicted in varying degrees by technical, administrative, and political problems impeding their development. By 2009, most of these programs were running years behind statutory deadlines, mandated or not. The nation is still at serious risk from the toxic and hazardous waste problems that Congress intended to remedy with TSCA, RCRA, and Superfund and is still uncertain about the danger of endocrine disruptors. Serious doubt exists that these programs may ever achieve their legislative objectives without radical reformulation.

Regulatory Achievements: Few but Sometimes Significant

There have been a few conspicuous regulatory successes. Federal regulations have largely eliminated the manufacture of PCBs, chemicals used primarily in commercial electrical equipment such as capacitors and transformers. Of the billion pounds produced in the United States between 1929 and 1976 (when PCB production was halted), fewer than 300 million pounds are still used in millions of electrical devices.[40] High levels of PCBs in human tissue declined from 12 percent of the population in 1979 to virtually 0 percent in the late 1980s. Trace amounts, once found in as much as 62 percent of the U.S. population, have also declined significantly.[41]

In conjunction with the Federal Insecticide, Fungicide, and Rodenticide Act, the newer regulatory programs have largely eliminated all domestic uses of the pesticides DDT, aldrin, dieldrin, toxaphene, and ethylene dibromide and most domestic uses of chlordane and heptachlor, all known carcinogens. Asbestos is slowly being eliminated from domestic commerce and industry. U.S. production of asbestos has dropped by more than half since 1976, and practically all industrial and commercial uses are being eliminated. In 1978, the EPA banned the use of chlorofluorocarbons from domestic aerosol cans, an important first step in controlling the destruction of the atmospheric ozone layer. The elimination or reduction of these substances removes some of the most dangerous and widespread chemicals in the United States, yet these represent only a tiny portion of the chemicals known, or strongly suspected, of posing grave risks to humans or the environment.

The Toxic Substances Control Act and Resource Conservation and Recovery Act: Administrative Overload

TSCA and RCRA abound in delays and complications. Many of these problems arise from the volume and complexity of work thrust on the

EPA within a few years. The numerous failures in program implementation also testify to the difficulty in obtaining technical data, to protracted scientific disputes over regulatory decisions, to the lack of resources and experience in program management, and to past political interference that plunged the EPA into demoralizing and acrimonious disputes with Congress.

One formidable problem is that each new law requires the EPA to assume the initiative for creating and interpreting a vast volume of integrated technical information. Obtaining the data often requires that chemical manufacturers, processors, consumers, and waste depositors provide timely, accurate information—information they previously guarded jealously. With this heavy burden of initiative, the agency would have been hard pressed to meet all its program obligations under TSCA and RCRA with even the most benevolent funding and generous personnel levels—neither of which it enjoyed.

The required testing of potentially harmful chemicals required by TSCA has been an exercise in frustration. Consider, for instance, the agency's attempt to create test rules for a whole category of chemicals. Some chemical groups are quite small, but others are voluminous—the aryl phosphates include about three hundred existing chemicals, with more being manufactured continually. The chemical industry complained that testing by broad categories would involve very high costs, would stigmatize many "innocent" chemicals along with dangerous ones in the same group, and would prevent the introduction of new chemicals until all existing chemicals in a category were tested.

In reality, EPA has been overwhelmed by TSCA's chemical testing requirements. As a 2009 GAO report concluded:

> EPA lacks adequate scientific information on the toxicity of many chemicals. One major reason is that TSCA generally places the burden of obtaining data about existing chemicals on EPA rather than on chemical companies. For example, the act requires EPA to demonstrate certain health or environmental risks before it can require companies to further test their chemicals. As a result, EPA does not routinely assess the risks of the over 83,000 chemicals already in use.[42]

The prognosis for improvement is, at best, guarded:

> The procedures EPA must follow to obtain test data from companies can take years.... [I]n 2008, GAO reported that [the] chemical assessment program—which provides EPA's scientific position on the potential human health effects of exposure to more than 540 chemicals—is at serious risk of becoming obsolete.... In May 2009, EPA announced reforms.... [I]f

the reforms are effectively implemented, they will ... provide a sound framework for conducting IRIS [Integrated Risk Information System] assessments. However, given the number of obstacles that can impede the progress of IRIS assessments, the viability of this program will depend on effective and sustained management.[43]

By 2009, the EPA had been able to test fewer than 200 of more than 62,000 commercial chemicals on its original TSCA agenda. In an effort to lighten its testing overload, the EPA resorted to an alternative strategy of encouraging chemical companies to voluntarily provide test data on about 2,800 chemicals produced or imported in amounts of 1 million pounds or more. However, the chemical industry would not agree to provide data on several hundred of these chemicals. Moreover, TSCA requires that the EPA determine whether a chemical about which it has received data will pose an "unreasonable risk" before the EPA can regulate its production or use. As a 2006 GAO report stated:

EPA officials say the act's legal standards for demonstrating unreasonable risk are so high that they have generally discouraged EPA from using its authorities to ban or restrict the manufacture or use of existing chemicals. Since Congress enacted TSCA in 1976, EPA has issued regulations to ban or limit the production of only five existing chemicals or groups of chemicals.[44]

It is also becoming evident that the number of potential waste storage and treatment facilities in the United States requiring corrective actions under RCRA is likely to exceed vastly the initial estimates. The EPA has estimated that perhaps 3,700 waste treatment and storage facilities will require cleanup under RCRA rules.[45] Moreover, the current list of 20,000 facilities subject to RCRA inspections is likely to grow as more facilities are discovered. If the estimates are accurate, the size and scope of the cleanup program would be as large as the expected Superfund cleanup and may cost more than $22.7 billion. The cleanup of all sites may not be completed until the year 2025.

The impediments to the RCRA program are those common to most federal regulatory efforts: cost and complexity, foot-dragging by regulated waste managers, insufficient money for needed oversight, and wrangling about cleanup terms. "The agency, the states, and companies often disagree on how cleanup should be pursued," explained a GAO report. "These disagreements prolong the cleanup process because more time is needed [to define] the cleanup terms, and companies must sometimes meet the duplicate requirements of both federal and state regulators."[46]

Superfund: "The Largest, Most Complicated, and Most Disliked"

The Superfund program has been a consensus choice as the most controversial, expensive, and problematic of all environmentalism's showcase legislation. Since Superfund's enactment in 1980, more than 1,600
abandoned hazardous waste dumps have been registered on the NPL of
the most dangerous sites. Another 11,500 sites are considered the next
potential additions. By George W. Bush's second term, EPA officials,
increasingly testy at the continued criticism of Superfund, were pointing
to significant improvements in the speed and economy of site cleanups.
The agency asserted that "recent cleanups are faster, with some sites
spending 8 years in the program"; the average before had been almost
eleven years.[47] That the EPA could soberly proclaim an eight-year site
cleanup to be remarkably speedy betrays much of the ambiguity and
disagreement still prevailing over the program's accomplishments. By
2007, EPA nonetheless claimed to be making "significant progress," and
pointed to its substantial accomplishment in cleaning up a total of 1,006
NPL sites.[48]

The EPA's annual Superfund reports remain relentlessly optimistic,
but the total Superfund costs cast a more pessimistic aspect. Superfund
long ago exhausted its originally authorized funding of $15.4 billion and
will greatly exceed the $26.4 billion that the EPA estimated in the early
1990s would be necessary to complete the entire program. Since 1981,
Superfund appropriations have totaled over $32 billion in nominal dol-
lars, or about $1.2 billion annually.[49] Careful estimates predict Super-
fund costs during the decade 2000–2010 alone will be approximately
$14–16.4 billion.[50]

Completed cleanups have averaged about $2.1 million each, but many
troublesome sites are creating enormous cost escalations. One hundred
fifty-four Superfund projects costing more than $50 million—such as
California's Stringfellow dump—have achieved "megasite" status because
of the time, technical complexity, and legal difficulties they entail.[51] About
20–33 percent of each Superfund site expenditure has been absorbed in
litigation and negotiation, which has become a growth industry for the
legal profession. One estimate suggests that approximately 20,000 lawyers are now engaged in Superfund litigation.[52]

The reasons for Superfund's plodding pace and bloated costs are clear.
The enormous legal costs generated by Superfund are largely the result of
the complexities involved in establishing liability for abandoned hazardous waste dumps and the difficulty in recovering damages from private
parties. In 1984, for instance, the EPA placed the Helen Kramer Landfill
in Mantua, New Jersey, high on the NPL and awarded $55.7 million for
the cleanup contract. To recover these costs through liability claims, the

federal government subsequently sued twenty-five private firms, and the state of New Jersey sued the same firms and twenty-five additional ones. A few of these 50 defendants sued 239 other parties who they claimed were responsible for these wastes, including the city of Philadelphia and other municipalities. And most of *these* litigants have sued their insurance companies.[53] The litigation is still active. So far, the EPA has been able to recover only a small fraction of cleanup expenses from parties alleged to be liable for the costs.

Another inducement to delay and expense has been controversy between regulatory officials and communities affected by Superfund over the appropriate amount of cleanup required to make sites safe. Because the Superfund legislation and its implementing regulations do not clearly establish cleanup criteria, Superfund officials have been under considerable community pressure to insist on the most stringent and costly standards for site restoration. When officials and communities disagree about the matter, litigation often results even before cleanup begins. In addition, the list of prospective Superfund sites continues to grow.

Unquestionable improvements have not pacified program critics, especially congressional Republicans who seldom, if ever, found much to like about Superfund. Less partisan experts and even many Superfund proponents, however, also believe additional reforms are imperative. Among the most important, in the opinion of a great many, is the development of a reliable method for ranking all Superfund sites according to the human and environmental health risks and allocating cleanup dollars on the basis of these risk priorities. Many observers believe the EPA needs to recover a much larger share of the site cleanup costs from private parties; the agency has been criticized for failing to recover more than $2 billion in cleanup costs just through careless bookkeeping.[54] Also, many observers assert that the EPA and the states need to reduce the time required to add a qualifying site to the NPL.

Congress and the White House have been under increasing pressure from insurance companies, private industry, state and local governments—indeed, practically all parties potentially liable to Superfund cleanup claims—to radically simplify the process by which liability for site cleanup is established and to create a cleanup standard that does not require the total elimination of all risk from site wastes. These, and many other reforms, have been repeatedly proposed in Congress since 1996, and many observers had hoped that Congress would finally pass a major Superfund reform measure after George W. Bush's election in 2000. Congress, soon preoccupied with other urgent matters, had neither time nor enthusiasm for such a contentious matter.

The NIMBY Problem

The Wyoming ranchers and stock raisers, whose ambivalence toward the prospect of giant wind farms close to home was introduced Chapter 1, would qualify as NIMBYs (recall that NIMBY stands for "Not In My Backyard"; see Chapter 2), but they are not typical. More often a NIMBY appears as a white-collar professional or executive, articulate, well educated, and politically sophisticated. She is often a housewife, an executive, or a professional. Such people personify the members of a growing citizen resistance movement known as NIMBY-ism.[55] It is

> a reaction or attitude towards any project, such as the siting of a hazardous enterprise or affordable housing projects, that is perceived to pose a threat to health or safety, status or reputation of a neighborhood or geographical area. NIMBYism can take the form of a protest against authorities or industry by the formation of action groups comprised by local residents. This response by the local population derives from a variety of reasons, including: a sense that they are being overrun by the authorities or industry to a genuine concern for the health and safety of residents of the community.[56]

NIMBY-ism is all too familiar to federal, state, and local officials attempting to implement state programs for issuing permits for hazardous waste sites as required by RCRA or trying to plan for the designation or cleanup of a Superfund site. It poses a formidable obstacle to waste site management under RCRA and Superfund. It is the environmental movement's problem, too. NIMBY-ism is a dissonance within the environmental ethic—a disturbing contradiction between the movement's commitment to participatory democracy and its insistence on rapid, effective environmental regulation.

NIMBY-ism thrives because of numerous, and still increasing, state and federal laws that empower citizen activism in the implementation of many different environmental laws and regulations. Most states now have legislation in which citizens are given some role in the writing, implementation, and enforcement of environmental laws. Seventeen states require the appropriate agencies to prepare environmental impact statements for their activities and mandate public notice and involvement in the process.[57]

Federal law provides many opportunities for citizen participation in environmental regulation. Major environmental laws, such as the CAA, the Clean Water Act, RCRA, and Superfund grant citizens the standing to sue federal agencies to compel their enforcement of environmental regulations. The Surface Mining Control and Reclamation Act (1977), the 1984 RCRA amendments, and the 1972 Clean Water Act amendments, among many others, require the responsible federal and state agencies to involve the public in writing and implementing regulations. Several federal environmental laws also permit citizens, or citizen organizations, to sue private firms for failure to comply with the terms of their pollution-discharge permits and to recover the costs involved in the suits. Public notice and hearings are routinely required of environmental agencies before major regulations are promulgated or permits are issued for pollution discharges or hazardous waste sites. Behind these generous provisions for citizen participation, legal scholar Michael S. Greve notes, is congressional distrust, a "reflexive suspicion that the executive, if left to itself, would systematically under-enforce the law."[58]

These statutory provisions have set in motion political forces powerfully abetting NIMBY-ism. One such force is the rapid proliferation of national and state organizations specifically committed to educating Americans about hazardous waste and to helping local communities organize politically to deal with local hazardous waste problems. Among the earliest and most visible national organizations is the Citizen's Clearinghouse for Hazardous Waste, created in 1981 by Lois Gibbs, a housewife whose experiences with the Love Canal waste crisis convinced her of a need to educate other communities about hazardous waste. There also has been an explosion of ad hoc state and local groups that have organized to deal with specific hazardous waste issues, ranging from the closing of city waste dumps to state policies for hazardous waste transportation.

Many existing state and national environmental organizations now give major attention to hazardous waste issues and provide technical assistance and education for concerned citizens. These groups believe they are ultimately contributing to better implementation of RCRA and Superfund by ensuring greater citizen understanding and acceptance of waste policy decisions made by government officials. Often, however, this activism arouses or emboldens citizen opposition to providing permits for local hazardous waste sites. Public officials and waste producers commonly complain that organized citizen groups too often agitate rather than educate in community waste issues.

Public resistance to hazardous waste site permits and management plans under RCRA or Superfund is a serious and unsolved political problem afflicting both programs. Coupled with litigation, the many political and administrative strategies available to citizen groups determined to prevent permits for local hazardous waste dumps can delay program implementation for years or decades.

State governments are not innocent of NIMBY-ism. Almost any hazardous waste proposal can arouse it. Public hearings on siting hazardous facilities, as political scientist Michael E. Kraft observed, can become "a perfect forum for elected officials and the general public to give vent to fears and concerns, and to denounce decision making on the siting question. The public hearing procedure ... facilitated the classic NIMBY response to siting unwanted facilities that impose localized costs and risks while offering diffuse national benefits."[59]

Many administrative strategies have been tried, but none seems to dispel NIMBY-ism. States that financially compensate local governments and citizens for the risks and other problems entailed in accepting a hazardous waste site are no more successful in gaining public approval for the siting than states using only scientific criteria for site selection. Evidence suggests that most citizens who oppose a hazardous waste site will not change their minds under any circumstances.[60] Opponents may occasionally be converted if they are convinced that the local community will have continuing, accurate information about the site status and continuing control over the site's management. But converts are few. Opponents to hazardous waste sites are numerous, vocal, and unyielding. Moreover, they are apt to win their fights.

NIMBY-ism will continue to be tough, stubborn, and durable, its ranks crowded with well-educated, socially active, organizationally experienced people. NIMBY-ism is rarely routed by better information, more qualified experts, improved risk communication techniques, and other palliative actions premised on the assumption that the public will be more reasonable about hazardous facility siting if it is better educated about the issues. All this belies the widespread belief among scientific experts and risk professionals that NIMBY-ism is rooted in the public's scientific illiteracy.[61]

Why is better risk communication not enough? Because NIMBYs usually distrust the *source* of governmental risk information: public officials and their scientific spokespeople. In addition, the critics of governmental hazardous waste management often have their *own* experts and information sources. The conflicting sides, notes Harvard physicist and science policy expert Harvey Brooks, tend to become "noncommunicating publics that each rely on different sources and talk to different experts. Thus, many public policy discussions become dialogues of the deaf...."[62] Often the true wellsprings of public anxiety about waste siting are not understood by technical experts; people worry about "potentially catastrophic effects, lack of familiarity and understanding, involuntariness, scientific uncertainty, lack of personal control by the individuals exposed, risks to future generations," and more.[63]

Critics often hold environmentalists responsible for NIMBY-ism. They assert that the environmentalist rhetoric favored by NIMBYs is little more than deceptive but respectable packaging for middle-class selfishness. In reality, argue the critics, most NIMBYs want somebody else to bear whatever risks are associated with hazardous waste sites while they continue to benefit from the products and economic activities that produce the waste. Even if NIMBY-ism is well intentioned, critics also note, it fails to solve waste problems. Eventually, waste has to go someplace. It is unfortunate, the critics conclude, that the waste often ends up at whatever sites are the least well defended politically, not at the most appropriate places. Thus, many environmental justice problems (as observed in Chapter 4) and numerous controversies between the states over high-level nuclear waste disposal (see Chapter 8) are created or intensified by NIMBY-ism.

Whatever its merits, the certain continuation of NIMBY-ism poses difficult problems for environmental regulation. Is it possible to secure informed public consent to the siting and management of hazardous waste facilities? If no public involvement techniques or risk communication procedures can produce public consensus or acquiescence to hazardous waste site planning under RCRA and Superfund, must solutions be imposed by judicial, administrative, or political means? Is there danger that continuing the promotion of public involvement in making these decisions will enshrine procedural democracy at the expense of social equity—in effect, will citizen participation gradually result in selectively exposing the least economically and politically advantaged sectors of the public to the most risks from hazardous waste? How much responsibility for the worst impacts of NIMBY-ism rests with the environmental movement? These questions can only grow in importance as the hazardous waste problem magnifies in the twenty-first century.

Conclusion

In no other major area of environmental policy is progress measured in such small increments as the regulation of toxic and hazardous wastes. The slow pace at which TSCA, RCRA, and Superfund have been implemented so far has produced a quality of regulation so tenuous and variable that a serious question often exists regarding whether regulation in any significant sense has been achieved. Hazardous waste in abandoned or deliberately uncontrolled landfills numbering in the thousands has yet to be controlled properly. Federal and state governments have yet to approve and implement on the appropriate scale the strategies required to ameliorate hazardous waste problems. The risks already associated with hazardous substances, and the many others that will become apparent with continuing research in the twenty-first century, are unlikely to diminish without a massive and continuing federal commitment of resources to implementing the programs as intended by Congress—a commitment of resources and will on a scale that has been lacking so far.

Even with sufficient resources, the implementation of TSCA, RCRA, and Superfund is likely to be slow because these laws raise technical, legal, and political problems on an order seldom matched in other environmental policy domains. First, no other environmental programs attempt to regulate so many discrete, pervasive substances; we have observed that the hazardous substances that may lie within the scope of these laws number in the tens of thousands. Second, regulation is delayed by the need to acquire technical information never previously obtained by government, to conduct research on the hazardousness of new chemicals, or to secure from corporations highly guarded trade secrets. Third, almost every major regulatory action intended to limit the production, distribution, or disposal of chemical substances deemed toxic or hazardous by government is open to technical controversy, litigation, and other challenges concerning the degree of risk associated with such substances and their suitability for regulation under the laws. Fourth, opponents of regulatory actions under TSCA, RCRA, and Superfund have been able to use to good advantage all the opportunities provided by requirements for administrative due process and the federalized structure of regulation to challenge administrative acts politically and judicially. Fifth, in many instances the states responsible for implementing the programs have been slow to provide from their own resources the means necessary to ensure proper implementation. None of these problems is unique to hazardous substance regulation, but few other environmental policies raise all these problems persistently and acutely.

From a broader perspective, the enormous difficulties in controlling hazardous substances once they are released into the ecosystem, together with the problems of controlling their disposal, emphasize the crucial role that production controls must play in hazardous substance management. Indeed, it may be that the human and environmental risks from hazardous chemicals may never be constrained satisfactorily once these substances are let loose in the environment. American technology development has proceeded largely with an implicit confidence that whatever human or environmental risks may be engendered in the process can be contained adequately by the same genius that inspired technology's development—a faith, in effect, that science always will cure whatever ills it creates. The risk to humans and the environment from the now-pervasive chemical substances created since World War II ought to prompt thoughtful reservations about the efficacy of technological solutions to technological problems. Toxic and hazardous substances pose for the nation a formidable technological challenge: how to reckon the human and environmental costs of technology development while technologies are yet evolving and, then, how to prudently control dangerous technologies without depriving the nation of their benefits.

Suggested Readings

Foster, Kenneth R., David E. Bernstein, and Peter W. Huber. *Phantom Risk: Scientific Inference and the Law.* Cambridge, Mass.: MIT Press, 1999.

Gerrard, Michael B. *Whose Backyard, Whose Risk?* Cambridge, Mass.: MIT Press, 1999.

Rabe, Barry G. *Beyond NIMBY: Hazardous Waste Siting in Canada and the United States.* Washington, D.C.: Brookings Institution Press, 1994.

Raffensberger, Carolyn, and Joel Tickner, eds. *Protecting Public Health and the Environment.* Washington, D.C.: Island Press, 1999.

Rahm, Dianne, ed. *Toxic Waste and Environmental Policy in the 21st Century United States.* Jefferson, N.C.: McFarland, 2002.

Wilson, Duff. *Fateful Harvest: The True Story of a Small Town, a Global Industry, and a Toxic Secret.* New York: Harper Collins, 2002.

Notes

1. From interview in Michelle Williams, "EPA's Chemical Backlog Long and Lingering," *National Journal Insider Interviews,* August 31, 2009, available at: http://insiderinter views.nationaljournal.com/2009/08/epas-chemical-assessment-proce.php (accessed December 20, 2009).

2. Quoted in Nick Madigan, "Largest-Ever Toxic Waste Suit Opens in California," *New York Times,* February 5, 1993, A17.

3. U.S. Environmental Protection Agency (EPA), "Superfund Success Stories," available at: www.epa.gov/superfund/randomize/thumbs3.htm (accessed March 25, 2004).

4. "Top 100 Verdicts of 2005," Verdictsearch, available at: www.verdictsearch.com (accessed March 10, 2007).

5. Ibid.

6. EPA, "Superfund Success Stories."

7. Quoted in Will Matthews, "Stringfellow Retains Reputation: 'Glen Avon' Backlash Underscores Lasting Stigma," *Inland Valley Daily Bulletin* (Ontario, Calif.), January 11, 2003, 1A.

8. Gallup Organization, "The Environment: People's Chief Concerns," April 2009, cited in "The Public Agenda Online," Gallup, available at: http://www.gallup.com/poll/116590/ increased-number-think-global-warming-exaggerated.aspx (accessed December 5, 2009).

9. EPA, "Environmental Progress and Challenges: EPA's Update," Washington, D.C., August 1988, 126. See also U.S. General Accounting Office (GAO), "Toxic Substances: Status of EPA's Reviews of Chemicals under the Chemical Testing Program," Report no. GAO/RCED 92-31FS, Washington, D.C., October 1991.

10. GAO, "Observations on Improving the Toxic Substances Control Act: Statement of John Stephenson, Director, National Resources and Environment," Report no. GAO 10-292, Washington, D.C., December 2, 2009, "Highlights."

11. These estimates, now more than a decade old, have not substantially improved. See, for example, GAO, "Environmental Protection Agency: Major Challenges," Report no. GAO 09-434, Washington, D.C., March 2009, esp. 6.

12. The number of carcinogenic chemicals includes those classified as "known to be a human carcinogen" and those "reasonably anticipated to be a human carcinogen." See U.S. Department of Health and Human Services, Public Health Service, National Toxicology Program, *Report on Carcinogens,* 10th ed. (Washington, D.C.: National Toxicology Program, 2002).

13. Keith Schneider, "Second Chance on Environment," *New York Times,* March 26, 1993, B16.

14. National Research Council, Committee on the Future Role of Pesticides in U.S. Agriculture, *The Future Role of Pesticides in U.S. Agriculture* (Washington, D.C.: National Academies Press, 2000), 33.

15. Philip Shabecoff, "Moderation Becomes Mainstream: The Nation Is Getting Ready to Cut Its Use of Pesticides," *New York Times,* April 16, 1989, 4, 6.

16. Ibid.

17. Philip Shabecoff, "EPA Pulls Back on Asbestos Rules," *New York Times,* March 9, 1985, 1, 48.

18. EPA, "2007 Toxics Release Inventory (TRI), Public Data Release Report," Report no. EPA 260-R-09-001, Washington, D.C., April 2009, 6.

19. EPA, "2007 TRI Public Data Release: Summary of Key Findings," April 2009, available at: epa.gov/tri/tridata/tri04 (accessed November 20, 2009).

20. EPA, Office of Solid Waste and Environmental Remediation, "Treatment Projects Applied to 62 Percent of Superfund Sites," March 10, 2004, available at: www.epa.gov/superfund (accessed March 26, 2004).

21. GAO, "Superfund: Estimates of Number of Future Sites Vary," Report no. GAO/RCED 95-18, Washington, D.C., November 1994, 14. See also Council on Environmental Quality, *Environmental Quality, 1992* (Washington, D.C.: U.S. Government Printing Office, 1993), 127.

22. Jennifer Lee, "Drop in Budget Slows Superfund Program," *New York Times,* March 9, 2004, 8.

23. EPA, "2007 Toxics Release Inventory."

24. Joseph G. Morone and Edward J. Woodhouse, *Averting Catastrophe* (Berkeley: University of California Press, 1986), 34–35.

25. U.S. Centers for Disease Control, "Cytogenetic Patterns in Persons Living near Love Canal—New York," May 27, 1983, available at: ww.cdc.gov/mmwr/preview/mmwrhtml/00000084.htm.

26. GAO, "Superfund," 1, 47.

27. Philip Shabecoff, "EPA Streamlines Cleanup Program," *New York Times,* May 14, 1983, 1, 6.

28. Estimates by Paul MacAvoy, *New York Times,* February 14, 1982, B3. See also Library of Congress, Congressional Research Service, "Six Case Studies of Compensation for Toxic Substances Pollution," report to the Committee on Environment and Public Works, U.S. Senate, no. 96-13, Washington, D.C., 1980.

29. Center for Bioenvironmental Research, Tulane and Xavier Universities, "Environmental Estrogens: What Does the Evidence Mean?" New Orleans, 1996; Center for the Study of Environmental Endocrine Disruptors, "Significant Government Policy Developments," Washington, D.C., 1996; Center for the Study of Environmental Endocrine Disruptors, "Effects: State of Science Paper," Washington, D.C., 1995.

30. Center for the Study of Environmental Endocrine Disruptors, "Effects," 12.

31. Center for the Study of Environmental Endocrine Disruptors, "Significant Government Policy Developments," 17.

32. Theo Colborn, Dianne Dumanoski, and John Peter Meyers, *Our Stolen Future: Are We Threatening Our Fertility, Intelligence, and Survival?* (New York: Penguin, 1996), 7.

33. "Toughest Decisions Still to Come in Pesticide Review," *USA Today,* August 30, 1999, 1A.

34. Marc Landy and Mary Hague, "The Coalition for Waste: Private Interests and Superfund," in *Environmental Politics: Public Costs, Private Rewards,* ed. Michael S. Greve and Fred L. Smith (New York: Praeger, 1992), 70.

35. Keith Schneider, "Rule Forcing Towns to Pick Big New Dumps or Big Costs," *New York Times,* January 6, 1992, A1.

36. Michael S. Greve, "Introduction," in *Environmental Politics: Public Costs, Private Rewards,* ed. Michael S. Greve and Fred L. Smith (New York: Praeger, 1992), 5–6.

37. Linda Schierow, "Summaries of Environmental Laws Administered by the EPA: The Toxic Substances Control Act, Congressional Research Service Report no. RL30022, Washington, D.C., 2006, 2.

38. Quoted in Christopher Harris, William L. Want, and Morris A. Ward, *Hazardous Waste: Confronting the Challenge* (New York: Quorum Books, 1987), 87.

39. Ibid., 90–91.

40. Council on Environmental Quality, "Environmental Quality, 1986," Washington, D.C., 1987, Table 9-6.

41. GAO, "Toxic Substances: EPA Has Made Limited Progress in Identifying PCB Users," Report no. GAO/RCED 88-127, Washington, D.C., April 1988, 3; Council on Environmental Quality, "Environmental Quality, 1986," Table 9-9.

42. GAO, "Observations," "Highlights."

43. Ibid.

44. GAO, "Chemical Regulation: Actions Are Needed to Improve the Effectiveness of EPA's Chemical Review Program," Report no. GAO-06-1032T, Washington, D.C., August 2, 2006, 1; see also Mary Cole, "When Superfund Expenses Go Mega," *Los Angeles Times,* January 26, 2007, 1A.

45. GAO, "RCRA Corrective Action Program," Report no. GAO/RCED 97-3, Washington, D.C., 1997; GAO, "Hazardous Waste: EPA Has Removed Some Barriers to Cleanups," Report no. GAO/RCED 00-2000, Washington, D.C., August 2000, 10–11. See also EPA, Office of Solid Waste, Economics, Methods, and Risk Analysis Division, "A Study of the Implementation of the RCRA Corrective Action Program," September 25, 2000, available at: www.coxcolvin.com/newsletter/CAImplemstudy.pdf (accessed May 15, 2002).

46. GAO, "RCRA Corrective Action Program," 2.

47. Reported in GAO, "Superfund: Progress and Challenges; Statement by David G. Wood, Associate Director, Environmental Protection Issues, Resources, Community, and Economic Development Division, before the Committee on Environment and Public Works, U.S. Senate," Report no. GAO/T-RCED 99-202, 7, Washington, D.C., May 25, 1999.

48. EPA, Region Six, "Superfund Success: EPA Continuing Cleanup Progress at Hazardous Waste Sites," December 2006, available at: www.epa.gov/Region6/6xa/superfund jump.htm (accessed March 30, 2007).

49. GAO, "Superfund Funding and Cost," Report no. GAO-08-841R, Washington, D.C., July 18, 2008, 4.

50. Robert Hersh, Michael B. Batz, and Katherine D. Walker, *Superfund's Future: What Will It Cost?* (Washington, D.C.: Resources for the Future), 131.

51. GAO, "Superfund Program: Current Superfund Program and Future Challenges," Report No. GAO-04-475R, Washington, D.C., February 18, 2004.

52. Landy and Hague, "Coalition for Waste." On the general problems with Superfund, see, for example, Steven Cohen and Sheldon Kamieniecki, *Environmental Regulation through Strategic Planning* (Boulder, Colo.: Westview Press, 1991); Daniel Mazmanian and David Morell, *Beyond Superfailure: America's Toxics Policy for the 1990s* (Boulder, Colo.: Westview Press, 1992).

53. Barnaby J. Feder, "In the Clutches of the Superfund Mess," *New York Times,* June 16, 1991, 3, 1.

54. Ibid.

55. On the sources and impact of NIMBY-ism generally, see Luther J. Carter, *Nuclear Imperatives and Public Trust: Dealing with Radioactive Waste* (Washington, D.C.: Resources for the Future, 1987); Clarence Davies, Vincent T. Covello, and Frederick

W. Allen, eds., *Risk Communication* (Washington, D.C.: Conservation Foundation, 1987); Roger E. Kasperson, "Six Propositions on Public Participation and Their Relevance for Risk Communication," *Risk Analysis* 6 (September 1986): 275–281; Patrick G. Marshall, "Not in My Backyard," *CQ Editorial Research Reports,* June 1989, 311.

56. Olurominiyi Ibitayo and Misse Herber, "NIMBYism," The Encyclopedia of the Earth, November 18, 2008, available at: http://www.eoearth.org/article/NIMBYism (accessed January 5, 2010).

57. Michael S. Greve, "Environmentalism and Bounty Hunting," *Public Interest* 97 (fall 1989): 15–29.

58. Ibid., 24.

59. Michael E. Kraft, "Managing Technological Risks in a Democratic Polity: Citizen Participation and Nuclear Waste Disposal," paper presented at the national conference of the American Society for Public Administration, Boston, 1987. See also Council on Environmental Quality, Executive Office of the President, "The National Environmental Policy Act: A Study of Its Effectiveness after Twenty-Five Years," Washington, D.C., January 1997.

60. William Lyons, Michael R. Fitzgerald, and Amy McCabe, "Public Opinion and Hazardous Waste," *Forum for Applied Research and Public Policy* 2 (fall 1987): 89–97. See also Michael E. Kraft, "Risk Perception and the Politics of Citizen Participation: The Case of Radioactive Waste Management," in *Advances in Risk Analysis,* Vol. 9, ed. Lorraine Abbott (New York: Plenum Press, 1990).

61. Thomas M. Dietz and Robert W. Rycroft, *The Risk Professionals* (New York: Russell Sage Foundation, 1987), 60.

62. Harvey Brooks, "The Resolution of Technically Intensive Public Policy Disputes," *Science, Technology and Human Values* 9 (winter 1984): 48.

63. Kraft, "Risk Perception," 7

Chapter 8

Energy
Nuclear Dreams, Black Gold, and Vanishing Crude

> *Not only are we committed to holding an inauguration that is the most open and accessible in history, but we are also committed to making sure that it is as environmentally friendly and sustainable as possible.... To reduce the inauguration's carbon footprint, attendees are being encouraged to carpool or ride public transit, even in evening gowns and tuxedos. If they must drive, they are being encouraged to use a hybrid vehicle or purchase carbon offsets.*
>
> Linda Douglass, chief spokesperson for
> Obama's inaugural committee, January 11, 2009[1]

Barack Obama had scarcely occupied the White House before presidential initiatives appeared that were intended to demonstrate that his promised new energy policy era had arrived. In mid-January 2009, Obama ordered the EPA to reconsider the Bush administration's earlier decision to deny California's request to set stricter emission standards than the federal government for new automobiles. Shortly thereafter came the president's exhortation that Congress raise American automobile fuel-economy standards to 40 miles per gallon, followed by a proposed billion-dollar investment in clean energy technology included in a massive economic stimulus bill, other actions to increase national energy efficiency, and much more—enough to prompt the National Resources Defense Council, a leading environmentalist organization, to decide that the new president "has done more in its first few months to protect our air, water and communities than we've seen in the last decade."[2]

The Obama election campaign had been rich in environmentalist substance and symbolism, and the inauguration was packed with events to dramatize it. Obama had committed early and often to an ambitious, new,

278

environmentally attractive energy agenda. The campaign platform had promised "an American clean energy industry," petroleum policies that "will curb our dependence on fossil fuels and make America energy independent," air pollution measures that "after decades of inaction ... will finally close the carbon pollution loophole by limiting the amount of carbon polluters are allowed to pump into the atmosphere," and much more.[3] The inauguration included "hundreds of people ... dispatched as part of a 'green squad' to pick up trash and recyclables along the Mall and parade route."[4] Catered events prescribed biodegradable containers, plates, and utensils. Plastics and Styrofoam were forbidden from official White House functions. Hors d'oeuvres were organic. There were volunteers fastidiously trailing parade horses, collecting the manure that was later sold to farms as compost together with leftover food, containers, and utensils. Within a few months, Michelle Obama and her daughters were planting the first White House vegetable garden (organic) since World War II.

All this was a prelude to what Obama had promised would become the policy pathway toward "a new energy future ... embracing alternative and renewable energy, ending our addiction to foreign oil, addressing the global climate crisis and creating millions of new jobs that can't be shipped overseas."[5] Riding a wave of massive environmentalist support, the Obama administration was preparing the energy policy foundation for the White House "green agenda" widely anticipated by environmentalists and the national media. Events soon demonstrated what all recent presidents have discovered—that the practical politics of transforming a new energy era from vision into policy and the stubborn realities embedded in the American energy economy pose inevitable, often daunting challenges inherent to American public policymaking.

A Different, Risky Energy Agenda

Despite environmentalist criticism, the Bush administration's energy program had been committed to modest energy conservation and improved energy efficiency.[6] The Obama energy policy agenda, however, was grounded in priorities and principles intended to depart sharply from the Bush presidency's preference for increased fossil fuel use and accelerated energy exploration, restrained environmental regulation, and reluctant engagement in global climate diplomacy. The Obama initiatives moved more aggressively toward creating an environmentally benign, energy-efficient, and resource-conserving energy economy. The policy foundations included:

- Authorization in the American Recovery and Reinvestment Act (ARRA) for more than $80 billion in the development of clean energy technologies and jobs

- Increased fuel economy standards for new automobiles
- New energy efficiency standards for common household appliances and federal government buildings
- Renewed U.S. commitment to negotiating a domestically binding global agreement to reduce global climate warming emissions
- Increased regulation of air pollution emissions from mobile and stationary sources and scientific updating of air quality standards
- Reduction of U.S. dependence on imported petroleum
- Modernization of the U.S. energy transmission system (the energy grid)

This agenda is freighted with more than ordinary political risks. These hugely expensive energy policies are emerging in the shadow of the nation's most severe economic recession since the end of World War II and huge federal budget deficits. The White House has created an enormous political investment in the success of energy programs authorized by the ARRA, the president's massive economic stimulus legislation, and especially in the numerous Department of Energy (DOE) activities, underwritten by $36.7 billion. As Box 8-1 illustrates, most of these projects are closely identified with Obama's "green agenda."

Box 8-1   *American Recovery and Reinvestment Act of 2009:*
             Energy Technology Investments

- $11 billion funding for an electric smart grid
- $6.3 billion for state and local governments to make investments in energy efficiency
- $6 billion for renewable energy and electric transmission technologies loan guarantees
- $6 billion for the cleanup of radioactive waste (mostly nuclear power plant sites)
- $5 billion for weatherizing modest-income homes
- $4.5 billion for the Office of Electricity and Energy Reliability to modernize the nation's electrical grid and smart grid
- $4.5 billion for state and local governments to increase energy efficiency in federal buildings
- $3.4 billion for carbon capture experiments
- $3.25 billion for the Western Area Power Administration for power transmission system upgrades
- $2.5 billion for energy efficiency research
- $2 billion for manufacturing of advanced car battery (traction) systems and components
- $3.2 billion toward Energy Efficiency and Conservation Block Grants
- $500 million for training of green-collar workers (by the Department of Labor)
- $400 million for electric vehicle technologies
- $300 million for federal vehicle fleets, to cover the cost of acquiring electric vehicles, including plug-in hybrid vehicles
- $300 million to buy energy efficient appliances

(continued)

Box 8-1 *(cont.)*

- $300 million for reducing diesel fuel emissions
- $300 million for state and local governments to purchase energy efficient vehicles
- $250 million to increase energy efficiency in low-income housing
- $600 million to clean up hazardous waste that threaten health and the environment
- $200 million to clean up petroleum leaks from underground storage tanks
- $100 million to evaluate and clean up brownfield land
- $400 million for the Geothermal Technologies Program

Total: $61.3 billion

Source: U.S. House of Representatives, Committee on Appropriations, "Summary: American Recovery and Reinvestment, Conference Agreement," Washington, D.C., February 13, 2009.

Thus, Obama's American energy politics will play out against a setting of high-stakes presidential initiatives, persistent economic turbulence, massive federal investments, and rapidly intensifying global issues affecting all energy policy domains. And no energy is more strategic in this politics than fossil fuel.

Fossil Fuel Nation: A Precarious Energy Economy

The United States has a ravenous energy appetite and most of the consumption is fossil fuel, as Figure 8-1 illustrates. Collectively, Americans constitute approximately 4.6 percent of the world's population and consume about 25 percent of the world's energy production; on average, one American uses more energy in a year than a European, a South American, and an Asian combined.[7] Many of the nation's major pollution problems are caused directly by current methods of producing and consuming this energy. Consider the environmental impact of fossil fuels. About 84 percent of all energy currently consumed in the United States comes from petroleum, natural gas, and coal.[8] The ecological consequences of this combustion are numerous:

- Transportation and other fossil fuel combustion annually produce 34 percent of the volatile organic compounds (VOCs), 78 percent of the carbon monoxide, 85 percent of the sulfur oxides, and 95 percent of the nitrogen oxides emitted into the air.[9]
- The land area disturbed by coal surface mining in the United States now exceeds 5.7 million acres, an area equal in size to the state of New Hampshire. Of this total, more than 3 million acres remains abandoned, creating an abandoned, sterile wasteland.
- During the first decade of this century, an average of more than nine thousand large spills of hazardous substances, mostly petroleum, were reported in U.S. waters yearly. More than 1 million gallons of petroleum and chemicals were spilled annually during the decade.[10]

Figure 8-1   U.S. Primary Energy Consumption by Source and Sector, 2008

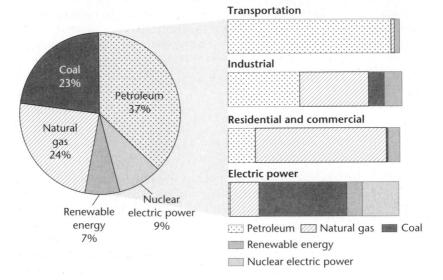

Total U.S. energy = 99.3 quadrillion Btu

Source: U.S. Energy Information Administration, "Annual Energy Review 2008," Washington, D.C., June 2009, Tables 1.3, 2.1b–2.1f.

Note: Sum of components may not equal 100% due to independent rounding.

So intimate is the association between energy and environmental quality—a link revealed again by the emerging problems of global climate warming—that the nation's energy agenda in the second decade of the twenty-first century will become environmental policy by another name.

In addition to the adverse environmental impact of fossil fuels—particularly coal—America's current energy consumption is doubly precarious. With the exception of coal, the fossil fuels providing most of the energy that drives the national economy comes from nonrenewable, generally receding energy stocks that are required to provide more than two-thirds of the nation's energy supply well into mid-century. Moreover, the petroleum accounting for more than one-third of national energy consumption, and powering virtually all domestic transportation as well as 40 percent of industrial production, increasingly flows from insecure, progressively more competitive foreign supplies, primarily in the Middle East, Asia, and Africa. Not surprisingly, Barack Obama has joined every U.S. president since Richard Nixon in his preoccupation with reducing national dependence on imported petroleum and mitigating the environmental impact of other fossil fuels.

Fossil Fuels: Consumption or Addiction?

U.S. dependence on imported oil declined sharply in the years immediately following the second oil shock created by Iran's sudden 1978 cutback in U.S. petroleum exports, and it seemed for a few years that the United States had learned the lesson of the oil embargoes. But imports rose again, and by 2009 the nation was importing almost 62 percent of its annual petroleum consumption, far more than the 38.8 percent imported when the first Arab embargo hit.[11] Moreover, an increasing proportion of this imported oil—currently about one barrel in four consumed in the United States—originates in the politically volatile Persian Gulf. At the same time, U.S. oil production is dwindling slowly. By 2009, U.S. production was at its lowest level since 1954 and was not ever expected to increase.[12]

The nation's surging dependence on imported oil occurs amid considerable uncertainty about the duration of the global petroleum supply and increasing international competition for access to known petroleum reserves. The International Energy Agency, for instance, predicts that mainland China's rapid economic growth will increase its dependence on imported petroleum from 22 percent of its annual petroleum consumption in 2000 to 77 percent by 2020, and that, during the same period, European dependence on imported oil will rise from 52 to 79 percent of annual demand.[13] The economic and political assumptions undergirding all these predictions about future world energy supply are at best informed speculation, often confounded easily by unanticipated events. Given these uncertainties, and the enormous ecological, economic, and security risks entailed in continuing its heavy dependence on foreign oil, the United States has reason to consider imported oil to be a major problem. Moreover, energy production and consumption, particularly fossil fuel combustion of all kinds, are the major sources of air pollution and significant water degradation. From an environmental perspective, coal is an especially potent polluter. More than 80 percent of the nation's electric power is generated from coal at the cost of enormous environmental degradation and impaired public health. Currently, however, few short-term alternatives exist to coal as a utility fuel or to petroleum and its byproducts as motor fuel or feedstock for thousands of industrial and commercial products such as plastics, cosmetics, and medical equipment. Most often considered among these alternatives are increased energy conservation, increased use of commercial nuclear power (shortly to be discussed), and increased use of renewable energy (solar, thermal, wind, and hydroelectric power). Until the latter years of the George W. Bush presidency, neither a revived nuclear power industry, quickly accelerated energy conservation, nor widespread governmentally mandated renewable energy had acquired the popular appeal, or political allure, that would significantly diminish the apparently implacable national dependency on fossil fuels.

The Revival of Renewable Energy

When the Bush administration needed $135,000 to print copies of its 2001 energy plan, the money came from the DOE's solar and renewable energy conservation funds.[14] This became a bleak preview of the apathy toward renewable energy and, especially, energy conservation that customarily prevailed throughout George Bush's first term, dissipating only in the administration's closing years with the steadily rising environmental and economic costs of alternative energy (see later in the chapter). In addition, energy conservation has been more often praised than enthusiastically promoted by the White House ever since Jimmy Carter's term. At Barack Obama's inauguration, all forms of renewable energy provided only 7 percent of the nation's total energy consumption (see Figure 8-2). Conventional hydroelectric facilities and wood fuels together provide almost 80 percent of renewable energy (45 and 34 percent, respectively). Although national renewable energy consumption has risen by modest increments since 1970—particularly when the energy crisis of the 1970s prompted momentary congressional attention to alternative fuels—the

Figure 8-2   Renewable Energy Plays a Role in the Nation's Energy Supply, 2008

Source: U.S. Energy Information Administration, "Renewable Energy Consumption and Electricity 2008," Washington, D.C., July 2009, Table 1.

Note: Sum of components may not equal 100% due to independent rounding.

White House, Congress, and the public have feebly and inconstantly embraced renewable energy and conservation compared to the national investment in fossil fuels. Indeed, the federal government, without public objection, dismantled within a few years almost all the most potent incentives for energy conservation and renewable energy production that had been created during the short-lived energy crisis of the 1970s.

By George Bush's second term, the adverse impacts associated with the continued national dependence on imported oil and fossil fuels hastened passage of the National Energy Policy Act of 2005 (EPAct), the Bush administration's most important national energy plan and most substantial commitment to promoting renewable energy and conservation. EPAct created numerous federal subsidies, tax incentives, and research support for the development of new energy-efficient technologies and improved energy conservation practices in the domestic economy. The important energy conservation and efficiency features included $4.19 billion in tax credits for the production of renewable energy (biomass, wind, solar, thermal, and hydroelectric) and increased energy efficiency in existing homes, new energy standards for a large variety of appliances, tax credits for hybrid vehicle purchases, and increased federal spending and tax incentives for production and blending of biofuels in domestic motor vehicles. Although these programs seem unambitious compared to the ARRA, they constitute a foundation on which the Obama administration expects to mount its vastly more expansive and expensive energy renewal and conservation efforts. The Obama administration's massive financial and political investment in enormously amplified renewable energy and energy conservation programs would, if successful, create an important and possibly enduring transformation of the American energy infrastructure.

Renewable Energy's Rewards and Risks

"Every gallon of oil each one of us saves," remarked Jimmy Carter in the aftermath of the nation's first, nationally disruptive energy crisis, "is a new form of production." Similar affirmations have become ritual in every subsequent American presidency, but it has taken almost three decades of national energy policymaking to transform renewable energy into a national policy imperative. Renewable energy, or at least a celebration of its virtues, has now become almost irresistibly appealing to national policymakers confronted with the political and economic turbulence created by the nation's increasing energy problems. However, the virtues of renewable energy are bundled with problematic trade-offs and risks that policymakers must also confront.

The Good News. Renewable energy's potential is substantial and widely advertised. The nation's renewable energy sector has experienced incremental expansion with episodes of rapid growth and retrenchment, depending largely on the state of the economy and the governmental incentives available. Predictions about the beneficial impact of renewables on the national energy economy have been impressive. For example:

- Biomass in the form of the leftover refuse from logging and milling operations on the federal lands could produce enough cellulosic ethanol to displace 8 percent of current gasoline consumption.
- Renewable energy, which presently accounts for about 7 percent of U.S. electric power production, could produce as much as one-quarter to one-third of the nation's future electric power if the price of competing fuels were to rise significantly.
- A year's worth of solar energy on 1 acre of Texas prairie could produce the energy equivalent of 800 barrels of oil, and solar-panel farms covering 100 acres or more in California's Mojave Desert could produce enough electric power to supply a small city.
- The total amount of electricity that could potentially be generated from wind in the United States has been estimated at 10,777 billion kilowatts annually—more than twice the electricity generated in the United States today.

Renewable energy can also generate employment. The Solar Energy Industries Association, which estimates that the domestic solar industry created almost 20,000 new jobs across the United States in 2009, predicts that as many as 45,000 new jobs could be created in a year with the proper federal tax and grant incentives. Given favorable sites and economic incentives, national corporations have been alert to the advantages of renewable energy.

- FedEx Corp will install solar panels covering about 3 acres and capable of generating 2.42 megawatts of electricity atop its distribution hub in Woodbridge, New Jersey; when completed, it is expected to be the largest rooftop solar facility in the United States, producing about 30 percent of the facility's electricity needs.
- Wal-Mart, whose ultimate goal is to produce 100 percent of its power with renewable energy, is installing solar panels on 10–20 stores and distribution centers in California by 2011; the company has already installed solar panels on 18 Wal-Mart and Sam's Club stores in California and Hawaii, where each solar project will create enough energy to power the equivalent of 2,600 homes.

While the federal government's commitment to renewable energy waivered throughout the Bush administration, the states seized the initiative to create some of the most convincing demonstrations of public-sector confidence in renewable's potential. By 2010, twenty-seven states had adopted Renewable Portfolio Standards (RPS) requiring utilities to obtain a percentage of their electric power, varying among the states from 4 to 30 percent, from renewable energy. California, often a leader in environmental innovation, enacted legislation requiring (perhaps too optimistically) that 20 percent of its electric power be obtained from renewable energy by 2010.

Trade-offs and Risks. Renewable energy also poses often unadmitted economic and environmental risks, and sometimes difficult trade-offs, to policymakers. One major concern is that renewable energy and its technologies are highly vulnerable to the vicissitudes of the marketplace. Changes in the price of competing fuels, unanticipated international trade events, the cost of technology development, and much else can produce chronic or sudden economic difficulties. For example, "[p]rices for turbines and solar panels, which soared when the boom began a few years ago, are falling," reported the *New York Times* in early 2009. "Communities that were patting themselves on the back just last year for attracting a wind or solar plant are now coping with cutbacks."[15] The onset of the severe economic recession in 2007 created a credit crisis for the industry—the eighteen large banks and financial institutions extending credit to underwrite wind turbines and solar arrays shrank to four lenders within two years.

The renewables industry also depends heavily on federal government patronage to provide economic incentives in the form of subsidies, research and development grants, and tax breaks that stimulate production and consumer interest. Federal and state regulations are another constant concern. Regulatory restrictions on carbon dioxide emissions prompted by global climate change, for instance, will probably raise electric power prices and perhaps make the additional costs entailed in adding renewable energy to the mix unwelcome for consumers (some estimates suggest that the cost of wind power may be more than 50 percent higher per kilowatt than conventional electricity produced by coal).

A persistent trade-off entailed by renewable energy production—and to environmentalists the most vexing—is the potential adverse environmental risks to be balanced against the attractions of renewables. The implications can pit environmental advocates against each other and arouse accusations of NIMBY-ism from one side or another. For example:

- "By 2030, environmental and lobby groups are pushing for the U.S. to be producing 20% of its electricity from wind. Meeting that goal, according to the Department of Energy, will require the U.S. to have about 300,000 megawatts of wind capacity, a 12-fold increase over 2008 levels. If that target is achieved, we can expect some 300,000 birds, at the least, to be killed by wind turbines each year."[16]
- State Renewable Portfolio Standards will increase the domestic demand for biofuels, such as ethanol, and possibly produce undesirable agricultural impacts, such as impaired water quality from fertilizer runoff and erosion, decrease water quantity and quality, degrade air quality and threaten wildlife habitat.
- The planned development of solar-panel farms covering thousands of desert acres in California, Arizona, Utah and other western states has frequently been vigorously opposed by coalitions of environmentalists and local residents intent on preventing the intrusion into their lifestyles, the risk to endangered species, and the possible disruption of the native ecosystems.

Many of these problematic aspects are likely to become increasingly evident and publicly contentious as the Obama administration attempts to implement its ambitious renewable energy programs.

Shifting Public Moods

Public concerns about imported petroleum, fossil fuel dependency, and the energy supply were hurried toward extinction by the Ronald Reagan administration's rapid elimination of the energy conservation and regulatory programs enacted in the late 1970s and by the return of ample world petroleum supplies creating lower petroleum prices. Neither the George Bush nor Bill Clinton administrations seemed interested in disturbing the public reverie. Thus, George W. Bush entered the White House inheriting both a superheated energy economy and two decades of apathetic energy planning reinforced by public disinterest. Throughout Bush's first term, however, events gradually revived public alertness to national energy issues and concerns about the energy supply. By 2006, a comprehensive survey of public polls since 1970 reported that:

> concern about the U.S. energy situation is as high now as it was during the nation's energy crises of the 1970s. While attitudes about traditional sources of energy are strongly influenced by current economic conditions, citizens are increasingly receptive to alternative sources of energy (e.g., nuclear energy). Citizens also support policy changes that involve the government encouraging conservation through energy efficient appliances, vehicles, and homes and offices.[17]

At the beginning of the Obama administration, the public mood appeared to elevate energy issues to a level of civic discourse unknown since 1973. Another comprehensive national opinion poll in 2009, for instance, reported that "a majority of the public sees the price of energy and dependence on foreign oil as troubling problems" and "a substantial consensus [exists] on the proposals that the nation should pursue, particularly alternative energy, conservation and incentives to become more efficient." These "seem promising to the public," the study authors also cautioned "but they may not have realistic assumptions about how quickly and easily these alternatives can be achieved."[18]

Caution was advisable because the public also appeared largely uninformed or mistaken about many fundamentals of energy production, distribution, and governance. For instance, nearly four out of ten Americans (39 percent) could not name a fossil fuel; still more could not identify a renewable energy source and more than half the public (56 percent) said incorrectly that nuclear energy contributes to global warming.[19] These revelations are consistent with numerous public opinion polls taken over the last several decades concerning environment matters, which also suggest that public opinions about policy issues are often meagerly grounded in facts and shallow in understanding the implications of policy preferences. Nonetheless, public opinion matters. At the very least, public attitudes establish a national mood, a receptivity or resistance to policy options, thereby creating more or less opportunity for civic debate, while becoming venues for public education and consensus building, all critically important in creating a civic setting for policymaking and change.

The intricate interdependence of energy production and environmental quality can be appreciated by examining three national energy issues in greater depth. Conventional nuclear power and coal, both important energy sectors, pose significant ecological risks likely to continue as long as the United States builds its energy future on a foundation of fossil fuel. And the sudden emergence of a new nuclear issue—the staggering financial and technical task of cleaning up the nation's military nuclear weapons facilities—threatens to create costs so massive and work so protracted that it will be the most expensive federal environmental program through most of the twenty-first century.

Nuclear Power: Looking for a Renaissance

It certainly was not business as usual at the U.S. Nuclear Regulatory Commission (NRC). The federal regulator of the commercial nuclear power industry had last received an order for a new facility in 1973. By October 2008, however, new applications with their voluminous paper baggage were arriving "so fast that the Nuclear Regulatory Commission, which had almost forgotten how to accept an application, has gone into a frenzy of hiring, bringing on hundreds of new engineers to handle the crush of applications."[20] Twenty-three companies had filed applications to build thirty-four nuclear utilities, new reactor-manufacturing facilities appeared, and four to eight new reactor units could come on line by 2018.[21] Florida Power and Light (FPL) was adding a small billing surcharge to finance three new nuclear utilities that it expected to construct within the next decade. Improbably, even Greenpeace, the epitome of traditional environmentalist opposition, now professed cautious approval.[22] Commercial nuclear power is unexpectedly riding the crest of a resurgence in national interest hardly imagined at the century's onset.

The Substance of Revival

At 2000, statistics about commercial nuclear power read like the industry's obituary. Since 1980, the Nuclear Dream—the vision of almost unlimited, cheap electricity generated by hundreds of nuclear reactors—had been dying. The commercial nuclear power industry was failing under a burden of economic and technological misfortunes, an increasingly hostile political climate, inept public relations, persistent environmental risks, and mounting regulatory pressures.

The industry's apparent recovery draws on several sources. One potent source might be called the "other greenhouse effect." With growing national and international attention to global climate warming (see Chapter 10), in the 1990s the industry initiated an increasingly aggressive strategy to promote commercial nuclear power as the most desirable economic and environmental alternative to the greenhouse gas emissions associated with fossil fuel combustion for generating electric power.

Another powerful stimulus has been the federal government's vigorous political and economic initiatives, especially since the George W. Bush administration. The industry was enormously encouraged when the Bush administration declared in its 2001 National Energy Plan that a "dramatic improvement in U.S. nuclear power plant performance over the last 25 years" had occurred and that the industry "has established a strong foundation for the expansion of nuclear energy in the next two decades."[23] In 2004, the DOE proposed building fifty new power plants and prolonging the operating life of numerous existing facilities to the year 2020. The EPAct's very substantial commitment to nuclear power development in 2005 seemed to the industry's advocates a confirmation that industry was, at last, truly reviving.[24] In keeping with a half century tradition of massive federal governmental subsidies, research grants, and other economic patronage, EPAct provided financial incentives for the construction of advanced nuclear plants amounting to $18.5 billion, which the industry has requested be increased to $100 billion.[25] Barack Obama added additional momentum to the nuclear resurgence when, much to the disappointment of most environmentalists, his campaign platform endorsed the continued development of commercial nuclear power, a commitment further reinforced when his 2010 State of the Union speech advocated "a new generation of safe, clean nuclear power plants" and proposed to triple public financing for nuclear power.

Underlying these events, and doubtless encouraging them, has been rising public approval for commercial nuclear power to the point where in mid-2009 the Gallup Poll reported "new high levels of support," with 59 percent of Americans favoring domestic nuclear energy.[26] Adding to this beneficial mix has been an anticipated 30 percent escalation of the U.S. demand for electric power; a very substantial increase in nuclear output capacity; and the absence of potentially catastrophic, high-visibility facility accidents or security lapses. The industry also contends that the planned new generation of reactor technologies (Generation III) will be considerably more efficient, safer, and more economical than present operating models.

This recent good fortune evolves despite the industry's history, a tarnished past of frequently flawed performance, misconceived governmental promotion, and regulatory criticism compounded by technical difficulties. That history has nurtured a deep distrust of commercial nuclear power that has been slow to dissipate among environmentalists, much of the scientific community, many public officials, and (until recently) the public.

The Peaceful Atom and Its Problems

Peaceful atomic power began with the Dwight D. Eisenhower administration's determination to demonstrate to the world that the United States was concerned with more than the military uses of nuclear power and the prevention of global nuclear proliferation. The federal government offered to the electric power industry massive subsidies and other powerful incentives to create a nuclear electric power infrastructure. Once the electric power industry agreed to the bargain, the regulation and management of the new technology were invested in the Atomic Energy Commission (AEC) and in the Joint Committee on Atomic Energy, a new congressional watchdog for the commission.[27]

The industry prospered due to benevolent regulation; huge infusions of generous federal subsidies; public and political favor; and unique governmental concessions never given its competitors, such as the Price-Anderson Act (1957), which limited a nuclear utility's insurance liability to $540 million for any single reactor accident, thus ensuring that the industry would obtain the necessary insurance coverage. Until the 1970s, all but a handful of scientists, economists, and public officials associated with the new technology seemed, according to economists Irvin C. Bupp and Jean-Claude Derian, so "intoxicated" by the enterprise that they largely ignored grave technical and economic problems already apparent to a few critical observers.[28] When problems could not be ignored, they usually were hidden from public view; when critics arose, they were discredited by Washington's aggressive defense of the industry. By the beginning of the Obama presidency, the industry had received by conservative estimate more than $77 billion in federal subsidies—approximately 60 percent of the total federal energy research expenditures and far exceeding Washington's support for any other energy. In 1975, the Nuclear Dream seemed most resplendent: 56 commercial reactors had been built, another 69 were under construction, and 111 more were planned. Then came the near-catastrophic reactor meltdown at Three Mile Island, near Harrisburg, Pennsylvania, in March 1979, the most politically damaging episode in the program's brief history, forcing national attention on an industry already in serious trouble. The industry's grave technical and economic problems had been evident even in the early 1970s. The accident at Three Mile Island, however, was a catalytic political event, powerfully altering public consciousness about nuclear power and strengthening the credibility of the industry's critics. Moreover, the industry's serious economic, technical, and environmental problems continued to worsen as the 1980s progressed. The May 1986 core meltdown at the Chernobyl nuclear power plant in Soviet Ukraine was one more catastrophe in a series of baleful events hastening the extinction of the Nuclear Dream. As the twentieth century ended, the domestic industry was almost moribund.

The Nuclear Industry Today

In 2010, there were 104 operating nuclear reactors licensed to U.S. electrical utilities, down from a peak of 112 in 1990. Most reactors are located along the East Coast, in the Southeast, and in the Midwest (see Map 8-1). These reactors currently represent about 21 percent of U.S. net electricity-generating capacity. Under their original schedule, the licenses for these reactors were issued for forty years and half of the reactors would have ended their legal operating lives between 2005 and 2015; the remainder would have shut down before 2075. In short, commercial nuclear power would disappear within a few generations unless the present facility licenses were extended and new reactors were constructed because U.S. utilities had ordered no new reactors since 1979 and simultaneously had cut back sharply on planned construction. In 2000, however, the NRC began to renew utility licenses through a prolonged process involving

Map 8-1   U.S. Commercial Nuclear Power Reactors and Years of Operation, 2009

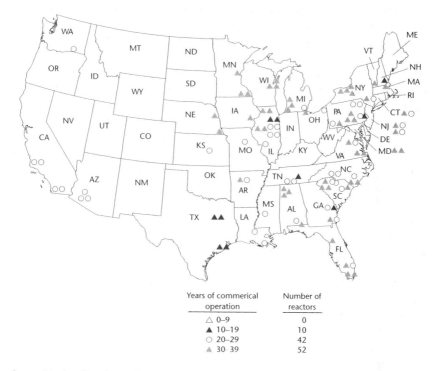

Years of commerical operation	Number of reactors
△ 0–9	0
▲ 10–19	10
○ 20–29	42
⬤ 30–39	52

Source: Nuclear Regulatory Commission, "Nuclear Reactors," 2009, available at: http://www
.nrc.gov/reactors/operating/power-reactors-map-sm.jpg (accessed January 20, 2010).

Note: There are no commercial reactors in Alaska or Hawaii.

extensive NRC safety reviews, public meetings, and state consultation. By
mid-2009, the NRC had extended the licenses of fifty-four reactors and
anticipated an additional thirty-one applications by 2013.[29]

Despite notable improvements in the industry's safety procedures,
technology, and operating efficiency since Three Mile Island, its troubles
remain substantial, including economic and technical difficulties, unsolved
waste management problems, and a regulatory regime uneasy about the
possibility of terrorist attacks on nuclear facilities.

Economic Ills. The gloss applied to the industry's public image by its
partisans cannot quite conceal some problematic economics. The cost of
constructing and maintaining commercial nuclear power plants climbed
so steeply between 1980 and 2000 that investment capital has been scarce
and costly. Capital investment is likely to be even more elusive in the

aftermath of the 2007 economic recession and the bloating estimates for new plant construction. Early in 2008, the *Wall Street Journal* and several other publications carried headline news stories about the skyrocketing cost projections for new nuclear facilities, indicating that it might cost $9–12 billion to build a single new nuclear power plant. FPL's first estimate for a large plant off the Florida Keys reached $12–18 billion. Progress Energy's proposed plan for a similar Florida plant was predicted to cost $17 billion, triple the previous year's estimate.[30]

The major reasons for this cost escalation are concerns about public safety and environmental protection. The time required to secure the many governmental licenses that ensure a facility will meet safety and environmental standards had steadily lengthened through the 1990s. Despite more recent efforts to streamline the review process, surmounting the regulatory hurdles still requires four to eight years and may involve almost a hundred different federal, state, and local governmental permits. Industry officials also complain about the costs imposed during plant construction through regulatory ratcheting by the NRC (its habit of requiring facilities to make new safety modifications or other expensive design changes many years after plant construction). Additional costs have also been imposed on many utilities by protracted litigation involving environmental groups and others challenging various aspects of plant design and safety. These costs have reduced the market competitiveness of nuclear-generated electricity compared to fossil-fuel-burning plants, especially in the West and Midwest. Nuclear power's greatest potential market appears to be in the East and Southeast, assuming the rampant cost estimates can be contained. Moreover, the industry's economic ills cannot be blamed wholly on the regulators and environmental critics. Operating plants acquired a lackluster efficiency image because many performed below design levels throughout the 1980s and 1990s, although the industry's annual capacity rate reached 90 percent by 2007.[31] And serious, expensive technical problems continue to beset the industry.

Technical Problems. Proponents of nuclear power argue correctly that its safety record, notwithstanding the accident at Three Mile Island, is excellent and that critics have exaggerated its technical problems. However, continuing revelations of technical difficulties suggest serious deficiencies in the basic design and operation of the plants and frequent carelessness or incompetence in plant management. Whatever their real significance, these problems have worked against the industry politically. Continuing admissions of safety risks and technical difficulties at a time of growing public apprehension about nuclear terrorism continue to inspire the opposition.

Several technical problems have been especially damaging to the industry. Materials and design standards for many plants currently operating or under construction have failed essential safety requirements. Reactor parts, for instance, have aged much faster than anticipated. Steam generators meant to last a plant's lifetime—approximately fifty years—are wearing out much sooner than expected; this is a particularly serious problem in New York, Florida, Virginia, Wisconsin, and South Carolina.[32] Mistakes have been made in plant specifications or construction. Pipes have cracked and "wasted" (the walls becoming thinner) from extended exposure to radiation. As early as 1988, the GAO recommended a mandatory inspection of all plants for pipe deterioration after finding that nearly one-third of the plants it surveyed did indeed have pipe deterioration. The NRC betrayed its own misgivings about plant safety in 1979 when it repudiated its 1974 estimate, contained in the Rassmussen report, that a potentially catastrophic reactor accident would occur only once in 10 million years of reactor operation—as probable as a single meteorite striking an individual on Earth. The NRC failed at the time to provide an alternative safety estimate.

Finally, continuing revelations of plant mismanagement, administrative bungling, and secrecy raise serious questions about the competence of plant managers and technicians. The industry must still contend with disclosures such as the NRC's announcement in early 2007 that it had downgraded the safety rating of the nation's largest nuclear plant, subjecting it to more inspectors and a level of scrutiny shared by just one other plant in the nation. As the Associated Press reported,

> The NRC's announcement ended three years of problems in various safety systems at the Palo Verde nuclear plant west of Phoenix. Inspectors in September found that one of its emergency diesel generators had been broken for 18 days. Emergency generators are critically important at nuclear reactors, providing electricity to pumps, valves and control rooms if the main electrical supply fails. Only FirstEnergy Corp.'s Perry nuclear plant in Ohio has a safety rating as bad as Palo Verde's, NRC spokesman Victor Dricks said.[33]

Industry officials insist that critics have misrepresented the safety record of commercial nuclear utilities by seizing on these disclosures as if they characterized the entire industry. Indeed, many utilities have a virtually uninterrupted record of safe operations and skilled management. Still, after more than thirty years of operation, the industry continues to experience serious design, management, and engineering failures. The Union of Concerned Scientists' verdict seems fair:

> Is nuclear power in the United States safe enough today just because a reactor has not experienced a meltdown since 1979? The answer is a resounding no. In the 27 years since the TMI [Three Mile Island] meltdown, 38 U.S. nuclear power reactors had to be shut down for at least one year while safety margins were restored to minimally acceptable levels. Seven of these reactors experienced two-year-plus outages. Though these reactors were

shut down before they experienced a major accident, we cannot assume we will continue to be so lucky. The number and length of these shutdowns testif[y] to how serious and widespread the problem is.[34]

Moreover, the industry has not solved its grave waste disposal and emergency management problems.

The Waste Nobody Wants. No problem has proved more politically troublesome to the nuclear power industry and its federal regulators than where, and how, to dispose of the enormous, highly toxic, and mounting volume of nuclear wastes in the United States. The problem, never anticipated when commercial nuclear power was first promoted, has been especially difficult because reactor wastes incite great public fear and chronic conflict among federal, state, and local officials concerning where to put them.

The wastes temporarily stored on site at commercial nuclear power plants joins an immense stock of additional radioactive materials from uranium mining, military nuclear weapons programs, hospitals, educational institutions, and research centers. The current controversy involves four categories of waste:

- *High-level wastes.* This category of waste comprises highly radioactive liquids created through the reprocessing of reactor fuels. These wastes are generated by both civilian and military reactor programs. Currently, more than 100 million gallons of high-level wastes are stored in temporary containment facilities in Idaho, New York, South Carolina, and Washington state.
- *Transuranic wastes.* Some of the elements in these radioactive byproducts of reactor fuel and military waste processing remain dangerous for extraordinarily long periods. Plutonium-239, with a half-life of 24,000 years, and americum-243, with a half-life of 7,300 years, are among the transuranics. Other, more exotic transuranic elements have half-lives exceeding 200,000 years.
- *Spent nuclear fuel.* About 63,000 metric tons of spent fuel rods and other radioactive trash, mostly from civilian reactors, are stored temporarily in cooling ponds at reactor sites.
- *Low-level wastes.* Any material contaminated by radiation and emitting low levels of radioactivity belongs in this category. This includes workers' clothing, tools, equipment, and other items associated with nuclear reactors or nuclear materials. Low-level wastes currently are stored at repositories in Nevada, New York, and South Carolina.

Map 8-2 shows where the wastes from commercial reactors and military activities are stored. In the early years of nuclear power promotion, it was assumed that spent fuel from civilian and military plants would

Map 8-2   Current Locations of Spent Nuclear Fuel and High-Level
Radioactive Waste Destined for Geological Disposition

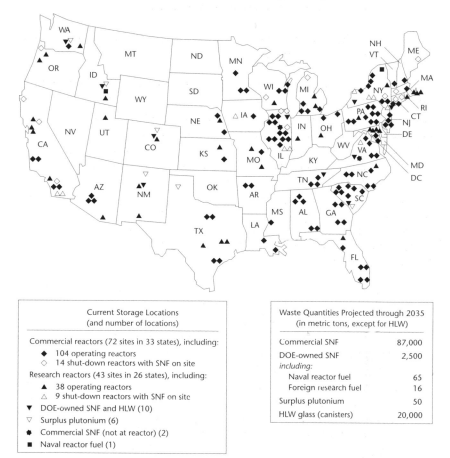

Current Storage Locations (and number of locations)	Waste Quantities Projected through 2035 (in metric tons, except for HLW)	
Commercial reactors (72 sites in 33 states), including:	Commercial SNF	87,000
◆ 104 operating reactors	DOE-owned SNF	2,500
◇ 14 shut-down reactors with SNF on site	*including:*	
Research reactors (43 sites in 26 states), including:	Naval reactor fuel	65
▲ 38 operating reactors	Foreign research fuel	16
△ 9 shut-down reactors with SNF on site	Surplus plutonium	50
▼ DOE-owned SNF and HLW (10)	HLW glass (canisters)	20,000
▽ Surplus plutonium (6)		
✱ Commercial SNF (not at reactor) (2)		
■ Naval reactor fuel (1)		

Source: U.S. Department of Energy, Office of Civilian Radioactive Waste Management, www.rw.doe.gov/wasteaccept/snflocationspic.jpg (March 27, 2001).

Note: HLW = high-level radioactive waste; SNF = spent nuclear fuel. Symbols do not reflect exact locations.

be reprocessed; the fissionable materials, primarily plutonium, could be recovered to be used again as reactor fuel, and the remaining high-level waste eventually would be contained and isolated at appropriate disposal sites. In the planners' early view, the high-level and transuranic wastes remaining after reprocessing posed a largely technical and readily solvable problem of finding the appropriate containment materials and geographical location for permanent storage. They did not anticipate the failure of civilian reprocessing and the resulting volume of nuclear waste. They did not foresee the necessity of storing military wastes for decades longer than the containment structures were designed to last. They did not anticipate the political repercussions of trying to find a place to put the waste.

Existing and planned commercial facilities were designed to store temporarily no more than three years of accumulated spent fuel in cooling ponds until the fuel assemblies were reprocessed. Since the early 1970s, however, virtually all spent fuel has been stored in these cooling ponds. Space and time are running out. The United States continues to reprocess its spent military fuel, thereby generating most of the high-level liquid wastes accumulating at military nuclear reservations. Until 1982, the federal government had no comprehensive plan for the permanent storage of these nuclear wastes. The federal government and the states quarreled for more than a decade over how a permanent waste depository would be designed and which states would be depository sites—nobody wanted it.[35] Idaho and South Carolina, already accommodating large volumes of high- and low-level wastes from other states, were increasingly reluctant to accept more. In 1976, California ordered a moratorium on the construction of commercial nuclear facilities until Washington, D.C., could certify that a permanent repository for their spent fuel existed. The nuclear waste issue was approaching a crisis.

The States Play Nuclear Keep Away. In 1982, Congress finally passed the Nuclear Waste Policy Act (NWPA), which was intended to create a process for designating and constructing the first permanent repositories for nuclear waste. The act appeared to end a decade of nasty legislative infighting during which each state scrambled to write language into the law ensuring that it would not be a candidate for the repository. The legislation assigned the site-selection task to the DOE and created what appeared to be a meticulously detailed, impartial, and open process by which all possible sites would be studied thoroughly and reduced to a few from which the president would eventually select two, one east and one west of the Mississippi River.

Following procedures required by the NWPA, the DOE in 1985 recommended three permanent western sites to the president from which he was to select one: Deaf Smith County, Texas; the Hanford Nuclear Reservation in Washington state; and Yucca Mountain, Nevada (near the Nevada atomic test site). The political leadership of both parties in all three states complained vehemently that their states had been improperly designated and attempted to overturn the designation in the courts. Environmental groups in each state went to court, challenging the designations on technical and procedural grounds. Rather than abide the continuing controversy, Congress found a simpler solution to the designation problem. In December 1987, Congress suddenly renounced the procedures it had ordered in the NWPA and summarily designated Nevada to be the first permanent waste site. As a consolation, Nevada was assured of receiving up to $20 million annually to manage the job. Nevada legislators were outraged. It "will turn our state into a federal colony," accused Republican representative Barbara F. Vucanovich.[36] "Instead of leadership and principle, it's a gang-rape mentality," added a spokesperson for Richard Bryan, Nevada's governor.[37] Nevada has continued its unremitting resistance to the Yucca Mountain facility with every political resource it has available.

This trench warfare slowed the facility's construction to a crawl, but Congress in 1997 left little doubt that Nevada was still the nation's most eligible nuclear waste bin. Both the House and the Senate passed legislation, over the vehement objections of the state's leaders, that created a temporary repository near the Yucca Mountain site for the high-level nuclear waste that was still awaiting the completion of the permanent Nevada site.[38] In the keep-away politics of nuclear waste, the most weakly defended constituency was still "it."

Repository Problems

"It's fair to say we've solved the nuclear waste problem with this legislation," Sen. Bennett Johnston, D-La., assured his colleagues with premature optimism after they awarded the waste site to Nevada. But after more than two years of preliminary work and an expenditure of $500 million at the Nevada site, the DOE announced in 1989 that it was abandoning its initial repository plan because it lacked confidence in the technical quality of the proposal.[39] The DOE predicted that the repository would be delayed until at least 2010, even though it was committed to accepting high-level wastes from commercial reactors by 1998 and the commercial utilities had already paid $3 billion in taxes to use the repository. However, by 2007 it was evident that the DOE would not be ready to receive the wastes at even a temporary repository and that the availability of a permanent repository remained equally speculative. "A realistic date for having a permanent repository operational keeps receding farther into the future," concluded a 1993 GAO report.[40] Frustrated by these continuing delays, the Bush administration in 2002 declared its intention to open the site by 2010; requested a large budget increase to underwrite accelerated site construction in 2003; and was promptly sued by the state of Nevada and numerous other plaintiffs, thereby relegating the Yucca Mountain facility to a judicial limbo and an uncertain future once again. The repository's destiny was further muddled when President Obama pledged to eliminate its federal funding while simultaneously continuing its operation until the complex legal path to its termination is completed.

Meanwhile, reports on the DOE's other nuclear waste management projects have been unrelieved bad news since the late 1980s. In mid-1989, the DOE announced that it was delaying the opening of its Waste Isolation Pilot Project (WIPP) near Carlsbad, New Mexico. The WIPP, begun in the late 1970s, was intended to store the plutonium wastes generated at the Rocky Flats nuclear military facility near Denver, Colorado, where space for the liquid wastes was fast disappearing. The underground repository had been scheduled to receive its first shipments in 1992, but the DOE's scientific advisers urged a delay of two or three years because the DOE needed to complete technical diagrams of twenty-one systems already built into the structure, including the electrical, radiation control, and fire protection systems.[41] In fact, the WIPP did not receive its first nuclear waste until 2001.

The WIPP's delay added another chapter to the already protracted, acrimonious debate about the safety of that facility and raised doubts that the WIPP will ever be used. Thus, the nation still lacks a permanent repository for its civilian and military nuclear wastes. Waste storage capacity at civilian utility sites continues to dwindle. At the same time, military waste-containment structures are deteriorating dangerously at places such as the Hanford Nuclear Reservation, where 440,000 cubic yards of high-, low-, and extremely long-lived nuclear wastes are stored, some since 1943, awaiting permanent deposition.[42] This is not, however, the whole of the national nuclear waste problem. The controversy attending reactor waste deflects public attention from the emerging problem of disposing of the nuclear facilities themselves after they have outlived their usefulness.

Decommissioning Problems

Once a civilian or military nuclear facility has finished its useful life, the NRC and the DOE require that the owners decommission the facility by removing from the site the radioactive materials, including land, groundwater, buildings, contents, and equipment, and by reducing residual radioactivity to a level permitting the property to be used for any other purpose.[43] Because a commercial reactor's life span was originally expected to be fifty years, an increasing number of the nation's reactors had to be decommissioned beginning in the 1990s. Five reactors have completed the process and sixteen more were undergoing decommissioning by 2007. However, no utility has yet completely decommissioned a large plant, and none expects to do so until a permanent high-level waste depository is available. Instead, the utilities plan to partially decommission their facilities and put them in so-called safe storage while awaiting the completion of a permanent repository.

Little is known about how to take apart large facilities and render them safe. Few of the nation's utilities have done much practical planning for decommissioning their own plants. No reliable estimates are available for decommissioning costs, which have been calculated to range from tens of millions to $3 billion for each facility.[44] The NRC currently requires utilities to set aside $105–135 million for decommissioning, but many experts believe these estimates are too low. Utilities are also required to have decommissioning plans, cost estimates, and written certification that they will meet the NRC's cost estimates. While some utilities have created decommissioning funds, assessed their rate payers for the costs, and filed complete decommissioning plans with the NRC, many other utilities have virtually suspended the process in the absence of a permanent high-level waste repository and in the brightening prospect of license renewal.

The DOE's responsibility for decommissioning the nation's military reactors presents even more formidable problems. Investigations of the nation's military nuclear facility management beginning in the late 1980s revealed appalling negligence in waste storage and management, leaks of dangerous radioactive materials for decades into the surrounding environment and civilian settlements, and deceit and secrecy in managing information about the lethal dangers created both onsite and offsite from waste mismanagement. This legacy of negligence leaves the DOE with a conservatively estimated cost of $230 billion to decontaminate and decommission its nuclear facilities.[45] Many experts believe the costs will climb much higher, so intolerably high that the sites will be, as some plant engineers privately predict, "national sacrifice zones" never decontaminated adequately.[46] Waste management and nuclear plant decommissioning problems will trouble Americans for centuries and remain a reminder of the technological optimism and mission fixation that inspired the approach by Washington, D.C., to nuclear technology development. Indeed, the politics of civilian nuclear power development has been as important as its science in shaping the economic, ecological, and technological character of the industry. So it will continue.

The Nuclear Regulatory Commission in the Middle

The NRC works in the vortex of controversy over commercial nuclear power regulation. Critics of the nuclear power industry almost ritually indict the NRC for its regulatory failures. But even its proponents recognize a problem. It was an NRC commissioner newly appointed by

President Reagan, a pro-nuclear spokesperson for a pro-nuclear administration, who publicly complained shortly after assuming office about the "surprising lack of professionalism in the construction and preparation ... of nuclear facilities" and "lapses of many kinds—in design analysis resulting in built-in design errors, in poor construction practices, in falsified documents...."[47] The NRC's regulatory deficiencies arise, in large part, from the political circumstances of its origin and the outlook of its professional staff. The NRC was created in 1974 when Congress abolished the AEC and vested that agency's regulatory authority in the new NRC. The new agency could not readily dissolve the strong congenial professional and institutional relationships linking former AEC staffers to the nuclear power industry, nor could it eliminate the impulse to promote and protect the industry so deeply rooted in the AEC's history. In addition, the NRC remains unapologetic about its commitment to nuclear power. "People who serve on this commission and on its staff do believe in the nuclear industry," retorted one staff member to a critic.[48] Successive NRC commissioners and their staffs often tried to regulate without prejudice and sometimes succeeded, but institutional history and professional experience often—the critics say *usually*—prevailed against regulatory rigor.

In the aftermath of Three Mile Island, the NRC has made an effort to be a more aggressive and foresighted regulator, and its relationship to the industry has become more complex. The NRC required a multitude of changes in plant management that cost utilities an average of $50 million. It has been quicker and harsher in assessing regulatory penalties, but the commission is still cited for serious regulatory lapses. For example, a GAO study of five nuclear facilities between 1986 and 1987 disclosed that "despite records of chronic safety violations, NRC did not close them. With only one exception, a safety incident occurred that made continued operation impossible or the utilities shut them down when the problems grew severe." Regarding plant safety standards, the study noted that the "NRC may take from several months to 10 or more years to resolve ... generic issues, including those NRC believes pose the highest safety risk."[49] A GAO investigation of the NRC's supervision of the decommissioning of eight small reactors in 1987 found that the "NRC fully or partially released two sites for unrestricted use where contamination at one was up to 4 times, and at the other up to 320 times higher than NRC's guidelines allowed.... Also, among five facilities that buried waste, NRC does not know the types and amounts of radioactive waste that have been buried at four of the sites."[50]

Defenders of the NRC assert that many of its regulatory lapses result from understaffing and underfunding, and that the regulatory changes required by the NRC often take years for utilities to accomplish. Some observers argue that the NRC must be doing its job reasonably well because it is also a frequent target of criticism from the nuclear power industry itself. One certainty is that the NRC operates in a radically different political environment from that prior to the accident at Three Mile Island. Relentless public exposure, politically potent and organized critics from the scientific and environmental communities, fading congressional enthusiasm for nuclear power, and technical controversy over the safety and economic prospects of nuclear power all produce a politically volatile regulatory climate in which the NRC is expected to operate. The transcendent political question for the NRC at the beginning of the twenty-first century, however, is whether it will be presiding over the death of the Nuclear Dream.

The Cold War's Wasteland: Nuclear Weapons Facilities

At the dawn of the twenty-first century, it appears that the largest environmental program in U.S. history will be the environmental restoration of military facilities, especially the numerous sites now administered by the DOE in which military nuclear weapons research, production, and testing have been conducted since the 1950s. The luckless DOE inherited the weapons facilities from the AEC when the commission was abolished in 1974. However, private corporations continued to operate the facilities under contract to the DOE, which was assumed to be exercising regulatory oversight. Some of the resulting environmental problems were accidents or mistakes, perhaps inevitable ones. But contractors and their federal watchdogs alike too often behaved as if the regulations were irrelevant. The legacy is environmental damage on a scale inviting disbelief.

Carelessness, incompetence, and the willful evasion of regulations compounded with criminal negligence afflicted the weapons program from its inception, tainting public and private participants alike. Most of these acts were concealed by a wall of military secrecy until the 1970s. By the early 1990s, however, the wall was thoroughly breached. In 1992, for example, the federal government admitted a shared responsibility with its contractors for environmental crimes at the Rocky Flats weapons facility. One contractor, Rockwell International, admitted guilt for ten crimes, including five felonies, and paid an $18.5 million fine. The DOE itself admitted that during the 1980s it had deliberately resisted any effort by the EPA and state environmental agencies to make its weapons facilities comply with environmental laws.[51] The DOE's evasions were inspired, in good part, by fear of multiple lawsuits from state governments, facility employees, and other private interests if Washington, D.C., admitted liability for environmental negligence or crimes. The suits came anyway.

"The Toughest, Most Dangerous Work in the World"

Site restoration now involves 17 major locations in 12 states and more than 50 smaller sites—in all, more than 122 facilities in 30 states and the Marshall Islands. The DOE estimates suggest that cleaning up all the sites—if the appropriate technologies can be created—will take at least seventy-five years and require at least $230 billion, or more than the costs of the Mercury, Gemini, and Apollo space programs combined, and could exceed $300 billion. Alone, the nuclear weapons cleanup would become the largest public works program in U.S. history. If it is extended to the more than 11,000 other military facilities where various kinds of mixed (that is, radioactive and chemical) hazardous waste currently exist, the total cost of environmental restoration of national military facilities could exceed a half-trillion dollars and require the better part of a century. However, the cost and time estimates are educated guesses, the bottom line of which has been increasing steadily since the late 1980s.

Former secretary of energy Hazel O'Leary's description of the cleanup as the "toughest, most dangerous work in the world"[52] seems appropriate in light of the DOE's own grim appraisal of its task:

> Many facilities are old and deteriorating and present serious threats to those who work in and around them. The complex is regulated under a mix of internal and external regulatory and advisory bodies that administer a maze of laws, regulations, directives, orders, and guidance. The result is intense frustration through DOE's workforce, serious overlaps and gaps in regulatory requirements, and a failure to address hazards according to their relative risks, costs and benefits.[53]

The Wastes

The radioactive and chemical wastes now contaminating the DOE facilities have been accumulating since the beginning of World War II. Some of the most dangerous wastes, such as liquid radioactive chemicals at the Hanford site and at the Rocky Flats facility have been stored since the early 1940s in badly deteriorating containment tanks designed to last less than twenty years. Only after George Bush's administration initiated an aggressive investigation did the extent of the environmental contamination begin to appear. As the investigation widened under the Clinton administration, it became clear that accurate estimates about the extent of the chemical contamination remaining on the sites and migrating offsite were difficult to make. The DOE has estimated that at least 500 waste streams, or flows of waste from weapons sites, exist together with at least 500,000 cubic meters of mixed wastes.[54] Many of the liquid and solid chemical wastes, particularly high-level and

Figure 8-3 Historical and Projected Cumulative Volumes of Untreated High-Level Waste in Storage

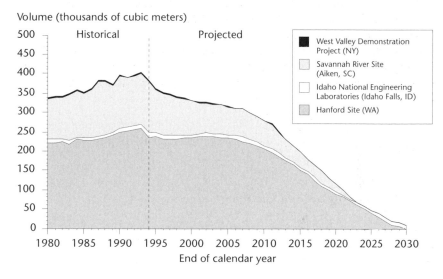

Source: U.S. Department of Energy, *Spent Fuel Storage Requirements 1993–2040* (Washington, D.C.: U.S. Government Printing Office, 1996), 38.

transuranic substances, can be dangerous to humans and the environment for 100,000 years or more.

Damage estimates are problematic because accurate records at the weapons sites are elusive—in some cases, for instance, monitoring of waste streams moving off military reservations created in the 1940s was not initiated until the early 1990s. The DOE may be only partially responsible for these conditions, but it bears most of the legal and administrative liability for site restoration and becomes the lightning rod in the political turbulence sure to arise. The DOE must characterize the wastes involved, stabilize any dangerous waste-containment structures, remove all nuclear and hazardous materials from the sites, and sequester them in safe repositories. Many of the highly dangerous radioactive liquid and solid wastes are not well understood. Technologies for managing many wastes have not been developed. Safe and permanent repositories for the most dangerous wastes do not yet exist. Site cleanup will also require a prolonged collaboration with a multitude of other agencies, including the Department of Defense, the EPA, the DOI, and all the state governments whose jurisdictions are affected by site work. Figure 8-3 depicts the past and projected magnitude of the high-level wastes accumulating at the four major DOE nuclear facilities.

The DOE, with desperate optimism, describes its task as the

vigorous challenge of cleaning up and safely containing waste for a thousand years. Scientific, environmental, and technical professionals must work closely with managers, educators, lawyers, innovators, and communicators to find the best solutions for cleaning up the environment and safely managing waste now and in the future. DOE's cleanup goal is one of the most difficult and vital tasks of our time.[55]

A brief examination of the conditions at the most thoroughly investigated site, the Hanford Nuclear Reservation near Richland, Washington, suggests how intimidating the challenge is.

Billion-Dollar Burps and Cleanup Careers

The Hanford Nuclear Reservation is almost half the size of Rhode Island. Its highly radioactive military wastes dating from the early days of World War II will become the costliest, most complex, and most technically challenging restoration facing the DOE. The most dangerous of Hanford's wastes are 54 million gallons of highly corrosive liquid radioactive materials stored in 177 tanks designed in the early 1940s to last for no more than several decades. More than 1 million gallons of these materials have leaked from sixty-six of the tanks since 1960, most of it into subsurface soil and groundwater.[56] Much of this waste has migrated to major surface waters, including the Columbia River. Federal investigation has revealed a long history of administrative and technical bungling by the prime contractor, Westinghouse, largely concealed with bureaucratic obfuscation.[57] The DOE reports indicated that workers at the facility were exposed to toxic gas leaking from the liquid containment tanks at least sixteen times since 1987, and some workers suffered permanent lung damage. Cleanup at the site was originally predicted to cost perhaps $50 billion, but estimates continue to climb inexorably. The cost of a treatment plant begun in 2001 to stabilize and prepare the site's liquid radioactive wastes for safe disposal, for instance, has soared from $4.3 to $11 billion.[58] "People's careers are going to be over before this is done," remarked a spokesperson for Westinghouse.[59]

The witch's brew of problems posed by Hanford can be appreciated by considering Tank 101-SY, one of the most dangerous of the numerous liquid waste containments dating from the 1940s. Tank 101-SY holds 1.14 million gallons of extremely unstable, high-level radioactive waste stored so long that its chemistry and behavior are no longer well understood. The tank is known to contain potentially explosive concentrations of hydrogen gas that must be "burped" from the containment every hundred days. In 1991, videos revealed what looked like "a partly cooled lava inside a volcano, seething and lurching as it burps noxious and explosive gases ... produced by chemical and nuclear reactions.... The shifting wastes splash the walls and bend metal parts; a narrator describes 'rollover events' in which the tank agitates itself."[60] By the century's end, the chemical mixture was said to resemble "a giant radioactive soufflé." The tank wastes also offer unwelcomed excitement; as one reporter observed,

> Whipped up unexpectedly by a pump that was supposed to dissipate pockets of hydrogen gas, the waste has smothered one tube for vapor sampling, threatens other instruments and could eventually overflow.... In May workers stopped the growth, at least temporarily, by lancing the crust with high-pressure waste jets, but the hole they made is beginning to close.[61]

"I don't make any claims about this tank," admitted one DOE energy expert. "I'm not convinced anyone understands the chemistry and physics involved...."[62]

Hanford is the DOE's worst problem, and it bids to stay so. In 2008–2009, the GAO issued several scathing assessments of Hanford's management. Among the milder appraisals:

> DOE has not systematically evaluated whether its tank waste cleanup strategy is commensurate with risks posed by the wastes. DOE lacks credible or complete estimates of how much the strategy will cost or how long it will take. The total project cost of constructing the waste treatment plant alone grew from $4.3 billion in 2000 to $12.3 billion in 2006. Further, DOE's schedule targets have slipped, with end of treatment extending from 2028 to 2047.... DOE has also fallen short in terms of risk-informed decision making.[63]

The daunting complexities of site restoration prevail at most of the DOE weapons sites. Many experts believe that the full restoration of all the DOE sites will be technically and economically impossible, forcing Congress or the DOE to practice administrative triage by selecting the priority sites (a responsibility that the DOE fervently wishes to avoid, so nasty would be the congressional infighting).

If there is any political good news at the DOE sites, it is that restoration should be an economic windfall for communities and counties surrounding the facilities. DOE site cleanups will probably be a national growth industry. The DOE's Savannah River site, for instance, is one of South Carolina's largest employers, with more than 24,000 people, and is predicted to grow.[64] The economics of the DOE's cleanup has also complicated restoration because site cleanup has become a coveted local expenditure that attracts considerable congressional attention, generating a minefield of political pressures and calculations to which the DOE must respond in making any important site decisions.

Black Gold

Every U.S. president from Richard Nixon through George W. Bush has tried, in one way or another, to dam the flow of imported oil into the United States with a wall of coal. Coal is the nation's most plentiful fossil fuel. With reserves sufficient for 250 years at current consumption rates, it is inevitable that federal energy planners should repeatedly attempt to substitute abundant domestic coal for expensive, insecure, imported oil. Economic and environmental problems, however, continue to inhibit a massive national conversion to coal combustion. By the time Bill Clinton and George W. Bush entered the White House, climate warming had become the global signature for coal's environmental risks, an ominous offset to the powerful attractions of coal energy in a nation extravagantly endowed with coal. Barack Obama, lately a U.S. senator from a major coal state, was walking a political tightrope through the turbulence of coal controversies before his second year in the White House. His administration has struggled at finding some politically viable equilibrium among its seemingly incompatible commitment to encouraging coal combustion through the rapid development of "clean coal" technologies, actively advocating global climate change emissions control, and aggressively regulating air pollution regulation, all while increasing electric power production—issues with *coal* written all over them.

The Saudi Arabia of Coal

Coal represents about 90 percent of the remaining U.S. hydrocarbon reserves. The coal industry liked to remind Americans during the energy crisis of the 1970s that the nation had the equivalent of Saudi petroleum resources in coal. This coal rests in three geological reserves: Appalachia's wooded hills and hollows sprawling across parts of seven southeastern states, the midwestern plains, and the western plains and grasslands. After years of sluggish growth, regulatory battles, and relentless environmentalist criticism joined by public health professionals, the coal industry in the late 1990s began a political and economic revival as a plausible alternative to continued U.S. reliance on imported oil and a dependable answer for rapidly growing demand for electric power.

Currently, coal accounts for about 22 percent of U.S. energy consumption. Electricity utilities, the prime coal consumers, generate more than half their power from coal-fired boilers and have been increasing their coal consumption. Although U.S. coal production stays at record levels, the industry has been afflicted since the 1950s with declining employment, chronic labor violence, and boom-or-bust economic cycles. The industry's economic fortunes are closely tied to the electric-power and metallurgical industries, which consume 85 and 13 percent of annual coal production, respectively. Because more than 8 of every 10 tons of mined coal are transported by rail, many railroads have become heavily dependent on coal production for revenue. Presidential coal policies have always been rationalized by great expectations. In the midst of the first energy crisis, the coal industry, alert to political opportunity, was quick to proclaim coal the "great black hope of America" and to throw its political weight behind new White House coal initiatives.

There were several plausible reasons for coal's continuing attraction to energy planners despite related economic and environmental problems. According to some estimates, accelerated coal combustion might displace as much as 2.5 million barrels of imported petroleum consumed by the United States daily. A coal boom might bring 100,000 new workers to Appalachia, reviving its stagnant economy, and perhaps 50,000 more workers to the West; coal-related income in the West and Great Plains might rise by $850 million to $1 billion. Large "mine-mouth" electricity-generating plants, located adjacent to coal seams to reduce transportation costs, could provide dependable, secure electric power for the growing West and Midwest. Coal is secure energy, without menace from Middle Eastern politics and unpredictable world petroleum markets. Because coal combustion produces more than half the nation's electric power, if "clean coal" technology becomes a reality coal could provide an enormously attractive reserve for the future electric power industry. Coal could glitter as gold if only the new coal boom could be made environmentally and economically tolerable.

The Environmental Legacy of Coal Mining

The most significant adverse environmental impacts associated with coal use are created by surface mining and combustion. Many of the problems associated with coal combustion are examined in Chapter 6. The regulation of surface mining has been no less contentious.

Surface Mining. Virtually all coal mined west of the Mississippi River and half the coal produced in Appalachia is surface mined. Surface mining rapidly has replaced underground mining because it is cheaper, more

efficient, more profitable, and less labor intensive. Unless rigorously regulated, however, surface mining is environmentally catastrophic. More
than 1.5 million acres of American land have been disturbed by coal
surface mining; more than a million of these acres remain wrecked and
ravaged wastelands, long abandoned by their destroyers. More than one
thousand additional acres are disturbed each week by surface mining,
and more than thirty states have been scarred by unreclaimed surface
mines.

In Appalachia, surface miners roamed the hills virtually uncontrolled
for decades. The evidence is written in the thousands of sterile acres,
acidified streams and rivers, decapitated hills, and slopes scarred by abandoned mine highwalls. In the western prairies and grasslands, unregulated
surface mining left thousands of barren, furrowed acres buried under
spoil banks so hostile to revegetation that they seem like moonscapes to
observers. After decades of resistance, the mining industry has come to
recognize the necessity of environmental regulation of surface mining, but
vigorous controversy continues over the manner of this regulation and its
effectiveness.

President Carter signed the Surface Mining Control and Reclamation
Act (SMCRA) of 1977 and thereby created the first federal surface mining
regulatory program. The act, strongly promoted by environmentalists
against fierce resistance from the mining industry is intended to control
the environmental ravages of surface mining by restoring surface-mined
land to productivity whenever possible. The act's major features
included:

- Environmental performance standards with which all surface miners
  were to comply in order to operate. Standards were to be established
  for the removal, storage, and redistribution of topsoil; siting and
  erosion control; drainage and protection of water quality; and many
  other matters affecting environmental quality.
- Requirements that mined land be returned, insofar as possible, to its
  original contours and to a use equal or superior to that before mining commenced.
- Special performance and reclamation standards for mining on allu-
  vial valley floors in arid and semiarid areas, on prime farmland, and
  on steep slopes.
- Enforcement of the act through a mining permit program administered jointly by the federal government and the states, according to
  federal regulations.
- Protection of land unsuitable for mining from any mine activity.
- Creation of a special fund, financed from a tax on existing surface
  mining, to reclaim orphan mine sites.

- Creation of an agency, currently the Office of Surface Mining Reclamation and Enforcement (OSMRE) within the DOI, to enforce the act.

SMCRA remains a troubled and underfunded program. The OSMRE and the states confront a hugely expensive and complex problem in protecting public health and safety on America's abandoned coal mine lands. Estimates suggest the total cost of restoring these ravaged and deserted acres is $8.6 billion.[65] Among other tasks, restoration requires the remediation of 9,000 acres of unstable waste piles and embankments, 4 million linear feet of dangerous highwalls, 8,200 acres of subsiding soil, and 23,000 acres of clogged stream lands.[66] A succession of directors continues through the OSMRE's revolving door, and the amount of improvement in program administration remains questionable. The OSMRE struggles to improve its public image (perhaps in desperation, its Web site now includes a children's link where young viewers can download a coloring book and poster depicting surface mines).[67] It seems apparent, at least, that the OSMRE cannot or will not exercise dependable, vigorous administrative oversight of state enforcement programs.[68] Still, some observers believe that the controversies surrounding SMCRA have had constructive results, including greater sensitivity in Washington, D.C., to the needs of the states and greater economic efficiency through more flexibility in program regulations.

Mountain Top Removal. Surface mining along mountain tops has steadily enlarged into a pervasive, bitterly contentious issue as the practice spreads primarily through Appalachia and the Midwest. As science writer David Biello observes,

> The *litany of problems*—both to the environment and human health— caused by a practice that involves blasting the top off a mountain to get at the coal beneath it more easily [includes] heavy metals, sulfuric acid and other mine contaminants in waterways and drinking-water wells; deformed fish carrying toxic levels of selenium found in 73 of 78 streams affected by mountaintop mining; entire streams filled in by blasted mountain rock; and forests cleared to get at the mountaintop beneath them. Add to that the fact that this form of mining has increased exponentially in the past 30 years, supplying roughly 10 percent of U.S. coal, and you have a recipe for much of the environmental devastation visible across northern Appalachia.[69]

Mining companies argue that it is the only way to get at many coal deposits. "Coal in these areas is found in very narrow seams, and the surrounding rock geology is less stable than in areas of layer seams," explained Carol Raulston, senior vice president of the National Mining

Association, "It creates flat terrain on what was the top of the mountain but the mountain is still there."[70] Critics, however, say that the land is devastated, that people, property, and the environment endure severe collateral damage. Predictably, mountaintop mining opponents were critical of the decision by the Obama EPA to permit continued mountaintop removal if the mining is rigorously regulated and monitored. The mountaintop issue seems destined to stalk the White House, EPA, and OSMER for many years and remain an abrasive issue between Obama and his environmentalist constituency.

The Restoration Gamble. One ultimately important test of surface mine regulations is whether they result in an environmentally safer mining industry and a significant restoration of the many thousand orphan mine sites across the United States. The answer to this is elusive, partly because the restoration of surface mine sites is difficult under the best of circumstances and public resources to underwrite much of the restoration cost remain unpredictable.

Obscured in the controversy over SMCRA's enforcement has been an issue even more important to the future of surface mining: Is restoration of mined lands in the manner contemplated by the act achievable? Technical studies suggest that the capacity of mining companies to restore mined land to conditions equal or superior to their original condition is likely to be site-specific, that is, dependent on the particular biological and geological character of each mining site. Western mining sites are often ecologically fragile; relatively limited varieties of sustainable vegetation and scarce rainfall make the ecological regeneration of the land difficult. With only limited experience in the restoration of western mine sites, most experts are reluctant to predict that mine sites can be restored to ecological vitality even with good intentions, generous funding, and high-quality technical resources.

The prospects for restoration are less forbidding in Appalachia, where an abundance of precipitation, richer soil, and a greater diversity of native flora and fauna are available. Nonetheless, many experts believe that the disruption of subsurface hydrology and the drainage of acids and salts from the mines' spoil heaps may not be controlled easily even when surface revegetation is achieved. Restoration remains a gamble with nature. If restoration proves difficult, confronting public officials with the prospect that a major portion of all surface-mined land may remain virtually sterile for centuries, a further national controversy may erupt over continuing surface mining.

More than three decade's experience with SMCRA leaves only fragmentary evidence of its success. After studying SMCRA's enforcement among many states, for instance, political scientist Uday Desai concluded that the consequences have been mixed, at best. Environmentally safe conditions apparently were being maintained at active mine sites in Montana, Pennsylvania, and Wyoming. But in Kentucky, a major mining state, the law appeared to have had only a "marginal" impact, and in West Virginia, another important coal state, it "had not been thoroughly and rigorously enforced in many areas."[71] Desai's conclusion suggests how far SMCRA's enforcement has yet to go in achieving its purpose:

> It is not possible to make an unqualified overall national assessment, but the evidence ... indicates that, in most (but by no means all) cases, surface coal mining is being carried out in environmentally less destructive ways than before the Act. However, accomplishment of its ultimate objective has fallen far short of the expectations of many. In addition, there has been a serious deterioration of the situation on the ground in some states such as Kentucky.[72]

Despite the formidable challenges involved, OSMRE resolutely casts restoration in a benign light.

An Emerging Issue: Coal Ash. The regulation of coal-burning emissions, mostly from electric power generation, annually creates 125–130 million tons of toxic ash and sludge, enough to fill a million railcars; more than half this volume resides in ponds and pits, primarily on electricity utility property. This waste was virtually invisible politically until December 22, 2008, when an earthen dam containing a billion gallons of ash waste from the Tennessee Valley Authority (TVA) Kingston Fossil power plant, near Kingston, Tennessee, failed. The released slurry erupted through the containment "like a volcano," reported one resident, flooding 300 acres, including Kingston and the nearby Emery River with sludge containing elevated levels of toxic metals (including arsenic, copper, barium, cadmium, chromium, lead, mercury, nickel, and thallium) and other pollutants.[73] Kingston residents claim the residue continues to create serious health problems. A rapid EPA national survey disclosed 431 similar facilities, of which 49 were considered "high hazard" because their failure could endanger human life. These containments are a portion of more than 1,300 sludge and ash pits estimated to exist nationally, most of them unregulated and unmonitored.[74]

Coal ash becomes a problem because it resides in a regulatory twilight zone. Depending on where it appears and what it contains, it can be considered a solid waste, water pollutant, toxic waste, groundwater contaminant, or even an air pollutant, and it is therefore subject to various federal and state regulations—or perhaps to no specific regulation or to conflicting laws. Consequently, although most states regulate some aspect of coal ash deposition, there is little consistency in and considerable ambiguity about how environmental controls are applied and if the most effective management prevails.

The EPA has proposed new comprehensive ash pit regulations, but the EPA and officials in the White House OIRA (see Chapter 5) do not agree on how to proceed. The coal ash pits constitute a major regulatory challenge for the Obama administration that will be closely watched by environmentalists, many critical of what they believe is an irresolute and tardy White House response—in effect, this issue is becoming a test of the administration's political credibility with environmental advocates.

Conclusion

Even though the nation's coal production is constantly increasing, its future remains uncertain at the beginning of the twenty-first century. The nation's coal production was never greater, nor its future more uncertain, than at the initiation of the Obama administration. Amendments to the Clean Air Act added in the 1990s require that national sulfur oxide and nitrogen oxide emissions be reduced by about 50 and 10 percent, respectively—a policy that could bring economic recession to Appalachia's troubled coalfields. Increasing emission control costs will create strong incentives for utilities to seek alternative fuel sources when possible. Policies to mitigate global climate warming, such as the Kyoto climate treaty supported by President Clinton (see Chapter 10), all contemplate major reductions in U.S. fossil fuel combustion—another assault on Old King Coal. However, the Obama administration is committed to increased coal use with "clean coal" technology and to expansive new electricity utility construction. The industry's vitality remains tethered uncertainly to the commercial success of that "clean coal" technology and to compatible governmental regulation. Only the ecological devastation of coal mining is ensured. It will be the inheritance of unborn generations, a legacy written in Appalachia's scarred hills and acidified streams, in barren mountaintops and sterile mine waste plowed into moonscapes across the western plains and deserts.

Coal combustion and civilian nuclear power are two examples of the implicit and inevitable association between environmental quality and patterns of energy development. The United States is currently following a path of energy development that can make vast, and possibly irreversible, changes in the nation's environment. Continuing coal use perpetuates surface mining, along with all its environmental risks, across Appalachia and the West. Industrial and utility coal combustion can intensify problems of air pollution, acid precipitation, and possibly the greenhouse effect through the first decade of the twenty-first century. In addition, even if civilian nuclear power should fail to develop beyond the facilities currently operating or under construction, the risks of accidents and the institutional difficulties in managing nuclear waste and decommissioning the plants will remain significant well into the new century. Serious technical, administrative, and political difficulties exist in the enforcement of legislation intended to protect the nation from the most environmentally malignant impacts of these technologies.

Equally important are the environmental implications of current energy policy for the future. First, the United States today has no explicit, comprehensive program of energy conservation, nor does it have any governmental commitment to promoting the development and proliferation of energy-conserving technologies beyond what may be accomplished through the deregulation of energy prices. This implies that energy development is likely to place increasing stress on environmental quality and nonrenewable resources such as fossil fuels.

Second, the continuing U.S. dependence on nonrenewable energy resources, along with the adverse environmental impacts often associated with these resources, is slowly but resolutely moving the United States into a position where it may have to contemplate a severe energy-environment trade-off should a new energy crisis emerge. Public opinion polls have long suggested that environmental quality is most politically vulnerable to an energy crisis. Should the public and its officials feel they must choose between more energy and continuing environmental protection, there seems to be a strong disposition to opt for energy development. The continued reliance on environmentally threatening energy sources will leave U.S. policymakers with few options other than environmentally dangerous ones in the face of another energy crisis.

Third, it should be apparent from our discussions of coal and nuclear power development that many of the environmental risks associated with these energy sources are created or exacerbated by the failure of institutional management or design. Stated somewhat differently, the problems of decommissioning reactors and finding a safe and publicly acceptable repository for nuclear waste illustrate the failure of policymakers to anticipate the institutional arrangements essential to ensuring the safety of energy technologies. An essential aspect of government planning in the future development of energy technologies—synthetic fuel technologies, nuclear fusion, or something else—should be a careful and prolonged consideration of the institutional arrangements essential to ensure the technologies' safety, a sort of institutional risk assessment that raises tough and realistic questions about the impact of technologies on governmental institutions and on their capacities to manage such technologies in an environmentally sound way.

Suggested Readings

Duffy, Robert J. *Nuclear Politics in America.* Lawrence: University Press of Kansas, 1997.

Flynn, James, James Chalmers, Doug Easterling, Roger Kasperson, Howard Kunreuther, C. K. Mertz, Alvin Mushkatel, K. David Pijawka, Paul Slovic, and Lydia Dotto. *One Hundred Centuries of Solitude: Redirecting America's High-Level Nuclear Waste Policy.* Boulder, Colo.: Westview Press, 1995.

Freese, Barbara. *Coal: A Human History.* New York: Perseus Books Group, 2003.

Nye, David E. *Consuming Power: A Social History of American Energies.* Cambridge, Mass.: MIT Press, 1997.

Notes

1. Quoted in Richard Simon and Jill Zuckman, "The Nation; Inauguration's Theme: Green; Many Organizations Will Celebrate Their Pet Causes on Jan. 20. But It'll Be the Environment That Cleans Up. (No Styrofoam, Please.)," *Los Angeles Times,* January 11, 2009, A14.

2. National Resources Defense Council, "NRDC—Obama Administration's First-Year Environment Record," January 11, 2010, available at: http://www.zimbio.com/Natur al+Resources+Defense+Council/articles/ATK3B85EGvC/NRDC+Obama+Administrat ion+First+Year+Environment (accessed January 20, 2010).

3. White House, "Energy and Environment," March 2009, available at: http://www .whitehouse.gov/issues/energy-and-environment (accessed November 23, 2009).

4. Simon and Zuckman, "The Nation."

5. White House, "Energy and Environment."

6. The Energy Policy Act of 2005 (EPAct), for example, created many new programs with evident environmental appeal. These included more than $14 billion in various tax incentives over the next three decades for increased energy conservation and efficiency, substantial support for research on biofuels such as ethanol, various research and development incentives for the creation of a "hydrogen economy" based on hydrogen fuel cells, and other proposals for increased energy efficiency. EPAct temporarily put to rest the administration's controversial plan to expand energy exploration in the Arctic National Wildlife Refuge (ANWR).

7. U.S. Department of Commerce, Bureau of the Census, *Statistical Abstract of the United States, 2000* (Washington, D.C.: U.S. Government Printing Office, 2001), 584.

8. U.S. Energy Information Administration (EIA), "Energy Basics 101," available at: www.eia.doe.gov/basics/energybasics101.html (accessed January 3, 2009).

9. Council on Environmental Quality, *Environmental Quality, 1992* (Washington, D.C.: U.S. Government Printing Office, 1993), 331.

10. U.S. Department of Commerce, Bureau of the Census, *Statistical Abstract of the United States, 1997* (Washington, D.C.: U.S. Government Printing Office, 1998), 273.

11. EIA, "Overview of U.S. Petroleum Trade," *Monthly Energy Review,* March 2007, 17.

12. EIA, *U.S. Crude Oil, Natural Gas, and Natural Gas Liquids Reserves: 2005 Annual Report* (Washington, D.C.: U.S. Government Printing Office, 2006), Chap. 3.

13. International Energy Agency, *World Energy Outlook, 2002* (Paris: International Energy Agency, 2002), 90, Table 3.1.

14. Thomas Doggett, "Bush Tapped Solar Energy Funds to Print Energy Plan." Reuters News Service, March 29, 2002, available at: www.solar-energy.net/bushtappedsolaren ergyfunds.htm.

15. Kate Galbreth, "Dark Days for Green Energy," *New York Times*, February 4, 2009, B1.

16. Robert Bryce, "Windmills Are Killing Our Birds," *Wall Street Journal*, September 8, 2009, A19.

17. Toby Bolsen and Fay Lomax Cook, "The Polls—Trends in Public Opinion on Energy Policy: 1974–2006," *Public Opinion Quarterly* 72 (summer 2008): 364.

18. Scott Bittle, Jonathan Rochkind, and Amber Scott, *The Learning Curve* (San Francisco: Public Agenda, 2009), "Summary of Findings."

19. Ibid., 15.

20. Michael Grunwald, "Nuclear's Comeback: Still No Energy Panacea," *Time*, December 31, 2008, available at: http://www.time.com/time/magazine/article/0,9171,18692031,00. html.

21. Ibid.; World Nuclear Power Association, "Nuclear Power in the USA," available at: http://www.world-nuclear.org.

22. Patrick Moore, "Going Nuclear: A Green Makes the Case," *Washington Post*, April 16, 2006, B1.

23. U.S. Department of Energy/Nuclear Power Industry, "Strategic Plan for Light Water Reactor Research and Development," Washington, D.C., February 2004, Executive Summary.

24. Ibid., 8.

25. World Nuclear Power Association, "Nuclear Power in the USA."

26. Jeffrey M. Jones, "Support for Nuclear Energy Inches Up to New High, Majority Believes Nuclear Power Plants Are Safe," Gallup, March 20, 2009, available at: http:// www.gallup.com/poll/117025/support-nuclear-energy-inches-new-high.aspx (accessed June 14, 2009).

27. On the history of U.S. commercial nuclear power, see Irvin C. Bupp and Jean-Claude Derian, *The Failed Promise of Nuclear Power* (New York: Basic Books, 1978); Steven L. Del Sesto, *Science, Politics, and Controversy: Civilian Nuclear Power in the United States, 1946–1974* (Boulder, Colo.: Westview Press, 1979).

28. Bupp and Derian, *Failed Promise of Nuclear Power*, Chap. 5.

29. World Nuclear Power Association, "Nuclear Power in the USA."

30. Rebecca Smith, "New Wave of Nuclear Plants Faces High Costs," *Wall Street Journal*, May 12, 2008, 1; Michael Grunwald, "Nuclear's Comeback: Still No Energy Panacea," *Time*, December 31, 2008, available at: http://www.time.com/time/magazine/ article/0,9171,1869203-1,00.html.

31. EIA, *Annual Energy Review 2002* (Washington, D.C.: U.S. Government Printing Office, 2002), 254. See also Max Schulz, "Nuclear Power Is the Future," *Wilson Quarterly* (autumn 2006): 98–107.

32. Matthew L. Wald, "As Nuclear Reactors Show Age, Owners Seek to Add to Usable Life," *New York Times*, June 22, 1989, A1.

33. "Safety Rating for Nation's Biggest Nuclear Plant Lowered," Associated Press, February 22, 2007, available at: www.cnn.com/Nuke%20Safety%20Problem07.html.

34. David Lochbaum, *Nuclear Tightrope: Unlearned Lessons of Year-plus Reactor Outages* (Washington, D.C.: Union of Concerned Scientists, 2006), 1.

35. Walter A. Rosenbaum, "Nuclear Wastes and Federalism: The Institutional Impacts of Technology Development," in *Western Public Lands: The Management of Natural*

Resources in a Time of Declining Federalism, ed. John G. Frances and Richard Ganzel (Totowa, N.J.: Rowman and Allanheld, 1984). See also Luther J. Carter, *Nuclear Imperatives and Public Trust* (Washington, D.C.: Resources for the Future, 1987), Chaps. 4–5; Edward J. Woodhouse, "The Politics of Nuclear Waste Management," in *Too Hot to Handle? Social and Policy Issues in the Management of Radioactive Waste,* ed. Charles A. Walker, Leroy C. Gould, and Edward J. Woodhouse (New Haven, Conn.: Yale University Press, 1983), 151–183.

36. Quoted in "Nevada to Get Nuclear Waste, Everyone Else 'Off the Hook,' " *Congressional Quarterly Weekly Report,* December 19, 1987, 3136–3137.

37. Quoted in ibid.

38. "Nuclear Waste: House Approves Temporary Storage Bill," *Greenwire,* April 16, 1997.

39. Matthew L. Wald, "U.S. Will Start Over in Planning for Nuclear Waste Dump," *New York Times,* November 29, 1989, A1.

40. GAO, "Nuclear Waste: Yucca Mountain Project behind Schedule and Facing Major Scientific Uncertainties," Report no. GAO/RCED 93-124, Washington, D.C., May 1993, 4.

41. Keith Schneider, "Nuclear Waste Dump Faces Another Potential Problem," *New York Times,* June 3, 1989, 1, 8. See also GAO, "Nuclear Waste: Storage Issues at DOE's Waste Isolation Pilot Plant in New Mexico," Report no. GAO/RCED 90-1, Washington, D.C., December 1989.

42. "Limited Reopening of Plutonium Plant in Washington State," *New York Times,* December 15, 1989, B14. See also GAO, "Nuclear Energy: Environmental Issues at DOE's Nuclear Defense Facilities," Report no. GAO/RCED 86-192, Washington, D.C., September 1986, 2–4.

43. GAO, "Nuclear Regulation: NRC's Decommissioning Procedures and Criteria Need to Be Strengthened," Report no. GAO/RCED 89-119, Washington, D.C., May 1989, 2–3. On decommissioning problems generally, see Cynthia Pollock, *Decommissioning: Nuclear Power's Missing Link* (Washington, D.C.: Worldwatch Institute, 1986).

44. Pollock, *Decommissioning,* 25–33.

45. U.S. Department of Energy, *Estimating the Cold War: The 1995 Baseline Environmental Management Report* (Washington, D.C.: U.S. Government Printing Office, 1996).

46. Keith Schneider, "The 29-Year Ordeal to Tear Down One Building," *New York Times,* October 31, 1988, A14.

47. Quoted in "U.S. Nuclear Official Criticizes Industry Planning," *New York Times,* December 12, 1981, B12.

48. Quoted in Matthew L. Wald, "Shoreham: Arguing over the Next Step," *New York Times,* January 21, 1985, L1.

49. GAO, "Nuclear Regulation: Efforts to Ensure Nuclear Power Plant Safety Can Be Strengthened," Report no. GAO/RCED 87-141, Washington, D.C., August 1987, 2–3.

50. GAO, "Nuclear Regulation: NRC's Decommissioning," 2–3.

51. Matthew L. Wald, "Bomb Plant Case Draws More Fire," *New York Times,* November 2, 1993, A18.

52. Quoted in Lawnie H. Taylor Sr., *Ten Year Cleanup of U. S. Department of Energy Waste Sites: The Changing Roles of Technology Development in an Era of Privatization* (Washington, D.C.: Department of Energy, 1996), 5.

53. Ibid., 10.

54. U.S. Department of Energy, Office of Environmental Restoration and Waste Management, *Fact Sheets: Environmental Restoration and Management* (Washington, D.C.: U.S. Government Printing Office, 1991), 21.

55. Ibid., 2.

56. GAO, "Understanding of Waste Migration at Hanford Is Inadequate for Key Decisions," Report no. GAO/RCED 98-80, Washington, D.C., March 1998, 3.

57. Matthew L. Wald, "4 Decades of Bungling at Bomb Plant," *New York Times*, January 25, 1992, available at: http://www.nytimes.com/1992/01/25/us/4-decades-of-bungling-at-bomb-plant.html (accessed May 11, 2010). See also GAO, "Nuclear Waste: Problems and Delays with Characterizing Hanford's Single-Shell Tank Waste," Report no. GAO/RCED 91-118, Washington, D.C., April 1991. In 1968, for instance, a major safety lapse involving an overheating and partial fuel melting at a nuclear weapons assembly plant was reported as "an improbable mechanical failure." Wald, "4 Decades."

58. GAO, "Hanford Waste Treatment Plant: Contractor and DOE Management Problems Have Led to Higher Costs, Construction Delays, and Safety Concerns," Report no. GAO-06-602T, Washington, D.C., April 2006, 1.

59. Quoted in Matthew L. Wald, "At Old A-Plant, One Sure Thing Is the Volatility," *New York Times*, June 21, 1993, A1.

60. Matthew L. Wald, "Hazards at Nuclear Plant Festering Eight Years after Warning," *New York Times*, December 24, 1992, A11.

61. Matthew L. Wald, "Nuclear Site Is Battling a Rising Tide of Waste," *New York Times*, September 27, 1999, A14.

62. Quoted in ibid.

63. GAO, "Uncertainties and Questions about Costs and Risks Persist with DOE's Tank Waste Cleanup Strategy at Hanford," Report no. GAO-09-913, Washington, D.C., September 2009, "Summary."

64. Matthew L. Wald, "Carolina Plant to Encase Atomic Wastes in Glass," *New York Times*, November 28 , 1990, B6; *New York Times*, August 5, 1993.

65. U.S. Department of the Interior, Office of Surface Mining Reclamation and Enforcement, "Abandoned Mine Land Reclamation: Update on the Reclamation of Abandoned Mine Land Affected by Mining That Took Place Before the Surface Mining Law Was Passed in 1977," Washington, D.C., 2003, 20, available at: http://www.osmre.gov/aml/remain/zintroun.htm.

66. Ibid.

67. U.S. Department of the Interior, Office of Surface Mining, "Mining and Reclamation Coloring Book," January 23, 2002, available at: www.osmre.gov/coloring.htm (accessed April 7, 2004); U.S. Department of the Interior, Office of Surface Mining, "Mining and Reclamation Poster," February 28, 2002, available at: www.osmre.gov/poster.htm (accessed April 7, 2004).

68. GAO, "Surface Mining: Interior Department and States Could Improve Inspection Programs," Report no. GAO/RCED 87-40, Washington, D.C., December 1986, 3. See also Richard Miller, "Implementing a Program of Cooperative Federalism in Surface Mining Policy," *Policy Studies Review* 9 (autumn 1989): 79–87; Richard Harris, "Federal-State Relations in the Implementation of Surface Mining Policy," *Policy Studies Review* 9 (autumn 1989): 69–78.

69. David Biello, "Mountaintop Removal Mining: EPA Says Yes, Scientists Say No," *Scientific American Observations*, January 8, 2010, available at: http://www.scientificamerican.com/blog/post.cfm?id=mountaintop-removal-mining-epa-says-2010-01-08. See also Margaret A. Palmer, E. S. Bernhardt, W. H. Schlesinger, K. N. Eshleman, E. Foufoula-Georgiou, M. S. Hendryx, A. D. Lemly, G. E. Likens, O. L. Loucks, M. E. Power, P. S. White, and P. R. Wilcock, "Mountaintop Mining Consequences," *Science* 327 (January 8, 2010): 148–149.

70. Jennifer Weeks, "Coal's Comeback," *CQ Researcher*, October 5, 2007, 825.

71. Uday Desai, "Assessing the Impacts of the Surface Mining Control and Reclamation Act," *Policy Studies Review* 9 (autumn 1989): 104–105.

72. Ibid., 105.

73. David A. Fahrenthold, "Still Unresolved, Tennessee Coal-Ash Spill Only One EPA Hurdle," *Washington Post*, December 22, 2009, A1.

74. Shaila Dewan, "Huge Coal Ash Spills Contaminating U.S. Water," *New York Times*, January 7, 2009, available at: www.nytimes.com/2009/01/07/world/americas/07iht-sludge.4.19164565.html (accessed September 5, 2009).

Chapter 9

635 Million Acres of Politics
The Battle for Public Lands

For many westerners, particularly those in the Rocky Mountain states, the sport appeals to the urge for unfettered—and fast—exploration of large swaths of terrain. But environmentalists say the snowmobile's continued presence [in Yellowstone Park] represents the triumph of commercial interests over conservation.

Representatives of both camps were standing within 50 feet of each other on Tuesday afternoon as Old Faithful spewed velvety veils of water into the cold, sunny air. O'Neal Browder, 63, an accountant from Birmingham, Ala., who has snowmobiled into the park half a dozen times in the past 25 years, called those who would ban the machines "a bunch of elitists." Nearby, Norman Ashcraft, a former Manhattanite now living in Connecticut, rested on his ski poles. Told that [Secretary of the Interior] Norton was nearby, he grimaced and said, "She's the enemy."

—*New York Times*, February 17, 2005[1]

Buried toward the back of the two-hundred-page-thick national energy plan conceived by the George W. Bush administration was a proposal guaranteed to embroil the White House, Congress, energy developers, and environmental advocates in a national controversy smoldering for more than a decade and involving millions of acres of land most Americans will never see and could not locate on a map. The conflict swirls about the Arctic National Wildlife Refuge (ANWR), 19.6 million acres of pristine polar wilderness in the remote northeastern corner of Alaska, among the wildest and most inaccessible of U.S. public lands (see Map 9-1). ANWR is huge and resplendently wild, a sprawling panorama of tundra marshes and lagoons, interlaced with glacier-fed rivers and lodged between the foothills of the soaring Brooks Range and the expansive frigid Beaufort Sea. All parties to the conflict agree—it is stunningly beautiful. They agree on little else.

Map 9-1 Arctic National Wildlife Refuge

— Refuge boundary
·········· Wild river
o   Community
▓▓▓▓ Dalton Highway
■ ·■ · U.S.–Canada border

ALASKA
Fairbanks ·
Anchorage ·
Juneau *

Beaufort Sea

Prudhoe Bay O   O Deadhorse
Kaktovik
*Kaktovik Inupiat
Corporation Lands*

1002 Area

WILDERNESS

AREA

C
A
N
A
D
A

Arctic Village   O

*To Deadhorse
239 miles*

Coldfoot o

*To Fairbanks
258 miles*

0   50 miles

O Fort Yukon

Source: U.S.Fish and Wildlife Service, http//arctic.fws.gov/shade.htm. Map reproduced by International Mapping Associates.

ANWR is also another flashpoint of political conflict over access to the nation's public lands. Such conflicts have flared repeatedly through-out U.S. history. In many ways, ANWR is a microcosm of the larger political forces, actors, and institutions historically drawn into these unrelenting conflicts over the use of vast natural resources held in trust by the federal government for the people of the United States. Beginning with a brief description of the actors and issues involved in the Alaskan dispute, this chapter explains why the nation's public lands have always been a battleground between advocates of contending, and often sharply conflicting, uses for the natural resources involved. The explanation involves the ambiguous, and often confusing, congressional legislation intended to determine which interests shall have access to these resources; the impact of the environmental movement on public land politics; and the constantly embattled federal agencies, especially the U.S. Department of the Interior (DOI) and the U.S. Forest Service (part of the U.S. Department of Agriculture), which are responsible for the politically arduous job of simultaneously preserving these lands, promoting use of their resources, and protecting their most valuable ecological functions. Using the national forests and wilderness areas as examples, the narrative illuminates currently significant public lands controversies.

The Arctic National Wildlife Refuge: Public Land Politics at a Boil

The national energy plan recommended that the "President direct the Secretary of the Interior to work with Congress to authorize exploration and, if resources are discovered, development of the 1002 area of ANWR."[2] But Congress should "also require the use of the best available technologies and should require that activities will result in no significant adverse impact to the surrounding environment." To the U.S. energy production industries and their allies, this proposal seemed reasonable and plausible, a long overdue, practical remedy to the nation's dangerously growing dependence on imported oil. The proposal infuriated environmentalists, conservationists, and their allies. Environmentalists frequently characterize ANWR as "the crown jewel of America's refuge system" and predict that further energy exploration there will result in catastrophic air pollution, habitat destruction, wildlife decimation, and ecological degradation. Arrayed among these colliding forces were a multitude of other interests that, in differing combination, are commonly drawn into disputes over the use of the public lands.

"The Biological Heart" of a Wilderness

As with most public lands owned by the federal government, ANWR's size and purpose are defined by Congress, and the responsibility for its oversight is vested in the DOI. ANWR was created in 1980 from federal lands within Alaska for the purposes of wildlife conservation, habitat preservation, wilderness protection, promotion of recreation, and energy exploration—an example of a multiple-use designation that almost ensures a constant battle among the contenders for different uses. Much of ANWR's 19.6 million acres has been opened to oil and natural gas exploration. The Trans-Alaskan pipeline, created in 1971, has been producing almost 1 million barrels of petroleum daily from Prudhoe Bay on Alaska's North Slope, and 90 percent of the adjacent coastal lands remain open for gas and oil leasing. However, about 1.5 million acres of the coastal plain, considered to be the most biologically rich and vulnerable within ANWR, has been restricted from energy exploration unless such activity is specifically authorized by Congress. This region, often called the 1002 Area, in reference to its authorizing legislation, is the epicenter of the political conflict over ANWR.

The ecological riches of the 1002 Area are undisputed. This natural endowment includes 160 bird species; the most important onshore denning area in the United States for polar bears; the principal calving ground for 130,000 migratory porcupine caribou; habitat for grizzly bears, arctic foxes, wolves, wolverine, and numerous whales; and many endangered plant and animal species. Ruggedly beautiful wilderness and vast Arctic panoramas invite recreation and tourism. This language of ecological values, biological conservation, and environmental aesthetics resonates powerfully among environmentalists. Much of this, they believe, would be sacrificed to produce exaggerated quantities of petroleum unlikely to alleviate significantly the nation's energy problems.[3]

At Stake: America's Energy Security?

Proponents of energy exploration in the 1002 Area speak primarily about national security, energy supply, and coexistence between energy production and environmental protection. They assert, for instance, that drilling in the area could yield as much as 16 billion barrels of oil, an amount equal to thirty years of oil imports from Saudi Arabia. They also assert that newer, more efficient energy production technologies will limit the amount of land that would be disturbed by energy production to a few thousand acres and, in any case, that the ecological disruption involved is vastly exaggerated by environmental opponents. Most important, proponents of further energy production argue that the reserves now untapped under the 1002 Area will significantly improve U.S. security by decreasing dependence on imported oil, which threatens to increase in the future. All these arguments speak to the nation's sensitivity to its petroleum dependency, rising energy needs, and domestic security awakened in the aftermath of the September 11, 2001, terrorist attacks.[4]

The Play of Politics

Since 1980, the DOI has been ready to sell energy exploration leases on the 1002 Area, but, because Congress must first agree, the political battle over exploration has been waged largely within Congress and the White House. In 1996, President Bill Clinton vetoed congressional authorization to permit the leasing. Since then, similar legislation has been approved in the House of Representatives eight times and then defeated, usually in the Senate.[5] In July 2003, the Senate unexpectedly rejected an ANWR leasing proposal vigorously promoted by the Bush administration. Still, the White House ANWR campaign persisted with dependable support from the entire Alaskan congressional delegation and from the DOI (whose ANWR Web site, for instance, pointedly includes a "How Long Would Your State Run on ANWR Oil?" chart to demonstrate the value of ANWR to each state).[6] Although the Bush administration's FY 2008 budget had assumed that legislation would be approved to open the ANWR to energy exploration, Congress took no further action, leaving the decision to the Obama White House. Barack Obama had repeatedly voted in the Senate against ANWR exploration and drilling and again declared his opposition during his presidential campaign. However, the Obama administration has become more ambivalent on the issue. Secretary of the Interior Ken Salazar declared in March 2009 that he would consider tapping oil from Alaska's ANWR by drilling outside its boundaries if it can be shown that the refuge's wildlife and environment will remain undisturbed. However, Salazar emphasized that the Obama administration stands firm that the Alaska refuge "is a very special place" that must be protected and that he is not yet convinced that directional drilling would meet that test, thus leaving the fate of the 1002 Area insecure and destined for continual contention among a multitude of political and economic interests.

Some of the stakeholders in the ANWR conflict have been highly visible; Congress, the White House, the DOI, environmental advocates, and energy industries rarely escape national attention. Another important stakeholder is the state of Alaska. Many states benefit from economic royalties received from resource exploitation on public lands in their jurisdiction, but Alaska's situation is unique. Royalties from energy production are the state's economic foundation. Every Alaskan resident—man, woman, and child—is reminded about this economic dependence by an annual check (currently about $1,100) representing his or her share of more than $660 million in annual dividends from state oil royalties.[7] Alaskans largely support energy exploration in the 1002 Area, believing energy production and environmental protection are compatible. Many resent what they consider interference by Washington, D.C., and other interests, including environmentalists, in what they believe should be

Alaska's own affair. Not surprisingly, Alaska's Republican governor Frank Murkowski complained about "America's extreme environmental community" after the Senate's rejection of ANWR energy leasing in 2003 and promised that he would open as much as a million acres of state-owned offshore waters to energy exploration.[8] Many of Alaska's Native Americans, however, were unlikely to cheer. The Inupiat Eskimos and the Gwich'in Indians, an indigenous subsistence culture, are among the native tribes heavily dependent on the 1002 Area's continued ecological vitality for food and fuel. The state's commercial fishing interests were also disturbed by the possible degradation of their offshore stocks.

The stakeholders in ANWR's resources include local, state, and federal governments; the federal bureaucracies administering the public lands; the economic interests seeking to exploit resources and the interests determined to protect them; and foreign governments, including Japan and China, that might become large consumers of the petroleum produced from the 1002 Area. In brief, ANWR epitomizes the pluralistic political struggles over natural resources in the public domain that have erupted continually throughout U.S. history.

A History of Contested Access

The controversy over ANWR renews an environmental struggle begun long before the concept of environmentalism was imagined. Fierce political contention over the use of the public domain runs like a dark and tangled thread throughout the fabric of U.S. history, reaching to the republic's inception. During the first century of American independence, the conflict was largely between the states and private economic interests to obtain as much public land as possible for their own advantage. Only in 1976, in fact, did the government of the United States officially end its policy of conveying huge expanses of public lands to private control. By then, more than 1.1 billion acres of land, an expanse larger than Western Europe, had been surrendered to the states, farmers and trappers, railroads, veterans, loggers and miners, and canal builders—in other words, to any interest with the political strength to make a persuasive claim to Congress. Land shaped the American character more decisively than did any other aspect of the nation's environment. With the mobilization of the conservation movement in the early twentieth century, the federal government began to restrict the private control of the public domain in the interest of the American people. Although vastly reduced, the public domain remains an enormous physical expanse embracing within its continental sprawl, often accidentally, some of the nation's most economically and ecologically significant resources, a biological and physical reserve still largely unexploited. The struggle to determine how this last great legacy shall be used constitutes, in large part, the substance of the political struggle over public lands.

At one time, most of the land in the United States was public domain. Over the past two centuries, the federal government has owned almost 4 of every 5 acres on the continental United States. This land, held in trust for the people of the nation, is governed by Congress, in whom the Constitution vests the power to "dispose and make all needful Rules and Regulations respecting the Territory or other Property belonging to the United States."[9] Until the beginning of the twentieth century, Congress had been concerned primarily with rapidly divesting itself of the lands, turning them over to the states or to private interests in huge grants at bargain-basement prices. Only belatedly did Congress, powerfully pressured by the new American conservation movement, awaken to the necessity of preserving the remaining natural resources in the public domain before they were wholly lost. By this time, most of the remaining public lands lay west of the Mississippi River; much was wilderness too remote and inaccessible to be exploited easily or was grasslands and rangelands seemingly devoid of economic attraction.

The Public Domain

Today, the federal government owns approximately 635 million acres of land, about 28 percent of the total U.S. land area (Map 9-2). Many western states are largely public domain; more than half of Alaska, Idaho, Nevada, Oregon, Utah, and Wyoming are federally owned, and public lands constitute more than one-third of Arizona, California, Colorado, and New Mexico. Much of this land, originally ceded to the western states when they joined the Union, was rejected by the states as useless for timbering, grazing, or farming; some was held in trust for Native American tribes by the federal government. Only later, well into the twentieth century, did exploration reveal that vast energy and mineral resources might reside under the tribal reservations, wilderness, timberland, and grasslands remaining in the public domain. The economic value of public lands increased greatly in 1953, when the United States joined other nations in redefining the limits of national authority over offshore waters. Before 1953, the traditional standard had limited national sovereignty to 3 miles offshore. In 1953, Congress passed the Outer Continental Shelf Lands Act despite the vigorous opposition of coastal states such as Florida and California. The act declared federal government ownership of outer continental shelf (OCS) lands extending as far as 200 miles offshore. The legislation, ratifying an international treaty negotiated by the State Department, ended a long-standing dispute between the federal and state governments over control of offshore energy resources by immediately

Map 9-2   Federal Land as a Percentage of Total State Land Area (excluding trust properties)

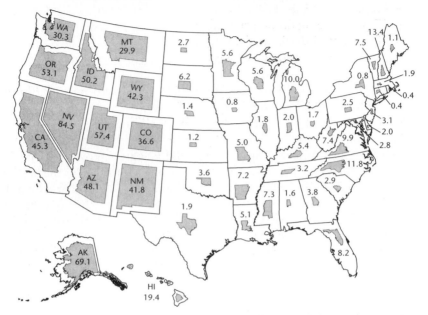

Source: U.S. General Services Administration, *Federal Real Property Profile,* 2004, available at: http://www.gsa.gov/Portal/gsa/ep/contentView.do?noc=T&contentType=GSA_DOCUMENT&contentId=13586.

vesting in the federal government control over almost all of the 1.1 billion acres of submerged continental shelf land. By accident and design, that third of the nation, together with its spacious offshore lands, now controlled by the federal government, has become a public trust of potentially huge economic value. And the land is a moneymaker. In recent years, for example, federal collections from user fees, mineral and fossil fuel extraction, land sales, timber production, and other economic activities added more than $1 billion annually to federal government income.

An Unanticipated Bounty

The magnitude of mineral, timber, and energy reserves in the public domain remains uncertain. Many areas, including much of the gigantic Alaskan wilderness, have yet to be inventoried fully. Estimates of the resources on more accessible lands also can be controversial. However, commonly cited figures concerning estimated resources on public land suggest the reasons why public lands have assumed such importance to major economic interests in the United States:[10]

- 35 percent of U.S. petroleum
- 39 percent of U.S. natural gas
- 42 percent of U.S. coal
- 17 percent of hydropower
- 50 percent of geothermal energy
- 30 percent of untimbered forests

Beyond those resources on which a price can be placed, the public domain contains both incalculable natural treasures whose worth has become evident to generations—Yosemite, Yellowstone, the Grand Canyon, and the other national parks—and nameless wild and free places, the wilderness that the naturalist Aldo Leopold has called "the raw material out of which man has hammered the artifact called civilization" and to which, he reminds us, we need often return, in fact and imagination, as to a sanctuary.[11] Indeed, much of what remains undisturbed on the American earth, still available to this generation in something like its original condition, can be found only in federal wilderness areas. Whether wilderness is or should be a thing beyond price and beyond exploitation remains among the most bitterly controversial of all environmental issues.

Diversity within the Public Domain

The public domain has been divided by Congress into different units committed to different uses and administered by different executive agencies. The most important of these uses are:[12]

- *National Wilderness Preservation System.* Created by Congress in 1964, the system currently comprises 105.8 million acres of land, including more than 50 million acres of Alaskan wilderness added in 1979. By legislative mandate, wilderness lands are to be set aside forever as undeveloped areas.
- *National Park System.* Created in 1872 with the designation of Yellowstone National Park, the system currently constitutes 66 national parks and 388 national monuments, historic sites, recreational areas, near-wilderness areas, seashores, and lake shores, altogether embracing more than 83 million acres. Closed to mining, timbering, grazing, and most other economic uses, the system is to be available to the public for recreational purposes.
- *National Wildlife Refuge System.* The system currently includes more than 96 million acres, two-thirds in Alaska but also distributed among all fifty states. The more than five hundred refuges are to provide habitat for migratory waterfowl and mammals, fish and waterfowl hatcheries, research stations, and related facilities.

- *National Forests.* Since 1897, Congress has reserved large forested areas of the public domain and has authorized the purchase of additional timberlands to create a forest reserve, to furnish continuous timber supplies for the nation, and to protect mountain watersheds. Forest lands are to be managed by a multiple-use formula that requires a balance of recreation, timber, grazing, and conservation activities. Currently exceeding 190 million acres, national forests are found principally in the far western states, the Southeast, and Alaska.

- *National Rangelands.* The largest portion of the public domain, located primarily in the West and Alaska, is made up of grassland and prairie land, desert, scrub forest, and other open space collectively known as rangelands. Although often barren, a substantial portion of the 404.7 million acres of rangeland is suitable for grazing. Federal agencies issue permits to ranchers for this purpose.

Such a classification implies an orderly definition of the uses for the public domain and a supporting political consensus that do not exist. Behind the facade of congressionally assigned uses stretches a political terrain strewn with conflicts of historical proportions over which lands should be placed in different categories, which uses should prevail among competing demands on the land, how much economic exploitation should be permitted in the public domain, and how large the public domain should be.

Since 1970, two national public land policies have provoked the most significant of these conflicts: (1) the congressionally mandated practices of multiple use, or balanced use, for much of the public domain and (2) the creation of vast tracts of highly restricted wilderness areas and roadless areas precluding all or almost all human development. This chapter examines the ecological and political context in which multiple-use and wilderness conflicts arise and the participants that are drawn into the struggles. These conflicts characteristically pit federal resource management agencies, state and local governments, commodity producers and users, and environmentalists against one another over issues that long predate the first Earth Day.

Conflicts over Multiple Use

Disputes over multiple use of the public domain customarily evolve in roughly similar political settings. Conflict focuses on land administered by one of the federal resource agencies, usually the DOI's Bureau of Land Management (BLM) or the Department of Agriculture's Forest Service, that are charged with the stewardship of millions of acres of the public domain under a multiple-use mandate.

Struggling to interpret an ambiguous congressional mandate for land management, the resource agency will commonly find several parties in conflict over the interpretation of *multiple use*. These parties include the states within whose jurisdictions the land resides, the various private economic interests with a stake in the decision, congressional committees with jurisdiction over the agency's programs, and perhaps the White House. Especially since 1980, environmental interests have been important and predictable participants. Sometimes the issues are resolved—that is, if they are resolved—only by congressional reformulation of land-use policy.

The Land-Use Agencies

Management of the public domain is vested principally in four federal agencies whose collective jurisdiction, more than a million square miles, exceeds the size of Mexico. The Forest Service, the National Park Service, the BLM, and the Fish and Wildlife Service control about 90 percent of all the land currently in the public domain. The Forest Service and the BLM control by far the largest portion of this collective jurisdiction. Unlike the National Park Service and the Fish and Wildlife Service, the Forest Service and the BLM are required by Congress to administer their huge public trusts under the doctrine of multiple use. The two agencies come to this task with strikingly different political histories and territorial responsibilities.

The Forest Service. Created as part of the Department of Agriculture in 1905, the Forest Service is one of the proudest and most enduring monuments to America's first important conservation movement. Founded by Gifford Pinchot, one of the nation's greatest conservationists, the service has a long and distinguished history of forest management. Widely recognized and publicly respected, the service has been adept at cultivating vigorous congressional support and a favorable public image—who is not familiar with Smokey the Bear and other service symbols of forest preservation? The service's jurisdiction covers 191 million acres of the land, including some grasslands, within the U.S. forest system. With more than 38,000 employees and a budget exceeding $2.0 billion, the Forest Service historically has possessed a strong sense of mission and high professional standards. "While the Forest Service has frequently been at the center of political maelstroms," political scientist Paul J. Culhane writes, "it has also been regarded as one of the most professional, best managed agencies in the federal government."[13] Operating through a highly decentralized system of forest administration, local forest rangers are vested with great discretion in interpreting how multiple-use principles will apply to specific forests within their jurisdictions.

The Bureau of Land Management. The BLM manages more than 264 million acres of public domain and leases another 200 million acres in national forests and private lands, but the bureau remains obscure outside the West. The BLM's massive presence throughout the West is suggested by Map 9-3, which identifies the proportion of state lands currently managed by the agency and suggests, as well, why western political interests have been so deeply implicated in the BLM's political history. The BLM has struggled to establish standards of professionalism and conservation that would free it from its own long history of indifference to conservation values and from unflattering comparisons with the Forest Service.

Map 9-3   Percentage of State Acreage Managed by the U.S. Bureau of Land Management, 2003

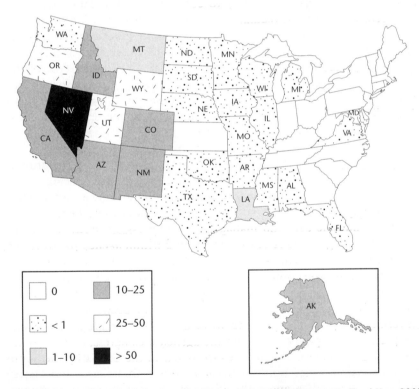

☐ 0	▨ 10–25
⠂ < 1	⟋ 25–50
▨ 1–10	■ > 50

Source: U.S. Department of the Interior, Bureau of Land Management, *Fiscal Year 2003 Annual Report: Shared Community Stewardship for America's Public Lands* (Washington, D.C.: U.S. Goverment Printing Office, 2003), 73.

The BLM was created in 1946, when President Harry S. Truman combined the DOI's old Grazing Service and General Land Office to form the new bureau with the largest land jurisdiction of any federal agency. Starting with responsibility for managing federal grasslands and grazing lands, the BLM gradually added to its jurisdiction other lands with mineral resources and, more recently, 78 million acres of Alaskan lands, including many large wilderness areas. The BLM has inherited a great diversity of lands with different dominant uses: the Alaskan wilderness, more than 2.5 million acres of prime Douglas fir timber in western Oregon, and 146.9 million acres of grazing lands. The BLM also is responsible for arranging the leases for mineral exploration on all public domain lands and on the OCS.

Lacking the prestige of the Forest Service and burdened with a long history of deference to the ranching and mining interests that form a major portion of its constituency, the BLM has struggled to achieve greater professionalism, more sensitivity to conservation, and more aggressive enforcement of land-use regulations within its jurisdiction. Throughout its history it has suffered from chronic understaffing and underfunding—its budget and staff are less than one-third of that of the Forest Service despite its greater jurisdiction. And the BLM has never enjoyed the relative insulation from top departmental management that the Forest Service has experienced. This, to many environmentalists, is one of its chronic problems. According to resource expert James Baker, "The multiple-use concept suffers at the BLM because management decisions are influenced by top policy personnel appointed by the administration in power, who inherently focus on one single use, such as mining, and ignore or give short shrift to such other legitimate uses as wildlife and recreation."[14]

The BLM and the Forest Service work in a political milieu whose character is shaped by the ambiguous, and sometimes inconsistent, requirements of multiple-use land management; by pressures from the private interests seeking access to resources on land within agency jurisdictions; by conflicts with environmentalists over the appropriate balance between environmental protection and resource use, both of which the agencies are expected to promote; by frequent conflicts between the president and Congress over their respective authority over the agencies; and by state governments, particularly in the West, determined to press their claims for preference in policymaking on the agencies, Congress, and the White House. All these conflicts were exacerbated in the 1980s by the White House's determination to force major changes in the existing understandings about such issues and in the 1990s by the growing political strength of the wise use movement that arose in opposition to environmentalist pressures on federal land management agencies.

An Ambiguous Mandate

In carrying out their assigned tasks, managers in these agencies often must walk an administrative tightrope fashioned from the inconsistencies and vagaries of their legislatively defined missions. Three different federal statutes charge the BLM and the Forest Service with administering the lands in their trust according to multiple-use principles. The most elaborate definition of the doctrine, ripe with the ambiguities that create so many problems in its implementation, is found in section 530 of the Multiple Use–Sustained Yield Act (1960):

> "Multiple use" means: the management of all the various renewable surface resources of the national forest so that they are utilized in the combination that will best meet the needs of the American people; making the most judicious use of the land for some or all of these resources or related services over areas large enough to provide sufficient latitude for periodic adjustments in use to conform to changing needs and conditions; that some land will be used for less than all of the resources; and harmonious and coordinated management of the various resources, each with the other, without impairment of the productivity of the land, with consideration being given to the relative values of the various resources, and not necessarily the combination of uses that will give the greatest dollar return or the greatest unit output.[15]

The intent of this complicated mandate is to make sure that in land management "any use should be carried out to minimize interference with other uses of the same area and, if possible, to complement those other uses."[16] But it provides to agency managers scant information concerning how these differing values are to be defined and balanced when differing claims on land use must be resolved. Such problems are commonplace because almost 60 percent of all public lands are held by federal agencies under some form of multiple-use law, and conflict over their resolution is predictable. The BLM, for instance, has wrestled for years with managing desert areas east and north of Los Angeles to the satisfaction of both conservationists and vehicle-racing enthusiasts. Each year the BLM processes more than one hundred applications for motorcycle races, some annual events with as many as three thousand competitors. Conservationists have argued that the races permanently scar the land, alter native ecological balances, and create noise and other disruptions for other recreationists.[17] In trying to reduce the impact of such racing, the BLM must determine the proper balance between recreation and conservation values in terms of these specific desert lands. Any decision becomes controversial.

The agencies frequently discover that multiple use also leads to a conflicting mandate. The Forest Service is expected to protect the national forests from excessive timbering but at the same time assist state and private forest owners in obtaining access to federal forests. Wildlife refuges are supposed to protect and preserve the ecologically viable habitat for endangered species but also provide grazing, hunting, and perhaps mining opportunities to private interests.

But the multiple-use doctrine also gives both agencies, and particularly the local resource managers who must often translate the doctrine into operational terms, a means of managing the conflicting interest pressures on the land. Multiple use requires a balancing of uses, and concern for a variety of claims, without ensuring that any one is dominant. This formula leaves resource managers with the opportunity to balance and negotiate among interests claiming the use of public resources. It also promises constant pressure on the agencies to create or alter interpretations of multiple use by whatever interests feel that existing interpretations discriminate against their claims on the land.

The Pluralistic Politics of the Public Lands

Multiple-use legislation is a mirror to U.S. resource politics, capturing the continual competition between a multitude of public and private interests for access to the public domain. The balance of forces changes over time, as we will continually observe, but the conflict plays out across lines of political cleavage created by federalism, the separation of powers, and interest group liberalism so deeply embedded in U.S. political culture.

State, Regional, and Private Interests

State governments, particularly in the West, historically have been deeply concerned with federal land-use policies and for more than a century have pressed Washington, D.C., for greater control over the public lands within their boundaries. Because the public domain constitutes so large a portion of many western states, decisions made at the federal level affecting land use can have an enormous economic, political, and social impact on the western governments. The states have a direct economic stake in multiple-use management. Approximately 20 percent of Forest Service receipts for timber sales are returned to local governments in lieu of property taxes on federal lands. More than one-third of the BLM's annual receipts for mining royalties and other uses of its land is returned to the states.

The Sagebrush Rebels. Regional politics is also deeply implicated in resource controversies. In general, the western states have long believed that they have been denied a properly influential voice in decisions affecting their lands. They often perceive themselves to be governed by a remote and unresponsive bureaucracy insensitive to their special concerns. In particular, the western states want a louder voice in determining grazing rights, in setting conditions for mineral exploration, in establishing timbering quotas, and in deciding how revenues from resource use in the public domain will be allocated. Many states, such as Utah, have insisted that the federal government ought to divest itself of much of the land within the state borders, turning the land and all its resources over to the states. By the 1980s, the western determination to assert greater state and regional control over federal lands had assumed a political identity known as the Sagebrush Rebellion. The rebellion found powerful spokesmen in President Ronald Reagan, a former California governor, and James Watt, his combative secretary of the interior, who promised—but eventually could not deliver—the liberation from Washington's public land controls so long coveted in the West.

President Clinton reignited the volatile mix of political resentments that had fueled the earlier western Sagebrush Rebellion by his decision, without congressional cooperation, to designate 43 million acres of western national forest lands as roadless areas, thereby virtually precluding any form of economic development. Western political interests again found a presidential champion in newly elected George W. Bush, himself a westerner, an oil man deeply committed to domestic energy development, and a political conservative unsympathetic to the Clinton administration's restrictive public lands policies. Bush left no doubts about his political inclination by appointing Gale Norton as secretary of the interior. Norton was another westerner with a political pedigree strongly reminiscent of Watt's, the *beau ideal* of the Sagebrush Rebels. (Norton and Watt had once even worked for the same conservative public interest law firm in Colorado.) Congressional conservatives, especially Republicans, were strongly encouraged by these congenial presidential signals to mount an aggressive legislative assault on the roadless-area designations and related Clinton land-use regulations. The situation foreshadowed numerous early barbed confrontations between the new Bush administration and environmentalist interests that were a prelude to Bush's turbulent relationship with environmentalism following his inauguration.

This persistently combative environment, prevailing throughout the Bush administration, was expected to turn considerably more benign with the advent of the Obama presidency and the appointment of Ken Salazar as secretary of the interior. Optimistic expectations, however, often prove fragile in the volatile policy conflicts that sooner or later erupt between public land policymakers and environmentalists—often divided among themselves—during any presidency.

Energy Conflicts. Given the conflict over ANWR described at the chapter's outset, it is understandable that the concepts energy and energy crisis evoke particularly intense political emotions among environmentalists concerned with public lands. They also raise federal-state resource conflicts in yet another context. A long historical shadow reaching back to the 1980s falls over any current discussions of either issue.

The 1980s were characterized by unusually open and bitter conflicts over the management of the public domain, particularly energy resources, triggered by the Reagan administration's vigorous attempts to change land policies in a manner that angered conservationist and environmental groups throughout the United States while attracting support from many western states. The protracted controversy profoundly alarmed environmentalists and many of the more traditional conservationists. It left the environmental movement with a lingering suspicion about Republican energy policies, a lingering paranoia about western political intentions, and a deeply embedded antipathy toward any individuals or political impulses even faintly reminiscent of resource politics during the Reagan years.

Energy development has been historically inseparable from the politics of U.S. public lands since the beginning of the twentieth century. Energy exploration and production have been powerful justifications for the development of public lands, and the related array of organized economic interests embraces many of the nation's largest and most powerful corporations and politically potent state and regional political coalitions, especially those historically identified with the midwestern and western "oil patch." Between 1981 and 1988, the Reagan administration and its opponents waged a conflict of historic proportions over the fate of energy and related resources on public lands. The administration began the 1980s with a determination to open public lands to energy and mineral exploration and to transfer tracts of public lands to state and private control on a scale unmatched by any other administration in the twentieth century. These grand designs for resource development were frustrated by resistance from moderates of both congressional parties, a fierce opposition campaign by environmentalists and their conservationist allies, and inept political promotion by Reagan administration spokespeople. Perhaps most important, domestic energy supplies recovered rapidly with the collapse of the OPEC oil embargo, petroleum prices fell, and public concern for an energy crisis evaporated. Reagan's Republican successor, George Bush, largely avoided confrontations with the environmental community over resource management.

Clinton, in contrast to Reagan and Bush, deliberately and repeatedly frustrated efforts by energy developers to expand their access to fossil fuel resources on continental public lands and on the OCS. Clinton's sweeping designation of new roadless areas and other restrictions on public land development during his final years in office, described earlier, especially antagonized domestic energy producers, who looked to George W. Bush for redress.

And so it was left for Bush to propose aggressive new energy development in his national energy plan and thereby demonstrate how close to the surface of American life the political tensions of the Reagan years remain. When Bush announced within a few weeks of assuming the presidency that the nation faced another energy crisis, it was inevitable that environmentalists would respond as if another Republican-led assault on public lands was forthcoming, particularly because energy interests had contributed substantially to Bush's presidential campaign. Moreover, Bush was also a westerner, and his energy policies tilted strongly toward the interests of western states. The Bush national energy plan, and its subsequent legislative proposals, seemed to confirm environmentalist suspicions that Bush was enthusiastically resurrecting Reagan's public lands policies with further embellishments. Environmentalists pointed to initiatives such as the acceleration of oil and gas exploration permits on public lands, a drastic slowdown in the designation of new wilderness areas, the relaxation of environmental restrictions on mineral mining on federal land, and a revocation of limits on off-highway recreation vehicles on public lands to demonstrate that Bush "threatens to do more damage to our environmental protections than any other [president] in U.S. history."[18] Although environmentalists and their allies were able to defeat some of these initiatives in Congress, many other administration initiatives were accomplished because they could be implemented entirely by the White House or bureaucratic agencies.

The Ambivalent States. Despite Sagebrush Rebellion rhetoric, the states are often guilty of doublethink about resources in the public domain, as the controversy over land policy in the 1980s illustrates. Eager to reap the economic advantages of greater resource use on lands within their domain—more royalties, more severance taxes, and greater industrial development—the states were equally determined not to pay calamitous ecological and economic costs for rapid resource exploitation. The federal government's new public lands policies often aroused not enthusiasm but hostility among the western states. These states wanted resource development *and* environmental protection.

Conflict between the federal government and the states was focused most sharply on the federal government's proposal for accelerated leasing of exploration rights to oil and gas on the OCS. In 1978, Congress had passed the Outer Continental Shelf Lands Act Amendments to increase greatly the environmental safeguards required for OCS exploration. To this end, extensive federal consultation with the states was required prior to any lease sales off their shores. The federal government's announced intention to sell thirty-two oil lease tracts off the central California coast sent California to the federal courts seeking an injunction to prevent the leasing. Citing federal failure to consult with the state under terms of the 1978 legislation, the court issued the injunction and the DOI subsequently withdrew most of the disputed tracts from auction.

Responding to pressure from California state officials, including the new Republican governor, most environmental groups, and most of the state's congressional delegation, Congress in 1982 and 1983 further restricted lease sales off the northern and central California coast by denying appropriations to implement the leasing. In 1984, Congress banned leasing in several OCS basins off Florida and Massachusetts. Often, states have taken unilateral action to impede or prevent the development of OCS lands. Even Bush family values could not prevail against state interests on energy matters when, in mid-2002, Gov. Jeb Bush of Florida successfully opposed federal efforts to commence oil exploration in Florida OCS waters, which his brother, the president, had supported. Thus the OCS states have largely succeeded in substantially reducing, at least temporarily, the scope of offshore energy exploration through a combination of legal and political strategies. Environmentalists, however, remain uneasy about the future because substantial OCS leasing is still permitted.[19] As if to confirm the worst environmentalist suspicions, Congress passed new legislation in late 2006 opening about 8.3 million acres of OCS to exploration in the eastern Gulf of Mexico and rewarding Louisiana, Mississippi, Alabama, and Texas with 37.5 percent of all new energy production revenues.

Resource conflicts at the boundaries between federal and state power are inevitable, grounded in the bedrock of the U.S. constitutional system itself. As long as the federal government continues to push aggressively for greater energy exploration and production on public lands or asserts its regulatory control over the public domain, the states will continue to press with equal determination for greater influence, if not control, over decisions about such activities within their own borders.

Private Resource Users

Interests using resources in the public domain, or ambitious to be among the elect, are important participants in the process of making public land-use policy. Each of the major federal land-use agencies has its "clientele," that coalition of organized groups with a major economic or ideological stake in the agency's programs. In general, resource users want to expand their access to resources in the public domain, to use the resources as cheaply as possible, to protect the continuing availability of renewable resources, and to maintain or enhance their influence within the agencies making decisions about resources strategic to them. For example, sheep and cattle ranchers customarily participate actively in the political struggles over BLM rangeland regulations; individual timber companies, such as Weyerhaeuser and Crown Zellerbach, and timber trade associations, such as the National Forest Products Association, are involved in Forest Service determinations about allowable timber harvests; and Peabody Coal and Climax Coal, two of the largest coal-mining companies in the United States, are found with the spokesperson for the National Coal Association actively attempting to influence the BLM or the Fish and Wildlife Service in writing regulations for coal leasing on land within their agency jurisdictions.

This intimate and historical involvement of clientele in land agency politics often has been criticized sharply, first by the earlier conservation movement and currently by environmentalists. Critics have asserted that agencies are easily "captured" by the clientele, who then promote resource exploitation at the sacrifice of balanced use and, particularly, with little regard for environmental values. Conservationists once dismissed the BLM as the "Bureau of Livestock and Mining." Similarly, environmentalists routinely sued the BLM in the 1980s for allegedly failing to enforce surface mining regulations on coal lessees in New Mexico and Wyoming. The Forest Service's exemplary reputation has been no shield from accusations that it sanctions clear-cutting and other timber practices abhorrent to environmentalists because the service allegedly has come to define its mission largely as timber production in response to commercial timber company demands. Agency administrators, however, often have a legislative mandate to promote resource use within their jurisdictions, and, as a consequence, some community of interest with resource users is inevitable. As we have often observed, the right of access by affected private groups to those administrators making decisions affecting such groups is regarded as a fundamental principle in U.S. politics. Both tradition and law make the continued involvement of resource users in agency decisions inevitable and their self-interested pressures on the agencies a continual threat to the concept of balanced use. Often environmental and conservation groups constitute practically the only politically active and effective force for balanced use within the private pressure group system.

Congress and the Public Domain

Congress ultimately decides how the public domain will be used. Although it cautiously shares some of this authority with the president, Congress traditionally has been a jealous and vigilant guardian of its prerogatives to decide finally how the states, federal land management agencies, private resource users, and others shall use the lands it holds in trust for the people of the United States. This authority flows from Article IV of the Constitution and from numerous Supreme Court decisions affirming the primacy of legislative authority in determining the character of the federal lands. Recent Supreme Court decisions have compelled Congress to share with the president the power to withdraw public lands from private use, but Congress has been quick to challenge presidents and their executive agencies when it has felt they were usurping a legislative prerogative in land management.

As in other policy areas, congressional control over the public domain is exercised through the committees and subcommittees in each chamber with jurisdiction over federal land management agencies. Although Congress vigorously defends its authority to define agency programs, it has also left the agencies with enormous discretion in deciding how lands within their jurisdictions will be used; the many multiple-use laws enacted in the past several decades leave to local land managers great latitude in establishing the character of specific land uses. These agencies, as a result, operate in a politically risky milieu, in which discretion is always subject to congressional challenge. When the presidency and Congress are controlled by the same party, conflicts between the two branches over agency decisions are seldom prolonged or serious. But the situation becomes ripe for conflict when different parties control the White House and one, or both, congressional chambers. Then agency managers, exercising what they believe to be their discretionary authority on behalf of the president's program, may find themselves and their agency under congressional attack. Many of the most publicized conflicts over the Reagan administration's land-use policies erupted as battles between the secretary of the interior and Democratic-controlled House committees with jurisdiction over the department's land programs. During the Clinton presidency, the situation was reversed, with a Democratic president and secretary of the interior usually defending the administration public lands policies against a largely critical Republican majority in both congressional chambers. Feeding the conflict were partisan disagreements over which programs the department should implement and traditional disputes over the limits of executive discretion.

In the past several decades, Congress has demonstrated an increasing concern for environmental values by enacting legislation requiring federal land management agencies to give conservation greater importance in land-use decisions. The Wilderness Act of 1964, an early manifestation of this growing ecological sensibility, designated by statute for the first time more than 9 million acres of public lands as wilderness and provided for additional future designations. Later, the National Environmental Policy Act

(NEPA) of 1970 required federal land management agencies, among many other executive agencies, to create environmental impact statements (EISs) in which the environmental consequences of land-use decisions had to be identified and considered in decisions affecting the public domain. Other major multiple-use laws passed in the 1970s (and examined later in this chapter), explicitly required the relevant federal agencies to incorporate ecological protection among the uses to be protected in the affected public domain. This concern for environmental value demonstrated in good part the rising political strength of environmental groups in the legislative process. Congress, particularly the House, came to be the principal institutional bastion within the federal government from which environmentalists mounted their attack on Reagan's land-use policies at the DOI.

The Environmental Movement and Public Lands

Environmentalists always have given the management of public lands a high priority. Both the National Park Service and the Forest Service were created near the beginning of the twentieth century in response to vigorous promotion by the great American conservation movement, the ideological and political predecessor of the existing environmental movement. Historical legal and political battles had been waged by the Sierra Club, the Audubon Society, and other environmental groups against ecologically reckless projects promoted by federal water resource agencies long before the environmental era was named. In the 1970s, environmentalists achieved a number of legislative and judicial victories that vastly expanded their influence in federal land management activities and compelled even the ecologically primitive BLM to develop, at least fitfully, an environmental conscience.

Among the most important of these achievements was passage of NEPA. As defined by the Council on Environmental Quality, which is responsible for its implementation, NEPA required that EISs be prepared by federal land management agencies for major land-use decisions affecting the environment—in effect, for most major land management planning. Draft statements had to be circulated for public review and comment prior to completion, and agency officials were obligated to give the statements careful consideration in all relevant decisions.

In practical terms, the EISs became an early warning system for environmental groups, alerting them to the implications of numerous agency policies whose importance might otherwise have gone unnoticed. Environmentalists had the opportunity to organize a political strategy for influencing land management decisions. Further, the statements often forced agencies, such as the BLM, to give greater attention to the ecological impacts of their management practices. Not least important, the EIS was a legally enforceable procedure; environmental groups skillfully exploited many opportunities to use the federal courts to delay or frustrate agency decisions they opposed by challenging the adequacy of impact statements.

Federal courts, often with the explicit approval of Congress, greatly expanded the environmentalists' standing to sue federal agencies for alleged failures to give environmental values sufficient attention in land-use planning. This greatly liberalized standing often enabled environmental interests to compel federal agencies to give them a voice in agency proceedings. Critics charged, sometimes justifiably, that environmentalists were seizing on these new strategies primarily to disrupt administrative procedures and thereby to harass their opponents even when their case lacked merit. But the environmental activities inspired by the enhanced standing, as well as the impact statement procedures, quite often resulted in valuable ecological improvements in federal land management and greater federal attention to the balanced use of land, to which many agency managers previously had given little more than lip service.

Finally, congressional attempts to encourage greater public involvement in the making of land management decisions by the Forest Service, the National Park Service, and the BLM also provided environmentalists with effective strategies for influencing federal policies, particularly at the local level at which so many land-use decisions were made. Indeed, environmental groups have perceived correctly that generous provision for public involvement in federal land-use planning has been among the most effective structural means of giving them access and influence in the administrative process generally. For this reason, they have been acutely concerned about the enforcement of these participation provisions in federal land law and convinced that any attempts to narrow such opportunities, by law or administrative manipulation, were covert attacks on their political bases.

In many respects, the 96 million acres of pristine federal land now congressionally protected from development under the Wilderness Act are a monument to environmentalist activism and to the laws and administrative regulations that enormously enlarged the environmentalists' administrative and congressional influence. As political scientist Craig W. Allin observed, provisions for public involvement in federal land-use planning at the local level provided wilderness advocates with the incentive and resources to expand their power at the congressional grassroots.

> Wilderness advocates quickly overcame their initial organizational disadvantage in local areas. Grassroots organizations sprang up, meeting the demands for public participation and pressing for inclusions of favored areas [in the National Wilderness Preservation System]. National conservation organizations assisted through local chapters and by publishing information about successful tactics.[20]

In a political system in which localism dominates congressional life, this ascent of environmentalist power from the grassroots was an instance of capturing the political base from the opposition.

The Wise Use Movement Emerged, Submerged, and Revived

Out of the political turbulence inspired by the Reagan administration's aggressive attempt to promote greater private access to public lands, the wise use movement emerged in 1988. The movement is a loose alliance of public lands user groups: resource developers seeking more public resources such as timber and fossil fuels; grazing and ranching interests opposed to increased user fees on public lands; and a multitude of other economic, regional, and political interests whose assorted agendas share a desire to diminish severely the federal government's restrictions on access to the public domain. Under the wise use banner march groups that are in other respects very dissimilar, such as the National Inholders Association (private property owners within public lands), the National Farm Bureau Federation, the Western Cattlemen's Association, the American Freedom Coalition (a part of the Reverend Sun Myung Moon's Unification Church), the Blue Ribbon Coalition (off-road vehicle manufacturers), off-road vehicle owners, timber interests, and petroleum companies. It is not, however, simply another incarnation of the Sagebrush Rebellion. The idea of property rights as a legal and philosophical basis for action—a strategy that greatly expanded the movement's political appeal beyond the West—has given the wise use movement a national reach and an intellectual depth. As political scientist Sandra K. Davis explains,

> The idea of protection of property rights was borrowed from the property rights movement, which originated in eastern states, and derived its basic concept from the libertarian party. It has been nurtured by intellectual leaders such as Richard Epstein, a law professor at the University of Chicago, and Roger Pilon of the Cato Institute. The Wise Use Movement's adoption of the property rights issue has facilitated its appeals for political support and its likelihood of succeeding in legal cases.[21]

The ideological underpinning of the movement is provided by various economic theories and theorists who argue that the private use of many presently protected natural resources—timber, fossil fuels, and grazing lands especially—would constitute a more economically efficient and nationally beneficial policy (or wise use) than the present restrictions on public resource exploitation. In this respect, wise use is in many ways a modern reprise of the progressive movement's conviction that the "highest and best use" of the public domain often implied its economic development. By grounding its arguments in economic theory, moreover, the movement gains a measure of intellectual respectability and a breadth of appeal to political and economic conservatives that is lacking in arguments based solely on often-arcane disputes over specific resource economics. The movement also shares a hearty dislike for environmentalists that occasionally erupts into vitriol, such as one leader's assertion that the movement intended "to destroy the environmental movement once and for all."[22]

The wise use movement packed a potentially powerful appeal but lacked a charismatic national political leader and proven political impact at the polls. It also lost much of the financial support provided by large resource-dependent corporations, such as Boise Cascade, Coors, and Weyerhaeuser, which were disappointed by the movement's feeble political impact and overheated rhetoric. Instead, corporate promoters of wise use have turned increasingly to think tanks such as the Cato Institute, the Heritage Foundation, and the Heartland Institute, which appeal to a much broader intellectual and social constituency while offering a greater promise of political return on their investments. Nonetheless, the environmental movement regards the wise use idea with considerable apprehension. Many environmentalists believe that wise use ideas, if not the name, were revived in the land use philosophy of important Bush administration land managers such as former secretary of the interior Gale Norton, former secretary of agriculture Ann Veneman (whose political background and land use philosophy closely resembled Norton's), and many of their subordinate administrative appointees.[23]

The Department in the Middle

The DOI is inevitably the focus of controversy over energy exploration in the public domain. More than 200 billion tons of coal, perhaps one-fourth of the nation's coal reserves, lie below western lands under the DOI's jurisdiction. Since passage of the Mineral Leasing Act of 1920, the secretary of the interior has had the discretionary authority to sell leases and to establish conditions for private mineral and energy exploration on public lands. Such leases, to be sold at "fair market value," must be "diligently developed" into mining operations within a decade; both federal and state governments charge royalties for coal production within their boundaries. Until the 1980s, however, the department promoted coal and other resource exploration on its lands rather indifferently, and during the 1970s, leasing was virtually suspended while the DOI, Congress, and the White House struggled to fashion a comprehensive leasing program. One finally emerged in the late 1970s, but it soon was challenged by the Reagan administration's new coal programs.

The change in coal-leasing philosophy under the Reagan administration was immediate and dramatic. In 1981 alone, the DOI leased more than four hundred times the acreage for coal exploration than it had the previous year. Proponents of a greatly accelerated leasing program asserted that the nation needed the energy resources lying unused in the public domain, that federal regulations could protect the lands from the ravages of surface mining, and that the economic productivity created by private use of the energy resources would generate more jobs and greater prosperity. Many of those within the DOI's political leadership would have said a hearty, if perhaps private, "amen" to the summary conclusion on the subject by the president of the American Mining Congress: "Our society is built on the stuff that comes out of the hole in the ground and if we don't unplug the red tape stuffing the hole, this country is going to be in one hell of a mess."[24]

The DOI's announced intentions to accelerate the sale of leases for oil and gas exploration on the OCS and its interest in leasing when legally possible even wilderness areas for exploration convinced environmental groups and congressional opponents of the Reagan programs that a massive public campaign to counteract the new policies was imperative. Congress became the institutional weapon.

The Politics of Checks and Balances

"The probability of our developing any meaningful dialogue with this Administration is low indeed," Russell Peterson, the politically seasoned president of the National Audubon Society, lamented after talking with White House officials less than a year after President Reagan's inauguration.[25] Most environmentalists agreed and turned instead to Congress, as they often did during those times, to exploit constitutional and partisan rivalries to their advantage in seeking an institutional restraint on the president's land policies. For environmentalists, constitutional checks and balances can become a lever with which to move the executive branch, or to frustrate presidential intentions, on resource matters. Such issues can easily arouse the institutional rivalries at the heart of the constitutional order. During the Reagan years, the White House programs awakened among many legislators, particularly those on House and Senate committees with oversight of the DOI's programs, a conviction that the department, with the White House's blessing, was abusing its delegated authority and subverting congressional intent in handling the new energy programs. Democrats on the oversight committees, especially in the House, sought opportunities to challenge and embarrass the White House by attacking its land programs. In the battle over land policy, the House Committee on Interior and Insular Affairs became the most aggressive congressional antagonist to the White House.

During the latter years of the Clinton administration, however, environmental and conservation interests frequently played the game of constitutional checks and balances in reverse. Republicans controlled both congressional chambers, and Alaskan legislators, among the most aggressive promoters of energy exploration on public lands, were the chairs of major Senate and House natural resource and energy committees. Then the environmental lobbies used presidential influence to thwart numerous efforts by these Republican-controlled committees to expand oil, natural gas, and timber production in ANWR, the Tongass National Forest, and Alaskan OCS areas.

With George W. Bush in the White House, environmentalists confronted yet a different situation through most of this administration, with Republicans controlling the presidency and, for most of the time, both congressional chambers. In this situation, environmentalists found that a strong bipartisan environmentalist bloc in the Senate could be used to counter the aggressive energy development plans favored by the president and House Republicans. With the return of Democratic congressional control following the 2006 elections, environmentalists expected much more aggressive congressional efforts to constrain the Bush administration's efforts to open the public lands to more commercial use and energy exploration.

The Politics of Presidential Leadership

The balance of political party strength in Congress may affect the environmentalists' agenda for good or ill, but the presidency is also a repository of formidable independent constitutional and political resources to promote or frustrate that agenda. The presidency offers opportunities for policy initiatives, for dramatizing and popularizing issues, and for invoking the constitutional prerogatives of the chief executive and his administrative authority in ways enabling the president—or his administrative appointees—often to achieve the president's environmental goals with little, if any, congressional collaboration. Presidential history from Reagan to George W. Bush amply illustrates the impact of this executive presence on public lands management.

Watt's resignation as secretary of the interior in October 1983 did not end the conflict over land policies initiated by the Reagan administration, nor did it diminish the administration's determination to open up the public domain to further energy exploration. Through the use of existing budgetary authority, established discretionary freedom, and "a thousand small changes," Watt had managed, in the face of formidable opposition, to move federal policy strongly toward more resource development on public lands.

Watt's successors created less public stir than their predecessor had while pursuing the same land policies more successfully throughout the tenure of the Reagan administration. Pressure to develop energy resources persisted.

George Bush's administration began on a more conciliatory note, with the president committing himself to an active environmental agenda and implicitly distancing himself from Reagan's public lands policies. But the environmental community was not pleased with the administration's new secretary of the interior. The president's choice, Manuel Lujan Jr., a former congressional representative from New Mexico, had been identified closely with mining, timber, and other corporate resource users during his legislative tenure. He was widely perceived within the environmental community as more antagonist than ally. Lujan's early pronouncements, including his advocacy of greater energy exploration on OCS lands, did little to dissipate this image.

The Clinton administration arrived in Washington freighted with environmentalist expectations of a major reversal in public lands policies that never occurred. Despite the appointment of Bruce Babbitt, an environmentalist paragon, as secretary of the interior and his outspoken commitment to turning away from the pro-development policies of the Reagan and Bush administrations, the White House seemed indecisive and uncertain in its land-use policies. As a result, Babbitt was frequently left without the president's apparent support in major clashes with Congress over forest management, energy exploration licenses, and grazing fees on public lands—all major concerns to public lands activists of all political persuasions. Furthermore, Babbitt's, and Clinton's, environmentalist reputation was progressively deflated. For a time, it appeared that the Clinton administration had been considerably more successful in stifling the pro-developmental momentum of the previous two presidents than in promoting a vigorous, strongly environmentalist land-use program of its own. However, Clinton's performance, especially during his final months in office, proved immensely gratifying to environmentalists and, in his final days, a spectacular demonstration of presidential authority over the public lands.

In December 2000, Clinton declared formally the creation of the largest nature preserve in U.S. history and thereby achieved a record unique to U.S. politics. With the addition of the new Northwestern Hawaiian Islands Coral Reef Ecosystem Reserve—a huge South Pacific expanse as large as Florida and Georgia combined and containing more than 70 percent of the nation's existing coral reefs—Clinton's administration had created more public lands for recreational and conservation purposes than any other presidency in U.S. history. The Hawaiian designation was the final flourish to an ongoing presidential performance that had been moving at breakneck speed through the final year of the administration in Clinton's determination to leave Americans what he called his land legacy. Altogether, Clinton's land legacy would be more than 50 million acres of new or newly protected public domain and the designation of 65 million acres of existing public forest land in Washington, Oregon, Idaho, and Montana as roadless areas, thereafter off-limits to commercial timbering.

Clinton's action left behind a lingering, bitter controversy. Wherever commercial access to natural or biological resources was prohibited, and that was virtually everywhere, the resource developers—timber companies, petroleum and natural gas corporations, ranchers, coal and mineral miners, and commercial fishermen among them—complained of national assets being locked up. Many members of Congress, and Republicans especially, were infuriated because Clinton's land-use decisions, especially during that last frantic year, were frequently made without congressional approval through authority granted unilaterally to the president by the American Antiquities Act of 1906. Moreover, Clinton was quick to blame Congress for its inaction. "Where Congress has been unable or unwilling to act," his spokesperson pointedly noted about the Hawaiian preserve, "this administration had not hesitated to use its full Executive authority to protect public health and the environment."[26]

Many western political leaders found additional reason to complain, particularly about the new roadless areas. Clinton's designation, for instance, had removed almost 20 percent of Idaho's land area from commercial timbering. "It's the kind of unilateral land management decision by the federal government that further deepens the distrust and skepticism that comes naturally to those of us in the West," protested Idaho governor Dirk Kempthorne.[27] Western ranchers denied access to grazing land by the same policy were incensed. "I think we Pacific Northwesterners," went one characteristic complaint, "ought to tell them Easterners to get the hell out of our area. Clinton, Gore, and whoever else is managing things back there: leave us alone!"[28] The U.S. Forest Service found the reaction of western resource developers so hostile that the service's Web site summarized the response as "Roadless Rage." Hawaiian commercial fishermen protested about the prohibition on their activity in the new ocean reserve. "The President's order," went one sarcasm, "gives the Great White Father in Washington control of Hawaiian resources."[29]

The Fate of the Forests

More than 1 in every 10 acres in the public domain could be used for commercial timber production. This land, about 89 million acres, lies mostly within the jurisdiction of the Department of Agriculture's Forest Service. Since the end of World War II, pressure has been unremitting on the Forest Service to increase the size of the annual timber harvest from the national forests to satisfy the nation's growing demand for wood products. Recently, there has been increased pressure to open many undisturbed old-growth timber stands and wilderness areas to commercial logging. Against this economic pressure, the Forest Service is required not only to enforce the doctrine of multiple use, which forbids the service from allowing timber cutting that will preclude other forest uses, but also to manage timber cutting to ensure a sustained yield from any forest reserve used for commercial timbering. Congress has left to the Forest Service the difficult and politically contentious responsibility of defining how much timber cutting is compatible with multiple use and sustained yield.

The struggle over competing timber uses is fought in the arcane language of forest economics—*nondeclining, even-flow* formulas, *allowable cuts,* and *allowable-cut effects*—but the larger interests and issues at stake are apparent. The struggle represents a collision between preservationist and developmental priorities for timber, between competing definitions of the nation's economic needs, and between differing definitions of the Forest Service's mission. It is a struggle likely to intensify well into the future.

A Disputed Treasure in Timber

About half of the nation's softwood sawtimber reserves and a substantial portion of its remaining hardwoods grow today in the national forests. The Pacific Coast region, particularly the timbered hills and lowlands of the Pacific Northwest, contains the largest of these timber stands within the public domain; the area contains almost half the pine, spruce, fir, and other softwoods in the national forests. These timber reserves, more than three times the size of all the private commercial forests in the United States and currently worth more than $20 billion, will increase in value.

Although timber cutting was permitted in the national forests from their inception, the demand for commercial timber in the forests assumed major proportions only after World War II. In the early 1940s, the Forest Service sold about 1.5 billion board-feet of timber per year; by 1973, the cut exceeded 12.3 billion board-feet. Driven by the nation's ravenous postwar desire for new housing, the demand for wood products rose steadily in the three decades following 1945. Private timber companies, approaching the limits of their own production, began to look increasingly to the national forests as an untapped timber reserve. This demand, if wholly satisfied, would probably result in a doubling of the annual timber harvest from the national forests, in keeping with the industry's estimates that the U.S. demand for wood products would double by the early twenty-first century.

Pressure to expand the allowable timber cut has been particularly intense in the Pacific Northwest. Many of the Douglas fir forests in Oregon and Washington are old-growth stands, virgin forests never touched by a logger's saw, growing in a continuity of development many centuries old. These forests are among the most ecologically diverse and historically unique of all timber stands in North America, reminders of a continent once largely timbered with a profusion of species greater than all of Europe's. Many virgin forests, together with other less spectacular timberlands, are on Forest Service lands that are still classified, or eligible for classification, as wilderness. To many environmentalists and to organized preservation groups such as the Sierra Club and the Wilderness Society, these lands are the living expression of the preservationist ethic, the values of the movement made visible. They are, in political terms, "gut issues."

The Greening of Forest Policy

The environmental movement has profoundly changed forest management policies since 1970 by altering its political underpinnings. Before the 1970s, as political scientist George Hoberg observed, "the forest policy regime was characterized by a dominant administrative agency, a strong orientation toward the development of timber resources, and little input from the public."[30] By the early 1970s, the organized environmental movement had acquired political muscle and, together with its political allies, had promoted new environmental laws and new federal agencies to implement them. Environmentalists aggressively used their newly expanded judicial access to fashion litigation into a potent political weapon. New statutory and administrative provisions for public involvement in the implementation of forest policy and greater congressional oversight of Forest Service policies expanded environmentalist influence in day-to-day forest management. These changes meant a new pluralism in forest management politics in which resource developers no longer dominated and in which environmentalists had become major players whose interests had to be acknowledged, along with their allies, in policymaking at all governmental levels.

Once again, as in other aspects of environmental policy, environmental organizations found the courts during the 1970s and early 1980s to be an effective ally. Especially important was the growing trend among federal courts to scrutinize carefully the Forest Service's management decisions to ensure they were compatible with newly enacted environmental laws rather than to defer, as the courts had done traditionally, to the Forest Service's professional expertise in cases in which the service's decisions were challenged. It was its success in overturning the historic

Forest Service practice of clear-cutting in the early 1970s, observed Hoberg, that demonstrated what this shift in judicial attitudes meant for environmentalists:

> Conservationists found an obscure provision of the original authorizing statute of the Forest Service ... requiring that harvested trees had to be "dead or matured" and that they had to be marked before being cut. Although these requirements were legislated even before the development of the forestry profession in the United States, the court refused to defer to the Forest Service's interpretation of the statute's meaning and enjoined clear-cutting in the Monongahela National Forest in West Virginia and the Tongass National Forest in Alaska. By outlawing the most common method for harvesting timber, these rules created a crisis of timber management. Congress was forced to rewrite management laws.[31]

The Forest Service did not respond warmly to most of these early provocations. Professional foresters and the Forest Service's rank and file often resented the challenge to their professional judgment and the environmentalist insinuations that they were ecologically unenlightened. The rise of politically organized and powerful environmentalism, moreover, spelled the end of the Forest Service's administrative autonomy, especially the customary judicial deference and the congenial congressional oversight it had come to expect. When Congress passed the National Forest Management Act (NFMA) in 1976, it compelled the Forest Service to open its forest management planning process from the lowest levels to environmentalist involvement and to set new standards for multiple-use decisions in which ecological values had to be given major consideration. Gradually, however, the Forest Service adapted to the new environmental realities, with the considerable assistance of progressive leaders within professional forestry itself. The academic training and recruitment of Forest Service professionals was transformed to include a much greater emphasis on environmental values and ecologically supportive practices in job preparation. The Forest Service adjusted its organizational structure and decision-making procedures to the new requirements of NEPA, the NFMA, and other judicial and congressional mandates to better incorporate environmental values in its policymaking.

Still, the Forest Service, like other federal land management agencies, must live with the multiple-use laws as the fundamental calculus for its land-use decision making, environmentalism notwithstanding. Thus, forest managers are never free of conflicting forces and values pressing constantly on them whenever major forest management policy must be formulated or implemented. Indeed, multiple-use legislation creates the fundamental political order out of which all forest management decisions must ultimately arise.

Multiple Use and Sustained Yield

Because Congress has chosen not to specify how it expects foresters to define *multiple use* or *sustained yield* in specific jurisdictions, the Forest Service has been left with enormous discretion in translating these formulas into practice. As with the multiple-use doctrine, the congressional definition of *sustained yield* is open to diverse interpretations; as section 531 of the Multiple Use–Sustained Yield Act suggests, "Sustained yield ... means the achievement and maintenance in perpetuity of a high-level annual or regular periodic output of the various renewable resources of the national forests without impairment of the productivity of the land."[32]

Conflict over the interpretation of multiple-use mandates has been intensified by requirements in the Resource Planning Act of 1974, as amended by the NFMA, that the Forest Service prepare comprehensive development and management plans for each of the more than 120 management units it operates. The Forest Service began this process in the late 1970s and still has not adopted final plans for all its management units. These management plans often become a catalyst for controversy among interests with competing demands on particular planning units. Moreover, the final adoption of a management plan does not necessarily end the controversy because arguments often continue over whether the plan is being implemented properly. The Forest Service often finds itself in the middle of a continuing, and often unresolvable, conflict over which pattern of multiple use is, or should be, implemented in a given forest tract.

Both the sustained-yield and multiple-use doctrines are important to the commercial timber industry because they provide the basis for the Forest Service's determination of the allowable cut in a given timber reserve, the amount of timber that can be removed from a particular resource area in a given time period. The Forest Service has interpreted sustained yield to require a nondeclining, even-flow policy, which limits the timber cut in a given area to a constant or increasing rate—but never a declining one. In effect, this has limited severely the cutting of old-growth forests, particularly in the Pacific Northwest, to the ire of the timber industry, local communities, and those economists who believe a larger cut of old-growth timber is more economically efficient and compatible with the multiple-use doctrine. Environmentalists generally support the protection of old-growth forests and advocate further reductions on the allowable cut elsewhere.[33]

In response to pressure from the timber industry and the Reagan administration's own preferences, the Forest Service began to increase the timber harvest substantially in the mid-1980s and to plan for increasing harvests through the 1990s. Between 1982 and 1989, the total timber cut in the national forests grew from 6.7 to 12.7 million board-feet.[34] Forest Service professionals contend that this expansion is consistent with the statutory mandate to maintain a sustained yield. But the timber industry wants more production. With its own reserves being depleted rapidly, the industry contends that only a timber harvest from the national forests significantly above the currently projected levels will provide enough wood for the U.S. economy in the next several decades.

Jimmy Carter's administration, responding to the rising cost of new housing, had ordered the Forest Service to depart "in a limited and temporary way" from its general sustained-yield principles and to open up some wilderness areas not specifically included in the National Wilderness Preservation System for timber harvesting. The Reagan administration, more sympathetic to the viewpoint of the National Forest Products Association, advocated that the Forest Service permanently modify its sustained-yield practices to permit greater timber cuts without violating the balanced-use principle. In keeping with this production bias, the Reagan administration's budgets substantially increased spending for Forest Service activities closely associated with timber production, such as new forest road construction.

The Forest Service asserted that it could meet the higher timber production levels demanded by the Reagan administration only by cutting deeply into the Pacific Northwest old-growth timber, including many of the nation's remaining virgin forests. Although towering stands of old Douglas fir and associated species within these forests provide incomparable vistas and sustain a great variety of plant and animal life, they are not particularly productive from an economic viewpoint. About one-quarter of the trees will rot once they mature. Most of these forests have already matured, and most of the timber has ceased to grow. In addition, the trees cover highly productive land on which second- and third-growth timber could flourish, producing much greater income during the twenty-first century than could be realized from its current use. Professional foresters associated with the commercial timber industry have asserted that protecting most of the old-growth forests from commercial cutting largely prevents decaying old forests from being converted to more productive young stands. Moreover, the Forest Service's critics note, higher timber cuts do not mean an end to all, or even most, of the old-growth stands but a selective cutting of some and the conversion of others to second-growth production.

Environmentalists have long opposed the logging of old-growth forests, citing the soil destabilization and ecosystem disruption they assert are almost inevitable. Nor do they find the economic arguments persuasive. The battles tend to be fought on a forest-by-forest basis as the Forest Service proposes the required long-range plans for each forest and then files the necessary EISs. Environmentalists often challenge the overall adequacy of the impact statements and the specific timber production goals. The struggle over timber use spills into the related issue of wilderness designation, where the Forest Service also exercises discretionary authority. George Bush's administration inherited one of these struggles, an especially emotional and public dispute provoked by Forest Service plans to permit greatly expanded timber cutting in old-growth northwestern forests. The plan might have succeeded, except for ecological serendipity in the form of the northern spotted owl.

The Northern Spotted Owl versus the Timber Industry

The spotted owl is now an icon of American resource politics, a symbol of the clash between competing approaches to valuing natural resources. In the mid-1980s the Forest Service had planned to permit commercial timber companies to make substantial cuts in the old-growth Oregon forests, whose 2.3 million acres represent the last 1 percent of the nation's original forest cover. In 1985, biologists in the DOI's Fish and Wildlife Service reported to the departmental leadership that the northern spotted owl, whose habitat was almost exclusively northwestern old-growth forests, was fast disappearing and should be designated an endangered species. Estimates indicated that about 1,500 nesting pairs of owls remained, all in the first-growth stands. One consequence of this designation would be to protect this habitat, if geographically unique, from almost all forms of development. The DOI's leadership initially overruled this recommendation under considerable pressure from the timber industry and a variety of local Oregon and Washington interests, including timber mills, community leaders, unions, local congressional representatives, and timber industry workers.

Spokespeople for these interests argued that designating the northern spotted owl an endangered species would virtually end logging on 1.5 million acres of old-growth timber in Oregon and Washington. The federal government estimated that between 4,500 and 9,500 jobs would be lost, but the timber industry asserted that the actual figure was ten times that amount. "You're talking about complete devastation of communities," protested then-senator Slade Gorton, R-Wash. The president of the Northwest Forestry Association, a trade group, repeated a familiar refrain among local economic interests in Washington and Oregon: "To devastate a regional economy over the spotted owl seems absurd. You're talking about affecting half our industry."[35] The timber industry's outrage was exacerbated further because much of the old-growth softwood timber was exported, primarily to Japan, where it could command several times the domestic price.

Environmentalists had opposed commercial logging in old-growth forests long before the specific tracts in Oregon and Washington had entered the dispute. Environmentalists have argued that intensive logging in old-growth forests, with the building of logging roads and disruptive soil practices sure to attend it, will greatly reduce the forest's ability to conserve water and to prevent soil erosion, thus violating the principle of balanced use. Spokespeople for environmental organizations also contend that much of the old-growth timber is found in poor soil—at high elevations and on steep slopes—and exposure to weathering will cause rapid erosion after logging begins. Moreover, they assert, these forests support a unique ecosystem with a great variety of important and irreplaceable flora and fauna. Finally, environmentalists challenge the presumption that a major increase in the timber harvest would significantly decrease housing costs. In any case, many acceptable substitutes for wood exist in the U.S. economy that can be had without sacrificing virgin forests, they note.

Except for the northern spotted owl, these arguments might have succumbed to the political weight of the local, regional, and national interests defending commercial access to first-growth timber. In fall 1988, environmental organizations obtained a federal court order that instructed the secretary of the interior to list the northern spotted owl as endangered, and in mid-1989 the DOI complied with the court's demand. The designation appeared almost to end commercial logging in northwestern first-growth forests, but it did nothing to diminish the rancor, or the economic stakes, involved in the continuing controversy over the appropriate use of the national forests.

Timber Sales Reform

George Bush's administration came into office committed to an active environmental agenda, explicitly distancing itself from the Reagan–Watt era in its goals for public lands. Although the environmental community had been displeased with the administration's choice of Lujan as the new secretary of the interior, it was considerably more receptive to the administration's proposal in early 1990 to reduce timber sales substantially in twelve national forests. The new proposal seemed to repudiate the previous administration's resource policies and to signal a major effort to reform traditional Forest Service sales practices, which had long been criticized by environmentalists.

The sales-below-cost controversy—political dynamite in the western states—seemed to set the new administration's public lands policy on a collision course with vast segments of the Forest Service's constituency.

The controversy had been simmering for decades. As the Conservation Foundation notes,

> The Forest Service typically constructs the roads and assumes other management and administrative responsibilities that allow private companies to harvest [public forest timber] economically.... However, several studies have alleged that the nation actually loses money (as well as valuable wilderness and wildlife habitat) in many cases, particularly in the Rocky Mountain region, because the Forest Service must spend more to allow the harvesting to occur than it receives from the harvests. The Forest Service denies that the economics of sales such as those in the Rocky Mountains and the Northwest are as unfavorable as many critics claim.[36]

Environmentalists, as well as critics within the Forest Service, had long asserted that this practice amounted to public subsidies for the commercial timber industry and a sacrifice of all other multiple-use values, such as recreation or wildlife habitat, to timber sales. "We think the Forest Service overestimates what is sustainable," argued a spokesperson for the National Wildlife Federation. "They overestimate how much timber a given area can produce, they overestimate the potential for the lands to be reforested and they underestimate the impacts on fish and wildlife. The bottom line is they are timber-dominated."[37]

When the Forest Service initiated a new bookkeeping system in 1987, the system appeared to demonstrate that the service was losing money on about two-thirds of its timber sales.[38] Critics cited Alaska's Tongass National Forest as an example of the losses disclosed by the new bookkeeping; the Forest Service had spent about $50 million annually to finance the cutting of 450 million board-feet of timber that brought less than $1 million to the government in revenue.[39] Nonetheless, the new proposal had many formidable opponents, including loggers, timber companies, state and congressional political spokespeople for the affected areas, and the Forest Service itself. Because much of the Forest Service budget was spent on preparing and auctioning acreage for commercial logging, a reduction in these sales would mean a substantial budget reduction for the service. In effect, the administration's plan represented the first major assault on a forest management practice that had endured for more than a half century, fortified by a powerful coalition of political and economic interests and defended by one of the federal government's most successful and respected public agencies.

The Clinton administration used the new bookkeeping system to considerable advantage in its efforts to restrain continuing efforts by the commercial timber industry and western state governors to expand allowable timber cuts in the national forests. The new system also worked to the advantage of conservation elements within the Forest Service who had been pressing for greater timber conservation for many decades. It was now possible to demonstrate not only that federal timber sales were not the financial asset they had been asserted to be but also that increased road building and logging in the national forests often increased the federal timbering deficit.

How Much Wilderness Is Enough?

A substantial portion of the 65 million undeveloped acres under the jurisdiction of the Forest Service—the roadless regions—could become part of the National Wilderness Preservation System and thereby be forever excluded from timbering. A large portion of this roadless area is eligible for assignment to timber production. Timber producers, environmentalists, the Forest Service, and Congress have disagreed since the 1980s over how much of this roadless area should be designated for multiple use—in other words, how much of the area should be open to timbering, mineral exploration, and other nonrecreational and nonconservation uses. Perhaps as much as a third of the whole national forest system, including many old-growth stands, is in these roadless areas.

Environmentalists have been apprehensive that any multiple-use designation for large undeveloped tracts will be an invitation not only to aggressive timbering but also to oil, natural gas, and coal exploration. They predict that energy industries, on locating energy reserves, will seek exceptions to environmental regulations. Air pollution from electric power plants and energy refining operations adjacent to public lands with energy reserves will result, and the quality of the lands will be degraded irreversibly. They would prefer that most of the roadless areas under the Forest Service's jurisdiction be included in the National Wilderness Preservation System.

With some justification, environmentalists also allege that the Forest Service's strong commitment to its traditional multiple-use doctrine makes it reluctant to turn large tracts of roadless areas over to a single dominant use such as wilderness preservation. This conviction led environmentalists to criticize the manner in which the Forest Service conducted its first major inventory of roadless areas within its jurisdiction in the early 1970s.

Nonetheless, the Multiple Use–Sustained Yield Act requires the Forest Service to include wilderness protection among other multiple uses of land within its jurisdiction. The NFMA also requires the Forest Service to draw up a master plan for the use of land under its jurisdiction that includes the consideration of wilderness designation. Thus, the Forest Service was given both ample authority and explicit responsibility to recommend to Congress additional roadless areas for inclusion in the National Wilderness

Preservation System. Although Congress alone possesses the authority to assign land to the system formally, the Forest Service's recommendations frequently influence the decisions. The White House, however, often has proposed its own plans for the roadless areas, sometimes at variance with Forest Service initiatives.

The Carter and Reagan administrations offered proposals to Congress for allocating the roadless areas between wilderness and multiple-use categories; both proposals departed in significant ways from the Forest Service's own proposals. The Carter administration's plan, the more conservative of the two, would have allocated about 10 million acres to wilderness and reserved another 10 million for further study. The Reagan administration, committed to increasing the size of territory open to timbering and energy exploration, rejected the Carter proposal. Congress, as it has often done, chose to follow its own agenda for wilderness preservation. Since the Reagan administration, relatively few new areas have been designated for wilderness because Congress and the White House could reach no agreement on priorities.

Conclusion

The struggles over energy exploration, mining, and timbering on public lands reveal a durable structure underlying the political conflicts over the use of public resources in the United States. The pattern tends to be repeated because it grows from political realities inherent in the U.S. governmental system.

At the center of the conflict is a federal executive agency guarding the resource as a public trust and wrestling with an ambiguous mandate for its management. Most often this agency will be part of the DOI or the Forest Service. The mandates will be vague because Congress must rely on the professional administrator to make expert resource decisions— hence the generality of the mandates—and ambiguous because Congress often shrinks from choosing between conflicting claims on resources. Thus, multiple-use prescriptions for forest or range management appear to offer something to recreationists, conservationists, and resource developers without really settling the competing claims. The administrative managers for the public resource inevitably will find their professional decisions politicized as conflicting interests seek to influence technical decisions to their advantage. Technical decisions themselves can often be made and justified in different scientifically defensible ways. All this means that resource administrators sometimes can exercise their professional judgment in the service of their own group and political loyalties. In all these ways, the resource management agency finds itself at the center of a political conflict over the public domain.

Further, both the White House and Congress will become partisan advocates of resource management policy, attempting to influence administrative decisions relevant to resource management and responding to pressure from organized interests with a stake in resource management. As we have observed in timber, wilderness, and energy development policies, Congress has the predictable tendency to intervene in administrative management to protect interests important to the legislators. So, too, Presidents Carter, Reagan, Bush, Clinton, George W. Bush, and indeed every president before them for a half century, have directed the DOI and the Forest Service to pursue specific objectives in resource management compatible with their ideological biases and political commitments. Indeed, Congress and the White House often compete in attempting to influence administrative determinations affecting the public domain. The president, despite the illusory title of chief executive, has no guarantee of success in the struggle.

The plurality of organized interests involved in resource decisions means that Congress, the White House, and the administrative agencies are enmeshed in a process of coalition building with organized groups during resource policymaking. These organized interests, moreover, involve not only private interests but also the states within which the public domain resides and for which the use of the domain's resources have significant political and economic consequences.

Finally, policy struggles quite often are waged in the technical language of resource economics and scientific management. Perhaps more than most environmental issues, public resource management is an arcane business to most Americans, particularly those living where few public lands exist. In such circumstances, specialized private groups, such as environmentalists and resource users, tend to operate almost invisibly to the public. The outcome of the policy struggles depends particularly on the groups' organizational resources, technical expertise, and political adeptness in the administrative infighting and legal wrangling that often characterize resource policymaking. It is a political arena, more particularly, in which organized environmental groups often constitute practically the only expression of viewpoints not associated with resource users or administrators.

Suggested Readings

Clark, Jeanne N., and Daniel McCool. *Staking Out the Terrain: Power Differentials among Natural Resource Management Agencies.* 2nd ed. Albany: SUNY Press, 2000.

Lowry, William R. *Dam Politics: Restoring America's Rivers.* Washington, D.C.: Georgetown University Press, 2003.

Nie, Martin A. *The Governance of Western Public Lands: Mapping Its Present and Future.* Lawrence: University of Kansas Press, 2009.

Reisner, Marc. *Cadillac Desert*. Rev. ed. New York: Penguin Books, 2001.

Vaughn, Jacqueline, and Hanna Cortner. *George W. Bush's Healthy Forests: Reframing the Environmental Debate*. Boulder: University Press of Colorado, 2005.

Notes

1. Felicity Barringer, "Secretary Tours Yellowstone on Snowmobile," *New York Times,* February 17, 2005, A18.
2. National Energy Policy Group, *National Energy Policy* (Washington, D.C.: Office of the President, 2001), 5–9.
3. Defenders of Wildlife, "Arctic National Wildlife Refuge," available at: http: www .savearcticrefuge.org (accessed May 1, 2007).
4. Charli Coon, "Tapping Oil Reserves in a Small Part of the ANWR: Environmentally Sound, Energy Wise," August 1, 2001, available at: www.heritage.org/research/ energyandenvironment/em763.cfm (accessed April 14, 2004).
5. For a legislative history of ANWR, see M. Lynne Corn and Bernard A. Gelb, "Arctic National Wildlife Refuge (ANWR): Controversies for the 108th Congress," Report no. 1B10111, Congressional Research Service, Washington, D.C., 2003.
6. U.S. Department of the Interior, "Environmentally Responsible Energy Production in Alaska's Arctic National Wildlife Refuge (ANWR)," July 21, 2003, available at: www .doi.gov/anwr/index.html (accessed April 15, 2007).
7. Rachael D'Oro, "Alaska Environment, Development Co-Exist," November 17, 2003, available at: www.lists.envirolink.org/pipermail/ar-news/Week-of-Mon-20031117/010930 .html (accessed May 1, 2007).
8. Mike Chambers, "Alaska Governor Invites U.S. Oil Drilling," AP Online, April 1, 2004, www.highbeam.com/library/doc3.asp?DOCID=1P1:929982 (accessed April 6, 2004).
9. Article IV, section 3, clause 2.
10. Tom Arrandale, *The Battle for Natural Resources* (Washington, D.C.: Congressional Quarterly, 1983), Chap. 1; U.S. Department of the Interior, "About the Department of the Interior: Quick Facts," available at: http://www.doi.gov/facts.html (accessed January 23, 2010).
11. Aldo Leopold, *A Sand County Almanac* (New York: Oxford University Press, 1949), 222.
12. A useful survey of public lands can be found in U.S. Department of the Interior, Bureau of Land Management, *Managing the Nation's Public Lands* (Washington, D.C.: U.S. Government Printing Office, 1983).
13. Paul J. Culhane, *Public Lands Politics* (Baltimore: Johns Hopkins University Press, 1981), 60.
14. James Baker, "The Frustrations of FLPMA," *Wilderness* 47 (winter 1983): 11. See also Jeanne N. Clarke and Daniel McCool, *Staking Out the Terrain: Power Differentials among Natural Resource Agencies* (Albany: SUNY Press, 1985), Chaps. 4–5.
15. 16 U.S.C. § 530, 74 Stat. 215 (1960). On the impact of sustained use on the Forest Service, see Culhane, *Public Lands Politics,* Chap. 2.
16. 16 U.S.C. § 530, 74 Stat. 215 (1960).
17. Council on Environmental Quality, *Environmental Quality, 1979* (Washington, D.C.: U.S. Government Printing Office, 1980), 309.
18. Natural Resources Defense Council, "The Bush Record," available at: http://www .nrdc.org/ bushrecord/default.asp (accessed May 15, 2008).
19. On the history of recent federal OCS legislation, see Marc Humphries, "Outer Continental Shelf: Debate over Oil and Gas Leasing," Congressional Research Service Report to Congress, Washington, D.C., August 14, 2006.

20. Craig W. Allin, "Wilderness Policy," in *Western Public Lands and Environmental Politics,* ed. Charles Davis (Boulder, Colo.: Westview Press, 1997), 179.

21. Sandra K. Davis, "Fighting over Public Lands: Interest Groups, States, and the Federal Government," in *Western Public Lands and Environmental Politics,* ed. Charles Davis, (Boulder, Colo.: Westview Press, 1997), 23.

22. Quoted in World Resources Institute, *The 1994 Information Please Environmental Almanac* (New York: Houghton Mifflin, 1993), 159.

23. Sheldon Rampton, "Fish out of Water: Behind the Wise Use Movement's Victory at Klamath," *PR Watch* 10 (April–June 2003): 117–126.

24. Philip Shabecoff, "Debate over Wilderness Area Leasing Intensifies," *New York Times,* February 15, 1982, D6.

25. Ibid.

26. Quoted in Douglas Jehl, "In Idaho a Howl against Roadless Forests," *New York Times,* July 5, 2000, A10.

27. Quoted in ibid.

28. Quoted in ibid.

29. Jesse T. Holland, "Clinton Creates Largest U.S. Nature Preserve," *New York Times,* December 5, 2000, 1A.

30. George Hoberg, "From Localism to Legalism," in *Western Public Lands and Environmental Politics,* ed. Charles Davis (Boulder, Colo.: Westview Press, 1997), 48.

31. Ibid., 53.

32. 16 U.S.C. § 530, 74 Stat. 215 (1960).

33. Culhane, *Public Lands Politics,* Chap. 2.

34. U.S. Department of Commerce, Bureau of the Census, *Statistical Abstract of the United States, 1989* (Washington, D.C.: U.S. Government Printing Office, 1990), 656.

35. Timothy Egan, "U.S. Stand on Owl Seen Saving Trees in West," *New York Times,* April 27, 1989, A18.

36. Conservation Foundation, *State of the Environment: A View toward the Nineties* (Washington, D.C.: Conservation Foundation, 1987), 220.

37. Margaret E. Kriz, "Last Stand on Timber," *National Journal,* March 3, 1990, 509.

38. Philip Shabecoff, "Aid Is Asked on Recreation in Forests," *New York Times,* February 17, 1988, B5.

39. Timothy Egan, "Logging in Lush Alaskan Forest Profits Companies and Costs U.S.," *New York Times,* May 29, 1989, sec. 1, 1.

Chapter 10

Climate Change, Domestic Politics, and the Challenge of Global Policymaking

If we build the foundations of our climate-change policies so confidently and so single-mindedly on scientific claims about what the future holds and what therefore "has to be done," then science will inevitably become the field on which political battles are waged. The mantra becomes: Get the science right, reduce the scientific uncertainties, compel everyone to believe it ... and we will have won. Not only is this an unrealistic view about how policy gets made, it also places much too great a burden on science, certainly on climate science with all of its struggles with complexity, contingency and uncertainty.

—Michael Hulme, professor of climate change, School of Environmental Sciences, University of East Anglia[1]

Twenty years ago when we started worrying about global warming, we thought we'd have a generation to pay those bills off. But we were wrong—the planet was more finely balanced than we'd realized. The melting Arctic is the call from the repo man.

—Bill McKibben, American environmental scholar and activist[2]

On December 9, 2009, President Barack Obama was preparing for a journey to Copenhagen to join other world leaders and several thousand delegates gathered at the United Nations Climate Change Conference (COP 15; the fifteenth Conference of the Parties to the UN Framework Convention on Climate Change). He was shadowed by a large polar bear. The bear arrived first. Alongside the cavernous conference hall, the United States had erected a handsome pavilion visited daily by crowds drawn

363

from more than 40,000 participants and delegates attending this most important global climate change conference in a decade. Inside the hall, Secretary of the Interior Ken Salazar's press conference was underway. Visitors watched a video of the president's Nobel Prize address on a wall screen. Many, however, were more attentive to the sociable bear on his hind legs, animatedly describing his species' threatened extinction from the effects of global climate change, paws waving and wagging at the video, warning Obama to return from Copenhagen with a viable global climate change agreement.[3]

The polar bear was a temporary alter ego for the public lands director of the Center for Biological Diversity (CBD) who, uncomfortably encased within his costume, represented one of the environmental advocacy groups that successfully used litigation to force the U.S. Department of the Interior to list the bears as an Endangered Species. The bear, perhaps the most recognizable icon for global climate change, could as easily symbolize the most daunting environmental challenge confronting the White House—the bear's sojourn to Copenhagen a political metaphor for an issue destined to stalk Obama's administration—as it has done with a growing presence in every presidency since Ronald Reagan.

By the time Obama arrived in Copenhagen, the way to a global climate treaty had become a tortuous path leading from Kyoto in 1998 through the inhospitable Bush administration and culminating with COP 15 in December 2009. Nationally, the journey become a tangle of obstruction and delay compounded of White House opposition to an international treaty or comprehensive federal legislation controlling greenhouse gas emissions and congressional deadlock over domestic greenhouse gas (GHG) regulatory legislation. Meanwhile, sixteen states had seized the initiative and created their own state and regional GHG regulatory programs. Environmentalists and other treaty advocates, frustrated with a decade of Washington inertia, enthusiastically anticipated Barack Obama's election as a breakthrough for domestic and international GHG regulation. Obama had made a "green economy" and renewed federal and international action on a global climate treaty the centerpiece of his environmental platform. Thus, Obama entered the White House on a tide of high expectation among climate treaty advocates who were encouraged, as well, by national opinion polls generally revealing public receptivity to a new global climate agreement.

The climate change issue is evidence that the distinction between domestic and international environmental policy is rapidly eroding as both science and diplomacy force the recognition of their increasing interdependence. Climate change is one of numerous global environmental issues, such as acid precipitation and stratospheric ozone depletion, that now routinely compel attention on the White House domestic policy agenda. Climate change seems to be an especially formidable issue for policymakers. Unlike acid precipitation, there are no stunted and withered forests to dramatize the problem, no sprawling ozone hole visible with satellite imagery to translate stratospheric ozone depletion into immediately recognizable public form—in short, there is little readily understandable, unambiguous evidence that domestic policymakers can summon effectively to frame the issue. Moreover, many of the most ominous global consequences predicted from climate warming—for example, the northern migration of the global temperate zone or the extinction of an indigenous species—may be diffused and attenuated over decades or centuries, thereby easily inhibiting a sense of urgency and relevance among the public and its officials. Because climate warming is conceived globally on a scale never historically experienced by humans, public opinion studies often suggest that the average American can feel intimidated and personally helpless to do much about it. In addition, the potential domestic and international economic cost and worldwide scale of political action essential to mitigating climate change or adapting to it require international diplomatic and economic collaboration that is difficult to achieve. Above all, the primal vortex about which the domestic policy debate over climate change swirls, the most powerful engine driving the nationwide political conflict over the climate change issue, is contested science.

The Contested Science of Atmospheric Warming

The catalyst to the ongoing controversy over the scientific validity of global climate change predictions has been the Intergovernmental Panel on Climate Change (IPCC), established in 1988 under the auspices of the United Nations Environment Programme and the World Meteorological Organization for the purpose of assessing "the scientific, technical and socioeconomic information relevant for the understanding of the risk of human-induced climate change."[4] The IPCC reports have each engaged more than 2,400 scientists across the globe in a continuing process of collecting, integrating, and evaluating the vast diversity of scientific research on virtually every aspect of climate change. The IPCC "does not carry out new research nor does it monitor climate-related data. It bases its assessment mainly on published and peer reviewed scientific technical literature."[5] The goal of these assessments is to inform international policy and negotiations on climate-related issues. The IPCC has become the most globally visible and consistently controversial of the scientific institutions associated with climate change research. Although the IPCC periodic reports are as close to Holy Writ as exists within the scientific community associated with climate change advocacy, the IPCC has been consistently diligent to acknowledge explicitly the limitations which may be inherent to their assessment's data or conclusions, lest the reports lose their credibility.

The Four Intergovernmental Panel on Climate Change Assessments.
The First Assessment Report of the IPCC (1990), as well as a supplemental report prepared in 1992, supported the establishment of the United Nations Framework Convention on Climate Change (UNFCCC) at the United Nations Conference on Environment and Development (UNCED, commonly known as "The Earth Summit") held in Rio de Janeiro, Brazil, in 1992. The UNFCCC treaty, which the United States has signed, serves as the foundation of international political efforts to combat global warming.

The IPCC's reports were also influential at the first Conference of the Parties (COP) to the UNFCCC, held in Berlin, Germany, in 1995. COP conferences, at different national locations, have subsequently been held at regular intervals, the last (COP 15) in Copenhagen in December 2009. The first COP delegates produced the Berlin Mandate, setting out the terms for a negotiation process that would produce binding commitments by the industrial countries to reduce their heat-trapping emissions after the year 2000.

The significantly strengthened IPCC Second Assessment Report (SAR, 1996) provided key input to the negotiations that led to the adoption of the Kyoto Protocol to the UNFCCC in 1997. The Kyoto Protocol is an international agreement that established binding targets for reducing the heat-trapping emissions of developed countries. After the SAR was published, a number of technical papers and special reports were prepared on the impact of aircraft, land use, technology, and changing emission levels on global warming. The IPCC Third Assessment Report (TAR, 2001) concluded that temperature increases over the twenty-first century could be significantly larger than previously thought and that the evidence for human influence on climate change is stronger than ever. The level of acceptance of this assessment within the extensive community of IPCC scientists was quite remarkable. The Fourth Assessment Report (FAR, 2007) has become the most internationally influential scientific document currently involved with climate change research, representing what most atmospheric scientists and related professionals consider to be a thorough, carefully explained view of the state of climate change science in 2001.

The Intergovernmental Panel on Climate Change Fourth Assessment Report.

The FAR

provides the strongest statement to date on the extent and causes of climate change. This report expresses much greater confidence than past assessments that most of the observed warming over the past half-century is caused by human activities (greater than 90% certainty). It notes that the rates of warming and sea level rise accelerated during the 20th century, the latter representing a major new finding. It also notes other important changes such as more intense precipitation, drought, and to some extent tropical cyclones.[6]

Among the other significant scientific conclusions that appear in it: *Fourth assessment report*

- It is "unequivocal" that Earth's climate is warming, "as is now evident from observations of increases in global average air and ocean temperatures, widespread melting of snow and ice, and rising global mean sea level."
- Global atmospheric concentrations of carbon dioxide, methane and nitrous oxide have increased markedly as a result of human activities since 1750 and now far exceed preindustrial values determined from ice cores spanning many thousands of years. The global increases in carbon dioxide concentration are due primarily to fossil fuel use and land-use change, while those of methane and nitrous oxide are primarily due to agriculture.
- "[T]he warmth of the last half century is unusual in at least the previous 1,300 years. The last time the polar regions were significantly warmer than present for an extended period was about 125,000 years ago, at which time reductions in polar ice volume led to 13–20 feet of sea level rise."
- Most of the observed increase in globally averaged temperatures since the mid-twentieth century is very likely (with a greater than 90 percent probability) due to the observed increase in anthropogenic GHG concentrations.
- Discernible human influences now extend to other aspects of climate, including ocean warming, continental-average temperatures, temperature extremes, and wind patterns.
- For the next two decades, warming of about 0.2°C per decade is projected for the range of emissions scenarios considered. Even if the concentrations of all GHGs and aerosols had been kept constant at year 2000 levels, a further warming of about 0.1°C per decade would be expected.
- Continued GHG emissions at or above current rates would cause further warming and induce many changes in the global climate system during the twenty-first century that would very likely (with a greater than 90 percent probability) be larger than those observed during the twentieth century.[7]

Changes of this magnitude without mitigation would profoundly, and possibly catastrophically, affect much of the world. Low-lying areas, including many economically underdeveloped countries in Africa and Asia as well as island nations, would be inundated by seawater, their economic and ecological sustainability severely jeopardized. Economically and technologically advanced nations with exposed seacoasts or levee-protected lowlands would also confront formidable economic, engineering, and logistical problems in adjusting to rising sea levels. Generally, the world's temperate zones would probably shift further north, accelerating the desertification and deforestation of many continental areas in Asia, Africa, Europe, and North America, while transforming agricultural production in many others. Along with these transformations would come shifts in regional ecology and a multitude of other natural changes that are difficult to predict precisely. Not all the predicted changes would necessarily be adverse. Some experts have also predicted longer and more productive growing seasons for many crops as a result of increased ambient carbon dioxide, the transformation of some northern latitudes into new agricultural breadbaskets, and other benign consequences. In any event, the profound global alterations attending significant climate warming, however characterized, would apparently create a relatively swift, pervasive transformation of human societies and world ecosystems unprecedented in modern human history.

The FAR also doubled the top end of possible climate warming globally to 11°F over the coming century and predicted an acceleration of the trends causing concern earlier. According to the report, the twentieth century was the warmest in the past thousand years. During that period, the sea level rose ten times faster than the average rate over the past 3,000 years. While continuing to acknowledge the tentativeness of many of its conclusions, the FAR seemed to confirm a growing scientific consensus about the imminence of climate warming and to strengthen political pressure for international governmental responses. Since the first IPCC assessment report, numerous public and private institutions have also conducted extensive research to characterize the global and domestic implications of the assessments. If the FAR is substantially accurate in its conclusions, the consequences are expected to profoundly alter almost every aspect of U.S. domestic life, a transformation on an ecological, economic, and social scale without historical precedent, as the predictions in Box 10-1 suggest.

Dissent. Although the IPCC reports and related research appear to represent what has been called the consensus among climate scientists, the IPCC data and conceptual models constituting the foundation for its predictions about the magnitude of global climate change and its implications have been contested from the inception of international discussion about global climate change. As the IPCC has become

Box 10-1 Global Climate Change Impacts in the United States: Key Findings

1. Global warming is unequivocal and primarily human-induced.
Global temperature has increased over the past fifty years. This observed increase is due primarily to human-induced emissions of heat-trapping gases.

2. Climate changes are underway in the United States and are projected to grow.
Climate-related changes are already observed in the United States and its coastal waters. These include increases in heavy downpours, rising temperature and sea level, rapidly retreating glaciers, thawing permafrost, lengthening growing seasons, lengthening ice-free seasons in the ocean and on lakes and rivers, earlier snowmelt, and alterations in river flows. These changes are projected to grow.

3. Widespread climate-related impacts are occurring now and are expected to increase.
Climate changes are already affecting water, energy, transportation, agriculture, ecosystems, and health. These impacts are different from region to region and will grow under projected climate change.

4. Climate change will stress water resources.
Water is an issue in every region, but the nature of the potential impacts varies. Drought, related to reduced precipitation, increased evaporation, and increased water loss from plants, is an important issue in many regions, especially in the West. Floods and water quality problems are likely to be amplified by climate changes in most regions. Declines in mountain snowpack are important in the West and Alaska where snowpack provides vital natural water storage.

5. Crop and livestock production will be increasingly challenged.
Agriculture is considered one of the sectors most adaptable to changes in climate. However, increased heat, pests, water stress, diseases, and weather extremes will pose adaptation challenges for crop and livestock production.

6. Coastal areas are at increasing risk from sea-level rise and storm surge.
Sea-level rise and storm surge place many U.S. coastal areas at increasing risk of erosion and flooding, especially along the Atlantic and Gulf Coasts, Pacific Islands, and parts of Alaska. Energy and transportation infrastructure and other property in coastal areas are very likely to be adversely affected.

7. Threats to human health will increase.
Health impacts of climate change are related to heat stress, waterborne diseases, poor air quality, extreme weather events, and diseases transmitted by insects and rodents. Robust public health infrastructure can reduce the potential for negative impacts.

8. Climate change will interact with many social and environmental stresses.
Climate change will combine with pollution; population growth; overuse of resources; urbanization; and other social, economic, and environmental stresses to create larger impacts than from any of these factors alone.

9. Thresholds will be crossed, leading to changes in climate and ecosystems.
There are a variety of thresholds in the climate system and ecosystems. These thresholds determine, for example, the presence of sea ice and permafrost, and the survival

(continued)

Box 10-1*   *Global Climate Change Impacts in the United States:
Key Findings (cont.)

---

of species, from fish to insect pests, with implications for society. With further climate change, the cross of additional thresholds is expected.

10. Future climate change and its impacts depend on choices made today.
The amount and rate of future climate change depend primarily on current and future human-caused emissions of heat-trapping gases and airborne particles. Responses involve reducing emissions to limit future warming, and adapting to the changes that are unavoidable.

Source: U.S. Global Climate Change Research Project, "Executive Summary," *Global Climate Change Impacts of the United States* (New York: Cambridge University Press, 2009), 12.

---

increasingly assertive in its major conclusions, the scientific debate has become increasingly strident; this has occasionally escalated into venomous exchanges within the scientific community. But, more often, these exchanges have taken place within the political arena, where the issue has transmuted into a polarizing partisan confrontation between contending factions promoting competing claims concerning the scientific validity and political acceptability of the proposed solutions. IPCC dissenters not only have contested the IPCC's major scientific conclusions and supporting research but, in some instances, accused various scientific proponents and organizations of willfully conspiring to suppress and falsify scientific data inconsistent with the major premises of climate change.

Climate change dissenters (sometimes anointed "contrarians") range across a broad, extremely diverse social and scientific spectrum: scientists engaged in climate research and related fields, other scientific professionals, political partisans ideologically hostile to the proposed social or economic solutions for climate change, and corporations vulnerable to the regulatory controls required to control climate warming emissions. Proponents of the IPCC's conclusions and related initiatives to regulate climate-warming emissions have been especially vehement in asserting that many of the individuals and institutions opposing the IPCC's conclusions are proxies for the global petroleum corporation Exxon-Mobil, which has spent millions of dollars on its own corporate media campaign attacking the credibility of the IPCC and its allies. Moreover, Exxon-Mobil has a considerable number of corporate allies in the business of underwriting opposition to the IPCC, including numerous other corporations and advocacy groups associated with fossil fuel mining and combustion and with petroleum distillation and distribution.

The ongoing scientific debate swirls around a multitude of complex technical issues certain to confuse the public. The critics' favorite target has been the computer models used to generate climate warming predictions, which have been assailed continually for faulty assumptions and inadequate data about current climate trends. Some experts have asserted that many computer models are based on inaccurate measurements of historical temperature change, that climate warming models fail to describe the long-range physics of climate change, that other historical climate data are misconstrued or misapplied in climate modeling, and much more. Some experts cite other causes, such as solar activity and terrestrial volcanoes, to explain climate warming. Others rely on different models suggesting that the greenhouse effect is not inevitable. Still others do not believe sufficient evidence exists to make *any* responsible judgment about future climate warming.

The already fierce contention over climate change science was further exacerbated, and the critics enormously inspired, by the emergence of what has been called the "climategate" affair in November 2009, with its serious political repercussions. Hackers captured more than one thousand emails from scientists at the Climate Research Unit (CRU) at Great Britain's University of East Anglia, a major global climate change research center supporting the IPCC reports, and publicized the purloined emails internationally.[8] Climate critics asserted that the emails revealed (as they had always suspected) evidence of a conspiracy among global climate scientists to fabricate data supporting climate warming while suppressing contrary evidence. Coming less than a month before the COP 15, the revelation could not have been better timed to further confound the already difficult negotiations anticipated at Copenhagen. Climate critics asserted that the messages, covering a period of thirteen years, constituted an arsenal of "smoking guns" destroying the credibility of the IPCC FAR. Many of the emails revealed that the CRU scientists and their global professional collaborators were at times rude, dismissive of critics, intensely partisan to their own research, and sometimes manipulative in presenting their data in the best possible light. Collectively, however, the emails did not seem to vindicate the climate critics' worst allegations—that fundamental climate data was counterfeit. Nevertheless, the aftermath of the CRU affair was bad enough for climate warming partisans.[9]

In defense of the CRU scientists, many proponents of climate change and the related research argued that the critics hastening to discredit the CRU scientists had edited the messages selectively, presenting out of context words and phrases common among research scientists and ignoring email evidence contrary to their "smoking gun" theory. Moreover—and this was perhaps the most important rebuttal—climate warming partisans noted that voluminous evidence was available at many *other* research centers globally that corroborated the CRU researcher's conclusions. The whole affair, however, was politically damaging regardless of the ultimate credibility of the CRU critics. The CRU emails had seized global media attention, throwing climate proponents on the defensive and prompting numerous investigations, all of which incited further speculation about the validity of climate change science and invited public confusion, if not disbelief, concerning the validity of climate warming science.

In the United States, the CRU affair appeared to erode further, at least temporarily, the already receding domestic political support for American participation in a global agreement limiting climate warming emissions—this at a time when the embattled president was already in Copenhagen, struggling to salvage at least a symbolic triumph from the contentious deliberations. The decline in public confidence in climate warming's reality was already evident by the time Obama departed for Copenhagen, as Table 10-1 indicates.

By the end of 2009, in any event, climate warming was not among the most important environmental issues concerning the public and seldom rose from the lower depths of most opinion surveys reporting the matters most concerning the American public. Perhaps even more politically significant, public skepticism about climate warming's reality

Table 10-1 Changing Public Opinion about Global Warming

	April 2008 (%)	October 2009 (%)	Change (%)
Is there solid evidence the Earth is warming?			
Yes	71	57	−14
Because of human activity	47	36	−11
Because of natural patterns	18	16	−2
Don't know	6	6	0
No	21	33	+12
Mixed/Don't know	8	10	+2
	100	100	
How serious a problem?			
Very serious	44	35	−9
Somewhat serious	29	30	+1
Not too serious	13	15	+2
Not a problem	11	17	+6
Don't know	3	3	0
	100	100	

Source: "Fewer Americans See Solid Evidence of Global Warming," Pew Research Center for the People and the Press, October 22, 2009, available at: http://people-press.org/report/556/global-warming. Reprinted by permission.

Note: Figures may not add up to 100 percent because of rounding.

had diminished implicitly the credibility of climate change scientists and science, thus undermining the single most crucial foundation of climate warming action globally.

The domestic debate about the evidence for climate warming and the policy implications also unfolds within a broader world arena shaping the political contours of the domestic issue in important ways. This global setting creates the setting for what has been called the transboundry politics of environmental policymaking so characteristic of the climate issue.

The Domestic Setting of Climate Change Politics

The United States is second only to China in the volume of its global GHG emissions (see Figure 10-1), and the magnitude of these emissions has risen steadily throughout the last several decades. Until the late 1980s, however, the nation's emission of these climate-warming gases was largely a concern of scientists, a matter virtually unknown and, in any case, uninteresting to the public.

Figure 10-1   Top Twenty Countries' CO$_2$ Emissions, 2006

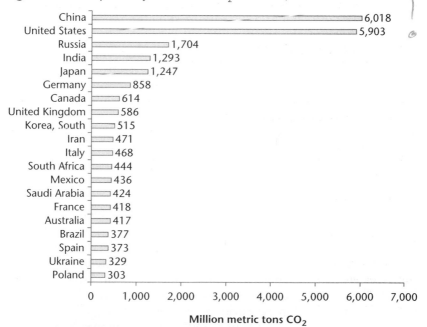

Million metric tons CO$_2$

Source: Union of Concerned Scientists, "Global Warming: Each Country's Share of CO$_2$ Emissions," available at: http://www.ucsusa.org/global_warming/science_and_impacts/ science/each-countrys-share-of-co2.html. Reprinted by permission of the Union of Concerned Scientists.

In mid-1988, James E. Hansen, director of the NASA Goddard Institute for Space Studies, testified before the members of the Senate Energy and Natural Resources Committee that it was "99 percent certain" that the unusually hot summer of 1988 was evidence that a global climate warming was underway.[10] That remark instantly caught the attention of Congress and the media. Suddenly, global warming, often called the greenhouse effect, bore the imprimatur of NASA science; it was speculation no more. Hansen had accomplished what the environmental movement could not despite many years of labor. Global warming had acquired political credibility.

In fact, the scientific evidence was less than compelling at the time, but global climate warming had arrived politically on a wave of international scientific advocacy, and presidents were compelled to act as if it were imminent. The U.S. involvement in global climate warming diplomacy was inevitable. Both the George Bush and Clinton administrations, uneasy with the science and politics of climate warming, initiated measures, albeit irresolutely, to mitigate the impact of global warming.

A great diversity of domestic political interests are caught up in the regulatory battle over GHG emissions, including electrical utilities, which account for 80 percent of all domestic coal combustion; automobile manufacturers and petroleum producers, whose products create significant carbon emissions; agricultural crop and livestock producers; and almost any other fossil-fuel-consuming industries. Throughout the 1990s, the domestic campaign for national and international controls on GHG emissions was led primarily by scientists, environmentalists, and segments of the national media. They were strongly supported by most European nations and Japan, which were prepared to negotiate a tough climate treaty by the early 1990s and brought considerable diplomatic pressure on the United States to act similarly.

Most of the segments of the U.S. economy that potentially would be regulated, led by the utilities, car manufacturers, and petroleum producers, were joined by organized labor in early opposition to any domestic or international agreements setting compulsory timetables and targets for cutbacks in fossil fuel emissions associated with climate warming. This domestic opposition was joined by most of the developing nations, which collectively account for 30–40 percent of current global GHG emissions. Some developing countries believed that the largely Western scientific community advocating climate controls could not speak to the interests of the developing world. Some poorer nations, for instance, resented calculations produced by the IPCC indicating that deforestation and livestock in developing nations contributed to global climate warming. From the perspective of developing countries, this unfairly stigmatized their difficult economic circumstances. In their view, "deforestation is a matter of desperation, not choice, and subsistence animals who provide a variety of useful functions cannot be compared with surplus, overfed stock in rich countries."[11] Developing countries also asserted that GHG abatement should be the industrialized nations' responsibility because developing nations needed all their resources for survival. "How can we devote our precious resources toward reducing emissions," asked Malawi's minister of Forestry, Fisheries and Environmental Affairs at the Kyoto conference, "when we are struggling every day just to feed, clothe and house our citizens?"[12] Nor did the developing countries find most economists helpful. Economists who asserted that developing countries could abate their fossil fuel emissions far more cheaply than could developed ones seemed to be feeding the appetites of the privileged nations while thrusting the abatement burden as much as possible onto others.

In any event, the estimated costs to the United States alone to reduce its carbon dioxide emissions would be enormous. The cost of abating carbon dioxide emissions in the United States would fall heavily on coal users and producers, particularly the electrical utilities, and on the auto industry. The capital cost of installing control technologies for carbon dioxide emissions—and no commercially proven technology yet exists—is estimated to be 70–150 percent of the entire cost of a new electricity-generating facility. This cost could raise the average American's electric bill by 75 percent.[13] Every American would feel some impact of the abatement policies on his or her lifestyle and pocketbook.

Until the early 1990s, scientific disagreement and public passivity forced policymakers to become scientific judges and scientists to become salespeople in the struggle to determine whose data would govern policy decisions. By the end of George Bush's administration in 1992, however, the combined scientific and diplomatic pressures, together with gradually emerging public concern about climate warming, forced the White House to confront the greenhouse effect diplomatically. At the 1992 Rio conference, the U.S. delegation reluctantly agreed to reduce voluntarily U.S. GHG emissions to 1990 levels by the year 2000. It was evident two years later that neither the United States nor several other industrialized nations would meet their voluntary emission abatement targets. President Clinton later agreed to negotiate a binding treaty at the 1997 Kyoto conference, convened at the initiative of the parties to the UNFCCC. Thus, the United States for the first time was apparently committed to a compulsory target-and-timetable agreement. But no consensus on the need for such a treaty existed within either congressional party or among the public as the negotiations began, leaving the outcome very much in doubt. Soon, Bill Clinton was absorbed in an epic impeachment struggle and the Senate, as expected, overwhelmingly rejected the agreement. The subsequent presidential election of George W. Bush in 2000 virtually ended active U.S.

domestic or international initiatives for comprehensive regulation of climate change emissions for eight years.

The failure of the Senate in 1998 to ratify the Kyoto Protocol, compounded by the subsequent election of a Republican majority in both congressional chambers and George W. Bush's presence in the White House, forestalled any further U.S. international initiatives on global climate warming until the Obama presidency. However, the states became so active in the absence of federal action that they had become the domestic leaders in climate change legislation at the conclusion of the Bush administration.

The States Take the Lead. By the time the Obama administration was inaugurated, sixteen states had adopted GHG emissions reduction targets, thirty-nine states had joined the multistate Climate Registry to monitor and report their GHG emissions, and state partnerships had formed three regional "cap-and-trade" programs: the eastern Regional Greenhouse Gas Initiative (RGGI), the Western Climate Initiative, and the Midwestern Climate Initiative.[14] In addition, California had enacted a regulatory program that exceeded federal standards for GHG emissions from the transportation sector, and twelve other states proposed the adoption of the standards as well. The state programs involve a mix of different provisions, which usually include:[15]

- *State climate change commissions.* Executive or legislative commissions that examine the possible consequences of climate change for a state and the costs and benefits associated with addressing them and that then develop recommendations for appropriate policies.
- *Climate action plans.* State-designed climate action plans to meet individual state conditions.
- *GHG reporting.* Mandatory or voluntary reporting of GHG emissions from major sources in many states, such as California, Wisconsin, West Virginia, and Hawaii. Most of these states also joined the national Climate Registry, a nonprofit organization measuring and reporting publicly GHG emissions through a consistently common, accurate, and transparent process across industry sectors and borders.
- *Economy-wide GHG reductions.* Emissions goals (usually voluntary rather than compulsory) for all major emission sources within the state.
- *GHG performance standards for electric power.* A requirement that all electric power generated within the state meet a common standard for GHG emissions. Most of the performance programs create a Renewable Portfolio Standard (RPS) requiring that electrical utilities

obtain a fixed percentage of their generated power from renewable sources such as wind, solar, biomass, and geothermal.

- *GHG performance standards for vehicles.* Federal law requires states to follow federal emissions standards for cars and light trucks or to follow California's higher standard. Eleven states had adopted, or planned to adopt, the California standard following a Supreme Court ruling in 2007 that the EPA had authority under the federal Clean Air Act to regulate CO_2, the principal GHG.

Belated Federal Action. The pall of inertia enveloping the White House during the Bush administration dissipated only in Bush's last year when the federal courts compelled the federal government to act on the climate issue. In 2006, Stephen Johnson, Bush's EPA administrator, against the advice of his own staff ruled that CO_2 was not a pollutant that EPA was compelled to regulate under the Clean Air Act (CAA). Later, again contrary to staff advice, Johnson decided that EPA would not issue a waiver allowing California to enact stronger automobile emissions standards than the federal government (the proposed California standards were intended, among other objectives, to reduce auto emissions of GHG). This waiver was permitted by the CAA and had customarily been granted to California when the state requested the authority to enforce other air pollution regulations that were more stringent than the federal standards. Moreover, eleven other states were prepared to adopt the California standards, as the CAA also permitted.

A coalition of states, asserting that the CAA did compel EPA to regulate CO_2, immediately challenged the EPA's contrary interpretation in the federal courts. In a landmark decision, the Supreme Court ruled in *Massachusetts v. Environmental Protection Agency* (2007) that CO_2 could potentially endanger human health or the environment as defined by the CAA. The Court then instructed the EPA to determine whether CO_2 was, in fact, a threat to humans or the environment (the "endangerment finding") and, if so, to write appropriate regulations to control domestic CO_2 emissions. The Court's decision accelerated a cascade of climate-warming bills, resolutions, and amendments already emerging from Congress—235 proposals in the 110th Congress (2007–2008) following the 106 from the previous session. Congress, however, was more preoccupied with other matters and never came close to enacting climate legislation before the end of Bush's second term.

Washington Revives: The Obama Administration. In keeping with his campaign commitment to reinvigorate federal climate change policy, one of Obama's first acts as president was to order his new EPA administrator, Lisa Jackson, to review the EPA's prior refusal of the California waiver, with the expectation that the EPA would now approve the state's request. At the same time, the president urged Congress to enact legislation creating a comprehensive domestic GHG regulatory regime.

With the advent of Democratic majorities in both congressional chambers and the Obama presidency following the 2008 elections, environmentalists had expected a renewed congressional effort to enact the comprehensive climate bill so long delayed. Throughout 2008 and early 2009, Congress ponderously struggled to produce a climate bill, but it was not until early 2009 that comprehensive climate legislation finally emerged from either congressional chamber. In June 2009, the House of Representatives, after an exhausting struggle and continual White House pressure, enacted the American Clean Energy and Security Act (ACES) by a vote of 219–212, sending it to the Senate, where its arrival late in the congressional session amid a multitude of other urgent issues precluded any Senate progress on ACES or an alternative.

The gargantuan ACES legislation, consuming more than eight hundred pages, would have been one of the longest, most complex congressional enactments ever written. Although Congress had to renew its effort to produce a major climate bill in 2010, ACES was a prototype in important respects for any future congressional climate legislation. Among the ACES provisions likely to reappear in future legislation was a cap-and-trade strategy for controlling GHG emissions. A version of cap-and-trade already existed in the CAA for the domestic regulation of SO_2 and NO_x, the major emissions from coal-burning electrical utilities. In addition, cap-and-trade had become a commonly proposed regulatory model for a global climate treaty.

Cap-and-Trade. At the time Congress began to consider climate warming legislation promoted by the Obama administration, several variations of cap-and-trade had already been created by American states as the framework for three regional GHG emissions control agreements: the eastern RGGI, the Western Climate Initiative, and the Midwestern Climate Initiative. The essence of a cap-and-trade program, the Pew Center explains, is that

> the government determines which facilities or emissions are covered by the program and sets an overall emission target, or "cap," for covered entities. This cap is the sum of all allowed emissions from all included facilities. Once the cap has been set and covered entities specified, tradable emissions allowances (rights to emit) are distributed (either auctioned, or freely allocated, or some combination of these). Each allowance authorizes the release of a specified amount of greenhouse gas emissions, generally one ton of carbon dioxide equivalent (CO_2e). The total number of allowances is equivalent to

the overall emissions cap (e.g., if a cap of one million tons of emissions is set, one million one-ton allowances will be issued). Covered entities must submit allowances equivalent to the level of emissions for which they are responsible at the end of each of the program's compliance periods.[16]

Allowance trading occurs among regulated facilities because

firms face different costs for reducing emissions. For some emitters, implementing new, low-emitting technologies may be relatively inexpensive. Those firms will either buy fewer allowances or sell their surplus allowances to firms that face higher emission control costs. Since a ton of carbon dioxide (CO_2) emitted from one source has the same warming effect as a ton emitted from any other, the location of a given emissions reduction does not matter. By giving firms a financial incentive to control emissions and the flexibility to determine how and when emissions will be reduced, the capped level of emissions is achieved in a manner that minimizes overall program costs.[17]

Proponents of cap-and-trade assert that it has numerous advantages as a domestic, regional, or international GHG regulatory regime:

- It provides a continuing incentive for firms to create new methods of emissions control because such innovation can significantly reduce regulatory compliance costs.
- It allows regulated firms to "bank" excess emissions credits to be later used or sold on the emissions market to other firms needing emission credits.
- It creates strict limits on emissions that can produce large pollution reductions.
- It promotes high compliance levels, transparency, and accountability.
- It is compatible with existing local, state, and regional emissions reduction programs.
- It is an economically efficient use of government resources.
- It is estimated to provide more benefits at less cost to regulated firms.[18]

The Search for a "Clean Coal" Technology. A cap-and-trade regulatory strategy comes equipped with some problematic elements, in part because local, state, and federal governments have had little experience with it. One of the most unsettled aspects of cap-and-trade concerns the availability of emissions control technology for the large electrical utilities that are the primary source of GHG emissions. Currently, no proven technically or economically feasible emissions control technology exists for these sources. Beginning in 2010, the United States will begin site experiments at the Mountaineer power plant near New Haven, West Virginia, with a "clean coal" technology called Carbon Capture and Sequester (CCS), the primary method now proposed for GHG regulation domestically. The CCS project will

> employ so-called chilled ammonia technology, which relies on ammonium carbonate chemistry to pull CO_2 out of the exhaust gases.... Mountaineer takes the captured CO_2 and compresses it to at least 2,000 pounds per square inch, liquefying it and pumping it roughly 8,000 feet down into the ground. That deep, the liquid CO_2 flows through the porous rock formations, adhering to the tiny spaces, slowly spreading out over time and, ultimately, chemically reacting with rock or brine.[19]

An enormous weight of expectations, political and economic, has been loaded on this and other "clean coal" technologies that are currently under domestic development. In effect, CCS may become either a gateway or a blind alley to the near future of domestic GHG regulation.

Transboundary Environmental Politics

Since the 1990s, three global issues—acid precipitation, stratospheric ozone depletion, and global climate warming—have dominated the nation's international ecological agenda and increasingly affected its domestic environmental policies. The United States has been a party to international environmental agreements since 1921, but the scope and pace of this global ecological involvement have increased significantly since the 1960s.[20] Before the 1980s, most of these ecological agreements, like the UN Law of the Sea Convention signed in 1984, dealt with protection and preservation of the marine environment and fisheries or, like agreements relating to Antarctica and outer space, with freedom of access to common global resources. Transboundary air and water pollution, and especially human-induced (anthropogenic) changes in global climate, received little, if any, diplomatic attention. The rapid rise after the 1970s of scientific concern about cross-national pollution and human-induced climate change, together with a growing volume of information, increasingly sophisticated global environmental monitoring, and the mounting political strength of global environmental organizations, encouraged increased worldwide governmental attention to transboundary pollution problems. As the geographical and climatological scale of scientific analysis expanded, the politics of international environmentalism was transformed. By the mid-1980s, the cross-national transport of pollutants and its global impact had become a major distinctive issue.

Historic Markers: Stockholm, Rio, and Kyoto

The rapid growth of U.S. involvement in global environmental diplomacy, and especially the nation's increasing engagement in problems of transboundary pollution, can be documented by three historic markers—the Stockholm, Rio, and Kyoto environmental conferences—spanning the years between 1972 and 1997. Growing U.S. activism began with the 1972 Conference on the Human Environment in Stockholm, Sweden, the first truly international conference devoted exclusively to environmental issues; it was attended by 113 states and representatives from 19 international organizations. The theme "Only One Earth" dramatized internationally for the first time the growing gravity and scale of global environmental problems ranging from population growth to outer-space pollution. Among the other significant accomplishments of the Stockholm meeting were the creation of the UN Environmental Program, initially supported vigorously by the United States, and the enactment of many other, largely symbolic measures that committed the United States to a major role in future international environmental activities.[21]

The second major international meeting, the 1992 Conference on Environment and Development (The Earth Summit) was held in Rio de Janeiro; it was attended by an even larger international delegation of representatives from 179 countries, including 116 heads of state. The new conference theme, "Our Last Chance to Save the Earth," invoked the growing sense of urgency about global environmental degradation that characterized the meeting, which focused special attention on the environmental concerns of developing countries. The Rio Declaration on Environment and Development, probably the most widely known of all the conference statements, proclaimed twenty-eight guiding principles to strengthen global environmental governance. Although U.S. delegates attended the conference and actively participated in almost all its proceedings, the official U.S. delegation, representing the viewpoint of President George Bush and his Republican administration, was widely and severely criticized for its reluctance to lead in conference policymaking and, in particular, for its refusal to join other industrial nations in agreeing to timetables and reduction goals for the GHG emissions that were assumed to be responsible for global climate warming.

Although environmentalists were deeply disappointed in the U.S. delegation's lackluster performance in Rio, The Earth Summit unleashed powerful domestic and international political pressures on the United States that resulted in the Clinton administration's commitments to the timetables and emission targets for the GHG reduction incorporated into the 1997 Kyoto Protocol.

By the time of the Kyoto meeting, the United States had also signed the 1987 Montreal Protocol on Substances That Deplete the Ozone Layer, limiting domestic production and consumption of chlorofluorocarbons (CFCs) and related chemicals that are destroying the global stratospheric ozone layer; it had resumed financial support for the UN Fund for Population Activities, earlier halted by the Reagan and Bush administrations; and it had ratified the Biodiversity Treaty and the UN Law of the Sea Convention, again reversing Reagan-Bush presidential policies. Although the United States seemed unlikely to sign the original Kyoto agreement in light of George W. Bush's outspoken opposition and the continued Senate disagreement over its details, worldwide diplomatic pressure virtually compelled the United States to remain involved in global climate-warming treaty negotiations. Thus, the U.S. diplomatic trajectory from Stockholm to Kyoto had led the country steadily, if unevenly, toward a broadening and deepening commitment to international environmental governance.

Environmental Diplomacy: Incentives and Disincentives

A multitude of events in the last quarter of the twentieth century, such as the development of satellite Earth-monitoring computer technology, new environmental sciences, and, especially, the growth of an international scientific community deeply engaged in ecological research, have all compelled national governments to recognize the reality of transboundary pollution while raising a new global consciousness of its scope and impact. Transboundary pollution eludes the jurisdiction of any national government. Its management—for example, combating pollution of the Mediterranean Sea—often requires local or regional collaboration among governments. But, as science becomes more sophisticated in its ability to monitor and to understand pollution processes, it increasingly frames transboundary environmental problems in terms of complex, intricately related, virtually global causes and effects. This impulse toward comprehensive conceptions of international pollution also animates modern science, however unintentionally, to continually push prospective solutions up the scale of international management.

State Sovereignty versus Ecological Stewardship. All international diplomacy occurs in a global setting that is frequently considered anarchic in the sense that there is no sovereign political regime—no determinate governmental institutions, laws, processes, or principles—to which national governments give dependable allegiance. In this sovereignless political arena, national relations are governed at different times and places by many principles in various combinations—political or economic power, cultural affinities, historical antagonisms, a regional or global superpower, technological and geographical resources, the rule of law, and much else—the nature of which is a source of unending preoccupation for diplomats and scholars. It is no surprise that the political foundation on which modern nations are expected to ground their international environmental diplomacy is at best precarious, a structure currently designed to satisfy two dissonant principles: national sovereignty over indigenous resources and national responsibility for environmental stewardship. Hence, it is inherently insecure.

Embedded in modern environmental diplomacy, therefore, is the fundamental tension between these two principles. Today, the United States and other nations recognize both principles as stated in Article 21 of the Stockholm Declaration (1972) and later reaffirmed by the Rio Declaration:

> States have in accordance with the Charter of the United Nations and the principles of international law, the sovereign right to exploit their own resources pursuant to their own environmental policies, and the responsibility to insure that activities within their jurisdiction or control do not cause damage to the environment of other states or of areas beyond the limits of national jurisdiction.

Article 21 prudently recognizes the reality of state sovereignty and self-interest and implicitly recognizes its primacy in international politics. Virtually all national policymakers, in any case, act as if state sovereignty and self-interest were a higher principle, even while genuflecting in the direction of environmental responsibility toward their neighbors. In effect, the United States conducts its international environmental diplomacy in a global political arena where its own self-interest and sovereignty, and those of every other nation with which it negotiates, are always at risk of conflict with U.S. environmental goals or with the global policies deemed essential to resolve satisfactorily an international environmental problem. Moreover, the U.S. government, superpower or not, cannot routinely or legally assert its sovereign will over other nations in environmental matters as it can often do in domestic political dealings with the states and other domestic political institutions.

National Costs and Benefits. Transboundary environmental issues, like domestic ones, involve an uneven distribution of costs and benefits, ones calculated in regional, international, and global metrics that involve money, sovereignty, national prestige, and historical experience. Virtually all transboundary problems, such as acid deposition, entail upstream-downstream relations in which one nation, or a group of nations, disproportionately bears the impact of pollution migration while the polluter is likely to reap the benefits, or to believe it does. This upstream-downstream disjunction is rich in political, social, and economic cleavages sure to erupt whenever issues of pollution management arise.[22] The United States plays both roles in international politics. It is a major source of GHG emissions associated with global climate warming and of the airborne chemicals responsible for stratospheric ozone depletion, but it also shares the ecological and human health risks from both problems along with other nations. The United States is also producer and recipient of transboundary acid deposition. International environmental issues are typically first raised, often exclusively, by the downstream pollution recipients, as happened in the case of acid deposition.[23]

Many international environmental problems—such as climate change or the depletion of commercial fishing species—also involve significant cross-generational costs. The cost of this generation's failure to abate the rising depletion of commercial ocean species will be fully experienced by another, later generation that may be unable to earn a living at all from the once-thriving Atlantic tuna or cod fisheries. Rising global sea levels, shifting temperate climate zones, and other major impacts predicted by climate-warming studies may not create significant human problems for several decades or for a single generation. As with domestic issues, observes political scientist Lynton Caldwell, "policies are made or affirmed and implemented by people accountable to the present, not to the future generations. Therefore, the urgency of an issue as an object of policymaking is not necessarily a measure of its ultimate significance."[24] In the case of international issues, the problem of cross-generational impacts is further complicated because many of the most severe cross-generational consequences will be experienced by the world's smaller, or most economically or culturally disadvantaged, nations—those that can exert comparatively meager political leverage on international affairs and that are least able to mitigate or adapt to prospective ecological change.

Moreover, the so-called developing or underdeveloped nations habitually view international ecological issues through the lens of their political history, infusing their environmental diplomacy with ideologies, passions, and assumptions drawn from their colonial experience or from past diplomatic, political, or economic associations with Western and industrialized countries. The United States invariably wears distinctive mantles in the perceptions of such nations engaged in environmental diplomacy. It is "Western," "colonial," or "capitalist"; a "superpower," "Northern," or "white"—all perceptions, along with many others similarly derived, that inevitably affect the conduct of any ecological negotiations involving not only the United States but also other Western and industrialized nations. Postcolonial and other developing nations are likely to suspect initially that U.S. or other Western diplomatic initiatives concerning the environment are covert attempts at exploitation or subjugation. Latin American nations may suspect that U.S. environmental initiatives are a newer version of the deeply resented "big stick" diplomacy that the United States employed toward its southern neighbors earlier in the twentieth century. Nonetheless, people in developing societies are increasingly aware of and concerned about environmental problems.

Even if history casts no long shadow over environmental diplomacy, the natural rivalries and tensions among sovereign states and the omnipresent impulse to national power and sovereignty always threaten to create a chokehold on national environmental sensibilities; all nations appraise prospective environmental policy first by its apparent impact on their own sovereignty and power. The surest poison for any international environmental agreement is a conviction held by a national leadership that its country's sovereignty will be compromised. Thus, opponents launching an early attack on a possible U.S. agreement in Kyoto to limits on U.S. domestic GHG emissions were quick to conjure images of imperiled national autonomy. "We are taking national sovereignty away from every nation that signs this treaty," charged Sen. Chuck Hagel, R-Neb. "Would [a binding treaty] mean a United Nations multinational bureaucracy could come in and close down industry in the United States?" he queried, adding meddling bureaucrats to the menace.[25]

Almost as potent in shaping environmental diplomacy is national prestige and image; leaders recoil from negotiations that imply national responsibility for an environmental offense or that attack the legitimacy of domestic environmental practices. "Any attempt by states or international bodies to alter national [policy] regimes immediately brings into play questions of sovereignty and the competence of a national bureaucracy. Once allegations are made against countries or their subjects, powerful defensive impulses from those identified as polluters may be expected," notes European scholars Sonja Boehmer-Christansen and Jim Skea.[26] Negotiations get prickly when issues, or apparently impartial scientific data, are construed in a good guy–bad guy style that appears to create national villains and victims. As a cautionary tale, political scientist Marc Levy describes the result of this strategy during the 1993 negotiations among European countries over a treaty to reduce acid-rain-producing emissions. Using environmental monitoring data, "Swedish and Norwegian officials branded the United Kingdom an irresponsible renegade guilty of damaging Scandinavian resources. In one heated moment, Norwegian environment minister Thorbjorn Berntsen publicly called his British counterpart, John Gummer, a shitbag."[27] Negotiations will be far less impassioned, and usually more productive, when issues and technical data are constructively interpreted to emphasize a problem's solutions and alternative strategies.

Given the many risks and costs perceived in international environmental diplomacy, national governments are strongly motivated to assume a

wait-and-see attitude toward environmental initiatives generated elsewhere, especially if they can become free riders to multilateral agreements
made by other countries, in which—as in the case of climate change—
benefits cannot be reserved only for those countries signing the treaty.
International environmental agreements often require some sort of new
implementation structure, perhaps a regional or global monitoring system
for a pollutant, and this may also be an inducement for a government to
stay on the diplomatic sidelines. This is particularly likely when the scientific evidence supporting action is not compelling. Even so, hundreds
of environmental treaties exist, and more are being negotiated despite the
disincentives. In addition, a large and complex array of international
institutions functions to implement these agreements. Clearly, powerful
incentives compel nations to participate in international environmental
diplomacy.

Incentives to Cooperation. Perhaps the most compelling and common
incentive for nations to negotiate environmental agreements is the recognition of a shared problem or the possibility of mutual advantage. The
Montreal Protocol, the 1987 agreement in which forty-seven nations,
including the United States, pledged themselves to specific targets and
timetables for reducing their production and use of ozone-destroying
CFCs, was driven largely by persuasive scientific evidence of a large hole
in the ozone layer above the Antarctic and predictions of a disastrous
depletion of atmospheric ozone in less than a century. Significantly, the
original signatories negotiated further agreements in 1990 and 1992 to
accelerate the pace and scale of CFC reductions when additional scientific
data indicated that global ozone depletion was even more serious than
originally assumed. These agreements were greatly facilitated by a broad
scientific consensus on the problem, by the appearance of a vivid, visible
ozone hole, and by the recognition that the serious human health and ecological risks of continued stratospheric ozone depletion would be shared
globally. Nonetheless, developing nations such as China, India, and the
African states were initially reluctant to join the Montreal accords. They
were persuaded by a ten-year extension of their compliance deadline and
an assurance of financial assistance in finding CFC substitutes through
a special multilateral fund established for that purpose. This instance of
side payments (incentives designed to encourage reluctant nations to join
in multilateral agreements) illustrates a strategy often used in environmental, as well as other, international agreements.[28]
    Like expediency, prestige also works to the advantage of environmental
diplomacy. Nations often join international agreements—especially when
the apparent costs are minimal—when the perceived gain is prestige,

improved national image, or political advantage. France, Belgium, and Italy, for example, signed the 1979 Convention on Long Range Transboundary Air Pollution not only to wear the halo of a good environmental citizen in Europe but also because they anticipated that the national emissions reduction goals to which they agreed would be achieved even without the agreement.[29] In a similar vein, the Clinton administration agreed in 1992 to stabilize GHG emissions at 1990 levels by the year 2000, thereby reversing the Bush administration's policy, a decision that won environmentalist approval and obscured much of the international censure of the United States for its opposition at the Rio conference to such goals. However, the administration's implementation plan relied largely on voluntary compliance and other nonregulatory strategies, which many domestic critics charged were relatively costless economically or politically and were ultimately ineffective.

National security and other military considerations can become potent incentives for international environmental cooperation. The United States, like almost all other nuclear powers, has entered into a variety of international weapons management and disarmament agreements, such as limits on the above-ground testing of atomic weapons and the global dispersion of nuclear weapons and materials. In a broader perspective, the growing evidence of global environmental degradation and the concurrent recognition of the mounting capability of technologies to profoundly alter the physical and biological bases of all global life—indeed, to eliminate it in some instances—are promoting a growing perception among policymakers that national security and environmental protection are becoming inextricably linked for virtually all nations.

Political and economic power, often wielded not so subtly, are also common weapons in environmental diplomacy. With its huge presence in the global economy, for instance, the United States can use access to its domestic market as a potent inducement for agricultural exporting nations to accept U.S.-promoted controls on pesticides and other potentially toxic chemicals on commodities shipped abroad. Nor has the United States been reluctant to use foreign aid or the promise of other kinds of economic or technical assistance to facilitate environmental agreements on climate diplomacy, hazardous waste management, the protection of Antarctica, and many other diverse matters.

The Crucial Role of Science. Scientists and science have assumed an important and sometimes (in the case of current global climate issues) decisive role in promoting environmental issues to international significance. The relatively recent ascent of environmental science as a crucial force in setting the international environmental agenda has many explanations: the proliferation of and collaboration among scientific organizations at all international levels; the growing technical capability and sophistication of the physical and biological sciences, abetted by increasing national investments in environmental research among the technologically advanced countries; the rapid elaboration of highly efficient global communications systems; and the exponential growth of global environmental monitoring and assessment data.[30]

A striking aspect of contemporary science is not only its capacity to compel international attention to environmental issues but also its success in doing so on the basis of predictions, computer models, and other extrapolations. The effect has been to project politics and policy issues far into the future, thereby linking present-day decision making in concrete and explicable ways to what has been traditionally treated as a remote, and quite frequently irrelevant, social world. This amounts to a subtle but ongoing and pervasive redefinition of political time and space for the world's key policymakers; a lengthening of the conceptual horizons in policy thinking; and frequently a forced, and not necessarily welcome, confrontation with the long-term consequences of today's decisions defined in the more or less authoritative language of science.

The resources and authority of modern environmental science originate primarily among the world's technologically advanced and largely Western societies, especially in the United States, Western Europe, and Japan. Because of its enormous scientific infrastructure, American science frequently assumes a major, often dominating role in Western scientific undertakings. Although the environmental science driving global ecological concerns draws considerable strength from its pervasive American and Western character, this becomes an impediment to global environmental diplomacy when non-Western and developing nations suspect, as they often do, that Western science is manipulated to serve Western political and economic interests.

Global Politics Is Different

Even a brief depiction of the global political arena illuminates its vast differences from the domestic setting of U.S. environmental politics. Unlike the constitutionally sorted and ordered division of U.S. domestic governmental power, no sovereign authority—no widely understood, accepted, or explicit apportionment of power—predictably directs international affairs. Rather, it is a world of competing national sovereignties where power in all forms is customarily the real legitimating and coercive force in international agreements. It is a world of highly pluralized political interests that become yet more fragmented as traditional nation states are increasingly forced to accommodate, and often compete with, nongovernmental organizations, multinational corporations, regional and international governmental bodies, and other entities for diplomatic influence. It is also a world as yet untouched by the moderating influence of a liberal democratic civic culture or of any common cultural grounding at all. It is a world of dangerous ideological and cultural cleavages, where the hold of environmental governance is still tenuous. In this setting, environmental diplomacy has only just begun to temper the force of power and sovereignty, and a global environmental consciousness is but recently emergent.

The Kyoto Agreement

By the time the Kyoto conference convened in December 1997, national opinion polls indicated strong public support for U.S. action to limit climate warming, even unilaterally if necessary, and the IPCC report released that year added further impetus for action.[31] Nonetheless, the Clinton administration, facing an unsympathetic Republican congressional majority and continued domestic opposition from almost all the prospective regulated interests, seemed irresolute and confused, leading environmentalists and their allies to doubt that the United States would agree to tough GHG emissions controls despite previous promises. Because any agreement signed at Kyoto would require Senate approval, the congressional mood constantly preoccupied the U.S. negotiators. The Senate characteristically viewed the proceedings through political bifocals, continually scrutinizing the international implications for U.S. sovereignty and then the likely domestic economic impacts, particularly in home states. With Senate Republicans generally skeptical and Democrats divided on the treaty's merits, the U.S. delegation knew that eventual Senate approval of any agreement would be problematic.

With 120 nations attending and worldwide media coverage, Kyoto became one of the century's historic international environmental conferences. To the considerable surprise of environmentalists and others expecting an indecisive performance, the U.S. delegation eventually committed to what many observers considered a rigorous schedule of emissions reductions.

In the United States, however, the Kyoto Treaty was doomed before the negotiations had even begun. There was virtually no enthusiasm for the agreement in the Senate, whose approval is mandatory for any international treaty. The most vociferous Senate criticism focused on the failure of China, India, and other rapidly industrializing nations to accept compulsory GHG emissions limits, but numerous other treaty provisions evoked disapproval on both sides of the partisan divide in Congress. Moreover, the president was embroiled in his impeachment battle and had neither time nor resources to invest in international climate diplomacy.

After the change of administration, George W. Bush's early opposition to the agreement seemed additional assurance—if more were needed—that the protocol would never survive Congress in its original form. Moreover, public concern about climate warming, although still rising, lacked the intensity to elevate the matter to a high priority among the nation's most important public issues, even though it was increasingly identified as a major *environmental* problem. The Gallup Poll reported in mid-2004, for instance, that the proportion of the public that reported worrying about climate warming "a great deal or a fair amount" had declined from 72 percent in mid-2000 to 51 percent by Earth Day 2004.[32] On Earth Day 2007, Gallup noted that "overall, Americans' concern about global warming has not generally shown much fluctuation since Gallup first asked the question in 1989."[33] Numerous members of both parties have pledged their opposition unless the developing nations also agree to mandatory domestic emissions cutbacks, which they have so far vigorously rejected. Other major senatorial concerns involve fears of lost sovereignty and adverse domestic economic impacts. Somewhat unexpectedly, tentative support for the agreement emerged among some segments of the automobile manufacturing, petroleum, and electrical utility industries, but powerful opposition remains. Further, many scientists believe that the Kyoto Protocol is at best a first step toward what must be a greatly accelerated timetable, with much greater emissions reductions among all major industrial nations if the worst impacts of a future climate warming are to be averted.

Ambiguity and Impasse at Copenhagen

However, by the time the president joined the Copenhagen Conference in December 2009, the national political mood was considerably less benign about a climate treaty. In the aftermath of climategate, a major national poll reported that public approval of the president's management of the climate issue had fallen from 65 percent in early 2009 to 45 percent in December 2009 and that 40 percent of the respondents had responded that they trusted "not at all" what "scientists had to say about the environment."[34]

By the time Obama arrived in Copenhagen, the meeting had become the most important international climate change conference in more than a decade, attended by 190 nations, more than 8,000 delegates, over 500 nongovernmental organizations, and 40,000 other participants. To the dismay of climate treaty advocates, the already fragile prospects for a meaningful treaty seemed to evaporate as Copenhagen evolved into an international spectacle of angry national conflicts, hardening disagreement between regional blocs of nations, and rapidly darkening prospects for compromise or conciliation between the large developed nations and the smaller underdeveloped ones. Obama's dramatic intervention in the conference's closing hours to broker a compromise among the major developing nations produced what became the Copenhagen Accord, the most important, and highly controversial, agreement that could be salvaged from the conference. Obama was careful to acknowledge the substantial limitations of the accord. "Today we made a meaningful and unprecedented breakthrough here at Copenhagen," he announced. "But it is going to be very hard, and it is going to take some time to get a legally binding treaty." Such a treaty, he concluded "was not achievable at this conference."[35]

In the aftermath of Copenhagen, the accord's ambiguities and contingencies have created a legacy of continuing disagreement about its achievements and importance to the United States, sharply dividing environmentalists over the document's ultimate value. "The Copenhagen Accord is clearly a work in progress," concludes a carefully balanced assessment by the Union of Concerned Scientists (UCS), a major environmentalist organization, "with key details such as the emission reduction targets for industrialized countries and emission mitigation actions of developing countries to be filled in later." Then, noting a primary source of conflict about the agreement, the UCS adds, "It is also a voluntary framework, with negotiations to continue in 2010 towards a legal binding instrument that would either accompany or supersede the Kyoto Protocol."[36]

The major elements of the Copenhagen Accord and its supporting documents that proponents consider an important step forward include:[37]

- *Global temperature limits.* The accord acknowledges that "deep cuts in global emissions are required ... so as to hold the increase in global temperature below 2 degrees Celsius," and it pledges countries endorsing the accord to "take action to meet this objective consistent with science and the basis of equity."
- *Emissions limitation pledges.* The accord sets a deadline that encourages most of the major emitting countries to put forward pledges of what they were prepared to do to limit their emissions of carbon dioxide and other heat-trapping gases. Initial commitments and actions are to be submitted to the UNFCCC secretariat by January 31, 2010, for compilation in an information document.
- *Developing country reporting.* The accord calls on developing countries to increase their frequency of reporting on their national

emissions inventories and actions to limit emissions to every two years, "with provisions for international consultations and analysis [of these reports] under clearly defined guidelines that will ensure that national sovereignty is respected." This was, notes the UCS "the hardest-fought phrase in the whole agreement, with President Obama and others pressing for greater transparency on whether countries like China are meeting their emissions limitation goals. This language is essential to assure the U.S. Senate that the world will be able to track progress by China and other major emitting developing countries."

- *Reducing emissions from deforestation and forest degradation.* The accord recognizes the critical role of reducing emissions from deforestation and forest degradation (REDD) in the overall effort to address global warming and calls for "the immediate establishment of a mechanism ... to enable the mobilization of financial resources from developed countries" for this purpose.
- *Climate finance.* The accord commits developed countries to providing "new and additional" financial resources of $30 billion over the next three years for developing countries' actions to reduce deforestation, deploy clean technologies, and adapt to the impacts of climate change. Developed countries also "commit to a goal of mobilizing jointly $100 billion a year by 2020 to address the needs of developing countries."
- *Technology.* The accord calls for establishment of a technology mechanism to accelerate technology development and transfer, to be "guided by a country-driven approach." The demonstration and deployment of clean technology, for both mitigation and adaptation, would be eligible for support from both the short-term and longer-term resources pledged under the accord.

But the Copenhagen Accord is also, at best, highly limited and often ambiguous in its implications, with many recognized deficiencies, including:[38]

- *Level of ambition.* Assuming that industrialized and major developing countries put forward only their current offers on emissions targets and actions, the collective level of effort will not put the world on a track to stay below the 2°C temperature limitation goal that the accord endorses. The accord was largely negotiated among three countries—the United States, China, and India—that have resisted calls from others to put forward a greater level of ambition in limiting their emissions; this has led many to wonder whether the accord will prove adequate to the task, or as some fear, represents a "coalition of the unwilling."

- *A move away from legally binding.* The accord, with its voluntary framework on emissions limitations, its lack of any compliance provisions, and its open-ended review in 2015, does little to calm concerns about enforcement. Without the creation of a legally binding framework for the United States, it is clear that Japan, Russia, and Canada will refuse to accept deeper reduction targets for the next commitment period of the Kyoto Protocol; thus, that instrument will wither away after 2012—and with it, the whole framework of meaningful, legally binding, international commitments on climate change.

- *The negotiations process.* The way the accord was hammered out, in a process starting with just twenty-eight countries in the room and ultimately being decided after President Obama walked in, uninvited, to a coordination meeting of Brazil, China, India, and South Africa, raises questions about the continued relevance of the whole United Nations negotiating process. Although the UN process leaves much to be desired and can allow small groups of countries—or even individual negotiators—to hold the process hostage for a time, it is not clear that replacing it with a less transparent process of dealmaking among a handful of powerful countries will produce superior results, either in terms of overall ambition or equity.

Where Do We Go from Here?

The formal negotiations will continue in 2010, with a negotiating session in Bonn, Germany, in June 2010 and the COP 16 held in Mexico November 29 to December 10. In addition, the issue of climate finance and perhaps other aspects of the Copenhagen Accord will be on the agenda for the G-20 leaders' summits in Canada in June and South Korea in November 2010. And the Major Economies Forum (MEF) process will probably continue, with an expected focus on climate-friendly technologies, emissions registries and monitoring, and other relevant issues; no dates for future MEF meetings have yet been set.

Many eyes will also be on the U.S. Senate to see whether it joins the House in passing comprehensive climate and energy legislation. The failure of the Senate to act before Copenhagen clearly limited the Obama administration's ability to negotiate a more comprehensive agreement. Prompt Senate action would improve negotiators' ability to nail down the gains made in the Copenhagen Accord, particularly those involving actions by major developing countries such as China.

Conclusion

Something profound, and as yet but vaguely conceived, happened to political cognition in the latter third of the twentieth century. To this phenomenon we have ascribed the inadequate word *environmentalism*. The artifacts of this movement are the most visible and, ultimately, the least important aspects of it. Beginning with Earth Day 1970 in the United States and comparable political stirrings elsewhere in the industrialized world, a structure of domestic laws, institutions, and cultural practices has evolved in the United States to translate *environmentalism* into a social force and presence. This already large and elaborate national structure (the focus of most of this book) has become a national pediment, among many throughout the world, on which a new regional and international regime of environmental management (the focus of this chapter) is emerging. This incipient globalization of environmental management is extremely tenuous and as yet largely unproven, still more symbol than monument. Yet it does exist, and it has never existed before in the history of human civilization. It is worth reflecting on the profound historical implications of an international protocol to manage climate change in the twilight of the twentieth century.

At the beginning of the new century, however, a better perspective on the future path of environmentalism might be gained by looking beyond its current political and governmental architecture, important as that may be, to its implications for our evolving national conceptions of political time, space, and causality. From this perspective, one of environmentalism's most profound impacts has been to accelerate the way in which science is transforming public policymaking. Environmental science, embodied in the technical underpinnings of current understandings of climate warming, ozone depletion, and intergenerational equity, is compelling policymakers to think in terms of policy problems and impacts, of the consequences of present decisions and future undertakings, and on a time scale almost unthinkable a few decades ago and unavoidable in the future. The genie of anticipatory environmental science is out of the bottle and, like the secrets of nuclear power, cannot now be ignored, however disconcerting it may be. Although our national political language has always been afflicted with vaporous rhetoric about "the future" and "concern for future generations," science today is providing policymakers with the intellectual tools and a scientific metric for characterizing the future impact of present public decision making that impose a responsibility quite new to public life.

Added to this increasingly sophisticated ability to describe and anticipate the environmental consequences of present policies, environmentalism has also made us aware, sometimes acutely, of the need to think deliberately about the long-term risks of technological innovation. As the U.S. experience with nuclear power amply demonstrates, it is not only the scientific risks of technology development that need to be appraised but also the institutional risks—the questions about whether we have, or can develop in appropriate ways, the institutional means of managing satisfactorily the technologies we create domestically and internationally.

Most important, the evolving impact of environmentalism on our politics and culture has made an especially persuasive case, for those who will listen, that we are beginning a new century not only with the technological ability to destroy the cultural and biological conditions for the survival of human life on Earth but also with the capability to alter the genetic foundations of human life and thus consciously shape human evolution in materially and spiritually beneficial ways. Environmentalism at its best is a challenge to develop the moral and ethical sensibilities to leaven this power with an enlightened stewardship of Earth.

Suggested Readings

Chasek, Pamela S., ed. *Global Environmental Politics*. 4th ed. Boulder, Colo.: Westview Press, 2006.

Conca, Ken, and Geoffrey D. Dabelko, eds. *Green Planet Blues*. 4th ed. Boulder, Colo.: Westview Press, 2010.

Edwards, Paul N. *A Vast Machine: Computer Models, Climate Data, and the Politics of Global Warming*. Cambridge, Mass.: MIT Press, 2010.

Hulme, Mike. *Why We Disagree about Climate Change*. New York: Cambridge University Press, 2009.

Pachauri, Rajenda K., and Andy Reisinger, eds. "Climate Change 2007: Synthesis Report." (Contribution of Working Groups I, II, and III to the Fourth Assessment Report of the Intergovernmental Panel on Climate Change.) Intergovernmental Panel on Climate Change, Geneva, 2008.

Susskind, Lawrence E. *Environmental Diplomacy: Negotiating More Effective Global Agreements*. Washington, D.C.: Island Press, 1999.

Notes

1. Michael Hulme, "The Science and Politics of Climate Change," *Wall Street Journal*, December 2, 2009, available at: http://online.wsj.com/article/SB10001424052748704 107104574571613215771336.html.
2. Bill McKibben, "President Obama's Big Climate Challenge," Environment 360, Yale School of Forestry and Environmental Studies, November 5, 2008, available at: http://e360.yale.edu/content/feature.msp?id=2082.
3. Andrew C. Revkin, "Polar Bear Warns Obama about Climate Failure," *New York Times*, December 10, 2009, available at: http://dotearth.blogs.nytimes.com/2009/05/07/polar-bear-protection-updates.
4. Intergovernmental Panel on Climate Change, "Climate Change 2007: Working Group I: The Physical Science Basis, IPCC Assessments of Climate Change and Uncertainties,"

2007, available at: www.ipcc.ch/publications_and_data/ar4/wg1/en/ch1s1-6.html (accessed May 15, 2010).

5. Ibid.

6. "Highlights from Climate Change 2007: The Physical Science Basis—Summary for Policy Makers," Pew Center on Global Climate Change, available at: www.pewclimate .org/ ... /IPCCSummary050407_050407_143632.pdf.

7. Adapted from "Highlights from Climate Change 2007"; "Findings of the IPCC Fourth Assessment Report: Climate Change Science," Union of Concerned Scientists, Global Warming, 2007, available at: www.ucsusa.org/global_warming/science/ipcc-high lights1.html.

8. Among the many sources for data concerning the CRU affair, those especially useful include the compendium of CRU emails, www.eastangliaemails.com/emails .php?eid=295&filename=1047388489.txt; "Global Warming: Debunking Misinformation about Stolen Climate Emails in the 'Climategate' Manufactured Controversy," http://www.ucsusa.org/global_warming/science_and_impacts/global_warming_con trarians/debunking-misinformation-stolen-emails-climategate.html; Union of Concerned Scientists, "Global Warming, 2009," www.ucsusa.org/global_warming/science_ and_impacts/global_warming_contrarians/debunking-misinformation-stolen-emails-climategate.html; Ronald Bailey, "The Scientific Tragedy of Climategate," *Reason Magazine*, December 1, 2009, available at: http://reason.com/archives/ 2009/12/01/the-scientific-tragedy-of-clim (accessed February 16, 2010).

9. Annenberg Public Policy Center, " 'Climategate': Hacked E-mails Show Climate Scientists in Bad Light but Don't Change Scientific Consensus on Climate Warming," December 10, 2009, www.factcheck.org/2009/12/climategate.

10. Philip Shabecoff, "Global Warming Has Begun Expert Tells Senate," *New York Times*, June 24, 1988, A1.

11. Jill Jaeger and Tim O'Riordan, "The History of Climate Change Science and Politics," in *Politics of Climate Change*, ed. Tim O'Riordan and Jill Jaeger (London: Routledge, 1996), 5.

12. Quoted in Calvin Sims, "Poor Nations Reject Role in Warming," *New York Times*, December 13, 1997, A7.

13. Matthew L. Wald, "Fighting the Greenhouse Effect," *New York Times*, August 28, 1988, sec. 3, 1.

14. Committee on Energy and Commerce, "Climate Change Legislation Design White Paper: Appropriate Roles for Different Levels of Government," Washington, D.C., February 2008, available at: http://energycommerce.house.gov/Climate_Change/ white%20paper%20st-lcl%20roles%20final%202-22.pdf.

15. Adapted from "State Legislation from around the Country," Pew Center on Global Climate Change, available at: www.pewclimate.org/what_s_being_done/in_the_states/ state_legislation.cfm (accessed February 12, 2010).

16. Pew Center on the States, *Climate Change 101: Cap and Trade* (Washington, D.C.: The Pew Center, 2008), 1–4.

17. Ibid.

18. Ibid. See also, U.S. Environmental Protection Agency (EPA), Office of Air and Radiation, "Cap and Trade," January 18, 2010, available at: http://epa.sownar.com/ airmarkets/cap-trade/index.html; Eileen Claussen and Robert W. Fri, *A Climate Policy Framework: Balancing Policy and Politics* (Queenstown, Md.: The Aspen Institute, 2004); A. Denny Allerman, Paul L. Jaskow, and David Harrison Jr., *Emissions Trading in the United States* (Arlington, Va.: Pew Center on Climate Change, 2003), Pt. III.

19. David Biello, "Burying Climate Change: Efforts Begin to Sequester Carbon Dioxide from Power Plants," *Scientific American*, September 22, 2009, available at: www .scientificamerican.com/article.cfm?id=burying-climate-change#comments.

20. Among the 152 multilateral environmental treaties and agreements adopted by the United States through 1990, 20 were signed between 1921 and 1959, 26 during the 1960s, 49 during the 1970s, and 48 in the 1980s. Marvin S. Soroos, "From Stockholm to Rio and Beyond: The Evolution of Global Environmental Governance," in *Environmental Policy in the 1990s*, 3rd ed., ed. Norman J. Vig and Michael E. Kraft (Washington, D.C.: CQ Press, 1997), 283.

21. For the history of international environmental negotiations, see Lynton Keith Caldwell, *International Environmental Policy: Emergence and Dimensions*, 2nd rev. ed. (Durham, N.C.: Duke University Press, 1990).

22. See, for example, Jill Jager and Tim O'Riordan, *The History of Climate Change Science and Politics* (London: Routledge, 1996); Sonja Boehmer-Christansen and Jim Skea, *Acid Politics* (New York: Belhaven Press, 1991); Duncan Liefferink, *Environment and the Nation State: The Netherlands, the EU, and Acid Rain* (New York: Manchester University Press, 1996); Oran Young, *International Governance: Protecting the Environment in a Stateless Society* (Ithaca, N.Y.: Cornell University Press, 1994).

23. Boehmer-Christansen and Skea, *Acid Politics*, Pt. II.

24. Caldwell, *International Environmental Policy*, 14.

25. "Four U.S. Senators Lobbying in Kyoto," *Washington Post*, December 3, 1997, A35, A42.

26. Boehmer-Christansen and Skea, *Acid Politics*, 19–20.

27. Marc A. Levy, "International Co-operation to Combat Acid Rain," in *Green Globe Yearbook 1995*, ed. Helge Ole Bergesen and Georg Parmanis (New York: Oxford University Press, 1996), 63.

28. See Richard Elliot Benedick, *Ozone Diplomacy: New Directions in Safeguarding the Planet* (Cambridge, Mass.: Harvard University Press, 1991).

29. Levy, "International Co-operation to Combat Acid Rain," 60.

30. On the role of science in international climate diplomacy, see Bert Bolin, "Science and Policy Making," *Ambio* 23 (February 1994): 25–29; Peter Haas, "Introduction: Epistemic Communities and International Policy Coordination," *International Organization* 46 (winter 1992): 1–35; Joseph Alcamo, Roderick Shaw, and Leen Hordik, eds., *The RAINS Model of Acidification* (Boston: Kluwer Academic, 1990); John E. Carroll, ed., *International Environmental Diplomacy: The Management of Transfrontier Environmental Problems* (New York: Cambridge University Press, 1988).

31. John Cushman, "Polls Show Public Support for Treaty," *New York Times*, November 11, 1997, A1. See also "Public Backs Tough Steps for a Treaty on Warming," *New York Times*, November 28, 1997, A36.

32. David W. Moore, "Americans Tepid on Global Warming Accord," The Gallup Poll Tuesday Briefing, April 13, 2004, available at: www.gallup.com (accessed April 16, 2004).

33. "Polls: Water, Warming, Travel, Youth, and Green Guilt," Environmental News Service, April 23, 2007, available at: www.ens-newswire.com/ens/apr2007/2007-04-23-03 .asp (accessed May 1, 2007).

34. Quoted in Jon Cohen and Jennifer Agiesta, "On Environment, Obama and Scientists Take Hit at Polls," *Washington Post*, December 18, 2009, available at: www.washing tonpost.com/wp-dyn/content/article/2009/12/18/AR2009121800002.html.

35. Quoted in Juliet Eilperin and Anthony Faiola, "Climate Deal Falls Short of Key Goals," *Washington Post*, December 19, 2009, 1.

36. "The Copenhagen Accord: Not Everything We Wanted, but Something to Build On," Union of Concerned Scientists, "Global Warming, 2009," available at: www.ucsusa .org/global_warming/solutions/big_picture_solutions/the-copenhagen-accord.html.
37. Ibid.
38. Ibid.

List of Abbreviations

ACES	American Clean Energy and Security Act
AEC	Atomic Energy Commission
AFO	animal feeding operation
ALF	Animal Liberation Front
ANWR	Arctic National Wildlife Refuge
ARRA	American Recovery and Reinvestment Act
BCA	benefit-cost analysis
BLM	Bureau of Land Management
CAA	Clean Air Act of 1970
CAFOs	concentrated animal feeding operations
CAGW	Citizens against Government Waste
CAIR	Clean Air Interstate Rule
CBD	Center for Biological Diversity
CCS	Carbon Capture and Sequester
CEQ	Council on Environmental Quality
CERCLA	Comprehensive Environmental Response, Compensation, and Liability Act of 1980 (Superfund)
CFCs	chlorofluorocarbons
COP 15	Fifteenth Conference of the Parties to the UNFCC
CPSC	U.S. Consumer Product Safety Commission
CPSRA	Consumer Product Safety Reform Act
CRU	Climate Research Unit
DDT	dichlorodiphenyltrichloroethane
DINP	diisononyl phthalate
DOE	Department of Energy
DOI	Department of the Interior
EIA	U.S. Energy Information Administration
EIS	environmental impact statement
ELF	Earth Liberation Front
EOP	Executive Office of the President
EPA	U.S. Environmental Protection Agency
EPAct	Energy Policy Act of 2005
FAR	IPCC Fourth Assessment Report

FPL	Florida Power and Light
FWPCAA	Federal Water Pollution Control Act Amendments of 1972
GAO	Government Accountability Office (until July 2004, Government Accounting Office)
GHG	greenhouse gas
IPCC	Intergovernmental Panel on Climate Change
IRIS	Integrated Risk Information System
MCL	maximum contaminant limit
MEF	Major Economies Forum
MPCA	Minnesota Pollution Control Agency
NAFTA	North American Free Trade Agreement
NASA	National Aeronautics and Space Administration
NEPA	National Environmental Policy Act of 1969
NFMA	National Forest Management Act
NIEHS	National Institute for Environmental Health Sciences
NIMBY	"Not in My Backyard"
NO_x	nitrogen oxides
NPL	National Priority List
NPS	National Park Service
NRC	Nuclear Regulatory Commission
NSR	new source review (Clean Air Act of 1970)
NWPA	Nuclear Waste Policy Act of 1982
OCS	outer continental shelf
OIRA	Office of Information and Regulatory Affairs
OMB	Office of Management and Budget
OPEC	Organization of Petroleum Exporting Countries
OSMRE	Office of Surface Mining Reclamation and Enforcement
OSTP	Office of Science and Technology Policy
PCBs	polychlorinated biphenyls
PSD	prevention of significant deterioration
RARG	Regulatory Analysis Review Group
RCRA	Resource Conservation and Recovery Act of 1976
REDD	reducing emissions from deforestation and forest degradation
RGGI	Regional Greenhouse Gas Initiative
RIA	regulatory impact analysis
RPS	Renewable Portfolio Standards
SAR	IPCC Second Assessment Report
SARA	Superfund Amendments and Reauthorization Act of 1986
SDWA	Safe Drinking Water Act
SMCRA	Surface Mining Control and Reclamation Act
SO_x	sulfur oxides
SUVs	sport utility vehicles

TAR	IPCC Third Assessment Report
TCDD	2,3,7,8-tetrachloridibenzodioxin
TMDL	total maximum daily load
TRI	Toxic Release Inventory
TSCA	Toxic Substances Control Act of 1976
TVA	Tennessee Valley Authority
UCS	Union of Concerned Scientists
UNCED	United Nations Conference on Environment and Development (The Earth Summit)
UNFCCC	United Nations Framework Convention on Climate Change
USTs	underground storage tanks
VOCs	volatile organic compounds
WCED	World Commission on Environment and Development
WIPP	Waste Isolation Pilot Project

Index

Note: page numbers followed by *f, t, m,* and *b* indicate figures, tables, maps, and boxes, respectively.